# WAR SO TERRIBLE

## SHERMAN AND ATLANTA

BOOKS BY THE AUTHORS OF
*WAR SO TERRIBLE*

JAMES LEE MCDONOUGH
*Shiloh—in Hell before Night*
*Stones River—Bloody Winter in Tennessee*
*Chattanooga—A Death Grip on the Confederacy*
*Schofield: Union General in the Civil War*
*and Reconstruction*
*Five Tragic Hours: The Battle of Franklin*
(with Thomas L. Connelly)

JAMES PICKETT JONES
*"Black Jack": John A. Logan and Southern Illinois*
*in the Civil War Era*
*John A. Logan: Stalwart Republican from Illinois*
*Yankee Blitzkrieg: Wilson's Raid Through*
*Alabama and Georgia*

# WAR SO TERRIBLE

## SHERMAN AND ATLANTA

### JAMES LEE McDONOUGH
### and JAMES PICKETT JONES

W · W · NORTON & COMPANY
NEW YORK  LONDON

The text of this book is composed in Goudy Old Style, with
display type set in Clearface Heavy Condensed.
Composition and manufacturing by The Maple-Vail Book Manufacturing Group.
Book design by Margaret Wagner.

First Edition

ISBN 0-393-02497-0

W. W. Norton & Company, Inc., 500 Fifth Avenue, New York, N. Y. 10110
W. W. Norton & Company Ltd., 37 Great Russell Street, London WC1B 3NU

1 2 3 4 5 6 7 8 9 0

To
Our Students

# Contents

# Illustrations

MAPS

# Acknowledgments

Two MEN can write a book, but they need an enormous amount of support and assistance from librarians, archivists, editors, typists, fellow historians, and friends. We must acknowledge the kind assistance of the people whose efforts on our behalf made this book possible.

The late Phil J. Hohlweck of Milwaukee generously made available for research his superb collection of regimental histories and assisted with photocopying pertinent information. Carolyn Wilson and Josephine Buffington of Nashville, Tennessee, assisted in locating and obtaining sources.

From across the country archivists opened their collections to us. We would like especially to thank Marilyn Bell Hughes of the Tennessee State Library and Archives, Sandra J. Boling of the Georgia Department of Archives and History, Carolyn Autry of the Indiana State Library, Cheryl Schnirring of the Illinois State Historical Library, and Susan Ravdin of the Bowdoin College Library.

Both authors received important assistance from employees at military parks and battlefields. Dennis Kelley, Retha Stephens, Horton Rucker, and Superintendent Ralph Bullard of the Kennesaw Mountain National Military Park opened their archives and supplied much valuable information, as did Robert Housch, Ed Tenney, and Superintendent Ann Belkov of the Chickamauga-Chattanooga National Military Park. We also thank Jeff Dean, Superintendent at the Pickett's Mill Battlefield, who served as a guide over the rugged, confusing terrain where Yank and Reb clashed in one of the little known, but bloody engagements of the war.

Staff members at the following libraries are acknowledged for their contributions: Duke University, the University of North Carolina, Emory University, the Atlanta Historical Society, Miami University (Ohio), William and Mary, the United States Military Academy, West Point, and the Huntington Library, San Marino, California.

Jan Gadel and Wanda Mitchell of Tallahassee, Florida, and JoAnn Harwell of Nashville, Tennessee, typed the manuscript; James L. Moon, Jr., of Nashville prepared the maps.

Four students provided assistance and encouragement to the authors. Our thanks go to Gena Wade Parker, Jack McElroy, and Bonnie L. Bellew. A special debt is owed David Coles whose huge library and knowledge of Civil War detail were called upon again and again.

To Olivia and Bill Bilenky goes our gratitude for their support and encouragement. Bill's computer literacy applied to the index brought two illiterates into the twentieth century.

Professor Thomas L. Connelly of the University of South Carolina provided valuable advice and encouragement.

Finally, deserving a special word of recognition, is James L. Mairs at Norton, for his interest, suggestions, and encouragement in helping us complete this book.

# Preface

*Atlanta. Sherman.* Perhaps no names associated with the American Civil War are more evocative—and with good reason. Sherman's Atlanta campaign was a more formidable challenge for the United States Army in some respects than any of the war. More important, it was a decisive campaign in humbling the Confederacy: one hundred thousand Federal soldiers in the Deep South (a vivid demonstration of the U.S. Army's strength, as well as a relentless force in the Union strategy of applying simultaneous pressure, both east and west, until the South collapsed); the fall of Atlanta, a city second to none as a Confederate war production center and rail crossroads; a major impact, possibly decisive, on the campaign to reelect President Abraham Lincoln, without which the Union well might not have survived; a correspondingly devastating blow to Confederate morale, to the Southern will to resist the might of Federal arms (for it had been thought by many Southerners that the defeat of Lincoln might assure the success of the Confederacy). These are the essential reasons why Sherman's Atlanta campaign was of paramount importance.

This book describes and analyzes that campaign, Federal and Confederate, more extensively than any volume previously published. The authors hope the style and manner of presentation will interest both the scholar and the popular reader. While some may wish more attention had been given to a particular subject, battle, or person in which they have a special interest, we had to pick and choose, not only to prevent a sizable book from becoming longer, but also because space generally should be proportionate to overall significance. Thus, for example, it seemed to us that the fights at New Hope Church and Pickett's Mill deserved more attention than that at Kolb's Farm.

Our goal was a balanced, objective presentation of the campaign, fair to both Yank and Reb. This statement, seemingly unnecessary if one has considered the responsibilities of historiography, is made because few subjects can stir the emotions of some people like the Civil War, even today, well over one hundred years after the event. A major reason for writing this book was the authors' conviction that the Atlanta campaign, from the Federal perspective especially, has never received the attention which it deserves. Yet, every effort has also been made to present a full and unbiased treatment of the Confederates.

We have often been asked how we worked together in coauthoring this book. The task was divided as evenly as possible. Whenever feasible, each author attempted to deal with topics of particular interest or knowledge. We did not always alternate chapters, each writing three in a row at one stage of the project. When finished, we went through the entire manuscript together, both for the purpose of making corrections and for adjustments of form and style in the interest of a more unified narrative.

Surprising perhaps is the fact that we really had no significant disagreements about interpretation—or problems "getting along" as coauthors. Writing the book together was a pleasant experience. We approached this study with a higher regard for General Joseph E. Johnston than we now hold after completing the manuscript. We began with a basically positive view of General William T. Sherman as an army commander, and a basically negative view of General John B. Hood. We found no reasons to modify either of those judgments, unless it be to further reinforce our favorable concept of Sherman.

Finally, a word of explanation is necessary about quotations. When quoting from soldiers' letters, diaries, and memoirs, rather than clutter the narrative with "sics," we decided to let improper grammar, misspelled words, lack of punctuation, etc., stand. (We also have retained dashes that the soldiers sometimes used in place of profane language.) We believe this helps to convey a better "feel" for the people and the time.

# WAR SO TERRIBLE

"We cannot change the hearts of the people of the South [but] we
can make war so terrible that they will realize [its futility],
however brave and gallant and devoted to their country. . . ."

*—General Sherman to General Grant*

# 1

# The Awful Scale of the War

THE telegram lay on the top of a barrel inside the tent. A candle burned beside it and dawn was graying the east as Confederate general Joseph E. Johnston talked with three men, all generals, at his headquarters on the Atlanta-Marietta Road. The date was Monday, July 18, 1864.

The telegram that had prompted the gathering of the generals was from Jefferson Davis, president of the Confederacy. It removed Johnston from command of the Army of Tennessee. "As you have failed to arrest the advance of the enemy to the vicinity of Atlanta, far in the interior of Georgia, and express no confidence that you can defeat or repel him, you are hereby removed from command of the Army and Department of Tennessee."

Now the focus of attention was upon the youngest of the four men, General John Bell Hood. The telegram had ordered Johnston to turn over command of the army immediately to Hood. Corps commanders Alexander P. Stewart and William J. Hardee had joined Hood in urging Johnston to withhold the order and retain command, since the Union army was making a general advance and the final outcome of the struggle for Atlanta appeared to be at hand. Johnston refused, replying that he was a soldier and a soldier's "first duty is to obey."

The old and the new commanders, conversing at the headquarters tent about halfway between Atlanta and the Chattahoochee River, were strikingly different. Joseph E. Johnston was a short man, small in frame, trim and alert. Twenty-four years older than Hood, Johnston sported a neat goatee, and made an appearance that arrested attention.

Hood, recently turned thirty-three, was old before his time. In 1861

3

the shy, six-foot-two Kentuckian with the sad face had been the idol of Richmond belles. Now, his stalwart frame weakened and maimed, he hobbled with a crutch to support the stump of an amputated right leg, caused by a wound at Chickamauga. Gettysburg had also exacted a heavy price, Hood's left arm hanging limp and useless at his side.

"Sam" Hood, wrote Mary Chesnut, was "the *simplest*, most transparent soul I have met . . . in this great revolution." Some soldiers, Robert E. Lee among them, questioned Hood's capacity to command an army. But Davis felt compelled to remove Johnston. For better or worse, both the fate of Atlanta and the Confederacy's main western army now rested in the hands of young General John Bell Hood.

Across the way in the Yankee lines, only a few miles to the north, the restless commander of the Union army was also awake. William Tecumseh Sherman usually arose at dawn, if not before. As yet the lean, grizzled, campaign-hardened Ohioan knew nothing about the change of com-

William Tecumseh Sherman.

mand in the Rebel army. If he had known, it is unlikely that he would
have done one thing differently that morning. Regardless of who commanded the enemy forces, Sherman intended to keep pressing relentlessly, just as he had since the campaign began.

Sherman was already at work. About the same time that the four
Confederate generals gathered at Johnston's headquarters tent Sherman
wrote to General George H. Thomas, who led the Army of the Cumberland, the largest force under Sherman's command. Headed "In the Field,
east of Chattahoochee River, July 18, 1864—6 a.m.," the communiqué
said: "GENERAL: I have this moment your letter of 8 p.m. last night. I
would like you to . . . feel down strong on Atlanta. General Howard has
already started and Generals Schofield and McPherson; I am on the point
of starting and will be near General Schofield. . . . I want that railroad
as quick as possible and the weather seems to me too good to be wasted.
W. T. Sherman, Major General, Commanding."


IN JUST three days it would be three years since Sherman and Johnston
first faced each other across a battle line of the American Civil War.
Then Johnston had commanded the Confederate forces at Manassas
Junction (Bull Run), the war's first engagement that could properly be
called a battle, while Sherman had led a brigade in the Union army.
They fought on Virginia soil, only a few miles from Washington. Then
the Confederacy, vital and confident, even arrogant, enjoyed military
strength equal, perhaps superior, to the United States. Then Johnston's
Southerners had driven the Federal army back to Washington, initially
in panic, finally in rout. And then the triumphant Confederates, many
of them, had thought the war would soon be over.

But three years later, Sherman and Johnston were fighting hundreds
of miles south of Manassas Junction. Now Sherman commanded a Yankee army with a significant manpower advantage, plus an overwhelming
superiority in all things material—from rolling stock to belt buckles to
fire power. Now the war was being decided not by dash and daring; rather
by Federal mass production, mass transportation, and masses of men.
Now the Confederate army had retreated to within less than ten miles of
Atlanta, and Johnston had been relieved.

Indeed the war had changed since Sherman led a Yankee brigade at
Manassas and Johnston commanded the Rebels in that first battle. And
much more than Johnston, the gods of war had placed Sherman in the
midst of the decisive campaigns. Soon after Manassas Sherman went
west, never to fight again in Virginia. That decision was fortunate for
the slim, nervous redhead, because the Civil War would not be won or

lost on the eastern front. There great, bloody battles were waged, the Seven Days, Antietam, Fredericksburg, Chancellorsville, and Gettysburg. Dramatic chapters, which now loom larger than life. One has only to think of Jackson, Lee, and Stuart to recognize this truth. But after three years of war in the East, no major army had been captured or destroyed by the other side and neither nation's capital had fallen. Rather the outcome of the conflict was ultimately decided beyond the northern Virginia theater, where the border between Union and Confederacy stretched for hundreds of miles. In that vast, sprawling region the Union had been turning the tide of war against the Confederacy.

By the early spring of 1864, the Federals had won West Virginia, most of Missouri, and much of Kentucky and Tennessee, along with parts of Louisiana and Arkansas. The Yankees had also occupied key islands around the 3,500 miles of Rebel coastline, penetrated the major rivers, captured several important cities including the largest, New Orleans, and clamped an ever-tightening blockade on the Confederacy.

Essentially the Yankees had been following a plan for total war: "Scott's

Joseph Eggleston Johnston.

Anaconda," as the strategy was dubbed by those who delighted, initially, in ridiculing it. But General Winfield Scott, overweight and gouty, retiring in the fall of 1861 at seventy-five years of age, lived long enough to have the last laugh, if he so desired, because the actual experience of war proved unquestionably that his concept was sound. Scott's plan recognized the North's great potential advantage of men and material, and was the first to emphasize the importance of the Mississippi Valley in the overall view of the war. Scott had advocated a naval blockade to cut off the Confederacy from European assistance; at the same time gaining control of the Mississippi River, thereby severing the Rebels from the cattle and other supplies of Texas, as well as from foreign aid that might come through the neutral ports of Mexico. Having seized all this the Union war machine, like a giant serpent, would firmly wrap itself tighter and tighter in a death hold about the Confederacy.

Thus the war's first really significant campaigning began on the great

Winfield Scott.

Mississippi's tributaries to the east, the Tennessee and the Cumberland rivers, which the Confederate authorities had neglected. In early February 1862 a combination land-water invasion force under U. S. Grant and Andrew H. Foote breached the Confederate defensive perimeter across southern Kentucky. Driving south up the Tennessee and Cumberland, they captured the supposed bastions protecting those vital waterways, Fort Henry and Fort Donelson.

The fall of Fort Henry opened the Tennessee River as an avenue of penetration all the way to the Alabama and Mississippi state lines. Advancing via the Tennessee River, a parallel line of the Mississippi, proved just as good as moving down the Mississippi itself. Actually it was better in some ways: it immediately broke one east-west railroad, the Memphis & Ohio, which crossed the Tennessee only seventeen miles south of Fort Henry, and soon resulted in taking out the all-important Memphis & Charleston line at Corinth, the Confederacy's main east-west rail link—as well as outflanking Memphis, which fell four months after Fort Henry.

The capture of Fort Donelson only ten days after the collapse of Fort Henry resulted in the taking of 15,000 Confederate prisoners, opened a second avenue of invasion to Tennessee's capital of Nashville, caused the collapse of the entire Confederate defensive line across southern Kentucky, and propelled General Ulysses S. Grant into the limelight as the North's first successful commander. When Nashville was abandoned a week later—the initial Confederate state capital to fall—the western Confederacy had lost its most important city for the manufacture and storage of all manner of war supplies, from heavy ordnance, to shoes, to flour and bacon. With the Rebel loss of Nashville and the area fifty miles to the west went the greatest iron ore producing region in the entire Confederacy.

On the Mississippi the grand advance of the Federals continued, as they applied pressure that gradually forced the Rebels to give up Island Number Ten, a strong fortification just south of Columbus, Kentucky, located in the southern end of a big loop of the river. Soon the Confederates were also compelled to evacuate Fort Pillow, only fifty miles north of Memphis, and the Federals then quickly closed in on the Bluff City, which was occupied by Union forces on June 6.

Meanwhile, at the mouth of "the Father of Waters" the onrushing Blue juggernaut had already taken the Crescent City, the impact of which was devastating to the Confederacy. The population of New Orleans was four times greater than any other Southern city. But the importance of New Orleans could not be recognized simply on the basis of the number of people dwelling there. New Orleans boasted the largest sugar refinery in the world, was the capital of King Cotton, and was the number-one export port on the American continent. The city was second only to New York in imports, and enjoyed the distinction of being the banking capital of the South.

From Fort Henry and Fort Donelson on the Confederacy's northern border to New Orleans on the southern, the decisiveness of the Union campaigning in the winter and spring of 1862 can hardly be exaggerated. Most of the results were never to be undone even briefly, and none permanently. Afterward, the fall of Port Hudson, and even the much-publicized fortress at Vicksburg, in the summer of 1863, were like an inevitable grinding to conclusion of forces set in motion by the momentous events of 1862.

And by late 1863 the Federals had finally secured, after a costly and frustrating series of engagements at places like Chickamauga, Lookout Mountain, and Missionary Ridge, the town long recognized as the gateway to the deep Southeast: Chattanooga, Tennessee. President Abraham Lincoln, who had developed appreciably as a strategist, penned his evaluation of Chattanooga's importance in the following words: "If we can hold Chattanooga and East Tennessee," he wrote on October 4, "I think the rebellion must dwindle and die."

Because of the Tennessee River, Chattanooga was a natural passageway between North and South. Even more significant, however, were its railroads. To the northeast lay the East Tennessee Railroad to Knoxville, Bristol, and Lynchburg. From the west came the Memphis & Charleston from north Alabama, and the Nashville & Chattanooga from middle Tennessee, with connection by the Louisville & Nashville to Louisville and the Ohio River. To the southeast ran the Western & Atlantic to Atlanta. From Atlanta were rail connections with Virginia through the Carolinas, as well as with munitions and iron centers of central Georgia and Alabama.

With the Union in possession of Chattanooga, the Confederacy's rail communications were severely damaged. Moreover, the Yankees were in a position, with Chattanooga as a major staging base, to carry the war into the Deep South. Chattanooga was the key to splitting the South along a second corridor, Nashville-Chattanooga-Atlanta, just as the Confederacy had already been split along the general line of the Mississippi. Chattanooga was the natural jump-off point for waging total war against the southeastern Confederacy, and by 1864 the town rested firmly in Yankee hands.

As the fortunes of war turned against the Southerners, William Tecumseh Sherman, caught up in some of the major action, had risen steadily in reputation and responsibility. Sherman commanded a division at Shiloh, where the Confederates barely failed in an all-out effort to turn back the Federal onslaught and gain a chance to recoup what had been lost in the western theater. Although surprised by the Rebel attack— only the day before the assault Sherman told a jittery fellow Ohioan that there was no enemy closer than Corinth, twenty miles away, and the colonel could "take his damn regiment back to Ohio"—Sherman recovered and performed well in a critical situation. Significantly for his future, the redheaded Ohioan also came to the attention of Grant at Shiloh, with whom he developed a close and important friendship, based upon mutual liking and respect.

In the Vicksburg campaign of 1862–63, which dragged on for months, Sherman commanded a corps under Grant; later at Chattanooga, he joined Grant in finally securing control of that strategic railroad town after the setback at Chickamauga. Thus when Grant went east in early 1864, as general-in-chief of the Federal forces and charged with the responsibility of coordinating the overall war effort, he had come to place more confidence in Sherman than any other general, a fact of far-reaching import in the months to follow.

DESPITE Federal successes, the winter and spring of 1864 constituted, both militarily and politically, a period fraught with uncertainty about the course of the war and the future of the Union. After three years of struggle, the military conflict still dragged on indecisively. Antietam, Gettysburg, and Vicksburg had not determined the war's outcome. Although Union victories in the West had cut deeply into the economic and military strength of the South, and the campaigns in the East had exacted a heavy price in draining its lifeblood, much of the vast heartland of the Confederacy was still intact, the will of the Southern people to resist had not been broken, and two formidable armies—one in Virginia and the other in northwestern Georgia—were poised again to challenge the Northern invader. The Confederacy had been weakened, unquestionably; but it was far from being beaten.

Meanwhile, the United States' goal of preserving the Union was encumbered by growing Northern war weariness and pronounced dissatisfaction with the Lincoln administration. More than a quarter of a century ago, Richard N. Current, in an essay published in Why the North Won the Civil War, wrote that the North's "overwhelming preponderance in most sources of economic power" made Southern defeat "all but inevitable," a point of view expressed neither for the first nor the last time by historians of repute. On the other hand, Herman Hattaway and Archer Jones, in the recent How the North Won, observe that "strategy, management, and execution weigh more than superior numbers and resources in dictating the outcome of wars," and then state that "the weaker side can win; the South almost did." The point is well made.

*And*, by 1864, beyond all considerations of numbers, resources, strategy, management, and execution, the will of the North to prosecute the war loomed like a gigantic question mark equal to, if not overriding, all other considerations. Northern war weariness was attributable to several factors. Foremost, of course, was the heartrending price exacted by the grim reaper. The nation had been shocked when the bloody cost of the first great clash, Shiloh, became generally known. By a wide margin, the engagement was, to that time, the biggest battle (in numbers engaged and in casualties) both of the Civil War and of American history. It was with the impressions of Shiloh fresh in his mind that Sherman wrote his wife about the horrid scenes he had witnessed and concluded that he did not expect to survive the war.

Yet, by 1864, a number of "Shilohs," both East and West, had been waged and were making—probably already had made—the Civil War the most costly conflict that the United States would fight, even to this present day. And the end was not in sight. Americans were killing each other at a rate that would eventually total approximately 622,000 people, more than were killed in all the rest of America's wars combined until several years into the Vietnam conflict. While the North had a larger manpower pool than the South—where one-half of the Southern white male population between the ages of eighteen and thirty would be either killed or crippled—the fact that the Northern percentage of loss was less than the Southern was hardly comforting when loved ones had been killed or wounded.

The awful scale of the war was clearly evident and deeply disturbing. Many were stripped of romantic illusions they once held about the glory of war, the expectation of a brief struggle, and the cause for which they fought.

The cause for which they fought—it was one way in which the war was harder for the North than the South. The Confederates fought for land, home, family, a way of life, and to be left alone; concrete issues around which they could rally with the deepest emotions as they strove to throw back the Yankee invader of their newly formed country. But the North fought for Union, a noble and worthy cause to be sure; yet a more abstract issue and an idealistic hope—hardly analogous, in its potential for generating intense fervor and determination, to the reasons why the South fought.

Also, by 1864, the North fought for emancipation of the slaves, indeed another noble and worthy cause. The war, however, did not begin as a struggle to free the slaves and many a Northerner resented the fact that the conflict had taken such a turn. While great numbers of Federals did approve the measure, and emancipation unquestionably helped the United States in the eyes of Europeans, especially Great Britain, thus making European interference on behalf of the Confederacy very unlikely; still the Northerner, even if he supported emancipation, often had never seen a slave before he tramped south in a blue uniform. The cause of emancipation was also relatively abstract, and undoubtedly less immediate, than those goals for which the South waged war. And the South had only to maintain itself, to keep from being defeated, while the North, once again, must gather strength to invade and conquer. By the winter and spring of 1864, growing Northern war weariness (although perhaps not widely, and clearly not fully, appreciated in the South) probably constituted the Confederacy's best hope of establishing itself as an independent nation.

The North had another major problem, one inevitably tied to the military difficulties: the political setting as the year 1864 came in. On this intriguing front the developments of 1863 were not fortuitous for the Lincoln administration. The conscripting of men for military service had led to scandal, violence, and rioting in a number of states. Arbitrary arrests, violating citizens' rights, numbered in the thousands. Taxation measures to support the war were, at best, accepted as a necessity of war and another part of the nation's sacrifice, although some decried taxation as further evidence of a general tendency toward increasing centralization of governmental powers. To Northern friends of States' Rights, and there were many of them, the measure seemed ominous. So too the centralized banking control, the employment of Federal martial law within a state, national pressure in state elections, and Federal judicial approval for irregular measures. It is a fact that such policies, for better or worse, were placing the states irreversibly in subordination to the Washington government. Many Northerners were convinced that it was for worse.

Then, at the end of 1863, Lincoln announced his amnesty policy and liberal plan for the easy and early restoration of the rebellious Southern states. Promising amnesty to all except a few high Confederate officials, the president proposed to reestablish civilian government in the conquered areas of the South when only 10 percent of the number of voters in 1860 took an oath swearing future loyalty to the United States Constitution and accepting emancipation. The result was a major squabble within the Republican party. The so-called radical element, many of whom favored a far-reaching, harsh reconstruction of the South, were at the point of an open break with the president, especially after Lincoln, with a pocket veto, killed their counterproposal—the Wade-Davis bill—

requiring 50 percent of the 1860 electorate to swear allegiance. The radicals were furious: Thaddeus Stevens of Pennsylvania, who would later head the Congressional Joint Committee on Reconstruction, called Lincoln's action "infamous." Relations between Lincoln and the radical element of the party had long been strained, but no previous event equalled the clash over reconstruction of the South.

The division within the Republican party seemed to occur at the worst possible time, as the presidential election was approaching. Many Democrats delighted in charging, like Clement L. Vallandigham of Ohio, that Lincoln had turned the war for the Union into a war for emancipation. Sounding a strong anti-black theme, Democrats claimed, in the typical time-honored politics of exaggeration and misrepresentation, that if Lincoln were reelected the amalgamation of the black and white races would follow. David Donald, in *Liberty and Union,* notes that the word *miscegenation* first appeared in an 1864 campaign document. Democrats would hammer at all the evidences of growing Federal power, and try to capitalize on the nation's war weariness. The war was a failure, they claimed. Lincoln, they said, was not only a failure, but a man to be feared—a would-be dictator. It certainly should be added that a lot of Republicans agreed.

In fact, many Republican favored another candidate as the election of 1864 approached and tried to keep the nomination from the president. Many felt Lincoln could not be reelected. Lincoln himself sometimes doubted he could win again. And if the president were to be defeated, the chances of maintaining the Union, in view of the conditions under which his challenger would emerge, were slim indeed.

Clearly then, if the triumph of the Union and of Lincoln—in a sense one and the same—were to be assured, the Federal armies needed to defeat the Confederates somewhere: to achieve something really significant, and in a decisive manner. Victory was the one obvious antidote for war weariness. Victory would silence the cries that the war effort and Lincoln were failures. Victory was the unifying cement that could make up for a multiplicity of alleged wrongs and assumptions of arbitrary power, and carry the Republican party and the cause of the Union safely through the presidential election of 1864.

# 2

# The Beginning of the End

THE train rocked its way northward from Nashville toward Louisville and Cincinnati. For a time the two friends tried to talk, but the noise made by the lurching cars made it impossible and they fell silent. And it was imperative that they talk one last time. In March 1864 momentous changes had come to the Union army's high command. Tired of stalemate in the eastern theater, Abraham Lincoln had summoned Ulysses S. Grant to Washington, offering him the three stars of lieutenant general and command of all Federal forces. Grant had accepted and in mid-March, after a final trip to his western army, he was on his way to the Army of the Potomac and his new and awesome responsibilities.

When Grant returned from that first trip to Washington he told William Tecumseh Sherman that he was to be commander of Union forces in the western theater. Although the two men, in whose hands Lincoln had placed the Union cause, were together in Nashville for several days, they had not had a quiet chance to discuss final plans for spring campaigns. Grant asked Sherman to accompany him to Cincinnati so that they might have that last talk. But the Louisville & Nashville's train was too noisy.

In Cincinnati Ellen Sherman met her husband and there was another delay. At last the two generals found a room at the Burnet House, broke out maps, and discussed their forthcoming campaigns against Confederate armies led by two renowned chieftians—Robert E. Lee and Joseph E. Johnston. Years later Sherman returned to the Burnet House, showed friends the room, and said: "Yonder began the campaign . . . we finally settled on a plan. . . . He was to go for Lee and I was to go for Joe

Johnston. That was his plan. No routes prescribed. . . . It was the beginning of the end."

The command Grant handed Sherman in March 1864 was the vast Military Division of the Mississippi, created in the fall of 1863. This military division, including the departments of the Ohio, the Tennessee, and the Cumberland, encompassed the region from the Appalachians to the Mississippi. After Grant's decisive victory at Chattanooga the troops in his command had gone into camp for the winter. The Army of the Ohio lay, for the most part, in eastern Tennessee around Knoxville. Most units in the Army of the Tennessee returned to the Mississippi Valley while the Army of the Cumberland spent the winter months around Chattanooga.

As the war's third year ended Grant considered plans for a renewal of the struggle in the West when better weather arrived in the spring. The winter might permit limited movements against the foe, but major action must await reorganization, massive accumulation of supplies, and spring skies.

It was clear which direction Grant's campaign would take. The Confederacy already had been divided along the line of the Mississippi River and Grant would next split the South along a line from Chattanooga through Atlanta to some point on the coast. In mid-January Grant wrote General Henry W. Halleck:

> I look upon the next line for me to secure to be that from Chattanooga to Mobile, Montgomery and Atlanta being the important intermediate points. . . . I do not look upon any points except Mobile, in the south, and the Tennessee, in the north, as presenting practicable starting-points from which to operate against Atlanta and Montgomery.

By the third winter of the conflict Lincoln, Grant, and Sherman had concluded that the Confederacy's defeat must come through a policy of exhaustion. Destroying the enemy army in the field had not proved possible. Herman Hattaway and Archer Jones conclude in *How the North Won* that the policy of "[a]nnihilation would fail because the mid-nineteenth century army was virtually invulnerable." Grant had been able to destroy enemy armies at Fort Donelson and Vicksburg by pinning them against navigable rivers, but, as Hattaway and Jones write, "It was hardly realistic to expect from the Confederate generals in the field in 1864 the kind of helpful performance provided in 1862 and 1863 by Floyd and Pemberton."

But the policy of exhaustion had its perils. In penetrating deeply into the South, vast amounts of supplies were needed. It was "these cursed

Ulysses S. Grant.

wagons and mules that bother us. . . . It is not 'villanous saltpeter' that
makes one's life so hard, but grub and mules," wrote Sherman. In driving
into the Deep South the Yankees would move beyond usable rivers. This
deeper penetration meant supply lines must be defended by men detached

Henry W. Halleck.

from the front. The Union army's numerical superiority would be diminished by defensive necessity. Grant explained: "As the enemy falls back he increases his strength by gathering in railroad garrisons whilst I am weakened by leaving behind protection for my avenues of supply." Once

Sherman had roared, "To secure the safety of the navigation of the Mississippi River I would slay millions." His attitude toward Rebel cavalry strikes at less important targets was different. Let them "rampage at pleasure in West Tennessee until the people are sick and tired," he wrote. In spite of Sherman's words, even those raids, by generals such as Nathan Bedford Forrest, did cause some concern.

In January when Grant told Halleck of his new line of attack, he added that he wanted "to be able to select my own campaign in the spring instead of having the enemy dictate it for me." Halleck agreed wholeheartedly. In dictating the campaign to the enemy Grant developed the strategy of exhaustion. This strategy aimed at destroying the Confederate military's logistical support. If Johnston and Lee were denied food, clothing, shoes, weapons, and ammunition their armies would be rendered ineffective without fighting battles. Furthermore, this war of exhaustion would also block the movement of replacements for men who were ill or who deserted, as well as wear down the will of Southern civilians to sustain their government. As Union armies sliced through the South, soldiers from the sections taken would grow anxious about their families and desertions would increase. If the Union invasion threatened railroad hubs—such as Atlanta—or factory towns—such as Selma, Montgomery, Columbus, or Macon—the Rebels would have to launch their own attacks against the Union front. Such defensive-offensives might allow larger Union armies to inflict heavy casualties on the attackers. This strategy of exhaustion was not merely the occupation of territory; it was aimed at wrecking the South politically, economically, and militarily.

The problems entailed in the policy were many. The supply and defense problems, discussed above, were obvious. So was the distance to be covered. Grant and Sherman faced a distance greater than that across Kentucky and Tennessee. And since they faced it without navigable rivers, more vulnerable railroads must be relied upon. In the upper South Unionist civilians occasionally aided the invaders, but in the Deep South the Federals could expect almost universal hostility.

Facing the virtual impossibility of annihilating Johnston's army and the several problems implicit in the policy of exhaustion, Grant and Sherman concluded that the latter was possible through a policy of raids in strength. Large forces would move rapidly to objectives, destroy them, and move on. Large occupation forces would not be necessary. This special kind of "raid" would bear little resemblance to the small-unit quick strikes common to both armies in the war's first three years. In *How the North Won*, Hattaway and Jones summarize Grant's idea:

Infantry, which would not have to flee so soon, would carry out the projected raids. Infantry armies would, with their engineers and large numbers
of troops, have the skill and manpower to do more thoroughly the job of
destruction of war resources.

A line through the Confederacy from Chattanooga to the Gulf was to
be the target of the offensive. Grant planned coordinated attacks from
Chattanooga toward Atlanta and from Mobile toward Montgomery.
Railroads would be destroyed, food both destroyed and consumed by the
invaders, and Lee and Johnston would go wanting for needed supplies.
The Federal armies would destroy along a strategic line, not occupy vast
expanses of territory. When Grant first developed this concept he planned
to lead the movement into Georgia himself, sending Sherman or General
James B. McPherson to march north from the Alabama coast.

When he began this two-pronged attack, Grant would unleash diversions from several points. Vicksburg's success was very much in his mind
as he planned his 1864 attack, and that victory had come in part through
heaping confusion on the enemy. If he could confuse them long enough
to advance without opposition for even a few days, the raid might be
another Vicksburg. If the Southerners quickly intercepted one force, the
other would move forward with little opposition because of Union manpower superiority. One other advantage of the raids was that if forced to
retreat, the army need not return to its original base. Federal naval power
along the Atlantic and Gulf coasts would allow the army to reach supplies and support in almost any direction. Thus the army moving from
Chattanooga to Atlanta would be much more secure and much more
flexible if the Mobile column could successfully penetrate central Alabama.

During the winter as Grant planned for the spring he decided to carry
out a combined infantry-cavalry raid into Mississippi. This strike had two
purposes. It would serve as a test of the principle of the raid in force
designed to carry out a policy of exhaustion. It would also serve to wreck
transportation and supplies in an area of the Deep South as yet unscarred
by the war, thus denying those resources to Johnston.

Sherman's Army of the Tennessee, from its camps along the Mississippi, would drive toward Meridian. At the same time, General W. Sooy
Smith would conduct a cavalry raid south from Memphis. If Sherman's
column could easily press on to Mobile it would do so; if not it would
return to Vicksburg. That this campaign was secondary to the projected
advance into Georgia and Alabama was evident when Grant wrote:
"Sherman will be instructed, while left with large discretionary powers,

to take no hazard of losing his army or of getting it crippled too much for efficient service in the spring." To assist Sherman and Smith, a diversion from Chattanooga toward Rome, Georgia, would be created, while naval forces off of Mobile would further distract the Rebels.

On February 3, Sherman, with 21,000 men, invaded Mississippi. Living off the land, the Blue column swung rapidly across the state. At Meridian the Yanks wrecked railroad facilities, storehouses, and arsenals. Sixty-one bridges, 115 miles of track, and twenty locomotives were also destroyed. General Leonidas Polk, commanding Confederate forces in the area, asked for reinforcements from Johnston. Troops were dispatched only to arrive after the raid had ended. Sherman said of the former cleric who commanded the Rebels in Mississippi, "I scared the bishop out of his senses."

The Mississippi raid was pronounced a success even though Sooy Smith's cavalry force was thrashed by Forrest at Okolona on February 22. The objectives hoped for by Grant and Sherman were achieved. The Confederates were confused and reacted slowly. Their transportation network lay in ruins and badly needed supplies had gone up in flames. The raid in force deep into enemy territory was possible.

There was another result, which would loom more important within weeks. Grant's faith in Sherman's command capabilities, already great, was strengthened. When Washington expressed concern Grant had replied, "with a man like Sherman to command, he is in no great danger," from concentrated Confederate forces. Grant had other campaign plans for the winter, but none was successful. The march to Meridian made the inactive months seem more productive.

Before Grant's well-crafted plan for the invasion of Georgia and Alabama could be put into effect, two events caused serious changes. Grant would never lead his new campaign. On March 3 a telegram arrived at his Nashville headquarters ordering him to Washington. On the ninth President Lincoln promoted the hero of Vicksburg and Chattanooga to lieutenant general and gave him supreme command of the Union army. Although Sherman urged Grant to exercise his new responsibilities from the western theater, Grant knew that he must go to Virginia. With no hesitation Grant suggested that Sherman, then commander of the Army of the Tennessee, take his place in the West. Lincoln approved, very pleased with his army's new command structure.

With Grant gone, Sherman would command the advance from Chattanooga. The march northward from Mobile would be led by General Nathaniel P. Banks, one-time speaker of the U.S. House of Representatives and a political general in the worst sense of the phrase. Before many days had passed it was evident that there would be no campaign from Mobile. Instead, Banks invaded Louisiana in the disastrous and mishandled Red River campaign, called by an angry Sherman "one damned blunder from beginning to end." Not only would Sherman not receive support from the south, but the 10,000 troops from the Army of the Tennessee sent to Banks would never join Sherman in Georgia. Banks's disregard of Grant's master plan for the West would place even greater pressure on Sherman's thin rail line from Louisville through Nashville and Chattanooga to Atlanta. In the lieutenant general's original plan, the raid from Mobile would open a supply line from the gulf that would help provide necessities for the army moving into Georgia.

In spite of these changes Grant wrote Sherman: "You I propose to move against Johnston's army, to break it up, and get into the interior of the enemy's country as far as you can, inflicting all the damage you can against their war resources." Demonstrating confidence in his lieutenant, Grant added: "I do not propose to lay down for you a plan of campaign, but simply to lay down the work it is desirable to have done, and leave you free to execute it in your own way." Six days later Sherman promised "thorough and hearty co-operation." He vowed: "I will not let side issues draw me off from your main plan, in which I am to knock Joe Johnston, and do as much damage to the resources of the enemy as possible." The western commander told his friend that he would remember "that Johnston is at all times to be kept so busy, that he cannot . . . send any part of his command against you or Banks." The Confederate use of interior lines to speed reinforcements from one theater to another, as at Chickamauga, would not be permitted. Grant also mentioned the possibility that even as Sherman pressed Johnston, the Rebel leader might abandon Georgia to join Lee. In that event Sherman was to follow Johnston "to the full extent of your ability." If Lee tried to reinforce Johnston, Grant promised to "prevent the concentration of Lee upon your front if it is in the power of this army to do it." Sherman's February raid to Meridian had been a rehearsal; by late April his army of over 100,000 men was poised to "knock Joe Johnston and do as much damage to the resources of the enemy as possible."

The general who would cut the Confederacy in half was, according to Walt Whitman, "a bit of stern open air made up in the image of a man." The two best known photographs of Sherman, taken in 1864 and 1865, as he was reaching the pinnacle of his fame, help us understand the poet's words. The two portraits are those of a stern and determined soldier. His unruly hair and somewhat shaggy beard frame a handsome, virile face whose most striking feature is its eyes. They are the eyes of restlessness and intelligence; the eyes of a man who would drive himself and ask no sacrifice of his men that he would not willingly share.

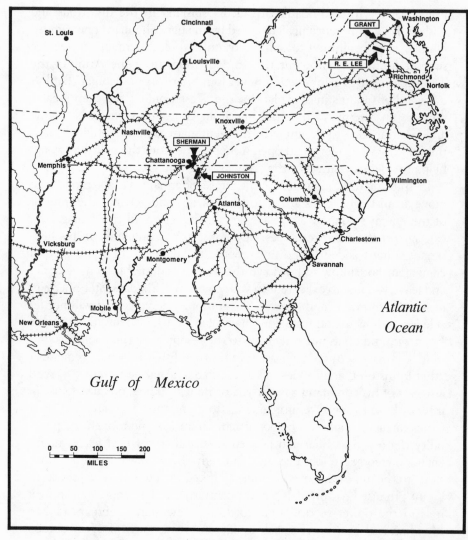

St. Louis

Cincinnati

Louisville

GRANT

Washington

R. E. LEE

Richmond

Norfolk

Knoxville

Nashville

SHERMAN

Chattanooga

JOHNSTON

Memphis

Wilmington

Atlanta

Columbia

Charlestown

Vicksburg

Montgomery

Savannah

Mobile

New Orleans

*Atlantic
Ocean*

*Gulf of Mexico*

0    50    100    150    200
MILES

Area Map, Spring, 1864.

Sherman was born in Ohio, and visited early by sorrow. His father died when he was two and his mother, who could not raise eleven children by herself, had to send Tecumseh—"Cump" as he was called by the family—to become a ward of the Ewing family. It was to his great good fortune. Thomas Ewing, a prominent lawyer and politician, gave the boy a sound education and influence that was able to open doors. Cump's new family even gave him a first name. Deeming Tecumseh, his only given name at birth, of heathen origin, the Catholic Ewings had him baptized. Since the ceremony occurred on St. William's Day, the lad became William Tecumseh.

In 1836 the young Ohioan, grown tall and slender, with the red hair he had hated as a child, entered West Point. He was popular with his fellow cadets, always ready for a bit of fun, willing to go to the area's most famous tavern for oysters and beer. But Cump was also a good student, finishing sixth in a class of forty-two in 1840.

As a boy he had grown close to his foster-sister Ellen Ewing. The two wrote regularly during his academy years and in 1850 they were married. The young officer served in California during the Mexican War, but after the conflict, low army pay and enforced separations from his family led Sherman to do what his future friend Grant and so many others had done—resign. He tried banking and real estate only to be flat broke after the Panic of 1857 struck the nation. It was a time of deep depression. "I look upon myself as a dead cock in a pit, not worthy of future notice," he gloomily told Ellen.

In 1859 a new job raised his hopes. The West Pointer became superintendent of a new military school in Louisiana; the school that eventually would become Louisiana State University. But Cump's duty in Baton Rouge was short lived. He got along well with Southerners, had no hostility toward slavery, but did not accept Southern theories of disunion. With the coming of secession, the Unionist traveled to St. Louis, working briefly for a street railway company before his opportunity came to return to the army.

Sherman led a brigade at First Bull Run and on August 7, 1861, he became the seventh-ranking brigadier general of volunteers in the army, eleven places ahead of Grant. In September Sherman went to Kentucky and began a difficult few months trying to organize Union forces there. His volunteers responded slowly, and the general's estimate of the number of troops needed to carry the war to the Rebels in the West was decried in the press as being insanely excessive. (It came to seem more realistic as the war years passed.) Sherman disliked journalists, and the dislike exploded into hatred over this incident. He ordered the press out of his command, and they branded him as insane. It was a label often used later by his foes, but also eventually used in jest by both his soldiers and the general himself. But it was not a subject of jest in 1861. He never forgave the journalistic profession for this treatment.

Sherman moved from Kentucky's contretemps to Cairo and then down the Tennessee to join Grant at Shiloh. He led the Fifteenth Corps in the Vicksburg campaign, then marched with Grant to Chattanooga to relieve the Army of the Cumberland as commander of the Army of the Tennessee. At Missionary Ridge Sherman's army was badly battered by Pat Cleburne's Confederates.

As the war dragged on, General Sherman came to realize the enormity of the task facing the Union. This realization came to Sherman sooner than to most Northern political and military leaders, and he wrote often on the subject. Since he wrote well and expressed himself firmly and with clarity, he has been called a "Fighting Prophet" by one biographer and "Soldier, Realist, American," by another. No American has spoken out more forcefully on war. No American of his time, with the obvious exception of Lincoln, has been more widely quoted.

In 1862 the general told Grant, if "we cannot change the hearts of the people of the South . . . we can make war so terrible that they will realize" its futility, "however brave and gallant and devoted to their country" they may be. In 1863 Cump wrote his brother, Senator John Sherman of Ohio: "It is about time the North understood the truth, that the entire South, man, woman and child is against us." That same year, when a Southern woman complained about the behavior of his troops, Sherman replied, "Madam . . . war . . . is cruelty . . . the crueler it is, the sooner it will be over." In 1864, when his policy toward occupied Atlanta produced an outcry, he wrote to Halleck: "If the people raise a howl against my barbarity and cruelty, I will answer that war is war and not popularity seeking." And, of course, there is his most famous quote of all, made long after the conflict: "War is hell."

And there would be other familiar statements. A Boston editor, after reading a Sherman letter in support of Grant said, "How his wrath swells and grows. He writes as well as he fights." In addition to his often-quoted remarks on war his "Atlanta is ours and fairly won," and "I present Savannah to the country as a Christmas present," were the kind of phrases that rallied a nation at war. After the war the general published highly readable memoirs that, given his turn of phrase and relentless honesty (as he saw it), provoked sparks of controversy. Perhaps his most famous statement on a subject other than war was the one made in 1884 when he was being courted as a presidential candidate by the Republican party: "If nominated I will not run, if elected I will not serve." With William Tecumseh Sherman there was little need to read between the lines. The force of his actions was matched by the force of his words. Undoubtedly Sherman relished being outspoken. In a letter to Grant soon after the war, which he instructed the general to show to President Johnson, Sherman stated what must have been obvious to Grant: "My opinions on all matters are very strong."

By 1864 the war had physically worn the western army's forty-three-

Scene of Sherman's Attack, Missionary Ridge.

year-old commander. A year earlier his wife told her father after a visit to Cump, "He looks more wrinkled than most men of sixty." Another who saw the general thought "I never saw him but I thought of Lazarus." Sherman's manner appeared nervous and restless. He smoked endlessly, puffing his cigar "as if it was a duty to be finished in the shortest time." Two excellent portraits of Sherman came from two staff officers. To Henry Hitchcock he was "a man of power more than any man I remember. Not general intellectual power . . . but the sort of power which a flash of lightning suggests—as clear, as intense, as rapid." John Chipman Gray saw in Sherman:

> the most American looking man I ever saw, tall and lank, not very erect, with hair like a thatch, which he rubs up with his hands, a rusty beard trimmed close, a wrinkled face, sharp, prominent red nose, small bright eyes . . . black felt hat slouched over the eyes . . . brown field officer's coat with high collar and no shoulder straps, muddy trowsers and one spur. He carries his hands in his pockets, is very awkward in his gait and motion, talks continually and with immense rapidity, and might sit to *Punch* for the portrait of the ideal Yankee.

Sherman possessed one of the Civil War's finest military minds. He understood the totality of war. His grasp of military problems allowed him to adjust his plans in the face of changing conditions. But he was not a great battlefield tactician. At Shiloh he was surprised by Albert Sidney Johnston's early attack and at Missionary Ridge he was confused by the terrain, costing his command heavy casualties. To Grant, Sherman's tactical shortcomings were more than offset by his broad understanding of war, his aggressiveness, and, perhaps most of all, his ability to work in harmony with his fellow Westerner.

Long after the event it seems inevitable that Sherman was elevated to command the western armies when Grant went east. Grant and Sherman had worked together for two years, and deep respect had developed between them. When Grant was promoted to lieutenant general he told Sherman and McPherson that they were "*the* men to whom above all others I feel indebted for whatever I have had of success." Sherman, two years older than the Illinoisan, recognized Grant's ability and was willing to play the subordinate. And Grant wanted to leave the army in the hands of an aggressive soldier.

But by 1864 the Union had developed a number of fine commanders, and any one of three, perhaps four, might have been given the Military Division of the Mississippi. Philip Henry Sheridan, who Grant took to Virginia to command his cavalry, might have replaced the new lieutenant general. Sheridan would eventually exercise an independent command in the Shenandoah Valley. Young James B. McPherson had made great strides and was a close friend of Grant and Sherman. Also, there was George H. Thomas.

Thomas, who outranked Sherman, had made a record as a subordinate commander in the West unmatched in either army. His war service had begun in the campaign of First Bull Run, but he was transferred to the West and served at Mill Springs and Shiloh. As a major general in the Army of the Cumberland under William S. Rosecrans, Thomas fought at Corinth, Perryville, and Stones River. At Chickamauga his tenacious defense of Horseshoe Ridge saved Rosecrans from a crushing defeat and won Thomas, already called "Old Tom," "Pap," and "Old Slow Trot," a new nickname—"the Rock of Chickamauga." Two months later the Army of the Cumberland, under Thomas's command, stormed up Missionary Ridge and drove Bragg's Confederates from the field.

Thomas's background was very different from those of Grant, Sherman, Sheridan, and McPherson. He was born in Southampton County, Virginia, and at fifteen he and his family were forced by Nat Turner's slave rebellion to flee their home. George Thomas entered West Point with the Ohioan Sherman, roomed with him for a time, and graduated six places behind him in 1840. The Virginian fought in Mexico and on the frontier under the command of two more senior Virginians, Albert Sidney Johnston and Robert E. Lee. With Virginia's secession Thomas refused to follow Johnston and Lee, remaining with the United States. His sisters were so upset by his action that they never reconciled with him.

Some have seen in Sherman's elevation over Thomas a conspiracy by the midwestern generals against a man from a different background. There is little evidence of such a conspiracy. The more obvious reasons for Grant's decision were his better ability to communicate with Sherman and the even more salient fact that his military temperament mirrored Sherman's, not Thomas's. Grant and Thomas had occasionally disagreed, whereas the Grant-Sherman relationship was more harmonious. Thomas, while undeniably successful, was more slow, deliberate, and methodical than either Grant or Sherman. Some of this difference is revealed in David Conyngham's observations of "the Rock of Chickamauga." Thomas was:

George H. Thomas.

quite the reverse of Sherman, both in manners and appearance. He is tall, stout, with brawny frame and shoulders. His head is slightly bent forward, as if drooping with thought and care. His hair and beard, which he wears cut pretty short, are rather dark, and slightly sprinkled with gray. He is about fifty years of age. . . . is very reserved; speaks little. . . . [is] calm and cautious; does everything by rule; leaves nothing to chance.

Conyngham's last sentence may best explain Grant's decision: he did not want a man who was too cautious. To his credit, Thomas hid any disappointment he felt and labored to prepare the Army of the Cumberland for the campaign. In a war in which both armies were plagued by thin-skinned generals standing on military protocol, Thomas's actions are as laudable as his combat record.

Much has been written of the Union's superiority in numbers as well as its superiority in the production of arms, ammunition, uniforms, and food. An equally vital superiority enjoyed by the Union lay in its command harmony. After struggling with its system for three years, the Federals enjoyed a working relationship in 1864 and 1865 that contributed significantly to eventual victory. The president, Grant, Halleck, and Sherman understood each other and operated together with a degree of unity never achieved in the Confederacy. A high degree of command harmony also existed in Sherman's army. It was strengthened and nourished during the winter of reorganization.

Thomas's Army of the Cumberland was reorganized during the winter months. By far the largest army in the Military Division of the Mississippi, Thomas's force numbered 72,938 officers and men by the time the spring campaign began. The Fourth Corps, with a troop strength of 20,538, was commanded by Oliver O. Howard. Widely known as "the Christian Soldier," Howard, from Maine, had graduated from West Point in 1854. He had served on the frontier and had begun his Civil War action at First Bull Run. Until the fall of 1863 he fought in the Army of the Potomac, participating in most of that army's battles. At Fair Oaks (Seven Pines) Howard was seriously wounded, losing his right arm. He led the ill-fated Eleventh Corps at Chancellorsville and Gettysburg and brought that unit west to reinforce Grant at Chattanooga. Devout and intelligent, Howard was an abolitionist. When the Eleventh was consolidated with the Twelfth Corps, Howard replaced Gordon Granger at the head of the Fourth. Granger's actions in the Knoxville campaign had angered Grant, Sherman, and Thomas, and he was sent to the Department of the Gulf. Howard was pleased with his new command, writing, "I like the 4th Army Corps," and admitting, "after the reverse at Chancellorsville, it was hard for me to cherish a feeling of confidence in the whole

of the old corps." Howard's was the only corps in Sherman's army that
had West Pointers—David S. Stanley, John Newton, and Thomas J.
Wood—leading all of its divisions.

The Fourteenth Corps of Thomas's big army would be led by John M.
Palmer. Forty-six years old, Palmer was an Illinois attorney who had been
a Democratic legislator before joining the Republicans after the passage
of the Kansas-Nebraska Act. Palmer was a delegate to the 1860 Republican National Convention, supporting Lincoln's nomination. He had
served all over the West, and was a veteran of Stones River and Chickamauga. Palmer's corps had 22,696 officers and men and its three divisions were commanded by Richard W. Johnson, Absalom Baird, and
Jefferson C. Davis.

Davis, with that interesting name for a Union general, is worthy of
special notation. A thirty-six year old from southern Indiana, he was one
of the best-known characters in Sherman's army. He was a private in the
Mexican War, commissioned in 1848, and was at Fort Sumter when the
firing started. Davis steadily rose in rank until a bitter feud with General
William Nelson in Kentucky threatened his career. Angered when "Bull"
Nelson called him a "damned puppy," Davis shot and killed the huge
Kentuckian. Because able officers were needed and because Indiana governor Oliver P. Morton shielded him, Jeff C. Davis was never tried. He
went on to serve at Stones River and Chickamauga. A slight man with

Jefferson C. Davis.

a shaggy beard, he was an officer noted for his sense of humor and for his use of strong language. Sherman liked the profane Davis and once slyly encouraged him to give full rein to his profanity in the presence of General Howard. Finally, "the Christian Soldier" with "distress all over his face, left, whereupon Sherman and Davis made the house ring with laughter." When one officer protested, Sherman replied, "that Christian-soldier business is all right in its place, but he needn't put on airs when we are among ourselves."

The third corps in the Army of the Cumberland was the 20,721-man Twentieth, created during the winter reorganization when the Eleventh and Twelfth were combined. The new corps, sporting a star taken from the old Twelfth Corps as its badge, had Alpheus S. Williams, John W. Geary, and Daniel Butterfield as its division leaders. Commanding the corps was one-time commander of the Army of the Potomac—Joseph Hooker. Always a center of controversy, "Fighting Joe" was also a capable leader who inspired his men. He was fifty; he had graduated from West Point in 1837, and had served in Florida, Mexico, and California before the war. A trail of confrontations followed him. By the outbreak of the Civil War he had clashed with Winfield Scott, Henry W. Halleck, and William Tecumseh Sherman.

Reactions to Hooker were almost always extreme. Sherman said he was "envious, imperious and [a] braggart." Supposedly Sherman and Hooker had battled in California before the war when both were in business there. The chief reason for Hooker's hostility in 1864 lay in the frustration he felt as his career plummeted following his May 1863 defeat by Lee at Chancellorsville. He considered Sherman his inferior. Hooker also outranked both Sherman and Thomas and was bitter at his subordinate role. Fortunately for the Union cause, Thomas managed the touchy general and acted as a buffer between "Fighting Joe" and Sherman.

There were those who loved and admired the Twentieth Corps commander. One of Hooker's brigade leaders wrote: "Hooker is *the commander*. I wish you could see him when a fight is underway. His enthusiasm is enough in itself to inspire any man."

The Army of the Cumberland mustered a cavalry corps of 8,983 troopers. General Washington L. Elliott, a regular army cavalryman who had served in Mexico and on the frontier, commanded the unit. Edward McCook, Kenner Garrard, and Judson Kilpatrick led the three mounted divisions. Sherman did not have great confidence in any of these men or in cavalry generally. McCook, just thirty and a member of the large clan, "the Fighting McCooks of Ohio," was a lawyer who had once served in the Kansas legislature. He had seen action at Perryville and Chickamauga. Garrard and Kilpatrick were both West Pointers. The former, in whom Sherman probably had the least faith, had fought in the East and been in charge of the Cavalry Bureau. The latter, an 1861 academy graduate, was only twenty-eight. After active service in the East, which included a badly led raid on Richmond in February 1864, the flamboyant Kilpatrick had been sent to lead one of Sherman's divisions—at Sherman's request. Probably Sherman wanted him because he was headstrong. Kilpatrick neither drank nor gambled, but his reputation as a ladies' man fit in well with the image cultivated by the mounted arm. One major who rode with him found Kilpatrick "a dashing fellow, more so than any cavalry officer I have met."

The huge Army of the Cumberland also boasted 130 pieces of artillery. Each division had two or three batteries of from four to six guns. Two smaller armies supported this formidable fighting machine. One of these, the Army of the Tennessee, would move against Johnston led by a new commander.

When Sherman was advanced, he and Grant agreed that the post Sherman had vacated at the head of this force of 24,380 should go to General James Birdseye McPherson. The thirty-five-year-old Ohioan had finished first in the West Point class of 1853. A talented engineer, McPherson served in that branch of the military before returning to the academy to teach. Fighting in all of the Army of the Tennessee's great battles, he was adored by his men and admired by his commanders. McPherson was a handsome, dignified soldier; both Grant and Sherman saw in him a future commander of the army.

McPherson was the only West Point graduate in the Army of the Tennessee above the level of brigade commander. None of his three corps commanders nor any of his seven division commanders had graduated from the academy.

In December when Francis P. Blair, Jr., took leave from his post as commander of the Fifteenth Corps to participate in Northern politics, John A. Logan was given the vacant slot. Not only had Logan come to the army from civilian life, he was excessively proud of it. An Illinois attorney, the man his troops called "Black Jack" had served as a Democrat in the Illinois legislature and as a representative in the U.S. Congress. His combat record was outstanding, but he was touchy about matters affecting his command and he often antagonized professional military men. He and Thomas clashed while the army lay in camp around Chattanooga. Logan's flowing black mustache made him noticeable everywhere he appeared. Logan's three divisions were led by Peter J. Osterhaus, Morgan L. Smith, and William Harrow.

Grenville M. Dodge commanded the two divisions of the Sixteenth Corps that would move against Johnston's Rebels. A third corps division had been sent to Louisiana, leaving units led by Thomas W. Sweeny and James C. Veatch under Dodge's direct supervision. The thirty-three-year-old Dodge, a New Englander who had moved to the prairies of Iowa, was a brilliant young engineer. When the war broke out he formed the Council Bluffs Guards and went on to be wounded at Pea Ridge. Dodge had served in the Sixteenth Corps since January 1863.

When the western theater's command dominos had begun to fall in March 1864, Sherman replaced Grant and McPherson replaced Sherman, leaving command of the Army of the Tennessee's last corps, the Seventeenth, vacant. By that time Frank Blair, Jr., ready to leave the political wars, was searching for a command. Rather than return to his earlier leadership of the Fifteenth Corps, already under Logan's command, Grant suggested the influential Missourian take McPherson's place with the Seventeenth. Blair agreed and found that part of this corps had also been sent to Louisiana. The remaining two divisions were led by Ohioan Mortimer D. Leggett and Marcellus M. Crocker of Iowa.

Blair, like Logan, bore the designation "political soldier," and, like Logan, was not altogether trusted by Sherman. Blair was a member of one of the nation's most prominent political families. His father, Francis P. Blair, Sr., a longtime power in Democratic party councils, had been a friend and confidant of Andrew Jackson. His brother Montgomery was Lincoln's postmaster general. Frank Blair, Jr., was a Princeton graduate who had served in Mexico. He led the Missouri Unionists at the war's start and was a significant force in saving that slave state for the Union. He had served two terms in the House of Representatives, resigning to enter the army in 1862.

For its Long Arm, the Army of the Tennessee had ninety-six pieces of artillery, with each division having either two or three batteries. Unlike the other two armies, McPherson's force had no cavalry divisions, only a few hundred riders used as couriers or scouts.

The third of Sherman's armies, the Army of the Ohio, numbered only 12,805 officers and men and was actually, by the spring, only one corps composed of three infantry divisions and one cavalry division, together with 592 artillerymen who served the unit's twenty-eight guns. Grant had ordered the army's Ninth Corps transferred to the East and left the Twenty-third for Sherman. Between December and February the Army of the Ohio had three commanders. The first, Ambrose Burnside, was relieved on December 12 and his replacement, John G. Foster, was too ill to handle the post.

In late January, Grant brought thirty-two-year-old John M. Schofield from his long service in Missouri to command the army. The plump Illinoisan had graduated seventh of fifty-two in the West Point class of

George Stoneman and His Staff.

1853, six places behind McPherson, and thirty-seven places ahead of Confederate general John Bell Hood. Schofield's receding hairline and long beard made him look older than his years, but his eyes were youthful and intelligent. Almost all of the army commander's war service had been west of the Mississippi. Leading Schofield's three divisions were Alvin P. Hovey, Henry Moses Judah, and Jacob D. Cox.

The Army of the Ohio listed mounted troops on its roster. A cavalry division of 2,951 riders was commanded by George Stoneman. A Military Academy graduate, the forty-one-year-old Stoneman was stationed in Texas at the outbreak of hostilities. He barely escaped capture by Texas authorities, winding up in Virginia where he led the cavalry corps of the Army of the Potomac. He had been transferred to the Army of the Ohio in early 1864.

The obvious inequality in size of the three armies Sherman would take into Georgia has sometimes led to criticism of the general's organization. He might have transferred men from Thomas's army to the other two, which Schofield suggested after the war. But Civil War troops had deep unit loyalty and "Old Tom's" men did not want to leave his command. Once the campaign was underway Sherman would be forced to detach parts of the Army of the Cumberland to cooperate with McPherson and Schofield. Twice this caused arguments as to command seniority, but the unequal size of his armies did not seem to concern Sherman and does not seem to have caused serious problems.

The organizational structure of Sherman's cavalry was a more serious flaw. With four divisions split between two armies, there was no united mounted force, although Sherman, not Thomas and Schofield, directly controlled the horsemen. Sherman has been faulted for poor use of his cavalry and he certainly had little faith in the horsemen. He never seems to have believed in the value of cavalry beyond scouting and protecting supply trains. He is credited in the western command with coining the saying "Who ever saw a dead cavalryman?" Sooy Smith's failure in the Meridian campaign had recently reminded Sherman of his doubts. In Meridian, waiting for Smith, he said, "It will be a novel thing in war if infantry had to await the motions of cavalry." Had Sheridan remained in the West the story might have been different, for Sherman had poor leadership for his cavalry divisions. Yet even then, the general's prejudice against the mounted arm might have curtailed its use in his campaign.

Three Union officers rarely mentioned in the story of Sherman's Georgia campaign are Colonels Daniel C. McCallum, Adna Anderson, and William W. Wright. Far from the front, this triumvirate was charged by the general commanding with creating, operating, and maintaining his lifeline with the rear. In his memoirs Sherman claimed, "The Atlanta campaign would simply have been impossible without the use of the railroads." The three colonels, therefore, were to make the campaign possible. McCallum was director and general manager of military railroads. Anderson led the Department of Transportation, which operated the supply trains, and Wright commanded the Department of Construction, which kept roadbed, track, and bridges operating.

The Union commander demanded that Wright's men be well drilled in rapid reaction to Confederate raids on his arteries. Through March and April these units practiced their tasks over and over. The American Civil War was the world's first railroad war. Sherman's army harnessed this transportation revolution to military use in a way not matched in the conflict.

From the day he succeeded Grant, Sherman began securing western railroads to his sole control. Civilian use was severely limited despite the outcry of citizens in east Tennessee and protests from Washington politicians, ranging from the War Department to the president. The general also fought with railroad executives who were not accustomed to his notions of work. He complained to Washington that "these railroad men are so accustomed to timetables that I believe they would run on a single track if a double one lay side by side." One executive, James Guthrie, president of the Louisville & Nashville, supported him, and soon the line was running cars into Nashville at a rate never before imagined.

Sherman's great supply depot was Nashville, by 1864 one of the nation's most important cities. In the new year's first months trains moved in and out incessantly as food, clothing, ammunition, and weapons hauled in from north of the Ohio were stockpiled. The general took a vigorous role in gathering his mountain of military necessities. His aides fanned out across the northwest purchasing the needed items; enough to be ready to move by April 25. Once when a quartermaster expressed doubts, Sherman roared, "I'm going to move on Joe Johnston the day Grant telegraphs me he is going to hit Bobby Lee; and if you don't have my army supplied and keep it supplied, we'll eat your mules up, sir—eat your mules up!" By April Nashville had become "one vast storehouse—warehouses covering city blocks, one a quarter of a mile long—stables by the ten and twenty acres, repair shops by the fieldful." New Springfield rifles were issued to some units, while others got the new seven-shot Spencer repeaters. Artillery batteries were outfitted with new gun carriages and caissons and new harness for their animals.

From Nashville these supplies were moved to the army's winter camps over the Nashville & Chattanooga Railroad. Once south of Chattanooga, Sherman's troops would seize the Western & Atlantic Railroad and his engineer colonels would extend their operations down the rails into Georgia.

To keep his army supplied Sherman estimated "65 cars a day were necessary to maintain an army of 100,000 and 30,000 animals." He added, "but for accidents and accumulation I laid my figures at 120 a day. To do this work from Nashville I aimed to get 100 locomotives and 1000 cars, expecting to lose two trains a week by accident and the enemy. . . . We attained nearly that standard before I got possession of Atlanta," Sherman concluded.

Union railroads ran for three hundred miles across Kentucky and Tennessee. To defend tracks, bridges, and tunnels against Rebel raiders, the Federals mobilized several thousand militiamen from the Midwest called to active duty for three months. South of Chattanooga Sherman would rely on more seasoned troops left in the rear to guard key points when the army pressed the enemy on toward Atlanta. Eventually the general assigned General James B. Steedman to command the District of the Etowah, a unit whose sole purpose was railroad defense. Sherman's preparations were so well carried out, and his railroad managers, engineers, and defenders performed their tasks so ably, that there was no significant interruption in the flow of supplies throughout the campaign's four months.

Well-functioning railroads would reduce Sherman's tie to the slow-moving mules and wagons he so despised. In the marching orders sent to each unit in April, wagons were limited. The general was determined to make his army "a mobile machine, willing and able to start at a minute's notice, and to subsist on the scantiest food." Unfortunately, the food available in north Georgia after three years of war and the passage of the two armies was to be very scanty. This planned lack of wagons, coupled with a shortage of food along the line of march, would tie the army more closely to the Western & Atlantic than Sherman had intended.

The campaigns of 1863 had been long and arduous. The marches into Mississippi and across Tennessee had been exhausting, and the great battles of Vicksburg, Chickamauga, and Chattanooga had taken a heavy toll in Union killed and wounded. After Grant's forces surged up Missionary Ridge on November 25, driving Bragg away to the south, most of the western army had gone into winter quarters. With the exception of occasional raids the Federal army rested, mended, and began slowly organizing for its next trial at arms. For most Union soldiers that trial awaited spring weather, so they had just over five months to recuperate, reenlist, and reorganize.

Sherman's large force was overwhelmingly midwestern. Of his 314 infantry regiments, 240 were from that section, 34 were eastern units, and 40 were from the Union slave states. The army had the distinct flavor of Illinois, Indiana, and Ohio, with 90 percent of the midwestern units from those three states. There was also a distinct immigrant flavor to Sherman's army. Many units, especially those from Missouri, Illinois, Indiana, and Ohio, were German-American. Orders were given in German or in strongly accented English. Names such as Osterhaus, Landgraeber, Wangelin, Kammerling, and Dilger were prominent on the army roster.

Quartermasters noticed these Westerners were taller and had larger shoe sizes than men in the Army of the Potomac. They were deeply tanned by their three years of marching across Kentucky, Tennessee, and Mississippi. These men wore their hair long, wore floppy hats rather than regulation military caps, and strode along with a rangy, swinging stride. When Easterners came west from the Army of the Potomac they gawked:

"This army looked quite unlike our own. . . . They were carelessly dressed, both officers and men; and marched in a very irregular way, seemingly not caring to keep well close up and in regular order."

The Westerners had deep contempt for the eastern army. That was evident in a letter from a Kentucky veteran:

> This is not a Potomac army. . . . That army was organized long before ours, has had all the caresses of the government, fed and clothed to its hearts content, has done nothing but march and countermarch, suffer defeat after defeat and now that three years have passed finds itself just where it began. Whereas this . . . army has driven the enemy back from 500 to 1000 miles, whipped them wherever they fought and . . . in the end get no credit for it. After we conquer all the cotton states we will have to take Richmond for the pampered, idle Potomac Army.

The reinforcements who had come west with Hooker before Chattanooga had initially been mistrusted, but by May 1864, although some rivalry remained, these units were deemed to be westernized enough to be acceptable.

Sherman's army fought hard and was combat-wise, but was careless of discipline and cynical about rules and regulations. The men were quick to jeer at other units and their own officers. When officers rode by on skinny mounts whole units cawed like crows. When Frank Blair drove his men hard on a forced march they bleated "Bla-a-a-i-r! Bla-a-a-i-r!" like angry sheep when he rode into sight. Many enlisted men called officers by their first names and yelled "Black Jack" and "Uncle Billy" at Logan and Sherman, two of their favorites. In characterizing Sherman's colorful army, Bruce Catton said it well when he wrote, "it seemed to be a combination of licensed freebooter and avenging angel, half instrument of destiny, half frontier mob."

In early 1864 many soldiers who had volunteered for three years in 1861 ended their terms of service in this army. Since it was vitally important for these experienced soldiers to remain under arms, a thirty-day furlough was offered to those who would "veteranize," as reenlistment was called. Officers made patriotic speeches and enlisted men urged each other to stay together to see the struggle to a victorious end.

Several inducements were offered. Promises of higher pay, new uniforms, as well as bounties: $402 according to Theodore Upson of the One Hundredth Indiana. Most Union veterans did reenlist and take their furloughs; for a time during the winter the army's strength was seriously diminished. Captain Alfred L. Hough watched men entrain for the North: "How happy they do look on their way home I expect they will cut up some shindys when they get there." He told his wife that she "must bear with them, for they are brave fellows and have only one short month of recreation before returning here to fight more battles." Hough added philosophically: "Being in the Army has a tendency to make spendthrifts of the boys. To be a first class soldier one has to learn to take no thought of tomorrow."

Those men who had not accumulated three years' service could not go home. Some regretted spending the winter in camp, while others were content to remain there. Many of those who went agreed with Illinois major James A. Connelly that, "It seems to me I was not at home more than a day." The men's return to the army bore little resemblance to their first enlistments in 1861. "War was no longer an exhilarating adventure to be entered upon in holiday mood, but rather a grim business to be got through with as quickly and expeditiously as possible." The men who "veteranized" that winter were the nucleus of Sherman's seasoned army. The furloughs helped raise morale, and once back in camp these veterans were confident that victory lay at the end of their 1864 campaign.

The army's winter quarters varied but were usually log huts or cabins housing five men. Mud filled the cracks between the logs and chimneys were made from rocks, barrels, or tents. The one great room in the hut served as kitchen, sitting room, and bedroom. The men slept on cots made by driving forked sticks into the ground. Crosspieces were placed on the forks with more flexible poles in between. Straw and leaves covered by blankets were used for a mattress.

Light in the cabins was supplied by the fireplace and by candles. When Illinoisan Joseph Whitney's unit ran short of candles he lighted his cabin with a "slut." Lest his wife misunderstand, he wrote: "I take bacon and fry the grease out, and put it in a low cup. Then I take a piece of rag and button and fix it so it will stand. Then I set fire to it and let it rip."

Alfred Hough found that most of the winter quarters were "comfortable." He also found that between mid-January and mid-February many units in Chattanooga had been moved into either north Georgia, Alabama, or southern Tennessee, ten to twelve miles from the city.

Living conditions for officers were usually better than for men in the ranks. In the north Georgia town of Ringgold, Major Connelly shared a house with his unit's surgeon. They had desks and cots and, with a "snug fireplace," they were warm. The house was owned by a merchant (whose children did not like the Federals). The family served tea and meals to the Union officers and Connelly wrote home, "I am living more comfortably than I have since I've been in the service."

At least one New York officer seemed determined to be comfortable and not let the war interfere with the style to which he had become accustomed in peacetime. James J. Gillette, attached to Twentieth Corps headquarters, wrote a friend in New York City asking that he take Gillette's diamond ring to Tiffany's to be fixed. He also ordered "brown linen duck breeches" from Brooks Brothers as well as a Panama hat—"a rakish one, you know, very wide brim." Not everyone in the army found war so terrible.

Perhaps it was a similar officer who ordered an Ohio regiment to wear white collars and gloves. James A. Congleton of the One Hundred and Fifth Illinois, bivouacked nearby, reported: "We are just shaking in our shoes for fear that we will be the next victims to the vanity of the shoulder straps." He vowed, "We enlisted to help put down the Rebellion not to be fitted out with white collars and white gloves . . . to be looked at as an ornament or toy." On May 2 when orders came to move toward the enemy, he gloated, "every man to have sixty rounds of cartridges. . . . White collars and white gloves I believe will be left in the rear where they should be."

While Confederates in north Georgia suffered from food shortages during the winter of waiting, Union troops were well fed. From Ringgold Ohio doctor Josiah Cotton reported good water and good food, and from Nashville, Ohio artilleryman Alpheus Bloomfield wrote on March 20: "We have plenty of rations, very good quarters . . . in fact we are seeing very good times."

The Sanitary Commission labored to supplement the soldiers' diet. Mother Bickerdyke, nurse and commission agent, received a pass allowing her transportation anywhere within the Military Division of the Mississippi. She was one of the few civilians permitted south of Nashville on Sherman's trains and steamers. In April she received potatoes, onions, sauerkraut, and pickles for distribution to the men in blue. In trying to supplement his army rations Private Lawrence Vetsch, a recent immigrant from Germany serving in the Fourth Minnesota, told his family that extra food was very expensive. According to Vetsch, "all the tings is very hi wit solgers." The private from Germany had trouble with the Indian name of the Tennessee city in which he was stationed. To Vetsch it was "Zat Anookey."

Disease was often a problem for armies packed into winter quarters. Sherman's force was no exception, although sickness was not widespread. Dysentery, diarrhea (which killed one of Illinoisan Joseph Whitney's friends), scurvy, and bilious fever were reported in the camps around Chattanooga. Major Connelly also reported measles and smallpox in his regiment and "indulged in the luxury of vaccination."

January and February were cold months. Snow fell in January and on

February 16 Connelly complained "think I shall almost freeze before morning. 'Sunny South,' eh? ugh!" By early March it appeared that spring had come. Orson Young, in an Illinois unit, felt "it is so much like summer that I took a stroll." Twelve days later the Yanks who believed that spring had come were shocked: "It has been snowing hard all day. Think of it! Snow in Georgia in the latter part of March!" Connelly said it snowed as hard as he had ever seen it in the North. After eight inches had fallen Whitney exclaimed, "The weather is treacherous here, as are the people." While some Union troops played in the snow, the men in blue do not appear to have engaged in the massive snowball battles that entertained the Rebels. By mid-April temperatures had risen, green crept up the mountainsides, and apple and plum blossomed. Only occasional rain slowed the army's preparations.

Although trips home and work toward the campaign ahead occupied Union soldiers, there was ample time for diversion in the five months in camp. At Christmas and New Year's the men celebrated with the best dinners they could muster in this alien land. April 1 was the occasion for practical jokes in the camps. The Yankees played poker, whist, and chess. Much time was spent reading. One enlisted man read dime novels "by the dozen, for there seemed to be un unlimited supply." Major Connelly and his wife, miles apart, read *David Copperfield* together and discussed the Dickens masterpiece by mail. The officer told her, "I must read something or my mind would become as rusty as a boy's jack knife that has been lost in a rubbish pile for a year or two." Alfred Hough admitted, "I spend *nothing* after living except for books." James Goodnow of the Twelfth Indiana read *Harper's Weekly* and the *Atlantic Monthly*, finding an article about the Creek War especially fascinating since he had fought through the same land.

There were more vigorous amusements available. James Congleton's captain tripped running the bases in a baseball game, broke his leg, and had to go to the rear. Hunting and fishing were popular diversions, as was sightseeing. Climbing Lookout Mountain to see the site of Hooker's "Battle Above the Clouds," as well as the view, was popular. Dr. Cotton wandered through the hills around Ringgold and soon his children in Ohio received "pretty stones" from their father away at war. Climbing a hill near Ringgold, Connelly looked to the northwest and saw smoke rising from Union campfires around Chattanooga. Turning to the south-east he saw smoke curling up from Johnston's camp near Tunnel Hill. But sightseeing in this country could remind men of the horrors of war. On that same jaunt the major found the graves of fourteen Ohio soldiers killed at Chickamauga.

Union soldiers sang, listened to both military bands and fiddlers, and went to dances. Sometimes they danced with each other, a rag around the sleeve designating the female partner. Luckier Yanks went to dances with local girls. Theodore Upson thoroughly enjoyed one such dance before fleeing when warned that Union provost guards were coming his way. Officers and men both drank to pass the time and fend off loneliness. Even generals were not immune. Fifteenth Corps commander John A. Logan, after some nagging from his wife Mary, told her in February, "I have quit drinking whisky."

On March 13 Illinois Major Connelly grumbled to his wife that "piety is a scarce article here." As the campaign neared, religious activity increased. There does not seem to have been a revival to match that which swept Confederate camps, but John Cope's report from the Ninety-eighth Ohio that "we have prayer meetings here nearly every evening," was fairly typical. General Howard wrote on April 25 that "the churches are full every evening and great religious interest is manifest." One week before the advance Illinoisan Orson Young informed his parents: "I have been serving the Devil. . . . I was being fast drilled in his tactics." "It is a hard place . . . to serve God, for we have to hear the sneers and scoffs of rude companions," he continued. Yet faith triumphed: "There are six of us in our company who have come out for the Lord. . . . We have not embraced any particular creed, but it is our intention to serve the Lord and do right."

The officers and men made every effort to maintain contact with political news from home. When told of opposition to the war Major Connelly believed, "Some of those Illinois copperheads need *killing just a little.*" By March, interest in the year's presidential contest had increased. Orson Young wrote home, "Give us Old Abe or Butler for President and we will fetch the rebels after a while." The Illinois soldier was too young to vote and he concluded, "I think that by the time I turn twenty-one, I shall have purchased my right to vote." One piece of April news created a stir. Forrest's Rebel cavalrymen took Fort Pillow on the Mississippi and massacred several hundred black soldiers. Connelly believed "it will create a hundred fold more sympathy in the army for the negro than ever existed before."

General Sherman was well aware of the effect of mail on the spirits of the men who followed his banner. Mail moved regularly, much to Theodore Upson's delight: "It is wonderful what an effect livly letters have." Connelly asked his wife to save his letters since "I would enjoy reading them myself twenty years hence, when the memory of these events . . . will have become blurred and faded like old daugerrotypes."

General James B. McPherson's inability to leave the army that winter had a special poignancy. Stationed in California in 1860, McPherson had met Emily Hoffman of Baltimore. The couple fell in love but the outbreak of hostilities prevented their marriage. Delay followed delay as the Ohioan's responsibilities increased. Finally, early in 1864, he received a twenty-day leave and went up the Mississippi to Cairo. There he learned that Grant had gone east, Sherman had been elevated, and he had been named commander of the Army of the Tennessee. Sherman, regretfully, told the young man he so admired that he must cancel the trip and return to his new command. Although they must have corresponded regularly, no letters between James and Emily exist. They were probably destroyed after the tragedy that lay ahead. McPherson did receive letters during the war from friends of the frustrated couple, and a picture of Emily Hoffman emerged from them. "I think you have won a prize for I never saw the woman whom I thought the equal of Emily Hoffman. I am sure you will be very happy," wrote one. When the army marched into Georgia, Sherman promised that when the campaign ended McPherson could go to Baltimore to be married.

Living for months in one place allowed Union soldiers an opportunity to observe "secesh" citizens. As with all invading armies, relations ranged from friendship to bitter hostility. John Wesley Marshall of the Ninety-seventh Ohio visited a Mr. Barrett "who altho somewhat . . . secesh nevertheless made the visit quite pleasant . . . and the evening glided swiftly by amid musick and mirth." Major Connelly found the woman with whom he boarded "a good woman, barring her secesh sentiments." Occasionally Yanks met east Tennessee Unionists. Walter Drew of the Ninety-sixth Illinois marched past a ninety-eight-year-old veteran of the War of 1812 "waving his hat and shouting for the Union." The men "gave him three rousing cheers."

Some Federals could not forgive the secession attitudes of these Southerners; others scoffed at the people they encountered. An Illinois soldier "saw one of Dixie's fair daughters, a number one of the southern chivalry. She was smoking and chewing tobacco and dipping snuff at the same time." And yet some Union soldiers reacted very differently to Southern women. Theodore Upson went to the wedding of his Hoosier sergeant and an Alabama girl. "The bride looked very pretty in her linsy wolsy dress . . . and she seems to be a nice modest girl," he wrote. "But no Southern girl for me!" vowed Upson, "There is a little girl in Indiana that is way ahead."

One widespread reaction was pity at the sufferings endured by the people of Tennessee and Georgia. Upson found a Tennessee family with a sick child. He took an army doctor to tend the invalid but they arrived too late to save the girl. "I am getting pretty tough but that hurt me aufuly," he admitted.

Almost all Federal units reported Confederate deserters coming into their camps during the winter and hoped it was a sign that the Rebel cause was collapsing. There was little fraternization between Union and Confederate soldiers since the two armies were not in close proximity. But, scouting along the Tennessee River, one squad of Indianans saw a group of Rebel scouts across the stream. They yelled to them, and coaxed one into rowing over. On the bank the enemies talked about the war, the Yanks giving the Reb coffee and newspapers before he rowed back.

One use of the time in winter quarters, especially in the weeks following the heavy March snowfall, was for drill. Sherman wanted his men prepared for hard marching and he wanted them to be able to respond quickly to enemy attack. For several hours each day they took target practice (far more than their Confederate opponents because of ammunition shortages in Rebel camps) built entrenchments, and fought practice battles. There were also reviews, but the Federal commander was more interested in exercises simulating combat than in fancy parades. Officers met to discuss tactics and weapon use, and to study maps of Georgia. Some read manuals—including Hardee's *Tactics*, written by a man they would soon face in battle.

By the last days of April the Union army was supplied, armed, and organized for battle. Officers and men were aware of their mission and confident of their ultimate success. On April 5 Sherman had promised his brother, "by May 1 I [shall] have on the Tennessee one of the best

A Group of Sherman's Veterans, Spring, 1864.

armies in the world." As the day for advance approached, the men who followed the Ohio redhead believed they were the finest army in the world. James A. Connelly wrote his wife, "We have a certain amount of whipping to give the rebels this summer and I am anxious to see the army getting at it," adding later, "The army is in fine fighting condition." As bugles sounded through the camps in May, Alfred Hough felt "the morale of our army is grand, it exceeds anything we had before, health good, spirits good."

Two of the army's most popular corps commanders shared this confidence. On May 1 Oliver O. Howard wrote his wife, "We are hoping that this campaign will end the war and I am more sanguine in that belief or hope than ever before." The Fifteenth Corps' chief, John A. Logan, had written his wife in March that he felt "buoyant as we are preparing for an exciting campaign." As the day neared for the advance he reported, "Our army is in fine health and spirits and will make one of its best fights this spring."

The high spirits that pervaded Sherman's western army was due in part to the respect officers had for their men and men for those who led them. No one expressed this bond better than Colonel Orlando M. Poe, Sherman's engineering genius.

> I care more for the respect and esteem of those brave soldiers, who have been tried in the fire with me, than I do of all the world beside. We *know* the measure of each other's value, a knowledge gained where there was no deception. . . . Theirs is that true chivalry inherent in the brave. It may lie under a rough coat, and rude manners and sometimes does—but it is not the less real, nor should it be anymore ignored than if it appeared under the courtly guise of the Knights of Old.

When Sherman moved his headquarters from Nashville to Chattanooga in April's final days the men knew the time had come. On April 5 the general had written his brother, "The war is not yet over by a d——d sight," and he was restless to be off. Sherman read census reports of the Georgia counties through which he must pass, observing to Grant that Georgia "has a million of inhabitants," and adding, "If they can live, we should not starve." Grant said in amazement, "He bones all the time while he is awake, as much on horseback as in camp or in quarters." To McPherson Sherman quipped, "You know how I like to be on time"; and, anticipating the twin invasions in East and West, he wrote to a member of Grant's staff: "We saw the beauty of time in the battle of Chattanooga and there is no reason why the same harmony of action should not pervade a continent."

On May 1 excitement rippled through the army. Rumors that they were about to advance were easy to believe for one Ohio soldier who found "every way you cast your eye, infantry, artillery and cavalry are seen moving." At Ringgold on the third Connelly knew, "We will surely move very soon right into the heart of Dixie." As units spent their last nights in camp they celebrated. On a beautiful spring morning a Michigan artilleryman wrote his last letter home before breaking camp. He remembered the previous night: "Over 1000 campfires were burning and at least 70 bands were playing all around us. The music, campfires and clouds of smoke were a sight to see and hear." In one large encampment every soldier took a candle, lit it, put it on his tent pole, in his bayonet socket, or held it aloft and waved it. For miles across north Georgia the lights twinkled through the spring night and the men, amazed by the seemingly endless sparkle, sent up a cheer that rolled from one end of the army to the other. It was a lovely scene from such a deadly war machine.

On May 6 Grant moved into the Wilderness and Halleck telegraphed Sherman his orders to advance. The men of the western army moved out with confidence on what their commander would later call their "splendid legs," legs that were to take them across Georgia and the Carolinas to a grand, triumphant march through the nation's capital. Some would not live to see that day. Even before a shot was fired, the veteran army was reminded that the valley of the shadow of death might lie just ahead. Some passed Chickamauga and saw skeletons protruding from shallow graves: "hands sticking up . . . fingers curved as if beckoning—one, with index finger pointing upward."

On this spring day in 1864 Sherman and Grant had enlarged upon "the beauty of time" until their "harmony of action" spanned a continent. It was the beginning of the end.

# 3

# We Can Redeem the Past

GENERAL BRAXTON BRAGG was gone at last from command of the Army of Tennessee. Sour, quarrelsome, ill-starred Bragg—a man hampered by poor health all his life, which was probably partly psychosomatic and seemed to become more pronounced when his responsibilities increased, he was often despondent and frustrated. The general gave the appearance of being a man who could successfully command an army, possessing good qualities of campaign planning and organizational ability, energy, discipline, and a strong sense of duty.

Yet something was missing. At the critical moments of a campaign, Bragg would become inflexible, hesitant, and indecisive. And his physical infirmities caused him to be irritable and harsh, alienating the general from the affection of many of the troops and contributing to serious friction, which always plagued him, with some, and at times all, of his corps commanders, as well as several division commanders. From beginning to end, the haggard, austere North Carolinian was just what he seemed in his first great battle when he led a corps at Shiloh, a puzzling mixture of competence and ineptness.

Probably there was not a more controversial high-ranking general in the Confederate army than Braxton Bragg. He was, as his biographer Grady McWhiney has observed, too ambitious to be satisfied with himself or others and represented "an unusual combination of potentially dangerous eccentricities and high ability." Bragg had evoked such dissension in the Rebel high command—Kentucky brigadier Roger Hanson, for example, wanted to kill him when he learned of the assault order on the final day at Stones River, only to die himself in that terrible affair—

Braxton Bragg.

that twice President Jefferson Davis felt compelled to visit the army in order to sustain his general and friend.

Bragg was the commander who led the Army of Tennessee longer than any other, with only bloody Chickamauga as a victory to set against his defeats. Yet even that triumph had been clouded, both by the Yankee blunder of withdrawing a division from their front line just as the Rebels charged that sector and, worse, by the Confederate failure to seize the opportunities which their victory offered. Once more, as earlier in Kentucky and again at Murfreesboro, Tennessee, many corps and division leaders thought a great chance had been frittered away—and this time even though the enemy was driven from the field. The Army of Tennessee then faced a near-mutinous internal crisis—the worst of the war—followed by the humiliating disaster of late November at Chattanooga, when the center of the Confederate line collapsed atop Missionary Ridge. The army fell back in near rout to north Georgia and finally, Bragg resigned.

"I fear we both erred," Bragg afterward wrote Davis, as he reflected on the decision for him to retain command following "the clamor raised against me" after Chickamauga and during the siege of Chattanooga. Speaking of his "shameful discomfiture" in the Chattanooga operations, Bragg acknowledged they were "justly disparaging to me as a commander," but he nevertheless blamed others for the failure, lashing out against his generals.

Now it was all academic. Whether the fault of the corps and division leaders, the rank and file of the army (Bragg blamed them too), or Bragg himself, the strategic railroad staging base at Chattanooga was lost, controlled by the Federals as the new year, 1864, came in. Heavy damage had been done to Confederate morale. The number of soldiers absent without leave was never higher, and a new commander of the Army of Tennessee would have to deal with the military situation.

This man was General Joseph Eggleston Johnston. If the word "charisma" had been in vogue in the 1860s people would have said that Johnston possessed it. When the general arrived at Dalton, Georgia, to take command of the Army of Tennessee, a body of troops, with a band, marched to his headquarters to serenade him and called loudly for him to come out and show himself. He came to the front door, accompanied by one of the army's favorite veterans, General B. Franklin Cheatham, who introduced him with an affectionate pat on Johnston's bald head and said: "Boys, this is Old Joe."

Johnston graduated thirteenth in his class at West Point, where he was a classmate and friend of Robert E. Lee. "Old Joe" had an attractive appearance and the demeanor, some said, of a gamecock. He was fifty-seven years of age, stood about five feet, seven inches tall, and was still leanly but firmly built. Wearing his well-fitted gray cloak, which complemented his gray-shot sideburns and goatee, the Confederate general looked like a commanding officer.

There was a magnetism about Johnston that evoked intense loyalty and imparted itself to the rank and file of his army. Once in Virginia when a cannon was deeply mired in the mud, the general dismounted and, despite high-polished boots and gold braid, waded into the muck, took hold of a muddy spoke along with the artillerymen, and cried out: "Now, boys; all together!" The gun bounded clear and after that, said one of the cannoneers, "Our battery used to swear by 'Old Joe.'" When he was riding the railroad, Johnston would help "wood up" the engine, sometimes working hard enough to cause his wound from the Battle of Seven Pines to give him pain. He was warm and unpretentious in manner and usually kind to subordinate officers and the common soldier, but he had an unfortunate tendency to irritate his superiors. Independent, close-mouthed, and highly sensitive about personal honor and dignity, Johnston sometimes made enemies in high places.

Foremost among these was Jefferson Davis. The ill feeling between Johnston and Davis likely had a great impact on the Atlanta campaign, especially from Johnston's perspective. Some said the trouble between the two men went back to their days at West Point when there was an alleged fistfight over the daughter of Benny Haven, keeper of the famous tavern long frequented by cadets of the military academy. According to the story, Johnston won both the fight and the affections of the young lady. However, Johnston's biographers, Gilbert E. Govan and James W. Livingood, say no contemporary source substantiates the tale and conclude it is a fabrication.

If the rumored fight over the girl is untrue, then the bitterness between Johnston and Davis apparently stemmed from events that occurred shortly before the Civil War. In 1854, as secretary of war, Davis had turned down Johnston's application to be appointed colonel of a new regiment. Later, when United States senator from Mississippi, Davis had opposed Johnston's appointment as quartermaster general of the army. It was said that even their wives became involved in a quarrel in 1861. Undoubtedly Mrs. Johnston distrusted Jefferson Davis, telling her husband, when he decided to stand with Virginia and the Confederacy, that she questioned the wisdom of his decision, in part because of Davis, who "hates you, . . . has power and . . . will ruin you."

Soon after the war began, Johnston and Davis disagreed over the need to concentrate troops in Virginia. This clash was as nothing, however, when compared with the question of Johnston's rank in the Confederate army. Johnston had expected, because of the high position he had held in the United States Army, to be named the ranking officer in the Confederacy. But Davis placed Samuel Cooper, Albert Sidney Johnston, and Lee ahead of him in the list of nominations for full general sent to the Confederate Congress in the late summer of 1861. Outraged by what he considered an attempt by Davis "to tarnish my fair fame as a soldier and a man," Johnston penned a seething six-page letter of protest addressed to Davis. The Confederate president, obviously filled with a wrath that closely matched Johnston's, responded with two sentences, the second of which characterized the "arguments and statements" of Johnston's letter as "utterly one sided, and its insinuations as unfounded as they are unbecoming."

Then in 1862, Davis and Johnston repeatedly clashed about strategic matters in Virginia and the defense of Richmond. The general had been convinced by an incident shortly before Davis's inauguration that any military conversations with government officials would quickly be divulged in the hotel lobbys of Richmond. He also resented having his judgment subjected to continual scrutiny and thus became increasingly uncommunicative. Keeping his own counsel generally Johnston confered least with the president. Davis, under a terrible strain when the Federal army was less than ten miles east of Richmond in the spring of 1862, could not even get an assurance from Johnston that an all-out defense of the city would be attempted. But soon Johnston's severe wound at the Battle of Seven Pines forced him from command. Robert E. Lee took over and drove the Yankees back from Richmond, and several months passed while Johnston recuperated.

Johnston remained in Richmond until November. When he was considered well enough to return to active service, he was placed in command of a broad new theater: the Department of the West. It stretched from the Appalachian Mountains to the Mississippi River, encompassing the major forces of Generals John C. Pemberton and Braxton Bragg. Johnston's basic assignment was to coordinate the efforts of Bragg and Pemberton for the defense of Tennessee and the Mississippi. Despite the dislike which the president felt for Johnston, the new secretary of war, James A. Seddon, who was the driving force in creating this huge department, influenced Davis to give the command to Johnston. "Davis swallowed gall but approved the appointment," observed Frank Vandiver in his book *Rebel Brass.*

Seddon saw the war in large terms, believed in concentration of forces, and continually urged offensive action. Thus Johnston was to be the sole deviser of military plans in the Department of the West, using his discretion in combining the forces of his department to meet the Federals on a superior, or at least equal, footing. As envisoned by Seddon, and as actually arranged, the only responsibility Johnston had to the president or the War Department was to report his actions and request what he needed. The idea was for Johnston to operate in the same manner, except on a much larger scale, as Lee had been doing within the Department of Northern Virginia, coordinating the movements of his own army as well as all smaller forces.

The concept of such a theater command seemed highly promising—but Joseph Johnston was not the man for the job. His poor relationship with the president proved a stumbling block from the first and probably explains, in part, why he never seemed to thoroughly understand the nature of his new command. Johnston felt, probably correctly, that he had been appointed theater commander simply because only three available officers outranked Bragg. Lee was busy in Virginia, and P. G. T. Beauregard's relationship with Davis was even worse than Johnston's: therefore, Davis was left with Johnston as his only choice. At times Johnston also suspected that he had been given a nominal command, with little actual power but heavy responsibilities, to make him look bad. Repeated assurances to the contrary—that he really did have authority—by the secretary of war could never persuade the general, and Johnston could not bring himself to exercise personal control of either or both the major armies under his supervision.

Instead, from the very day of his appointment, Johnston protested the impossibility of his assignment, focusing upon the facts that Bragg's and Pemberton's armies were separated by several hundred miles and that both Major General U. S. Grant's army and the Tennessee River were between them. Consequently, Johnston never gave the assignment his best effort to see whether or not the theater concept might work. Contending with Davis over various matters, both major and minor, Johnston assumed a defeatist stance, became disgusted, and his huge department slipped away from him. Bragg and Pemberton went their separate ways, Vicksburg was lost, more of Tennessee was lost, and Davis felt confirmed in his negative judgment of the Virginia general.

Yet when Johnston took command of the Rebel forces in front of Dalton at the end of 1863, the bad blood between him and the president—detrimental though it was to the fortunes of the Confederacy—probably did not constitute the worst problem. Actually, the most foreboding factor was that Johnston had a major flaw as a military commander: he lacked an aggressive, competitive temperament when leading an army. From first to last, Johnston's military record in the Civil War belies the time-honored Confederate legend of the Atlanta campaign: that the general was a master of Fabian tactics.

Early on in the war Judah P. Benjamin, while serving as secretary of war, perhaps perceived Johnston more clearly than most, and spoke of his "tendencies to defensive strategy and lack of knowledge of the environment." As long as Johnston held field command in Virginia, whenever a Federal advance appeared in the offing, Johnston seemed always either to retreat or be anticipating a retreat. In mid-June of 1861 he abandoned Harpers Ferry, calling the pullout "a strategic withdrawal" under pressure from superior numbers. By late winter of 1862, when a second major Federal offensive seemed likely, Johnston told Davis that the Confederate army, positioned along Bull Run and the Potomac, could not block the multiple routes by which the enemy might move on Richmond. The Rebel forces must fall back, said the hero of the Battle of Manassas. When Davis wanted to know to what line the retreat would be, Johnston replied that he did not know, being unfamiliar with the country between Richmond and Manassas.

The president was understandably upset. "That a general should have selected a line which he himself considered untenable," Davis later wrote, "and should not have ascertained the typography of the country in his rear was inexplicable on any other theory than that he had neglected the primary duty of a commander." Granting that Davis did not care for Johnston, yet it is difficult not to agree with Davis's judgment.

Unannounced to the president, Johnston's pullback from the Bull Run line began while Davis was still urging him to hold on, assuring his general that he would be promptly and adequately reinforced. In fact, Davis spoke of strengthening Johnston's army to the point that he could take offensive action. But Johnston retreated to the line of the Rappahannock River, burning supplies and equipment which could not be carried off by civilians, and leaving heavy guns in their emplacements.

The long-awaited Union offensive started at last, except not in the north-to-south manner anticipated by the Confederates. Instead, the Yankees moved by water to the base of the peninsula between the James and York rivers, seventy miles southeast of Richmond, from there intending to move on the Rebel capital. Johnston shifted his forces to confront the invader, only to soon begin a retrograde movement up the peninsula. He could find no position that satisfied him. Abandoning the middle and lower stretches of the Chickahominy Creek, Johnston took up an intermediate position, only to relinquish it within two days and retreat to the very outskirts of Richmond. Another withdrawal and the Federals under George McClellan would possess the Confederate capital by default. And what Johnston intended next he would not divulge, as previously noted, even to the president. Finally, backed against the capital, he fought the Battle of Seven Pines, launching the one attack of his military career and suffering a severe wound in that confusing, badly bungled engagement. When Johnston eventually recovered and left Virginia to command the new Department of the West nothing had changed. Certainly he did not show much aggressiveness in Mississippi and Tennessee.

WHY then was Joseph E. Johnston chosen to command the Confederate Army of Tennessee in one of the war's last and most significant campaigns? The answer to that question bears heavily upon one of the widely propagated, long-popular concepts of the war: that the South had superior generals but the North won because it had superior resources.

The superiority of Southern generals is largely a myth. Like some other Southern legends—such as the Virginia Cavaliers and the happy and contented slaves—it is untrue. The circumstances of Johnston's appointment certainly contribute to the destruction of the legend, because a basic reason for the selection of Johnston to lead the Army of Tennessee was that President Davis simply did not have many choices.

When Braxton Bragg resigned command of the army to become Jefferson Davis's chief military advisor, General William J. Hardee was left in temporary charge of the Army of Tennessee. Hardee did not want permanent command, stating that he did not have the abilities for the position. Probably the matter was more complex. As one of Bragg's longtime critics, Hardee may have balked at the thought of bearing the chief

James Longstreet.

responsibility of replacing Bragg, even though Hardee was a good orga-
nizer, a solid corps commander, and likely did possess the qualities to
lead an army. Colonel T. B. Roy, Hardee's chief of staff, later wrote that
the general, deeply concerned about morale, felt that Beauregard or
Johnston could do more to rebuild the spirit of the rank and file. There
was too the fact that Johnston outranked Hardee in seniority. There were
no corps or division commanders in the Army of Tennessee, besides Hardee, who merited serious consideration for the position.

Upon learning that Hardee would not agree to take command, Davis
faced a very difficult decision: with James Longstreet out of the picture
because of his less than satisfactory performance in east Tennessee, Davis
either must send Lee west or appoint one of his longtime enemies, Beauregard or Johnston. If Lee went to the Army of Tennessee, there would
then be the question of who would command the Army of Northern
Virginia. Nevertheless, Davis tried for several days to persuade Lee to
take the assignment. However, just as when the turmoil had arisen to
oust Bragg after Chickamauga, Lee did not want the appointment; he
finally convinced the president that he should remain in Virginia.

With Lee eliminated, Davis apparently leaned toward Beauregard in
what was, for him, doubtless a question of picking the lesser of two evils.
But the president received considerable pressure from Johnston's friends,
as well as the anti-Davis bloc in the Congress—often one and the same—

P. G. T. Beauregard.

to appoint the Virginian. Even Davis's close and trusted friend, the bishop-general Leonidas Polk, wrote to urge the appointment of Johnston. Besides, if Beauregard were appointed, there would be the matter of picking a successor for him at Charleston. And Johnston was senior to Beauregard. Still, Davis wondered if Johnston could overcome what the president, like former Secretary of War Benjamin, now perceived as a natural inclination for defensive warfare. Manifesting "doubt and misgiving to the end," according to James Seddon, and without any possible selection that he really believed would be good, Davis finally concurred with his cabinet, which had concluded Johnston was the best man available. On December 16, Davis sent a telegram to Johnston, then at Bolton's Depot, Mississippi, directing him to turn over the Army of Mississippi to Polk and assume command of the Army and the Department of Tennessee in north Georgia.

JOHNSTON found his new command in poor condition. Private Sam Watkins sometimes exaggerated when he told the history of the First Tennessee Infantry, but his account is always lively and readable, even when he's painting a bleak picture. "The morale of the army was gone," he wrote. "The spirit of the soldiers was crushed, . . . They would not answer at roll call. Discipline had gone. A feeling of mistrust pervaded the whole army. A train load of provisions came into Dalton. The soldiers stopped it before it rolled into the station, burst open every car, and carried off all the bacon, meal and flour that was on board. Wild riot was the order of the day." The holiday season was "boisterous and stormy," according to Dr. W. J. Worsham of the Nineteenth Tennessee. He thought there was "more fighting and drinking in camp than usual," and observed that gambling "was again on the rampage." Another Confederate wrote on January 2: "The war appears to have demoralized everybody." He said "the girls smoke and chew tobacco and drink whiskey . . ." and "the rumor says that almost half the women in the vicinity of the army, married and unmarried, are lost to all virtue." Still another Confederate, observing that "war is a severe strain on religious habits," recalled an officer who, early in the war had led his men in prayer at evening roll call, but who was frequently seen drunk in public during the winter of 1863–64.

Demoralized by the embarrassing defeat at Chattanooga, the army's ranks were thinned from desertion, some troops having gone over to the enemy, many more having returned to their homes. There was a shortage of food, clothing, horses, wagons, artillery, weapons, and ammunition. (Disconcerting evidence of the shortage of ammunition may be found in Johnston's February 16 circular urging corps commanders to make every effort to recover the lead bullets used in target practice so that they might be melted down and used again.) General Hardee, during his temporary service as army commander before Johnston's appointment, had labored to secure more food and clothing, as well as granting furloughs to a number of soldiers. But it was obvious to Johnston that much more was necessary to place the army in fit form for active operations.

Arriving at Dalton to find an unsigned letter, dated December 18, 1863, from Secretary of War Seddon, stating the administration's hopes that Johnston would "assume the offensive" as soon "as the condition of our forces will allow," Johnston curtly returned it for a signature, informing the secretary (ironically one of the men who had urged the reluctant Davis to appoint Johnston), "This army is now far from being able to resume the offensive. It is deficient in numbers, arms, subsistence stores, and field transportation."

Johnston was not exaggerating. Especially during December and January, food was frequently scarce. Meat from government sources was available no more than three times a week. Soldiers often ate a monotonous and sparse diet of cornbread and sweet potatoes or, for variety, cornbread and peanuts. Packages from home were a great treat and helped the men survive the lean weeks. By late February and early March conditions were much improved and the army was being furnished with sufficient quantities of meat. The food shortage was largely resolved because Johnston established cordial relations with Georgia's volatile governor, Joseph E. Brown, an adamant States' Rights leader. (Brown, for example, insisted on calling the Georgia State Militia the "Georgia Regular Army.") The Western & Atlantic Railroad from Atlanta to Chattanooga was owned by the state of Georgia, and Braxton Bragg had engaged Governor Brown in a running controversy over the use of its equipment for moving the army's supplies. Johnston handled the touchy governor more wisely and tactfully than Bragg, with the result that provision trains started running regularly again.

The winter of 1863–64 was unusually cold, the temperature in January once reaching three degrees below zero in north Georgia, and snow covering the ground in late March. Living quarters for Confederate soldiers were similar to those of the enemy. The structures were crude yet adequate—if sufficient bedding and clothing could be obtained. Unlike the Union army, however, blankets were scarce for the Confederates and, worst of all, many men were without shoes. Johnston worked hard to resolve the problems. When a blockade runner came in from Nassau with a large load of shoes, Johnston secured thousands of them for the Army of Tennessee. There is no question that Johnston did more for the physical and mental welfare of the army than Bragg had achieved. "General Johnston seems to have infused a new spirit into the whole mass," an officer wrote to his wife in early April. "Our men are better clothed than at any previous time, while their food is better than one would have anticipated two months ago."

The strength of the army was increased by the return of several thousand absentees when Johnston proclaimed a general amnesty for all who returned to the ranks. Many who had gone home in despair after the defeat at Missionary Ridge came back, their fervor for the Confederate cause renewed by the policies of a new commander in whom they placed confidence. Johnston also instituted a system of furloughs by which the entire army, in detachments, was allowed to visit home on leave of absence. Of course some regiments, depending on where home was located, could not take advantage of the opportunity. Dr. Worsham wrote that only a few men of the Nineteenth Tennessee, "on account of the improbable chances of reaching home," due to Yankee occupation and bad weather, made the attempt. But all appreciated Johnston giving them a chance for a furlough.

The rise of army morale was particularly important at this time, because the terms of enlistment were about up for many of the soldiers who had originally volunteered for three years' service. Most of the veterans who were eligible for discharge did reenlist, the majority basing their decision on patriotism, knowing the Confederacy could not possibly survive without its experienced soldiers.

Sometimes, however, there were reenforcing influences—in fact intoxicating influences—employed to insure that army veterans reluctant to reenlist would be encouraged to make the proper decision. Such was the case with the Eighteenth Alabama Infantry, who were marched into an open field while orators delivered patriotic speeches and a detail passed out ample quantities of whiskey. After a time, the regimental colors were moved forward several feet and the men told that if they wished to reenlist for the duration of the war, they should move forward to the colors when the command "forward march" was heard. Meanwhile, those soldiers known to be willing to reenlist had been instructed to rush forward with loud yells at the command. The command was given. Officers and men who had been alerted charged up to the colors with a piercing yell. The others, "half drunk, many of them," hearing a familiar command, obeyed it. Thus did the Eighteenth Alabama, in its entirety, volunteer for the remainder of the war.

While Johnston's policies undoubtedly strengthened the Army of Tennessee, there is no way to determine with assurance what that strength actually was in terms of numbers. This uncertainty is due to different methods and categories used in the army for assessing manpower. With categories such as "effective strength," "total present," "aggregate present," and "present and absent," plus differing criteria for determining the total in each category—not to mention the fact that reports from the same period and using the same categories will sometimes give different totals—the task of calculating the manpower of the Army of Tennessee is frustrating indeed. Most students of this numbers game have placed Rebel strength, as the time to go to war drew near, between 50,000 and 60,000. Examining the differing "official sources" upon which such a determination must be based, one is highly reluctant to attempt any more specific assessment.

Whatever the precise number, it was too small. That, at best, there would be too few men to compete with the Federals on anything like an equal basis had been obvious to Johnston and other officers several months earlier. Engrossed in attempting to restore morale, find more soldiers, and convince Richmond that the army's condition was not nearly as strong as supposed, Joseph E. Johnston was only a few days into his new command when General Patrick R. Cleburne, without a doubt one of the very best division leaders the Confederacy possessed, dropped a bombshell (figuratively speaking) in a council of Johnston's generals.

Cleburne would solve the manpower problem by enlisting slaves in the Confederate army. The "black race of slaves" should then be granted freedom, said Cleburne, in return for faithful military service to the Confederacy.

Patrick Ronayne Cleburne was a thirty-five-year-old, slim but broad-shouldered six-footer, with gray-blue eyes and a heavy shock of dark brown hair. He was born on St. Patrick's Day in Ovens Township, County Cork, Ireland. His family's fortunes had seen hard times after the death of his father Dr. Joseph Cleburne. Young Patrick, scarcely fifteen, was chosen by his family to become a doctor like his father. But in 1846 Pat Cleburne failed the entrance examination at the Dublin Medical School. Fearing that he had disgraced the family name, Cleburne ran away to join the Forty-first Regiment of Infantry, rising by 1849 to the rank of corporal in Her Majesty's Army. Cleburne's family, meanwhile, seeking a better life, decided that same year to move to America. Young Patrick purchased his discharge from the British army with borrowed funds and joined in their Great Adventure.

Home in the New World eventually became Helena, Arkansas. In the decade before the Civil War, Cleburne rose rapidly in local society as a druggist and later as an attorney who was active in politics. Energetic, durable, and intelligent, he made his presence felt. The advent of the war saw the same steady, determined drive to achieve. As first a brigade and later a division commander, Cleburne's unsurpassed record became part of the history of Shiloh, Perryville, Stones River, and every other major western battle.

But even for a Confederate hero-general, one course was unacceptable in the American South of 1864, and that Cleburne now proposed: to free slaves. It was not that the Irish general failed to understand something of the sensitivity of the issue. In fact, the long paper he read at Johnston's headquarters advocating this truly breathtaking proposal had consumed his attention for days, according to Captain Irving A. Buck, Cleburne's assistant adjutant general. While Cleburne himself owned no slaves, and although his foreign background, in a non-slaveholding society, probably did develop in him a mind less racially prejudiced than the average Southerner, yet the General had resided for a decade and a half in the midst of an institution that as much as anything else had caused the war, which symbolized much that was Southern, and involved tremendous economic investment. Cleburne knew he was dealing with a revolutionary subject.

In the opening paragraph of his paper, dated January 1, 1864, a year

Patrick Cleburne.

to the day after Abraham Lincoln's Emancipation Proclamation became
official, the general acknowledged his subject was "so grave" and his
views "so new," that he sought suggestions before submitting the proposal to higher authority. He also chose to review the war, emphasizing
at length the Confederacy's dire situation, before ever stating his specific
proposal to free the slaves.

Cleburne was an intense patriot who would do anything to help his
adopted country win the war, whose logic had carried him to the conclusion that without more men, the Confederacy could never survive. He
wrote: "We have now been fighting for nearly three years, have spilled
much of our best blood, and lost, consumed, or thrown to the flames an
amount of property equal in value to the specie currency of the world."
The fruit of all this had been "nothing but long lists of dead and man-
gled." And now the Federals, with superior numbers "at every point,"
were endeavoring "to make the preponderance irresistable. . . . Every
soldier in our army already knows and feels our numerical inferiority to
the enemy." And, when the Confederate soldier "turns from the wasting

armies in the field to look at the source of supply, he finds nothing in the prospect to encourage him."

But Cleburne had found a source of encouragement. Of the Confederacy's something less than ten million people, according to the 1860 census, more than three million were slaves. Here, thought Cleburne, was the pool of manpower with which the Confederacy might still win the war. This was the surest, probably the only, means left for recruiting the army's dwindling, exhausted ranks. And so the general proposed that slaves be enlisted with the guarantee of "freedom within a reasonable time to every slave in the South who shall remain true to the Confederacy in this war." The South must free all its slaves, said Cleburne, first, because it was only fair, and second, because the black would not fight otherwise. The South would have to promise the Negro freedom, not only for himself but for his wife, his children, and all his race. The project should be done in a reasonable way, in order to prepare both races for the traumatic change, but it must be done.

This policy would have other advantages. Cleburne argued that slaves had become a military liability because they were being recruited into the Union army as it overran Southern states. The abolition of slavery also might encourage the long-desired recognition of the Confederacy by European nations. Cleburne concluded by saying that he thought the plan "will save our country. It may be imperfect, but in all human probability it would give us our independence. No objection ought to outweigh it which is not weightier than independence."

Although the paper was signed by four of Cleburne's brigade commanders and ten regimental commanders, the document startled both the high command of the Army of Tennessee and the Richmond authorities, just as Captain Buck had predicted when Cleburne first showed it to him. When Buck had warned Cleburne that slaveholders were "totally unprepared to consider such a radical measure," and that the general's chances for promotion (which seemed quite good after his success at Taylor's Ridge) would be destroyed by publication of the paper, Cleburne responded that the crisis upon the South was so grave he felt it to be his duty to bring the proposal before the authorities. Deep as was his attachment to his present command, Cleburne added that he would be willing to undertake the training and leadership of a black regiment. The most disastrous result, personally, could only be a court-martial and cashiering, said Cleburne, in which case he would, according to Captain Buck, "immediately enlist as a private in his old regiment, the Fifteenth Arkansas, then in his division; that if not permitted to command, he could at least do his duty in the ranks."

After Cleburne read the paper on the night of January 2, in the presence of Generals Johnston, Hardee, W. H. T. Walker, Alexander P. Stewart, Carter L. Stevenson, Thomas Hindman, and William B. Bate, a marked division of opinion erupted. Leading the attack on Cleburne's proposal, General W. H. T. Walker—a hotheaded, proslavery Georgian—stated his intention to forward a copy of the document to Richmond, together with a report as to which generals seemed to support it. Considering Walker's militant personality, and references in a letter to Bragg about "the treason and the . . . traitors" of "the abolition party of the South," perhaps Cleburne was fortunate that Walker did not challenge him to a duel.

At first, Walker intended to send the report through the War Department, but General Johnston forbade this, stating that the subject was not a military matter. Johnston, in fact, told Secretary of War Seddon in a later letter that he "regarded this discussion as confidential, and understood it to be so agreed before the party separated." Obviously Walker did not so regard it. Procuring a copy of the startling paper from the straightforward Cleburne, who apparently had few qualms about who saw it, Walker next addressed a circular letter to each general present asking whether he had supported the measure. General Hindman, for one, was so incensed by Walker's presumptiousness that he made no reply. When a shocked Jefferson Davis received these items, he quickly moved to suppress all knowledge of the proposal. Secretary Seddon assured Johnston that "while no doubt or mistrust is for a moment entertained of the patriotic intents of the gallant author of the memorial," the president wanted Johnston to squelch any further discussion of the matter.

Johnston cooperated fully. So did Cleburne. In fact, it was not until 1890 that Cleburne's paper was rediscovered, found in the personal effects of a member of his staff who died in California. Walker, however, was not yet willing to allow the matter to rest; not while it might still be used to promote his career. The key point in understanding General Walker is to realize that in the winter of 1864 he hoped to succeed to a corps command. Thus he continued to attack Cleburne, Hindman, and Cheatham (the latter was not even present at the January 2 conference at Johnston's headquarters) for their supposed part in an abolitionist conspiracy. Walker told Bragg, who had been at odds with Cheatham since the Battle of Murfreesboro over a year before, that Cheatham had approved of Cleburne's document. Reminding Bragg that Hindman had been Cleburne's law partner before the war, Walker reported that Hindman spoke at the meeting in favor of Cleburne's plan to free slaves. Walker's biggest guns were for Cleburne, of course, whom he characterized, as previously noted, as a traitor. General Joseph Wheeler also wrote Bragg, not only attacking Cleburne, Hindman, and Cheatham, but naming Hardee too as favoring the slave proposal. Bragg referred to Cleburne and the others as "abolitionist men" who should be "marked" and "watched."

The whole affair became a despicable mess, stemming from the best of motives on the part of Cleburne, but ultimately resulting in still more high-command dissension in the Army of Tennessee. And Cleburne, as Captain Buck had foreseen, would never be promoted above division command.

Cleburne, however, never seemed particularly concerned about promotion or lack of promotion. Determined to keep his division at the highest possible efficiency level, Cleburne conducted for some time at Dalton a daily school of instruction in the art of war. His log-cabin classroom was for the benefit of his brigade commanders, who in turn instructed their regimental officers, and these the company commanders. Cleburne's unit was also known for its sharpshooters. Using the Whitworth rifle, accurate up to two thousand yards when fitted with telescopic sights, the sharpshooters composed an elite force capable of quickly silencing a troublesome Yankee battery.

Still, not all of Cleburne's thoughts were on the war. In February, he took his first and only leave of absence from the army to serve as best man at the marriage of General Hardee. The trip was eventful and memorable, for in Mobile, Alabama, Cleburne met Susan Tarleton, a young woman who soon became his fiancée. All too soon, however, the Irishborn general had to return to Dalton and the army.

Certainly Cleburne was not the only officer who believed in drill and instruction—followed by more drill and instruction. Not only did Civil War generals think such would improve the fighting qualities of their commands, they also thought discipline and morale were strengthened thereby. Thus, whenever the weather permitted, the soldiers spent hours practicing the intricate maneuvers outlined in Civil War manuals of instruction. "Drilling is the order of the day now," wrote a Georgian in late March. "We have to go five miles to the drill ground and by the time we get through drilling and return to camps we have done a good days work." Target practice, formation drills, work on fortifications, marching, reviews, and mock battles were a large and integral part of the soldier's life.

Yet their officers could not keep the troops busy all the time. Leisure activities ranged from the more sedate, such as fishing, reading, and singing, to gander pullings, cockfights, and primitive baseball. Always, of course, there was poker. But the Dalton event longest remembered and most often recalled by a host of veterans in the years after the war was none of the foregoing. What the soldiers never forgot was "the Great Snowball Battle."

North Georgia seldom experiences much snowfall in any year, and certainly it is extremely rare in late March. But as the Southerners sleepily responded to reveille on March 22, 1864, they were astonished to see the ground turned white. During the night, while the army slumbered, a heavy snow had covered the area to a depth, some reported, of five inches. Soon after breakfast many soldiers were snowfighting all around their camps. Eventually good-natured skirmishes between small groups "snowballed" into larger bouts, conducted in more zealous fashion, and resulting in black eyes and bruised limbs, even broken bones. Large portions of divisions, such as William B. Bate's, Alexander P. Stewart's, and Cleburne's, became involved. The snowfighting included many officers. For example, Cleburne himself, directing a brigade, was "captured," then "paroled," only to be "captured" again.

But to judge from the accounts of soldiers who were present, a still more monumental battle than the foregoing occurred. According to some Confederates, the greatest snowballing in history involved B. Franklin Cheatham's Tennesseans against, appropriately in view of the clash about arming slaves between the two generals, William H. T. Walker's Georgians.

About midmorning, after several hours of sporadic snowfighting among themselves, the Tennesseans and Georgians, camped next to each other along a small creek bed, exchanged challenges. Word quickly spread through the camps and in all, some 5,000 men made ready for the fray, piling large stacks of snowballs in preparation along opposing hilltops. Then the Tennesseans, armed with as many snowballs as they could carry and stuff into pockets, charged the position of the Georgians, only to retreat when they ran low on "ammunition." The Georgians immediately launched a counterattack, with the same result as the Tennesseans had experienced. Charges and countercharges continued for several hours, with the most determined attacks aimed at the stockpiles of snowballs. Only when all were cold and wringing wet, most exhausted, and some bruised and cut from hits by balls containing rocks or other hard substances, did the clash seem at last to be subsiding.

But then Colonal George W. Gordon of the Eleventh Tennessee Infantry took command, riding along the ranks waving a large banner as he rallied the Tennesseans for yet another assault. Gordon ordered the charge and rode straight into the Georgia line. "The air was white with whizzing and bursting balls," wrote Gordon, describing how "men were tripped up, knocked down, covered with snow, or run over." The Tennesseans pushed the Georgians through their camps and into the woods beyond, then rejoiced in their victory. Some even rifled the Georgia camps of provisions and cooking utensils.

This apparently ended the full-scale fighting. However, some of the triumphant Tennesseans, not yet ready to stop the fracas, turned on each other, continuing a vigorous snowballing for quite some time. At last some diehard Georgians once more attacked a portion of the Tennesseans. When the Tennesseans drove them off and captured their leader, Brigadier General John K. Jackson, the general made a short speech saying he hoped the Tennesseans would whip the Yankees as handily as they had his Georgians. This seemed to touch a respondent chord and the men shouted with cheers for Georgia and Tennessee and at last returned to their quarters. The Great Snowball Battle had ended.

The late winter and spring of 1864 witnessed another phenomenon in the Army of Tennessee: a more pervasive wave of religious enthusiasm sweeping through the camps than in the Union forces. In his book *Confederate Morale and Church Propaganda*, James W. Silver wrote: "Throughout 1864 preachers called for a return to Christ as the means of putting the Confederacy back on the road to victory. More than ever they tended to minimize defeat and to exaggerate the importance of minor Confederate successes." There were other motivations as well as the salvation of the Confederacy affecting the men, to be sure. "The missionary influence of the enemy's cannon," as the Kentucky Confederate Johnny Green called it, was undoubtedly a factor in the conversion of some soldiers as time drew near for military campaigning to begin. Too, there is always an emotional mass consciousness involved in large-scale revivalism. When several persons are persuaded to the mourners bench, others are certain to follow if the preacher continues an emotional appeal. Presumably, of course, some of the men were sincerely converted, separate and apart from considerations of circumstance, what others were doing, or the impassioned oratory of evangelists.

In late April a Confederate wrote his sister that "a great many has joined the church and others are penetent," reporting that the previous night "there were 118 persons at the altar." Only a few days later another Southerner said that while sitting in front of his tent he could hear the voices of four different preachers at four different services, all within less than a quarter of a mile of his camp. Still another reported that "a revival spirit took hold of the men as well as the ministers, and each brigade had its 'Brusharbor.' Each afternoon and night, . . . when inspection and drill were not in order, . . . could be heard singing and shouting" from several arbors at the same time.

While clearing off the ground for one of the arbors in George Maney's brigade, a tall hickory tree had been left standing, which appeared to be sound. On the night of April 29, according to Dr. Worsham, "there were hundreds under the arbor, and about forty penitents. At one bench there were eight penitents and two others, who were Christians, talking to them, all kneeling, when, with no more warning than a sharp crack . . . , the tree came crashing through the arbor . . . killing the ten at once." Sam Watkins also wrote of the death of the ten, testifying: "God had heard their prayers. Their souls had been carried to heaven. . . . They joined the army of the hosts of heaven."

MEANWHILE, General Joseph E. Johnston finally had the army organized—although not in the arrangement he desired—for the spring campaign. Johnston had found the Army of Tennessee divided into three corps, two of which were infantry and the other cavalry. One infantry corps was led by Lieutenant General William J. Hardee. Known in Confederate legend as "Old Reliable," Hardee was famous as the author of *Rifle and Light Infantry Tactics*, commonly referred to simply as Hardee's *Tactics*, a manual of arms by which many of the soldiers drilled. He was a native of Georgia, a graduate of West Point (class of 1838) who had distinguished himself in the Mexican War, continued in the old army, and held the rank of lieutenant colonel when the Civil War began. His men had led the attack at Shiloh, the first truly great battle of the war, in the spring of 1862. Again, nine months later, they had streamed out of the dim light of early morning to stun the Federals, many of whom were still breakfasting in their camps, at Stones River. Hardee's men had successfully defended the right flank at Missionary Ridge only to be forced into retreat by the collapsing center of the Rebel line. His corps was a tough fighting unit, composed of divisions led by Cleburne, Cheatham, Stevenson, and Walker.

The other Rebel infantry corps, when Johnston first took command at Dalton, was led by Major General Thomas C. Hindman, a Tennessean with no formal military education. A former member of the United States Congress, who had fought in the Mexican War, Hindman was commissioned a Confederate colonel in 1861. Although he fought at Shiloh, his war service was primarily in the trans-Mississippi region until he joined the Army of Tennessee in the summer of 1863, soon fighting in the battle of Chickamauga, and also falling into the anti-Bragg camp. Hindman's division commanders were Patton Anderson, John C. Breckinridge, and A. P. Stewart.

Commanding the cavalry corps was Joseph "Fightin' Joe" Wheeler. A twenty-seven-year-old, five-foot-five, 127-pound major general, Wheeler was idolized by many a common soldier in the western Confederacy. Sometimes admiringly referred to by one newspaper correspondent as "the War Child," Wheeler was an 1859 West Point graduate. He was well known for a swashbuckling ride completely around General William S. Rosecrans's army shortly before the battle of Stones River, as well as a more recent raid on the enemy's supply line west of Chattanooga. That raid was followed by a reckless trek into middle Tennessee, which cost several hundred of his men in killed and wounded and a good many

Joseph Wheeler.

captured. In truth, Wheeler had all but wrecked his command before he got it once more on the south bank of the Tennessee River at Decatur, Alabama. While some praised Wheeler's dash and daring, infantry brigadier general Arthur M. Manigault was closer to a realistic evaluation when he wrote of Wheeler's October 1863 ride: "I am inclined to think that this raid, like a great many others, did us more harm than the enemy." Wheeler's corps was divided into four divisions, commanded by John A. Wharton, William T. Martin, Frank C. Armstrong, and John H. Kelly.

General Johnston was not at all pleased with his army's organization. He wanted the infantry divided into three corps, which he believed would provide greater flexibility. He asked Davis to approve the plan on the last day of 1863, and also asked that Major General William H. C. Whiting be sent to command the third corps. Again and again—twice in January and twice in February—Johnston renewed his request. At last learning that Whiting would not be sent, Johnston then asked for Major General Mansfield Lovell. In requesting first Whiting and then Lovell, Johnston picked two generals who had become identified as enemies of the Davis administration. Perhaps Johnston wasn't aware of the talk. If not, it was an unfortunate turn of events: Davis's increasing sensitivity to criticism and dissent, plus his longtime friction with Johnston, as well as Johnston's personal friendship with key anti-administration politicians, made it highly unlikely that Johnston's request would be honored. Indeed, Braxton Bragg ultimately conveyed the Confederate government's refusal to allow the formation of a third corps, with an explanation that the Army of Tennessee was too small to justify it.

The government then proceeded to organize the army according to its own desires. Such officers as Patton Anderson, John Breckinridge, and John Wharton were reassigned; Johnston was also denied E. P. Alexander, whom he wanted for chief of artillery; and most importantly, President Davis promoted John Bell Hood to lieutenant general, sending him to Dalton to replace Hindman as corps commander. Hindman was so angry that he offered his resignation. Ultimately he was prevailed upon to stay with the army, returning to the command of his old division since Patton Anderson had been sent to Florida. Major General William B. Bate was given command of the division Breckinridge had led, and that division was transferred from Hood to Hardee's corps in exchange for Carter Stevenson's division. Obviously Johnston could not have been pleased by the manner in which Richmond had dealt with his proposal for reorganizing the army.

In addition to all the other difficulties, the Confederates faced a major question of what should be their strategy. From the time that Johnston took command of the Rebel forces at Dalton in December until Sherman launched his campaign in May, the attempt to develop a western strategy continually plagued the Confederates.

Several factors contributed to this seemingly insoluble problem. One was that Richmond, convinced the Federals would begin another large-scale offensive against the Army of Northern Virginia in the Spring, could not conceive of the Yankees having the manpower and material resources to launch an equally strong, simultaneous offensive against the Army of Tennessee. Also, Richmond held an erroneous opinion of the condition of the Army of Tennessee, believing it was in better shape than first had been supposed after the defeat at Chattanooga.

For example, when Johnston took command of the army at Dalton on December 27, a letter—one that had to be disconcerting and irritating in view of the poor condition of the Confederate force—was already on its way from President Davis. In it, two days before Christmas, Davis wrote Johnston: "The intelligence recently received respecting the condition of the army is encouraging, and induces me to hope that you will soon be able to commence active operations against the enemy." Referring to positive reports from Colonel Joseph C. Ives and General Hardee, the president stated that, "The effective condition of your new command, as thus reported to me, is a matter of much congratulation." Davis then suggested—although prefacing the remark by saying that Johnston would "not need to have it suggested"—the "imperative demand for prompt and vigorous action," rather than "a season of inactivity."

Davis's letter clearly indicated also that the bleak specter of Braxton Bragg, even though removed from command, still loomed menacingly upon the horizon of the Army of Tennessee. The president wrote: "In a letter to me soon after the battle [Missionary Ridge], General Bragg expressed his unshaken confidence. . . . He says: 'We can redeem the past. Let us concentrate all our available men, . . . hurl the whole upon the enemy and crush him in his power and his glory. I believe it practicable.' " The aggressiveness of the enigmatic Bragg seemed to increase remarkably after he no longer commanded the army.

Making the situation worse, Richmond was not knowledgeable of the formidable topography problems presented by the east Tennessee countryside. Even Bragg, once he was in the position of military advisor to the president, apparently forgot about terrain and logistical problems that he had argued were impossible to overcome—when he had held field command. Thus Richmond wanted offensive action by Johnston in order to take the initiative from the Yankees at Chattanooga, to stop the alleged transfer (which was not occurring) of Union troops from west to east in a massive concentration against Lee, and also, in Lee's words, "to repossess ourselves of Tennessee."

But Johnston had no desire to take the offensive. His favored plan, he said, was to await Sherman in north Georgia, defeat and drive him back, and then advance into Tennessee as the Yankees retreated. And Richmond's unrealistic offensive plans and misinformation played into Johnston's hands, enabling him both to make sound arguments against those proposals and feel all the more justified in his own determination to stand on the defensive, awaiting Sherman's move.

Worse yet, Davis, Longstreet, Lee, Bragg, and Seddon were involved for several weeks in discussion and correspondence trying to devise a western plan of campaign for Johnston—without even consulting him. While there is no direct evidence that anyone was purposefully keeping Johnston in the dark, that he was left out of the strategic brainstorming further confirmed what "Old Joe" already thought—that Richmond could not be depended upon to deal with him fairly.

One of the plans for a western offensive, discussed in Richmond at some length before Johnston learned about it, stemmed from General Longstreet in east Tennessee. Briefly dallying first with an idea to invade Washington with his infantry corps mounted on mules and accompanied by Lee's cavalry, which he suggested to Lee on January 10, Longstreet hardly gave the ink time to dry on that proposal before broaching the subject, the very next day, of invading Kentucky to strike the Louisville & Nashville Railroad. Again, his corps was to be mounted on mules and horses. By early February Longstreet still liked the Kentucky plan, suggesting that all the cavalry in both Johnston's and Polk's departments should join his mounted infantry in central Kentucky. In fact, Longstreet seemed to become rather carried away with his strategic postulating and proposed that Lee join him for the Kentucky venture while Johnston's army would be shifted to Virginia.

No doubt this scheme seemed a bit unrealistic to Lee, who soon responded with an enumeration of several of its problems. He suggested as an alternative that Longstreet and Johnston should join forces to drive the Federals from east Tennessee. Longstreet was not persuaded, continuing to lobby, with various alterations, for his Kentucky strategy, but Richmond quickly latched onto the Tennessee project.

Davis and Bragg both liked it. So did Seddon. The idea was for Johnston to cut loose from his Western & Atlantic Railroad communications with Atlanta and march to a point forty miles or so south of Knoxville; there he was to join Longstreet, and together their forces would cross the Tennessee River, then move over the Cumberland Mountains, finally capturing Nashville before the Yankees at Chattanooga realized what was happening. Johnston was to be reinforced with 5,000 men from Polk and 10,000 more from Beauregard.

It was past mid-March when Johnston learned of this plan. In a letter to Bragg dated March 16, Johnston wrote: "I have had the honor to receive your letter of the 7th instant. . . . I beg leave to say that the plan of campaign to which you have twice referred, has not been communicated to me and that the scale on which preparations are to be made must depend on a knowledge of it and of the forces to be used." When Johnston at last learned of the campaign being discussed at Richmond he was appalled.

Logistically, as Johnston saw at once and informed Richmond, the campaign was an invitation to disaster. Inadequately supplied with wagons and sorely hurting for teams to pull them, Johnston would have to carry enough provisions to feed his army on a hundred-mile trek to the rendezvous point south of Knoxville, plus enough for both his force and Longstreet (who had said his 12,000 men, already on half rations, would have to rely on Johnston's provisions) to subsist on from the crossing of the Tennessee River over the Cumberland Mountains, another sixty-five or seventy miles, to where additional supplies could at last be obtained in middle Tennessee. Besides all this, another 150 wagons would be needed just to carry the pontoon train for crossing the Tennessee River.

Even if such logistical problems were not incapacitating, there were other major difficulties. Longstreet must evade a superior enemy force at Knoxville in order to join Johnston in the first place. The promised reinforcement from Polk and Beauregard was just that—a promise, for General Bragg had told Johnston they would join him, not at Dalton, but after the campaign began. One other problem existed, which was equalled only by the logistical difficulties. Johnston was correctly convinced that the Yankees were massing more than 100,000 men in the Chattanooga-Nashville sector. By rail, large numbers of these troops could be moved from point to point within a few hours. However, once Johnston and Longstreet left the Kingston-Loudon area south of Knoxville, they would face a hundred-and-sixty-mile struggle to Nashville, half of it through mountains, with the objective of their march fairly obvious to the highly mobile Federals.

Believing that Richmond's plan, which Longstreet also considered impracticable, possessed all the ingredients of a military fiasco, Johnston suggested, after explaining his misgivings, that if middle Tennessee were going to be invaded, it would be much better to do so by moving through north Alabama. Actually, Johnston did not favor this offensive either, fearing the strong Union army at Chattanooga might attack him in flank as he marched through northeastern Alabama; he was apprehensive too of the supply problems in crossing the mountain ranges of the area, and convinced that he would have to move beyond the Stevenson-Bridgeport sector to cross the Tennessee River because of the Federal strength protecting the railroad at those points.

Johnston was still sure that the best strategy was to await the Yankee offensive in north Georgia—"to bring on a battle on this side of the Tennessee"—but if Richmond insisted on an invasion, then the north Alabama route was much to be preferred to the expedition through east Tennessee. Also, Johnston suggested that Longstreet should reinforce him at Dalton.

Johnston's letter to Bragg of March 20, while conveying these weighty objections to the middle Tennessee campaign, was also characterized by a tone that Richmond doubtless found to be all too familiar. Avowing that the enemy "will advance as soon as he can, with the greatest force he can raise," Johnston, as in the past, thought basically in defensive terms. While he did ask "Would it not be easier to move into Middle Tennessee through North Alabama?" the query, taken in context, constituted merely a passing comment, tied with his refutation of a move through east Tennessee, and followed immediately by this unmistakable statement: "I believe fully, however, that Grant will be ready to act before we can be." Clearly, Johnston thought the true Confederate strategy, in his own words, "as soon as possible," was to "put ourselves in condition for successful resistance."

The general would go into detail explaining why Richmond's offensive plans could not work, but he never offered any details of an alternative to those plans; indeed he never offered any offensive suggestion at all, unless the mere mention of a move through north Alabama be so considered. Any references to a forward movement, whatever the circumstances, were always few and accompanied by vague qualifications of the type that politicians are wont to make, such as "whenever the relative forces of the opposing armies should justify me in such a measure"—the meaninglessness of which surely was not lost on the politicians and administrators in Richmond.

Without question, defensive strategy permeated Johnston's thinking, doubtless causing Richmond to take all he said, however well reasoned, less seriously than otherwise. His March 20 letter to Bragg contains an endorsement by Jefferson Davis, dated March 28, which reads: "Returned to General Bragg after being read with disappointment."

And so, as the time for the spring campaigning approached, the relationship between Johnston and Richmond (particularly Davis and Bragg) continued to deteriorate. Davis blamed Johnston for the massive concentration in front of Lee, allegedly marshalled with troops transferred from the West, which would not have occurred, thought Davis, if Johnston had acted offensively. Johnston could not convince Richmond that he faced as large an army as Lee did. Also, Richmond still believed the Army of Tennessee stronger than it really was—despite evidence to the contrary provided by investigation sponsored by the government—and increasingly harbored doubts that Johnston would ever act aggressively.

General John Bell Hood readily reinforced this concern, going over the head of his unknowing commanding officer with letters to Davis and Bragg, who apparently (on the basis of internal evidence) had instructed Johnston's new corps commander to keep them informed. In a mid-April letter to Bragg, Hood wrote: "I received your letter, and am sorry to inform you that I have done all in my power to induce General Johnston to accept the proposition you made to move forward," but the general would not consent. "I regret this exceedingly, as my heart was fixed upon going to the front and regaining Kentucky and Tennessee. . . . To regain Tennessee would be of more value to us than half a dozen victories in Virginia."

In an intriguing choice of words, Hood wrote, "I am not able to comprehend" when the army would be in better condition for an offensive. The future would prove that Hood was hardly the man to offer judgment on such offensive operations; nevertheless, in the spring of 1864, Davis and Bragg probably were listening to the tall, maimed hero of both the eastern and western theaters of war. He was saying what they wanted to hear, of course—likely knowing that fact. Perhaps he even acted calculatingly, although there is inadequate evidence to establish such a conclusion. Undoubtedly, Hood did harm to Johnston's already meager credibility with Davis and Bragg.

Thus the Confederacy's high command, in the spring of 1864, contrasted strikingly and forebodingly with that of the Union. While the working relationship between Sherman and Grant could scarcely have been better—strategy clearly defined and Sherman receiving strong support from the East, as well as President Lincoln placing marked confidence in both Sherman and Grant—the relationship between Johnston and President Davis, between West and East, festered with misunderstanding and distrust. The two men's variance centered upon strategy, organization, support and—sometimes the most difficult of all obstacles to surmount—events of the past. To a degree, whether they realized it or not, Johnston and Davis faced a formidable enemy in their own shared history as they attempted, in the words of Bragg, to "redeem the past."

# 4

## Turntable of the Confederacy

WHEN the mail coach stopped in the small north Georgia town of Marthasville, a twenty-three-year-old army first lieutenant got out and stretched. Boarding again, William Tecumseh Sherman rode the short distance on to Marietta, where he reported for six weeks of duty in February and March, 1844. The duty was routine and boring but the young Ohioan lost no opportunity to see the region. He was stationed in Charleston when he was sent to Marietta, and he had been charmed by the bright flowers and blazing sunlight of the Deep South. "I have almost renounced all allegiance to Ohio, although it contains all whom I love and regard as friends," he wrote his brother John.

In his weeks at Marietta Sherman rode up Kennesaw Mountain often, looking north to the Allatoona Mountains and south toward the Chattahoochee River and Marthasville. He took long horseback rides alone, looking at the rolling land of north Georgia, here and there slashed by lazy yellow rivers. His duty completed at Marietta, Sherman rode to Rome, Georgia, and on to Bellefonte, Alabama, before returning through Marietta, Marthasville, and Augusta. In the next two decades the young officer crossed the continent, but he did not forget the land in which he had passed those late-winter days. When he returned twenty years later he was Major General Sherman and little Marthasville was Atlanta, "the turntable of the Confederacy."

A decade before Sherman first reached Marthasville the traveler into this region of north Georgia would have found little human habitation. The Cherokees had been driven from the region, leaving the rolling land with its forests of pine and oak wide open for acquisition. The state's

73

population was centered along the Atlantic Coast and up the Savannah River. A few settlers moved into the north Georgia ridgeland in the thirties, but to that decade's end it was sparsely settled. In 1833 Hardy Ivy built a log cabin on the future site of Atlanta, and although few settlers followed him at once, the region's future had been guaranteed by 1837.

In that year the speculations of Georgia railroad promoters focused on the site soon to be called "Terminus." The Western & Atlantic was building northward toward Chattanooga while the Georgia Railroad was creeping westward from Augusta. In 1837 a stake was planted at Terminus designating the spot as the junction of the two rail lines. In spite of the railroad speculation Terminus grew slowly. By the decade's end locals said, "The railroads don't start nowhere or don't go nowhere," and most predicted the place would remain a cluster of log cabins and a few businesses. One young Georgian disagreed. Passing through the town, Alexander H. Stephens told a friend that he believed "a magnificent inland city will at no distant date be built here."

In 1842 the few citizens of Terminus witnessed the arrival of their first engine. Hauled on a large wagon, drawn by sixteen mules, the Western & Atlantic's "locomotive" arrived from Madison. A more auspicious beginning of steam locomotion came on Christmas Eve when the assembled and powered engine, trailed by a passenger coach and freight car, chugged the twenty miles to Marietta. Oddly enough, one year after Terminus really became a railroad terminus, the town's name was changed to Marthasville, in honor of Governor Wilson Lumpkin's daughter. With the railroad's arrival new settlers began to trickle in. Pioneer store owner John Thrasher and such early community leaders as Samuel Mitchell, Lemuel P. Grant, and Jonathan Norcross were involved in the development of the local economy as well as in the town's early political administration. Grant, an engineer for the Georgia Railroad, and Norcross, whose mill produced crossties for the Georgia Railroad, were both Maine Yankees. Mitchell and Grant, active in laying out the town, created the first streets, some of them still major arteries on the Atlanta city map: Peachtree, Marietta, Decatur, Alabama, and Pryor.

In 1845 the Georgia Railroad was completed to Marthasville. To recognize the great importance of railroads in the life of the little town, the official city seal showed a locomotive in a circle. By the mid-forties the name Marthasville was deemed not impressive enough, so Georgia Railroad superintendent Richard Peters asked railroad magnate J. Edgar Thomson to suggest a new name. Thomson replied: "Eureka—Atlanta, the terminus of the Western & Atlantic Railroad—Atlantic masculine,

Atlanta feminine—a coined word and if you think it will suit adopt it."
Soon railroad timetables and newspapers began using the new name.
Terminus had given way to Marthasville and Marthasville had become
Atlanta.

The city's development was accelerated with the arrival of a third
railroad, the Macon & Western, which entered Atlanta from the south.
Jonathan Norcross remembered the arrival of the new road's first train:
"I shall never forget it. It was a clear night and the whistle commenced
blowing way out by Whitehall . . . and the minute I heard it I started
on a full run for uptown. . . . When I got to the depot I found everybody
in town was on hand." Norcross was convinced that "the real growth of
Atlanta began right then." Four churches, six schools, about twenty stores,
3,000 people, and the railroads were included in the city's vital statistics
for 1848.

Atlanta's early days were filled with growth, hope, and the usual by-
products of life on the frontier. Living was primitive, many homes had
earthen floors, few buildings of any kind were pretentious. After dark,
drunken wagoneers yelled and fought with no one to stop them. Along
Decatur Street a section called Murrel's Row, after a well-known Southern outlaw, was lined with bars and places where both locals and transients gambled. Cockfights were a regular and popular occurrence. On
Whitehall a stretch called Snake Nation vied with Murrel's Row as a
pocket of lawlessness. On the edge of town near the Norcross mill lay
Slabtown, a section inhabited by both the poor and the lawless.

Stimulated by Atlanta's transportation network, new businesses came
to town in the late forties and early fifties. In 1850 the Western & Atlantic completed its tunnel through Chetoogeta Mountain, soon to be called
Tunnel Hill, completing the line's run form Atlanta to Chattanooga.
With the tunnel's opening, goods could be shipped from the Midwest
through Atlanta to the coast at Savannah and Charleston. The Western
& Atlantic was aptly named since it connected the Mississippi Valley
with the Atlantic Ocean. With this connection Atlanta's future in both
peace and war was sealed. In peace the region would grow and prosper;
in war the city would be a vital center for its nation and an obvious
objective for enemy armies.

In 1853 Atlanta's first map revealed a city shaped in a perfect circle,
two miles in diameter, centering near a point, later called "Five Points,"
at which Peachtree, Whitehall, Marietta, Decatur, and Line streets joined.
Within this two-mile sweep lay much that was still primitive. Forests
penetrated portions of that circle and streams wound through the town—
streams that often overflowed, making a morass of streets. Cows wan-

dered about the city and demands rose that they at least be stabled after dark. Gas lamps were placed at key points about the city, making night travel somewhat safer.

Railroads brought travelers with news from across the state and nation. Railroads also brought the telegraph, running parallel to the twin steel lines, and soon the rail hub had two newspapers. The *Intelligencer* was published by Jared I. Whitaker and the *Southern Confederacy* by Cornelius R. Hanleiter.

In the last decade before the Civil War, Atlanta experienced rapid growth and an increase in the accoutrements of civilization. New businesses opened, hotels welcomed travelers, and impressive new homes dotted the landscape. North Georgia's growing metropolis could not yet challenge Savannah and the older and more sophisticated tidewater for the refinements available within the smell of salt water, yet Georgians from the coastal counties sometimes built second homes in the interior and fled to Atlanta to avoid the humidity and disease of the summer. Some of those seasonal refugees liked what they found and stayed to become year-round Atlantans.

Business competitiveness and drive separated Atlanta from the more leisurely life of the tidewater and the plantations of central and southern Georgia. Contemporaries wrote that the city seemed more like a Northern city than a Georgia city. Elizabeth McCallie wrote of Atlanta in the 1850s: "There was no leisure class in Atlanta—no ladies who trailed silken garments over polished floors or gentlemen who walked the streets clad in fine broadcloth and satin waistcoats." She added: "This does not mean that some of the men and women in Atlanta had no broadcloth suits or silken dresses, but these were worn only on festive occasions."

Among the more prominent citizens in this busy and expanding city were Jabez Richards, who owned a book and stationery store on Whitehall Street, and Lemuel Grant, the engineer, who built one of Atlanta's most beautiful homes. Active in constructing the growing city's business buildings, civic structures, and churches was Maxwell Berry, who lived with his wife and five children on Fairlie Street. James and Ezekial Calhoun, the former an attorney, the latter a physician, lived on Washington Street; both were active civic leaders. A Vermont Yankee, Edward Everett Rawson, established a thriving hardware business on Pryor Street. Rawson's establishment was so successful that he soon built the city's best-known residence, "the Terraces," surrounded by beautiful gardens and lawns, where he lived with his wife Elizabeth and his daughter Mary. Perhaps Atlanta's wealthiest citizen was John Neal, whose fortune, amassed in trade and real estate, was believed to stand at half a million dollars.

Neal owned a home on Pryor Street as well as a "large, double brick" home at the corner of Washington and Mitchell.

As the frontier rail junction grew more affluent, time for recreation became available. In 1854 a theater opened in the city. The Athenaeum, on the second floor of a Decatur Street building, was home to a troupe of players led by Mr. and Mrs. William H. Crisp, billed as "the South's most accomplished Shakespearean actors." Picnics and barbecues were popular forms of entertainment as were the antics of street performers and magic lantern shows. For the city's men, drill with the Atlanta Guard was another form of recreation, more serious than picnics and barbecues to be sure, but recreation nevertheless. In their dark blue uniforms trimmed in gold, topped with a White-plumed black shako, the guard drilled regularly and performed on festive occasions throughout the year.

Although Atlanta became more diversified with each passing year, the city remained principally a railroad hub. Atlanta's life seemed to revolve around its depot, newer and larger by 1860, but still called "the car shed." The depot, between Pryor and Loyd Streets, and nearby State Square, brought together both people and goods flowing through the heart of what had come to be called "the Gate City." The name seemed appropriate and soon the city's militia company was the Gate City Guard, while a newspaper dubbed the *Gate City Guardian* began publication.

Joining the new depot was a new brick city hall and courthouse at the corner of Washington and Hunter, and a new and more secure city jail. At the corner of Butler and Jenkins Streets, Doctors John and Willis Westmoreland opened the Atlanta Medical College and on a little hill at Collins and Ellis streets, the Atlanta Female Institute began to provide education for the daughters of the Gate City's most prominent citizens.

This growth prompted an effort to move the state capital to Atlanta from Milledgeville. But the legislature was not moved by the case presented and the state house remained in Baldwin County until the late 1860s.

When Atlanta's first city directory was published in 1859 it revealed that the pioneer hostelry, the Atlanta Hotel, had been joined by the Gate City Hotel, the Washington Hall, the Planters Hotel, and the Trout House. The latter, with its four stories and one hundred rooms, was an Atlanta landmark. Alabama, Decatur, Marietta, and Whitehall streets were lined with business and office buildings. The 1859 directory listed six banks, seventeen insurance agencies, and seventeen major commercial buildings. Also listed were thirteen churches.

The 1860 census indicated that Fulton County's population had reached 11,572. The list, by occupation, had a strong railroad flavor. There were seventeen baggagemasters, eight boilermakers, two car inspectors, one depot watchman, fifty-nine locomotive engineers, sixty-six locomotive firemen, thirty-seven railroad conductors, thirty-seven train hands, one railroad president, and one railroad superintendent. Ninety residents of the Gate City claimed to be merchants, 41 were attorneys, and there were 41 doctors. At the opposite ends of the moral ladder were 17 clergymen on the one hand and 9 gamblers and 49 prostitutes on the other. The largest census listings were: laborer, 284; carpenter, 235; and clerk, 177. Among the odd listings in the Gate City's census were: at rest, 1; at rest for one year, 1; gentleman, 1; gone to California, 1; old loafer, 1; old maid, 1; pauper, 1; and young lady, 1.

As Atlanta grew, the nation struggled with its problems of growth. The people of the Gate City, concerned about "Freesoil" agitation in the Kansas Territory, strongly supported James Buchanan, the Democratic candidate for president in 1856. John Brown's raid on Harpers Ferry three years later revived the city's hostilities toward abolitionism. A New Yorker, working for a dry goods merchant, was forced to leave the city because he publicly toasted Brown. Atlantans talked about refusing to trade with the Northern states. "The times demand that no black republican or abolitionist shall profit by Southern trade, either directly or indirectly, from cupidity, nor from avarice," editorialized the *Intelligencer*.

During the 1860 presidential election Democrat Stephen A. Douglas spoke in the city on October 30. Accompanied by Alexander H. Stephens, who endorsed "the Little Giant's" popular sovereignty views, the Illinois senator told his audience that the Union must last forever and that there was no cause for secession. It was a sentiment many of those who listened did not share. Douglas's trip to Atlanta was a part of his journey across the South attempting to talk Southerners into resolving their problems within the Union. By the time Douglas reached the city, the divided Democrats were certain of defeat and Abraham Lincoln, the Republican nominee, was just as certain of victory.

On election day, November 6, Lincoln, of course, polled no votes in Fulton County. Douglas claimed 662 and John C. Breckinridge, Buchanan's vice-president, also running for president as a Democrat, garnered 1,853. The highest total in the county went to Tennessean John Bell, the standard-bearer of the compromise Constitutional Union Party. Bell got 2,264 votes. Thomas Maguire, from his home near Atlanta, wrote in his diary when he learned the national result: "Heard news occasioned by the late election that was not pleasant, but we will have to do the best under the circumstances. God defend the right."

On November 8 the Minute Men Associations of Fulton County, formed only nine days earlier, met to consider action in light of Lincoln's victory. Although the Minute Men did not speak for all Atlantans, their resolution spoke for many in their community as they threw down the gauntlet.

> RESOLVED, That as citizens of Georgia and Fulton Country we believe the time has come for us to assert our rights, and we now stand ready to second any action that the sovereign State of Georgia may take in asserting her independence by separate State action, or in unison with her sister States of the South in forming a Southern Confederacy.

Forty-two days after that resolution indicated that secession sentiment was strong in Atlanta, Georgia's neighbor, South Carolina, as one Palmetto State journal boasted, "has thrown the tea overboard, the revolution of 1860 has begun." The Gate City fired a one-hundred-gun salute in support of South Carolina's act of secession and an enthusiastic torchlight procession marched across the city. As a part of the celebration, Abraham Lincoln was burned in effigy in front of the Planters Hotel.

Thirteen days after South Carolina seceded from the Union, the citizens of Atlanta went to the polls to vote for delegates to Georgia's secession convention. The three candidates pledged to immediate secession won a ringing victory over the Cooperationists, who supported secession in theory but counseled delay in practice. The next day, a "clear and cloudless" January 3, a slight earthquake rocked Atlanta. The *Intelligencer* saw an omen in the minor tremor: "May not its coming and passing away so easily with the clear and bright sky, be symbolical of the present political convulsion in the country, which, in the South, will pass away so easily, leaving the spotless sky behind."

On January 19 Georgia followed South Carolina, Mississippi, Florida, and Alabama out of the Union. Guns were fired in Atlanta to salute the state's decision, but the celebration was not as noisy as that following South Carolina's secession in December. Also in January the city went to the polls to elect a mayor. Jared Whitaker was chosen, but he would not finish his term. In November, when Governor Joe Brown appointed Whitaker "Commissary-General of Georgia Troops," he resigned as mayor.

Whitaker's first task as mayor was to organize the city's reception for Jefferson Davis, who passed through Atlanta on his way to Montgomery to assume his post as Confederate president. On February 16 Davis arrived at the Western & Atlantic depot where he was saluted by the Atlanta Grays. A large crowd greeted Davis at the Trout House listening to the Mississippian deliver a stirring address greeted with applause and great excitement. One Atlanta schoolgirl who participated in the greeting to Davis later recalled, "My only remembrance of our great chieftain was that he was tall and thin and rather tired looking."

One month later Alexander H. Stephens, the Confederate vice-president, on his way from Montgomery to Savannah, arrived by rail. Again a distinguished visitor was greeted with gunfire and applause and again words that inspired the populace echoed across the city. "Little Alec" believed peace would prevail but he told the citizens that by preparing for war, peace would be made more certain.

In the Confederacy's first days, Atlantans attempted to convince the new government that their city would be an excellent site for the national capital. The *Gate City Guardian* proudly proclaimed: "This city has good railroad connections, is free from yellow fever, can supply the most wholesome food, and as for 'goobers,' an indispensable article for a Southern legislator, we have them all the time." These arguments did not prevail. Confederate solons would have to find their "goobers" in Virginia.

By April companies were being organized for the Confederate army. As the national crisis intensified, Atlanta's young men rallied to the Bonnie Blue Flag. They formed parts of eleven Georgia infantry units, two artillery batteries, and several state units. A spirit of dash and adventure accompanied the organization of these first companies with names such as "the Stephens Rifles," "Fulton Blues," or "Confederate Continentals." One romantic young woman thought the mustering in "was a beautiful sight!" She praised "wealthy, cultured young gentlemen voluntarily turning their backs upon the luxuries and endearments and affluent homes and accepting in lieu the privations and hardships of warfare." When one unit mustered in that spring, a ceremony at the state square was marked by the first raising in Georgia of a new flag, the Confederacy's "Stars and Bars." On April 1, in spite of a pounding rain, a large crowd gathered at the depot as the Gate City Guards left for service at Pensacola.

That spring was filled with the furious activity of a people going to war. A women's association was formed to make bandages for the city's soldiers. A committee of safety was organized to provide aid for the families of Atlanta's volunteers in uniform. Governor Brown brought gunsmiths to Atlanta to discuss establishing armories in the city. He began the retooling by appropriating forges in the Western & Atlantic's machine shops for the manufacture of gun barrels. A commissary department was also established in a central location in this important city.

On July 21 Atlantans cheered receipt of the news that their army had soundly defeated Lincoln's forces at Manassas. Predictions of an easy victory followed the Rebel success in Virginia. Grief also reached Atlanta in the wake of the battle. Two attorneys, John A. Puckett and James S. George, a well-known teacher, Anderson M. Orr, together with thirteen other Atlantans, were killed on the field of battle.

In October 1861 Samuel P. Richards moved to Atlanta from Macon to join his brother Jabez in the book and stationery business. Richards kept a diary that affords an excellent picture of daily life in Confederate Atlanta. On New Year's Eve the moderate Richards lamented: "But little hope of preserving the Union. The abolitionists and fire eaters are determined to destroy it."

On Christmas Thomas Maguire, who lived near Atlanta on his "Promised Land" plantation, noticed a subdued atmosphere in the city since "Abe's government has cast its shadow of war around the country and gloom and seriousness is the effect, even among the young and thoughtless." Maguire hoped for an early peace, and saluted Confederate soldiers who "as a wall of fire," were "standing between us . . . and the vandals of the North."

By the early days of 1862 prospects for a quick end to the conflict had diminished. In the year's first six months the confidence generated by Manassas was badly tarnished by Grant's victories at Forts Henry and Donelson and David G. Farragut's capture of New Orleans. The great bloodshed at Shiloh added a sobering note, as did the war's approach to Georgia. The Yankees took Savannah's Fort Pulaski, and Federal troops moved down the Tennessee River to Huntsville, Alabama, only fifty miles from the Georgia state line.

For many Atlantans James Andrews's raid on the Western & Atlantic, a further indication that the war had reached Georgia, was shocking. The Kentuckian Andrews and his twenty-two Union raiders aimed at cutting the railroad between the city and Chattanooga. On April 12 they seized the locomotive "General" and raced northward, cutting telegraph lines and obstructing the rails. When the Rebels chased Andrews in the locomotive "Texas," the "General" ran out of fuel and Andrews had to push on on foot. The entire force was taken and Andrews and seven others were tried and executed in Atlanta.

In May the city became a military post and three months later martial law was proclaimed by General Braxton Bragg. On September 3, according to Special Orders No. 206, habeus corpus was suspended. Strict new rules were applied to those who lived in this fortress-like city. Military units patrolled the streets and closely watched the comings and goings at the railroad station. Liquor was not to be sold to men in uniform and drunkenness was to be punished by immediate arrest. As the war rolled on, however, intoxicated men often reeled through the city's streets. The proclamation of martial law also forbade blacks to move about after dark. With Whitaker's resignation as mayor, James M. Calhoun assumed the post and carried on his duties as usual despite martial law. The definition of the line between civil and military authorities was not very clear, but Calhoun continued to exercise civil authority in a manner as close to prewar usage as possible.

By the second autumn of the war Atlanta had become a refuge for Confederate wounded. The rail system brought wounded soldiers to the Gate City in such numbers as to make it the medical center of the Deep South. The Female Institute became a hospital as did the Medical College, closed since 1861 because of a lack of students. The Concert Hall, several hotels, business buildings, and a large complex constructed at the Fair Grounds added to the city's facilities.

Caught up in the Southern cause, volunteering brought many Atlantans to the colors in 1861, but by April 1862, as the rush to the armed forces slowed, conscription began in the city and across the Confederacy. Before the year was out a notice was posted about town that warned "all delinquents and skulkers of their peril in attempting to evade the high and overruling obligation of coming up to their duty."

The designation "turntable of the Confederacy" was obvious since by 1862 Atlanta had become the most important rail hub in the South; "workshop of the Confederacy" would have been almost as fitting. With the refusal of the border states to secede, coupled with the collapse of the upper Confederacy, a string of medium-sized cities across the Deep South were converted to military production. By 1862 the Confederate military depended on all manner of goods produced in Meridian, Selma, Montgomery, Columbus, Macon, Augusta, and Atlanta. Out of Atlanta's factories came buttons, belt buckles, spurs, canteens, tents, revolvers, cannon, and cartridges. The Atlanta Rolling Mill produced plates for Rebel gunboats, including the ironclad *Merrimac*. A pistol factory, machine shop (to rifle cannon), sword factory, and several rifle factories funneled the necessities of war to grayclad armies in the field. Atlanta housed three tanneries and factories which produced such necessities as shoes, soap, clothing, and, sadly, wooden coffins. The Atlanta Machine Works, a Northern-owned firm, refused to produce munitions for the South whereupon it was taken over by Confederate authorities who soon had it turning out ammunition for the men in gray. Winship's Foundry made freight cars and other kinds of supplies in great demand in this railroad city. The Confederate Arsenal at Walton and Peachtree streets produced shells used by the Army of Tennessee against Grant's Union soldiers in the West. Those shell casings marked "Made in Atlanta" were noted so often by Grant's friend, General Sherman, that he became convinced the city must be wrecked if the Confederate cause was to be defeated. In addition to those and other factories, Atlanta was named headquarters of the Quartermaster's Department of the Army of Tennessee soon after the army's creation.

Railroads had built Atlanta and railroads remained the city's greatest resource. The four lines connected the city with agricultural and industrial sections of the interior South as well as with Rebel armies in the field in both East and West. The Western & Atlantic was the most direct line from the Deep South to Confederate forces in the West; the Georgia Railroad ran east to Augusta, connecting with roads that led to Charlotte, Richmond and Lee's army; the Macon & Western and the Atlanta & West Point Railroads connected with southern and western Georgia, the Atlantic coast, Alabama, and Mississippi. Many of the manufactured goods and much of the agricultural produce from the Deep South passed through the Gate City on its way north. Troops passed through Atlanta on their way to combat and invalids came to Atlanta for nursing or moved through the Georgia city on their way home from the war. As the struggle intensified private use of the trains was restricted. Atlanta's lines, especially the Western & Atlantic's tracks to Chattanooga, were strained to the utmost. At times trains ran so often on that road there appeared to be an endless line of cars all the way from Marietta to Atlanta.

Also strained by an increase in population, as well as by the increase in use generated by the war, were Atlanta's streets and Fulton County's roads. By 1863 inadequate maintenance and heavy traffic had created deep holes and ruts in the streets, at some points so deep as to make wagon travel difficult and often hazardous. In February 1864 the city council vowed that repairs should be started before spring rains added to the problems. Long before this project could repair Atlanta's thoroughfares, Sherman's long-range guns would turn holes into craters.

There were some efforts to entertain Atlanta's citizens in this second grim year of war. The Athenaeum brought actors to perform Shakespeare's *Richard III* and *Romeo and Juliet*. Of the latter performance the *Intelligencer* reported, "The audience was delighted." There was also "Barton's Southern Moving Panorama and Diorama of the Great Yankee Stampede at Manassas Plains." Samuel Richards went to City Hall "to hear Blind Tom, the wonderful Negro Pianist." "He is just twelve years old, and little better than an idiot," wrote the bookseller, "but he is truly one of the seven wonders."

The observant Richards watched the year go by in his diary. July 4, 1862, "passed very quietly," but at Christmas his family "had a fine rooster for . . . dinner which tasted quite as well as turkey. Santa Claus, as usual, brought the children some presents and they had a fine time." For Richards the new year brought "renewed hope that ere many months the dark tide of war will have passed away."

But in 1863 the war's "dark tide" moved closer to Georgia. At Murfreesboro, Tennessee, from December 31 to January 2 the armies battled only to have General Bragg allow the advantage to slip from his hands, the Army of Tennessee eventually withdrawing toward Chattanooga. In April and May Union Colonel Abel Streight rode into Georgia to cut the vital rail lines only to be routed and forced to surrender his 1,700 men to Nathan Bedford Forrest on May 3. So pleased were Georgians with their saviour Forrest that they gave him "a magnificent charger, completely caparisoned with fine bridle and halter" when he visited Atlanta in July.

Forrest might have saved Georgia for the time being, but distant military tidings were distressing. The Army of Northern Virginia was forced to retreat from Gettysburg, leaving dead Atlantans in its wake. In the West the news was even more upsetting. On July 4 Vicksburg fell, slicing the Confederacy in half and denying the Southern cause supplies from the Trans-Mississippi. The fall of Vicksburg made supplies from central Alabama and central Georgia even more important to the Confederacy than in the conflict's first two years. It also meant that Federal armies would inevitably turn their attention to this area. Grant's victorious Army of the Tennessee would soon be able to join William S. Rosecrans's Army of the Cumberland in advancing against Georgia's defenders, Bragg's Army of Tennessee.

Before that juncture could take place, Rosecrans advanced toward Chattanooga, which Bragg abandoned, luring the Yankees into northwestern Georgia. On September 19 and 20, along Chickamauga Creek, the aptly named "River of Death," Bragg struck Rosecrans. By the evening of the twentieth the Yanks were in full flight toward Chattanooga where Bragg set a siege line. Once again the Army of Tennessee's commander allowed the advantage to slip away. Grant replaced Rosecrans, Bragg divided his force and Union supplies began to trickle in, followed by reinforcements. In late November Grant's army hammered its way out of Bragg's tentacles, winning a smashing victory at Missionary Ridge on the twenty-fifth. When control of Chattanooga, the natural staging area for a further invasion of the Deep South, fell to the Federals, Lincoln believed that his army at last had a "death grip on the Confederacy." With the Army of Tennessee driven into north Georgia and Chattanooga in Union hands, Atlanta stood next on the list of Grant's objectives. The citizens of "the turntable of the Confederacy" were well aware of approaching danger. They also agreed when the *Intelligencer* told them "that if Atlanta should fall, the backbone of the Confederacy would be, for a time at least, broken." It was an opinion fully shared by Ulysses S. Grant and William T. Sherman.

As the sound of guns crept toward Atlanta, the city and state began preparing to resist what was as yet distant thunder. Governor Brown called for 8,000 militiamen and all Atlantans below the age of forty-five had to register at City Hall. Mayor James Calhoun urged citizens to join militia defense units.

The most obvious defensive effort mounted in 1863 was the fortification of the city. Colonel Marcus J. Wright, commander of Atlanta's defense force, met with Captain Lemuel Grant, chief engineer of the Department of Georgia, to discuss a line of forts to protect the city. Grant began by constructing protective barriers to cover fords and crossings on the Chattahoochee River north of the city. After completing these first forts, Grant sketched out a line more than ten miles long circling Atlanta, planned to contain from twelve to fifteen strong points at strategic locations so as to support each other.

When the work began slaves were pressed into service, their masters being paid one dollar a day for their labor. Grant's line used the region's waterways and north Georgia's hilly terrain to advantage, ringing Atlanta for just over ten miles and lying about one and one-quarter miles from the city's center. On December 1, 1863, the defensive perimeter was pronounced complete. During the winter of 1863–64 trenches and support positions were added so that by the early days of the new year "Fortress Atlanta" had been created.

As the inevitability of attack grew with the fall of Chattanooga, the facilities to sustain the Rebel army in the task just ahead were improved. The army's Commissary Department was headquartered at Pryor and Peachtree while the Signal Corps was established in the Gate City Hotel. On Whitehall Street the Transport Office was a scene of constant bustle as was the Provost Marshal's office on Wadley Street and the garrison of the Military Post of Atlanta positioned just north of Walton Street. Also on Pryor was the Remount Department, where horses and mules were prepared for the army. Richmond was the capital of the Confederacy and Millegeville the capital of Georgia, but by 1864 Atlanta had become the military capital of the Deep South.

The last days of 1863 and the first days of 1864 were trying times for the citizens of the Gate City. Already bulging with wounded, the city was inundated with seriously injured soldiers after Chickamauga and Chattanooga. In addition, 1863 had not been a healthy year for Atlanta's civilians. Smallpox struck and the disease grew so serious that victims had to be isolated in a hospital built in a remote section of the county. The fall was unseasonably cold and damp. Atlanta's populace had animals hauled off without compensation by the military, taxes rose, and inflation drove prices to unheard of levels. Flour cost $35 a hundred pounds, eggs $1 a dozen, coffee $4 a pound, bacon $1.50 a pound and potatoes $12 a bushel, an alarming increase since the beginning of the war. Holding that the theater was frivolous, given the seriousness of the times, the Athenaeum was closed except for patriotic programs for the benefit of the poor and destitute. Dances, often to raise money for the troops, continued through the chilly, bleak winter. The wife of a Confederate officer away at the front, believed, "They danced as only the women of the Confederacy, at that time and in that place, could dance—waltzing over the crater of a volcano, on the brink of a precipice."

By January 1, 1864, Atlanta's population had been greatly increased by the war. The 11,572 people listed in the 1860 census had been swelled by both permanent residents and transients. Population estimates range from 18,000 to 25,000 by the third year of the Civil War. Some fortunate Southerners fleeing to the Gate City could live with friends and relatives, but most refugees were forced to take shelter in tents or abandoned railroad cars near the depot. With this influx of refugees came deserters and those seeking a quick fortune; a rise of lawlessness resulted. Soldiers still in the army and deserters alike stole from homes, shops, and gardens. Those too young to join the army loitered about the streets, gambled, and were suspected of burglarizing the city's homes and shops. The Atlanta grand jury urged law enforcement officials to arrest these teenaged lawbreakers. The grand jury was also concerned with an increase in assault, murder, the sale of stolen food, and the distillation and sale of spirits. Public drunkenness and the firing of weapons at night was also on the increase by 1864.

Three newspapers joined the refugee tide to Atlanta. The *Chattanooga Rebel, Knoxville Register,* and *Memphis Appeal* (known popularly as the "Moving Appeal" as it fled across the South) set up operations in Atlanta for a time before moving south as Sherman's army approached. These three journals joined the four dailies already being published in the city: the *Intelligencer,* the *Southern Confederacy, The Reville,* and the *Commonwealth.*

In the first months of 1864, when weather and transportation permitted, citizens from Marietta and Atlanta boarded trains at 4:15 P.M. to travel northward to watch the parades and mock battles of their defenders—the men of the Army of Tennessee. They paid the Western & Atlantic's round-trip fare of $15.50 to take food, clothing, and other gifts to Johnston's soldiers encamped near Dalton. The journey to the Confederate camps became an important event of the winter social season for many Atlanta belles.

Even though the enemy stood on their north Georgia doorstep, many aspects of life in Atlanta appeared to be business as usual. The *Southern Confederacy* ran an advertisement offering $100 for George, a runaway slave, as well as ads for whisky, rye, cognac, "Havana Segars," and billiard tables. There were items for sale listed as "Received per steamer from Nassau," and on March 19 a jingle boasted: "Through the Blockade; At the Arcade; The Place of Trade!" Miller and Sons, on Marietta Street, offered the populace silk and linen handkerchiefs, toilet soap, fine shirts, and suspenders. On April 19 Atlantans were put on notice that the dog leash law would be enforced.

Atlanta newspapers regularly reported news from the camps around Dalton. The *Southern Confederacy* praised General Joseph E. Johnston as "one of the most consumate soldiers whom the great struggle has produced" and looked "forward with a high and hopeful spirit to the future of his great army." In March the paper told its readers that the Army of Tennessee was "[n]ewly clad and presented a very fine appearance and we can scarcely recognize in them that army which was hurled from Missionary Ridge, dispirited and broken through the incompetency of their leader."

As the winter passed and spring, with its threat of Federal advance neared, Atlanta's populace jammed churches to invoke the god of battles to strengthen their army. The city's best-known clergyman was Dr. Charles Todd Quintard, army surgeon, chaplain of the Army of Tennessee, and friend of bishop-general Leonidas Polk. Quintard, who had been rector of a Nashville church before the war, founded St. Luke's Episcopal Church on Walton Street when he arrived in the city. After a campaign led by the Tennessean raised $12,000, soldiers' labor helped build a wooden structure that held four hundred worshipers. On April 19, 1864, the first services were held in this church, doomed to last only four months before being closed by a combination of danger from Federal artillery and the southward flight of its communicants. In November 1864, St. Luke's was destroyed by fire, not to be rebuilt after the conflict.

Quintard had raised the morale of large army congregations who heard him preach in the field and his sermons had the same effect from his Atlanta pulpit. The Episcopal rector was indefatigable in his labors for the men in gray. He gathered needed supplies and wrote a prayer- and song book whose pocket edition, published in Atlanta, brought solace both to men in the ranks and their relatives at home. To one Rebel private, Quintard "was one of the purest and best men I ever knew."

Spring brought warm weather, clear skies, and appeals to the people of Atlanta for support against Sherman's hordes. To bring Atlantans to arms the *Southern Confederacy* hysterically portrayed the Union army in words that must have sent a chill of terror through the city's residents.

> We are fighting the good fight of home and family, of hearthstone and sepulchre, not only against the hosts marshaled at the North, but the refuse

of European prisons, of men who hire themselves to cut the throats of inno-
cent men, women and children.

After reading of Sherman's throat-cutting convicts, Atlanta's citizens
were told by the *Intelligencer*, "Georgia is the next state on the Yankee
program for invasion . . . as soon as spring comes." The Civil War had
turned Atlanta into a bustling city of great importance, but that very
importance made it a target. Two decades after he first visited Marthasville, Sherman was on his way back. And this time he was not alone.

# 5

## All Before Is Mere Skirmishing

THE stage was set at last. It was the fourth day of May and the drama no longer centered in the halls of power at Washington and Richmond, nor in the politics and intrigue of army headquarters. For Sherman's army the decisive campaign had begun. The warm spring sun, like a giant spotlight, fell upon the young men of the army, a hundred and ten thousand strong, as they moved slowly toward Johnston's well-entrenched positions along the hulking ridge known as Rocky Face and Buzzard's Roost gorge, northwest of Dalton, Georgia. With these veteran soldiers, some already tired and worn-looking beyond their years, together with others like them in Virginia, marched the hope for union of the United States of America.

The city of Atlanta lay 120 miles south of Chattanooga. It was an obvious target, and would become, eventually, the goal of the campaign. The immediate quest, however, was the Confederate army; to force a fight, if possible, and break it up. "Neither Atlanta, nor Augusta, nor Savannah, was the objective," wrote Sherman years later in his memoirs, "but the 'army of Joseph Johnston,' go where it might." At the time of the campaign Sherman confirmed his understanding of Grant's plans in blunt words: "I am to knock Joseph Johnston, and to do as much damage to the resources of the enemy as possible."

Whatever happened, Sherman's soldiers were to press close to the enemy and stay close. They must keep driving until either the enemy would be destroyed or finally accept terms of surrender. The Yankee army must stick close and make it impossible for Johnston to detach troops to succor Lee's Army of Northern Virginia, which Grant, Meade, and the

Federal Army of the Potomac were to press simultaneously with equal vigor.

If this occurred, the Confederacy, with a much smaller manpower pool from which to recruit troops, would ultimately be ground down and the triumph of the Union would be assured. It was the Federal foot soldier who must do the work. He must shoulder the great bulk of the sacrificing, fighting, suffering, and dying, without which the victory could not be achieved. And he must do it now, while there was still time before growing Northern war weariness and the ever-increasing strain on the nation's economy could combine to give the Confederacy renewed vitality.

Hindsight provides the historian with a seemingly invincible tool for analyzing and recognizing the far-reaching significance of Sherman's 1864 campaign. Also, in the memories of many veterans—who would live on to a great age and often look back, romantically glorifying and magnifying the war years—the impact of this campaign would come to stand clearly and starkly, requiring no embellishment. But even in that awful yet vital and decisive year of 1864, there were some, soldiers and civilians alike, who saw unmistakably the significance of the far-reaching events in which they were caught up.

Ringgold, Georgia.

Perhaps foremost among these was Sherman himself. To President Lincoln he described the impending campaign as one "on which the fate of the nation hung"; while to his brother he wrote that his actions then "would probably decide the fate of the Union"; and to his wife he said, "all that has gone before is mere skirmishing." An Illinois private phrased the matter quite differently, albeit in his own way seeming to grasp the reality rather well. This man, Thomas J. Frazee, wrote to his sister, "I think we can lick the Rebs like a book when we start to do it and I hope we will clean Rebeldom out this summer so we will be able to quit the business."

There were Southerners too who sensed with a sure instinct what the campaign meant. Sam Richards of Atlanta wrote in his diary on May 6: "If we are defeated in these battles, I fear the bright and cheering hopes of peace that now animate all hearts in the South, will be dissipated quickly." From atop Rocky Face Ridge Confederate lieutenant Lawrence D. Young, with disturbed feelings, watched the awesome Federal force come: "We could see extending for miles the enemy's grand encampment of infantry and artillery, the stars and stripes floating from every regimental, brigade, division and corps headquarters and presenting the greatest panorama I ever beheld. . . . It haunted me for days."

Joseph E. Johnston also saw and understood. All together, Johnston believed Sherman had 100,000 effective troops, most of whom were thought to be concentrating at Ringgold during the first week of May. But, as previously noted, Richmond blindly refused to credit Sherman with a force anywhere near that large. For the first three days in May the Confederate commander nervously received reports from scouts about Sherman's predicted advance. On the fourth, when intelligence indicated there was no doubt of the Federal onslaught, Johnston hastily telegraphed Richmond for reinforcements. As the campaign began Johnston's army numbered between 50,000 and 60,000 officers and men, with his infantry formed into two corps commanded by Hardee and Hood, while Wheeler led the cavalry.

The bastion of the Confederate position was Rocky Face Ridge, that formidable eminence which runs from a point a few miles north of Dalton southward almost to the Oostanaula River. Rising about eight hundred feet above the surrounding valleys, and named from the rocky outcropping on its western face, the rugged ridge was so imposing that Sherman would later contend that the Confederate geographical advantages offset the Federal superiority in numbers. Johnston, not surprisingly, disagreed—and the Rebel general probably was right.

Just as the center of the Confederate defensive line on Missionary Ridge had appeared more formidable than it really was, so too the defensive position at Dalton was actually more vulnerable than it seemed to

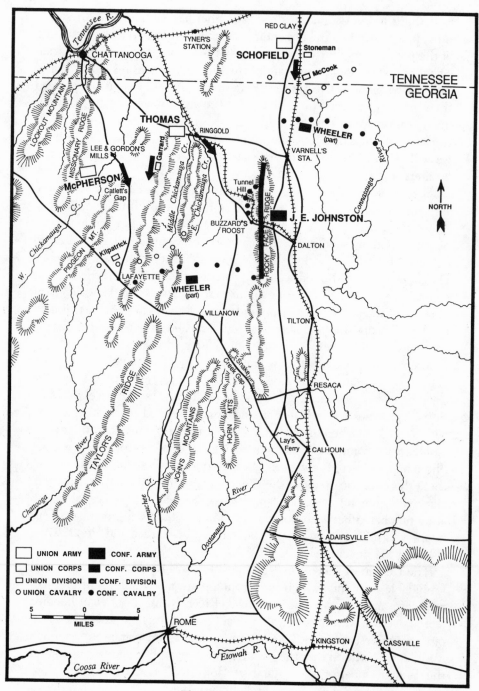

The Campaign Begins.

be. Deceptively impressive on the map, Dalton presented a precarious situation for the Army of Tennessee, because the very strength of the position dictated an enemy flanking movement and, with several such options available, a well-executed march by a strong portion of Sherman's superior force would be difficult to detect before it gained control of Johnston's railroad somewhere south of Dalton.

After the war Johnston claimed in his *Narrative of Military Operations* that he was aware of the weakness of the Dalton position, writing that "it had neither intrinsic strength nor strategic advantage. It neither fully covered its own communications nor threatened those of the enemy." Johnston contended that the position had been selected only because it was the site where the army halted in late November following the retreat after the disaster at Missionary Ridge. In fact, Johnston claimed he would have fallen back from Dalton except "for the earnestness with which the President and the Secretary of War . . . wrote of an early assumption of offensive operations and apprehension of the bad effect of a retrograde movement upon the spirit of the Southern people."

Yet, in his letters to the government through the winter and spring of 1864, Johnston never reported any specific vulnerability of the Dalton position, only a general comment that a Federal move through Rome would make it impossible to hold Dalton. In fact, during the winter Johnston had fortified his position so well that he believed it could be held against any attack. Trenches were dug along Rocky Face Ridge and across Crow Valley north of Dalton. Strong locations for artillery batteries were prepared. Great stones were maneuvered into position to be rolled off the ridge onto an attacking foe, and Mill Creek was dammed to form a lake that protected portions of his defensive line. If Johnston was seriously worried about the Dalton position neither his letters to Richmond nor his actions showed it. And, it is pertinent to note, throughout Johnston's career, as his papers clearly demonstrate, whenever he identified problems he did not hesitate to complain about them. Apparently, his concern for the Dalton situation came after the fact.

To understand the vulnerability of the Confederate position, a grasp of the nature of the terrain in northwest Georgia is imperative. The town of Dalton lay in a relatively narrow and somewhat rugged river valley. Through this valley, and slightly east of the town, the Connasauga River wound generally southward to join the Oostanaula, just southeast of the village of Resaca. From Resaca this larger stream continued the southward course, although gradually snaking several degrees to the west, until its confluence with the Etowah at Rome to form the Coosa. From Resaca also the river valley widened noticeably and the terrain soon changed abruptly, especially from Calhoun southward. The steep ridges, narrow gaps, and heavy woods that characterized the region north of the Oostanaula gave way to gently rolling hills and a sparsely settled farming region, with only a light cover of vegetation.

Rocky Face Ridge, lined with Rebels, lay a short distance west of Dalton, paralleling the southward flow of the Connasauga River for a distance of twenty-five miles. Farther to the west, Rocky Face was paralleled by the long Taylor's Ridge, with Missionary Ridge, Lookout Mountain, and the Sand Mountain–Racoon Mountain range still farther away, all paralleling one another and stretching in a generally southward but westward-bearing direction. The formidable Rocky Face Ridge could not be crossed except at one of the occasional gaps: Mill Creek Gap ("Buzzard's Roost" to the locals), a relatively wide passage near Dalton where the Western & Atlantic Railroad cut through the mountain; Dug Gap, a narrow opening about five miles south of Mill Creek Gap; and Snake Creek Gap at the southern end of the ridge, west of Resaca, where the northern end of Horn Mountain begins.

The Snake Creek Gap was especially dangerous to Johnston's position. It presented the most direct approach, via Ship's Gap through Taylor's Ridge, thence to Villanow and on through Snake Creek Gap to Sugar Valley in Johnston's rear at Resaca. Also, because of the ruggedness of Rocky Face south of Dalton, where the mountain is over three miles wide, a Federal strike could only be detected by posting troops at the western entrance to the gap. If Resaca fell to the Yankees, the Confederate army would be trapped in the narrow valley between Resaca and Dalton.

In addition to defending the three gaps in Rocky Face against a possible Federal movement, Johnston also had to consider other routes still farther to the south where Sherman could enter the valley. The Yankees might elect to turn south at Villanow, march on the road toward Rome for a distance, then advance around the southern tip of Horn Mountain, where they would still be north of the Oostanaula and within reasonable striking distance of the railroad at Resaca. Or they simply might continue on the road to Rome. The capture of Rome would be a disaster, severing both the railroad and pike to Alabama and reinforcements, not to mention the loss of the Rome industrial complex.

Johnston's northern flank was quite vulnerable too. Rocky Face Ridge, three miles north of Mill Creek Gap, faded away and presented, by way of the Appalachian Valley into east Tennessee, an inviting avenue for a Federal advance. By the first of May, Johnston knew the Yankees had moved south to Red Clay, only a few miles north of his Dalton headquarters.

Might Johnston have chosen better if he had moved forward and taken his stand along Taylor's Ridge, which he could have occupied earlier? The advantages of Taylor's Ridge (known as White Oak Mountain north of Ringgold) would have been that it blocked the Yankees more effectively because it extended for a much greater distance to both north and south (actually bearing northeast to southwest) than Rocky Face; was a formidable position without being so rugged, like Rocky Face, that information about Union operations to the west was difficult to obtain; and, of course, would have enabled the Rebels to begin the campaign a little farther to the north, a move which might have been expected to lift the spirit of the Southern army.

The problems with Taylor's Ridge, even though it would have allowed the Rebels to cover territory from the Rome industrial complex to the Tennessee State line, were formidable, especially in dealing with an enemy superior in numbers. The greater length of Taylor's Ridge, with more gaps to defend than Rocky Face, would demand constant and efficient scouting, as well as an army with excellent mobility, to counter a Federal advance. And if the Yankees did manage to execute a wide move around the northern flank of the Rebel position, admittedly more difficult than at Rocky Face, there then would be the same problem as Rocky Face: a broad valley over which the Federals could quickly march upon the Confederate rear.

Perhaps Calhoun, which Johnston later claimed he actually favored, would have provided a better defensive position then either Rocky Face or Taylor's Ridge. At Calhoun Johnston could have established a generally east-west line, thus eliminating the major threat to his right flank that the Dalton position entailed, taking advantage of good interior lines of defense, and placing himself closer to Rome in the event that the main Federal thrust should develop there. The problems of Calhoun would be the negative effect on Confederate morale of a further retreat, plus the risk of giving Sherman the opportunity to move south from Chattanooga earlier, consolidate his position, and start the campaign deeper in Georgia.

Yet another possibility for Johnston would have been to secretly prepare a strong position at Calhoun, while still holding Rocky Face. When Sherman advanced, Johnston could have fallen back to Calhoun, enticing Sherman beyond Tunnel Hill and then making an all-out effort with part of his cavalry to blow up the tunnel, thus confronting Sherman with a major railroad problem at the beginning of the campaign. Sherman still would have possessed a rail line, more circuitous to be sure, via the east Tennessee track from Chattanooga to Cleveland, and then south to Red Clay and Dalton. However, if at the same time that the tunnel were blown to block the direct route from Chattanooga, Johnston had sent a

Tunnel Hill, between Ringgold and Dalton.

strong, effective cavalry force after Sherman's railroads in middle Tennessee, just possibly the Union commander, who seemed more worried about the rail line than any other single factor, might have panicked. It might well have been worth a try. And even if Sherman's nerve held up, Johnston would still have possessed a better position at Calhoun than at Dalton.

In any event, Joseph Wheeler's failure to blow up the tunnel when the Federal advance began, which he assured Johnston would be done, constituted a major shortcoming of "Fighting Joe's" Civil War career. Whatever might have been, Johnston chose to make his stand at Dalton.

And Dalton was really not a bad position—if the gaps in Rocky Face had been covered adequately, as they should have been.

By early May, Johnston had decided that the most pressing danger would come upon his right or northern flank. Thus, no Confederate infantry were stationed between Resaca and Rome, while the weight of an inadequate cavalry command (less than 2,500 effectives) was placed in an arc north of Dalton to give early warning of an enemy advance from that direction. The remaining troopers were spread even thinner, picketing the Taylor's Ridge gaps. When Johnston's headquarters received word of heavy Federal activity at Ringgold, the Confederate commander, sure only of the enemy's approach from Ringgold and Red Clay, expected Sherman to demonstrate along Rocky Face Ridge, while marching the bulk of his army around its northern end into Crow Valley.

To meet this threat, the burden of defense fell upon Hood's corps, strengthened by two divisions, Major Generals William Bate's and B. Franklin Cheatham's, from Hardee's corps. Thus Hood commanded five of the army's seven infantry divisions as the campaign began, with Hardee's stripped command holding what Johnston anticipated would be the less important sector of the position. Concerning what Hardee, the army's senior lieutenant general, thought about Johnston's deployment, there is no record.

But Johnston was totally misled in his anticipation of Sherman's plans.

Clisby Austin Home, Near Tunnel Hill, Used by Sherman as Headquarters.

Worse, he lost touch with part of Sherman's army. While Johnston watched the area in front of his right flank, Sherman moved against his left.

FROM the perspective of the Union high command the campaign was to be determined by three things: the railroad, the terrain, and Johnston's movements. And when Sherman made his plans he had three basic choices. He could move by his left flank, slipping around the upper end of Rocky Face Ridge, for either a southward march down the Oostanaula Valley, attempting to take the railroad and the Confederates from the rear (a strike, however, that would uncover his base at Chattanooga); or he might opt for an immediate, face-to-face confrontation with John-ston's army in the open ground around Dalton, where there was some room to maneuver. This would force Johnston into a possibly decisive battle, outside his entrenchments, with Sherman's forces holding a two-to-one edge in manpower. Still, the Confederates would not likely be surprised and such a fight promised much bloodshed.

Another possibility, of course, was to attack the Rebel strength head-on at Mill Creek Gap. When Sherman directed his field glasses at the position of Confederate troops along the ridge, and strategically placed in the gap, he could readily see that an assault on such a bastion would cost far too many casualties—even if it succeeded, which it probably would not. Sherman certainly was not the only Union soldier with his eyes turned toward the mountainous ridge. Private Charles Benton, looking at Mill Creek Gap, (Buzzard's Roost), spied a buzzard lazily hovering over the gorge. Calling the ugly creature to the attention of his companion, Benton said his friend replied, "He's counting us."

Understandably, Sherman decided to take the third choice. He could move by his right flank, which itself opened other options, as previously noted. He thus determined to strike at Johnston's railroad, eleven or twelve miles south of Dalton at Resaca. Fortunately for Sherman, some of his scouts discovered Snake Creek Gap, leading directly to Resaca, about eight or nine miles to the east. Snake Creek was a wider gap than either Dug or Mill Creek gaps—and had been left completely undefended by the Rebels.

General Thomas originally suggested this plan, with his Army of the Cumberland playing the key role. While McPherson and Schofield moved into the position Thomas's men held in front of Ringgold, "the Rock of Chickamauga" would take his army down the west side of the ridge to its south end, then strike eastward through Snake Creek Gap for the West-ern & Atlantic. At the least, the Confederates would be compelled to fall back from their imposing mountain citadel in order to protect their supply line, possibly transforming the campaign into a war of maneuver at its inception, more favorable to the Union with its greater numbers. Possibly, too, the Rebels just might be taken by surprise, trapped between two strong Federal forces, and badly beaten.

The Union commander did not think the plan, as Thomas conceived it, was practical. The Army of the Cumberland was too large and unwieldly for such maneuvering. Probably secrecy could not be maintained, considering the problems involved in withdrawing 60,000 men from the immediate front of an alert enemy. The Confederate commander then might fall upon the smaller segment of the badly divided Yankee forces. Besides, Sherman considered Thomas a bit slow and lacked the confidence to entrust him with such a mission.

But as the energetic Ohioan with penetrating eyes mulled over the Thomas plan, he hit upon a modification that filled him with excitement. McPherson's Army of the Tennessee should do the work, Sherman decided. A force of 25,000, it was small enough to move rapidly, yet large enough to have considerable striking power. The Army of the Tennessee was the army that Sherman himself had led at Vicksburg and Chattanooga, and now, with his favorite McPherson commanding, Sherman felt good about its chances for success. Still better, the Army of the Tennessee was not yet in position in front of the Rebels; thus it required no shift from the enemy's immediate presence. McPherson could march south from Chattanooga, keeping hidden west of Taylor's Ridge, and suddenly strike east through Ship's Gap, Villanow, and Snake Creek Gap. He would surprise the Rebels and cut their railroad at Resaca, possibly before Joe Johnston even suspected what was developing. And while McPherson's soldiers marched, Thomas and Schofield would be busy engaging Johnston's attention at Dalton. The concept was excellent.

Eagerly Sherman issued the necessary orders. He brought Schofield's Army of the Ohio marching down the railroad to Red Clay, in preparation for launching a demonstration against the right flank of the Rebel position; Thomas's Army of the Cumberland was instructed to make ready for a push against the enemy on Rocky Face, threatening to break through at Mill Creek Gap and Dug Gap. Southward across the bloody Chickamauga battlefield came McPherson's Army of the Tennessee to Lee and Gordon's Mill, the jump-off point for his flanking move on Resaca.

Sherman set it up well. On May 4, all three armies began their separate but coordinated movements to turn Johnston out of his entrenchments. Meanwhile, Confederate reinforcements, some taken from coastal garrisons, were on their way to Johnston's army. Lieutenant General Leonidas Polk's Army of Mississippi (soon to become a third corps in the Rebel army) was also moving toward Dalton. All of these troops would not reach the Army of Tennessee until mid-May, but their presence would increase Confederate strength to nearly 70,000. And some would arrive just in time to make a difference at Resaca.

On May 7—as the Battle of the Wilderness, with its appalling harvest of casualties, was subsiding in Virginia—came the first real clash of the Atlanta campaign. General Thomas, with the Fourteenth Corps, supported by the Fourth, occupied Tunnel Hill, facing the Buzzard's Roost Gap, driving Wheeler's cavalry outpost back to the fortified lines at the gap, while the Twentieth Corps advanced on Thomas's right flank to Trickum, and Schofield's force began to close upon his left. On May 9 General Thomas's demonstration was very aggressive, "pushing it almost to a battle," according to Sherman's description in his After Action Report.

Indeed, a portion of Brigadier General John Newton's Second Division of the Fourth Corps did climb the northern end of Rocky Face Ridge. This unit was Brigadier General Charles G. Harker's Third Brigade. Leading the way as skirmishers was Colonel Emerson Opdycke's One Hundred and Twenty-fifth Ohio Regiment. A thirty-four-year-old Ohioan with a fiery reputation earned in most of the major western battles—from Shiloh, where he first led a charge, to Missionary Ridge, where his troops

Buzzard's Roost Gap, Georgia.

were among the first to reach the crest—Opdycke's reports are usually accurate and interesting.

"I saw but one practicable place of ascent on the western side," he wrote. "I moved to the northern point of the ridge and made a demonstration against the enemy's skirmishers, as if I intended to pass round to the eastern side and go up there; then suddenly withdrew my men and left other portions of the brigade to continue the skirmish while, under concealment of trees, I commenced to ascend obliquely the western side. We pushed up with all possible celerity."

Reaching the top, Opdycke and his men swept south toward Dalton, but soon met an advancing Rebel force. The firing was severe and men scrambled for cover behind the rocks that lay around. "I got a company front up and poured in several volleys," said Opdycke, "and then charged and drove the enemy a third of a mile." The rest of Harker's brigade soon ascended the ridge and came up to Opdycke's support.

The Yankees drove southward until they encountered the main Confederate line, which ran east down the ridge across Crow valley. Here their advance was stopped. Still in the forefront was the One Hundred and Twenty-fifth Ohio, whose Lieutenant Colonel David H. Moore "rushed ahead with about thirty brave men and got close to the enemy's works, but could not carry them," recorded Opdycke. Moore was hit three times, continued Opdycke, "but seemed to be miraculously preserved."

Moore himself, in a letter addressed "Dear Julia," and dated May 10, 2:40 P.M., described his experience: "In the charge last night I was hit four times, once by a ball which passed through a corporal's head, struck me in the back of the hip and lodged in the lining of my blouse; that only *stung*. Another stripped my right coat sleeve below the elbow, a fragment of another hit me in the left breast; still another struck my right lower bowels. These two last hurt, but are only *slight*; they do not lay me up. . . . Our loss in the 125th so far in killed and wounded is forty-eight." The corporal to whom Moore referred was L. S. Calvin and the bullet that diagonally pierced his head had shattered the right lower jaw. Calvin's comrades did not expect him to survive, but he did. In 1898, Moore wrote that he still had the bullet, bearing the indentations of Calvin's teeth.

The Federals next moved two pieces of artillery to the crest of the ridge but, even with their support, found the ridge top too narrow and too well protected by rock barricades and Confederate infantry to reach the Mill Creek Gap. Skirmishing continued at this point with no significant tactical change.

Meanwhile, Schofield moved his right, Brigadier General Henry M.

Judah's division, to the northern point of Rocky Face Ridge and connected with Thomas's left; and his own left, Brigadier General Jacob D. Cox's division, swung about a mile eastward toward Varnell's station to better protect his flank, both divisions skirmishing briskly with the Rebels. Schofield's center division, commanded by Brigadier General Alvin P. Hovey, remained in a reserve position.

There was considerable action south of Mill Creek Gap. Brigadier General John W. Geary's Second Division of the Twentieth Corps crossed Mill Creek and made a bold push against Rocky Face. The somewhat dramatic and verbose Geary often wrote After Action Reports that are longer than anybody else's. Geary was Hooker's best-known division leader. An engineer who fought in Mexico, the Pennsylvanian had then served as San Francisco's first mayor under the U.S. flag, and in 1856 helped to ease civil strife as governor of Kansas Territory. He fought at Chancellorsville and Gettysburg, lost a son who was under his command at Wauhatchie, and then played a key role in taking Lookout Mountain, a "feat that will be remembered," he said. Three times he had been wounded. Now he sent his men against Dug Gap.

Dug Gap had been left virtually unguarded except for a small force of Kentucky cavalry and Arkansas infantry, which arrived barely in time to stop the Yankees. When Polk's leading division under Brigadier General James Cantey had reached Resaca, Johnston ordered it held there to protect the Oostanaula crossings. Some 250 Arkansas infantry of Cantey's division were sent to Dug Gap, where they were soon joined by a regiment of Kentucky cavalry.

Austin Peay was one of these troopers, who later recalled the episode: "Reaching the Gap, we were dismounted, our horses left with holders at the foot of the mountain, and we were double-quicked to the top, and none too soon, for the enemy was swarming up the acclivity on the farther side." Two Federal assaults were repulsed after desperate fighting in which Southerners used stones as well as bullets.

"The attack was a most gallant one," according to General Geary, who reported "officers and men rushing through the few narrow apertures or clambering the precipice. Many of them gained the crest, but were met by a tremendous fire from a second line of works which were invisible from below, and were shot down and compelled to jump back for their lives. Here hand-to-hand encounters took place, and stones as well as bullets became elements in the combat, the enemy rolling them over the precipice, endangering our troops below. Failing to hold the crest after two separate assaults, our front line was withdrawn about a 150 yards and reformed in preparation for another effort."

Geary then sent the Thirty-third New Jersey Volunteers, which had just arrived, about half a mile to the south with orders to ascend the ridge; but this attack also failed. At nightfall the Yankees withdrew. Geary reported a loss of 357 men. As Geary's men fell back, Confederate troops from Major General Patrick Cleburne's division of Hardee's corps moved onto Rocky Face Ridge, to strengthen the defense with a continuous line from Hardee's left, at Dug Gap, to Hood's right, in Crow Valley.

Some of Cleburne's men, Texans of Granbury's and Lowrey's brigades, found the Kentuckians' horses at the foot of the mountain, and, "with a wild whoop," sprang into the saddles. "Mounted in the saddle once more," according to cavalryman Bennett Young, "they felt war's delirium and . . . shouting and yelling they galloped forward . . . to the succor of their hard-pressed comrades on the mountain top." One lively young Texan is said to have galloped up to Hardee and Cleburne, swung off his horse, and cried out, "Where am I most needed?" The effect was instantaneous, the two generals and their staffs experiencing a moment of comic relief as they burst into laughter.

Relieved by Cleburne's infantry, the Kentucky cavalrymen began filing down the mountain. Austin Peay remembered that Cleburne's veteran division opened the way to let them pass, many with heads uncovered. He heard remarks such as, "Boys, you covered yourselves with glory," and "We will never call you 'Butter-milk Rangers' any more." Peay said that some of Cleburne's men later told him they counted more than 400 enemy killed and wounded in front of the position. This seems consistent with Cleburne's report, who credited the Arkansans and Kentuckians with having "gallantly repulsed every assault," when he arrived at Dug Gap in person, about an hour before sundown, and "placed Lowrey and Granbury in position, which was done by night-fall."

No attack was made by Geary the next day. The Federals had determined that Johnston's position was too strong to be carried. Besides, the move on Rocky Face Ridge was designed only for a demonstration. As such it worked quite well. While the Yankees of Thomas and Schofield sparred with Johnston along Rocky Face, McPherson's Army of the Tennessee marched to accomplish its vital part of the Union plan. Having moved through Ship's Gap and Villanow, late in the evening of May 8 McPherson's advance units reached Snake Creek Gap and found it completely undefended.

"I'VE got Joe Johnston dead!" exulted Sherman. He had just learned that McPherson was within a few miles of Resaca. Outspoken and eminently quotable on war, perhaps the Union commander never uttered any words, except the "War is hell" pronouncement, that have appeared with such frequency in articles and monographs. Yet the exclamation about Johnston is well-nigh irresistable, because it is so typical of the grim but colorful Sherman. Plus, he very nearly did have the Confederate commander "dead."

The Rebel failure to block Snake Creek Gap rests primarily upon Johnston and secondarily upon Wheeler. Because of his immobilizing conviction, from first to last, that the main enemy thrust would be from the north against Dalton, Johnston disregarded the gap until, except for good fortune, it was too late to avoid Sherman's trap. Wheeler apparently was more interested in a grandstanding ride around Sherman's army (permission for which was refused), or a headlong charge, than in gaining information for his commander.

Not until the early morning of May 9 did Johnston demonstrate real concern—probably triggered by Cleburne's warning of ten o'clock the previous evening that the Yankees apparently were retiring from Dug Gap and moving southward along the west front of Rocky Face—about the location of Sherman's main force. Johnston acknowledged that he did not know if the weight of Sherman's army was west of Rocky Face or still on the line from Mill Creek Gap around the northern end of the ridge; twice he issued orders for Wheeler to find out where Sherman's main body lay. But the Confederate commander's chief of staff, W. W. Mackall, although he told Wheeler that Johnson was "anxious to obtain early information," first conveyed no specific orders, leaving the matter to Wheeler's discretion; and then later in the day said Johnston wanted "some cavalry in observation between this place [Dalton] and Resaca for fear of a surprise," only to immediately add his own opinion that, "I do not think Resaca in any danger; we have 4,000 men there." Thus Wheeler, ignoring Johnston's wishes, did not send any troopers to block the passes between Dalton and Resaca.

All of this is academic, except to illustrate the Confederate army's command problems, because Johnston's action was far too late, even had Wheeler been issued a specific order and carried it out immediately.

On that very morning of May 9, McPherson's Army of the Tennessee, debouching from Snake Creek Gap's eastern mouth, drove a handful of Confederate cavalry before it, and reached within a mile of Resaca. There the Yankees came under a heavy fire from the 4,000 Rebel infantry holding an entrenched, curved line extending from the Oostanaula on the south to the railroad on the north. The railroad north of Resaca bends slightly to the east, a situation drawing McPherson into a position between the Southern forces at Dalton and those facing him at Resaca. The latter, according to prisoners, constituted at least a division. McPherson felt out the Confederate defenses, and concluded they were strong.

Certainly McPherson, while he could not know exactly what confronted him, had not expected this much opposition. In fact, he expected none, although in war to expect the unexpected should be axiomatic. Haunted by the unknown, especially a nightmare scenario of Johnston hurrying large forces by the good road from Dalton to attack him while isolated from the rest of Sherman's army, McPherson decided to withdraw into the security of Snake Creek Gap. This he had done by nightfall, his front entrenched and his army secure against any surprise Johnston might have been contemplating.

When Sherman learned that his favorite subordinate had not taken Resaca his spirit sank—all the more because he had expected so much after McPherson's earlier report. Some accounts say he was enraged. Years later he wrote in his memoirs that McPherson "could have walked into Resaca. . . , or he could have placed his whole force astride the railroad above Resaca, and there have easily withstood the attack of all of Johnston's army, with the knowledge that Thomas and Schofield were on his heels. . . . Such an opportunity does not occur twice in a single life, but at the critical moment McPherson seems to have been a little cautious."

At the time, when Sherman again joined McPherson, still in Snake Creek Gap, he chided the Army of the Tennessee's commander, "Well, Mac, you missed the opportunity of your life!" Although then and later Sherman acknowledged that McPherson was "perfectly justified by his orders," he clearly felt that "Mac" had not been aggressive enough. The authors, confessing to a liking for McPherson, would find it preferable to contend that the young general was right in the decision, and fault Sherman for being overly critical. Actually, however, Sherman was right.

McPherson had 25,000 well-equipped veterans with him, hardly a paltry band. War always involves risk, and here the possible decisive gain—both securing the enemy's railroad and trapping him between the Federal pincers—makes the risk seem minimal. He should not have been surprised by some opposition at Resaca. While Sherman's later comment that he "could have walked into Resaca" is clearly an exaggeration, McPherson should have been able to take the town, or a least get a solid grip on the railroad, which would have been just as good. Johnston could not have detached heavily to drive him off without having to deal with an overwhelming enemy force at his back.

Ironically, and perhaps significantly for understanding Sherman's displeasure with McPherson, Sherman himself had had a similar opportunity at Missionary Ridge. He could have occupied the key point of the entire battle area at Tunnel Hill, the northern end of the ridge, before the Rebels manned it in strength. But he pulled up, in face of the unknown, rather than take the risk of meeting the enemy in force, when the rest of the Union army was not within immediate supporting distance.

From a Rebel viewpoint, General Cleburne, in his report dated August 16, remarked that how Snake Creek Gap "was neglected I can not imagine," and continued that, "as it was, if McPherson had hotly pressed his advantage, Sherman supporting him strongly with the bulk of his army, it is impossible to say what the enemy might not have achieved—more than probable a complete victory."

MEANWHILE, during the afternoon of May 9, Johnston received a report that John Logan's and Grenville Dodge's corps were in Snake Creek Gap. Thus he sent Hood with three divisions, Cleburne's, Hindman's, and Walker's, marching to Resaca. Hood was on the ground by night, aware that the Federals—though he did not know they were McPherson's troops—had pulled back, and so reported to Johnston the next morning. Johnston then ordered Hood back to Dalton, although Cleburne's and Walker's divisions were halted about halfway between Dalton and Resaca, at Tilton. Some of the relieving soldiers had never reached Resaca anyway and, significantly, none of the reinforcements were left there. Apparently, as Thomas Connelly concluded in Autumn of Glory, "Johnston and his commanders still believed the main thrust would be from the north against Dalton." General Hardee observed, on the afternoon of May 10, "there seems to be no force threatening us except on Rocky Face."

Actually, not until May 12 did Johnston finally realize that Sherman was moving around his left flank. Though Sherman was disappointed at McPherson's failure, he soon realized that an advantage had been gained nevertheless, and determined to join "Mac" with most of his troops. Anyway, the entire campaign was to be one continuous application of pressure, and if one movement failed, Sherman intended that another would immediately follow. Only Howard's Fourth Corps and some cavalry were left to watch Johnston at Dalton. The first Federals moved out on May 10, and on the following day, the roads west of Rocky Face became crowded with long columns of soldiers tramping south, Thomas's army in the lead, followed by Schofield's. White-topped wagon trains creaked slowly along. Gun carriages groaned as teams strained to pull them. Then the rain fell hard, beating against the ground in torrents, as the wind blew strongly and men were drenched. Some cursed; some engaged in lighthearted banter; some were too bored or lonely to register any reaction. In spite of the elements, by the evening of May 12, most of the Yankee troops had reached Snake Creek Gap.

On May 13, while halted near the gap for another unit to move ahead, an artillerist with the Second Regiment of Illinois Light Artillery recorded an amusing incident. Beside the road was a log shanty, and on a rudely constructed bench outside the door sat "a very good looking young woman of the southern 'cracker' type." She had been watching the Federals file past, ignoring their stares. Then some of the soldiers began to question her and the Union gunner remembered that the conversation went in the following manner:

"Are you married?"

"Yaas."

"Where is your husband?"

"Oh, he's down yonder. You'ens gwine down whar he is."

"Ar'n't you afraid we'll kill him?"

"Dunno. Maybe he'll kill you'ens."

"How many Rebs are there down yonder?"

"Dunno, a heep o'em. We'ens got a right smart crowd."

"What will you do if the Yanks kill your husband?"

"Dunno;" and then a smile seemed to creep over her face, which deepened into a grin, and she said:

"Dunno, I 'spect I'd hab to marry one ob you'ens." Her drawling response evoked a howl of laughter from the soldiers.

ON MAY 12 and 13 there was heavy skirmishing west of Resaca between McPherson's soldiers and outposts of Polk's corps. To the north General Johnston, still hoping to draw the Federals into an assault on his formidable lines at Dalton, was slow to accept the signs pointing to Sherman's flanking move. He had intelligence by midmorning of May 12 that Sherman's army was marching either toward Villanow or Snake Creek Gap. Later in the day reports arrived both from Cleburne, indicating that the enemy was massing in Snake Creek Gap, and from Wheeler, revealing that only two of the Yankee divisions remained in front of Dalton. Johnston still held on at Dalton until early morning of May 13. Then he ordered Hardee and Hood to hurry their corps to reinforce Polk at Resaca. The Rebel commander did have good roads south, and a shorter distance to cover than Sherman's Federals, but he risked too much in waiting so long to fall back.

It was late in the morning of May 13 before Hardee and Hood reached Resaca. If—and it is a big "if"—Sherman could have attacked during the morning, he probably would have taken the town and still trapped the Confederate army north of the Oostanaula River. The outspoken Union commander later said of Johnston: "Had he remained in Dalton another hour, it would have been his total defeat." The statement was an exaggeration. Sherman did not know what an opportunity lay before

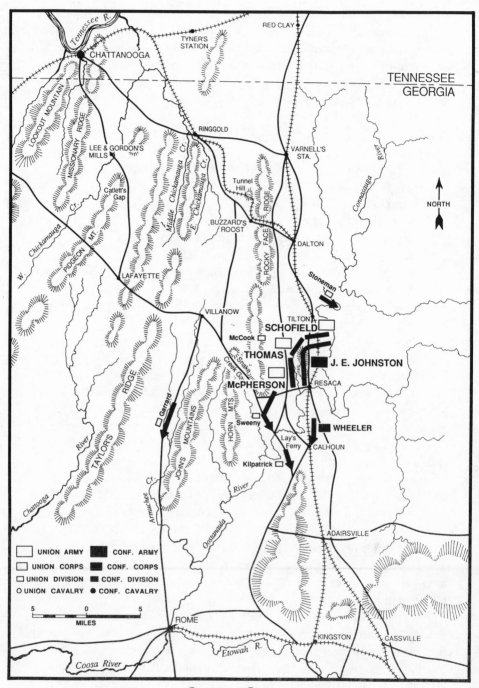

Situation at Resaca.

him and regardless, could not have pushed forward rapidly enough to attack during the morning hours. In fact, when his army finally moved within sight of Resaca, Hood and Hardee already had taken defensive positions around the town. In his After Action Report Sherman was more nearly accurate than in later years, saying, "Nothing saved Johnston's army at Resaca but the impracticable nature of the country, which made the passage of troops across the valley almost impossible." By the time the Federal army was deployed for battle on May 13, sundown was at hand, and nothing beyond skirmishing had taken place. Nevertheless, the day did see a notable casualty at a crossroads cavalry clash when Yankee brigadier Judson Kilpatrick took a bullet that put him out of action for several weeks.

The Confederate army deployed west of Resaca on the hills along the eastern side of Camp Creek. A single division of Polk's corps held the Rebel left, anchored on the Oostanaula. Hardee's corps formed the center of Johnston's line. Hood's corps held the right, angled northeastward across the road from Dalton, his line extending to the Connasauga River, which flowed into the Oostanaula east of Resaca. Cavalry was posted east of the Connasauga, while cavalry and infantry guarded the south bank of the Oostanaula.

The entrenched line, stretching for three miles over knolls and hills, had substantial strength—as well as weaknesses. Not only were the Con-

Battleground of Resaca, Georgia.

nasauga and Oostanaula rivers at the back of the Rebels, and their defensive line drawn at a right-angle position, but in front of their left flank lay several hills that, if occupied by the Union, would enable the enemy's artillery to strike the bridges, both railroad and pike, at Resaca. On these hills was posted only a skirmish line of Gray infantry.

As the Federals deployed for battle, McPherson, in the advance, held the right while Thomas, following behind, moved to the north and formed on McPherson's left flank. Schofield, advancing behind Thomas, moved farther north, joining up with Thomas's left flank. Howard's corps, following the Rebels south from Dalton, would come up on the left of the Army of the Ohio, to form the extreme Yankee left flank.

Many of the Federals were tired from forced marching. Possibly, none appeared more so than Sherman himself. Unshaven, weary-looking and rumpled, the general seemed drunk to a Union private who made the mistake of too loudly remarking on the matter to a companion. An aroused Sherman rebuked the young soldier, assuring him that his commander was not drunk, but had been up late, busy planning the army's next move.

If one could have seen across the lines and compared, the Confederate commander doubtless would have been the more impressive appearing of the two generals. On Saturday, May 14, Johnston rode from point to point along the line, wearing "a light or mole colored hat, with a black feather in it," sporting fluffy white side-whiskers, a neat mustache, and a chin beard. Small, trim and alert, Johnston inspired confidence and many of the Rebels cheered him.

Just as Sherman said, however, he had been planning. Skirmishing began at dawn on May 14, and by six o'clock heavy firing was taking place up and down the lines. Sherman's battle plan sent an infantry force under Brigadier General Thomas W. Sweeny reconnoitering farther south to the Oostanaula River, searching for a crossing at Lay's Ferry to threaten Johnston's communications at Calhoun, while a cavalry division under Brigadier General Kenner Garrard rode from Villanow toward Rome, if possible there to destroy factories and ironworks, and break the branch line railroad between Rome and Kingston. The bulk of the Union army would press against the Confederates at Resaca.

Skirmishing heavily at all points to cloud his purposes, Sherman made an assault in the early afternoon with the left center of his line. General Thomas's Army of the Cumberland gained nothing of significance, and Schofield's Army of the Ohio, plagued by rugged terrain, confusion, and a division commander's incompetence—not too mention fierce Confederate resistance—took a whipping.

First assuring himself that the Fourth Corps, advancing from Dalton,

Chester House Hotel, Dalton, after Federal Troops Moved Out, 1864.

would soon be within supporting distance of his left flank, Schofield ordered his troops to advance, develop fully the enemy's position, and attack. Jacob D. Cox's division was on the left flank, Henry M. Judah's division on the right, and Alvin P. Hovey's division in reserve. Cox was an able and vigorous leader. An Oberlin graduate who practiced law and was elected as a Republican to the Ohio Senate, he was a dedicated abolitionist and political ally of James A. Garfield and Salmon P. Chase. A keen observer, Cox wrote several books after the war, including a history of the Atlanta campaign. Across rough, broken ground, covered with dense woods and thick underbrush, and over a deep, narrow channel of Camp Creek, Cox's troops drove the Rebel skirmishers until they reached the foot of a ridge upon which the Confederate's first line of trenches was dug.

General Cox described the ensuing action: "A short halt was made, bayonets were fixed, and the whole command charged the hill and carried the line of rifle-pits on the crest, driving the enemy back upon a second line some 250 yards from the first. . . . The enemy immediately opened with both artillery and musketry from their second line, which extended far beyond both flanks of the division, and no troops being as yet in position on either our right or left, the division was halted. . . . Farther advance being entirely impracticable till supports should come up on right and left, the command was ordered to screen itself from fire, as much as possible, especially on the extreme right, which, from its greater proximity to the enemy's second line of works and its exposure to artillery fire from his batteries in position on its flank down the valley, suffered very severely."

In vain did Cox look to his right for support from Judah, who never got beyond the creek. An 1843 graduate of the Military Academy who had finished near the bottom of his class, Judah's Civil War service had mostly been in rear areas. He had a poor reputation as a commander. Judah's problem began to develop when the First Brigade, positioned on his division's right flank, found part of the Fourteenth Corps from the Army of the Cumberland across its front. Instead of waiting for that force to advance, which it was about to do, Judah ordered the First Brigade, in the words of Brigadier General Nathaniel C. McLean, commanding the brigade, "to march over them and advance immediately." Complying with Judah's "reiterated command," as McLean noted, he proceeded to "pass over the troops of the Fourteenth Corps and through the dense and tangled undergrowth of the forest." Some of the Fourteenth Corps, in the confusion, began to advance with McLean's brigade; thus interlaced, the two forces went forward together. In addition to the obvious command problem and chaos thereby created, the situation was made worse when Judah's Second Brigade, on his left flank, was left behind in the advance.

On surged the Federals, units intermingled and lines in disorder. Bugles were sounding the forward note continually and the mass of men plunged ahead through heavy timber and thick underbrush, across an open field, and then hit the barrier of Camp Creek. Colonel William Cross of the Third Tennessee (Union) reported the "creek was hedged on either side by thick bushes and was about waist deep and was very difficult to cross."

When the Yankees finally staggered past the creek they started struggling up a rather steep hillside that lay open in front of the Confederate works. Here they were swept by a galling musketry fire mixed with artillery. "To climb the opposite bank under such a murderous fire," reported General McLean, "was more than they could do, especially when we found the works so strong that with the force then attacking there was not the slightest chance of success. Under these circumstances we were forced back, leaving fully one-third of the attacking party killed and wounded on the field."

Efforts were made to reform and attack again, but many of the soldiers would not respond. The commander of the Twenty-fifth Michigan reported that "neither threats nor entreaties could induce those troops to expose themselves again to that terrible fire."

Only when Judah's First Brigade had been defeated did the Second

Brigade arrive and launch another unsuccessful assault. Brigadier General Milo S. Hascall succinctly summarized the episode: "My brigade had no fair chance at all in the attempt upon Resaca. It was rushed pell-mell through about three-quarters of a mile of thicket, and then, after the First Brigade had been defeated and routed, was suffered to go headlong over a precipice down into a creek bottom, where the men in great disorder were immediately confronting the enemy's works and exposed to his musket and artillery fire at short range. The result was what might have been expected, a most disastrous defeat."

Still General Judah talked about attacking. When General Hascall pleaded that his brigade was so decimated that it could hardly even render assistance, Judah turned to the One Hundred and Seventh Illinois Regiment, which had been held in reserve; professing that a single regiment could take the Rebel works, Judah said he would lead the charge in person. The general never made his appearance to personally lead however—fortunately for the men of the One Hundred and Seventh—and the bloody affair at last came to an end.

Rumors were soon circulating that Judah was drunk when he directed the advance. His division suffered the greatest loss of life of any that engaged in the fighting before Resaca, and the next morning Lieutenant Colonel Isaac R. Sherwood, commanding the One Hundred and Eleventh Ohio Regiment, would go to headquarters of the Army of the Ohio, complaining to Schofield that Judah was guilty of gross negligence. Within two days Schofield would replace Judah with General Hascall.

Meanwhile, as Schofield's Army of the Ohio struggled, a few hundred yards to the north the Yankee left flank came under attack. Schofield's assault had gone in against Major General Thomas C. Hindman's division of Hood's corps. While the assault was in progress, General Johnston sent word for Hood to probe the Union left flank. As Johnston hoped, Confederate cavalry discovered—in the language of Civil War dispatches—the flank was "in air," that is, neither anchored upon easily defensible terrain nor supported by adequate reserves.

The Rebels attacked with two of Hood's divisions, Major General Alexander P. Stewart's and Major General Carter L. Stevenson's, supported by troops taken from the center and left of the Southern line. Shortly after four o'clock in the afternoon the Confederates struck. Their full force went in against Major General David S. Stanley's division of the Fourth Corps, whose left flank First Brigade, under Brigadier General Charles Cruft, was still trying to get into position. Stanley was a West Point graduate of 1852, had fought in "Bleeding Kansas," and had refused the command of a Confederate regiment being organized in Arkansas. He served in the Trans-Mississippi before joining the Army of the Cumberland, eventually becoming the army's cavalry commander. He had assumed his infantry command the previous November. Stanley reported that "the Thirty-first Indiana, stationed upon a round-topped hill, found itself fired into from three directions. . . . The One Hundred and First Ohio and Eighty-first Indiana were soon driven back, and the enemy was bursting exultingly upon the open field when Simonson [Captain Peter Simonson, Fifth Indiana Battery] opened on them with canister, which soon broke and dispersed that attack. The enemy formed in the woods and attempted to cross the open field again, but met the same savage shower of canister."

Actually, the situation was much worse than Stanley, who later wrote that reinforcements were unnecessary for the Fifth Indiana to repulse the Rebel attackers, admitted. Not only had the First Brigade retreated in panic, but the Second Brigade, under Brigadier General Walter C. Whitaker, also gave way, leaving only the Fifth Indiana Battery to meet the Confederate attack. The artillerists raked the charging Southerners. They had packed their guns with canister, small metal fragments fired to produce a wide and devastating effect on the enemy. Captain Simonson could see and hear the Rebel officers shouting to their men, urging them forward, and some did get within fifty yards of his guns. Then they fell back, reformed, and came again from another direction, farther to the left of the battery. Hood's determined attackers apparently were on the brink of a triumph, if Federal reinforcements had not arrived.

Fortunately, Stanley had earlier requested a supporting division on his left flank. Just in time, Major General Alpheus Williams's division, the lead unit of Hooker's corps, came up to support the Fifth Indiana Battery before the Rebels overpowered it. Williams was a fifty-three-year-old graduate of Yale, from Connecticut, who had been a lawyer, publisher, and postmaster of Detroit before the war. Colonel James S. Robinson's brigade, leading Williams's march, quickly deployed, despite the hindrance of numerous routed troops from Stanley's command, and marched at once to support the battery.

The Blue brigade swept down the side of a steep wooded ridge, scrambled across Camp Creek at the base, and—changing front forward on the right regiment—surprised the attacking Confederates with, as Colonel Robinson reported, "a tremendous fire upon the overconfident foe." The opening volley against the Rebel flank threw the attackers into confusion. The Yankees immediately followed their fire with a charge, yelling and shrieking, as they drove the Southerners "clear over the hill out of sight in great confusion," in the appreciative words of the Fifth Indiana Battery's Captain Simonson. Darkness soon covered the field and neither side attempted any more fighting on May 14.

The Confederate commander was initially pleased as he reviewed reports of the day's action, and determined to renew the assault against the Federal left flank at dawn. Only later in the evening did he learn the disturbing news from General Polk that the Yankees had achieved a notable success at the other end of the battle line. General McPherson's Army of the Tennessee had forced Polk's skirmishers off the high ground west of Resaca and brought artillery onto the position with range to bombard both the railway and turnpike bridges close in the Confederate rear, thus endangering the line of retreat. Polk had made several unsuccessful attempts to retake the position. Worse, scouts reported that Federals in strength had crossed the Oostanaula downstream to the south at Lay's Ferry, near the mouth of Snake Creek, where they could soon threaten the Western & Atlantic Railroad. Intelligence reports also indicated that Union troops marching south from Dalton had arrived on the enemy's left flank.

Alarmed, Johnston countermanded Hood's attack order for dawn; immediately sent Major General W. H. T. Walker's division, from Hardee's corps, on a night march south to attack the Yankees at Lay's Ferry and drive them back across the river; and began preparation to withdraw the bulk of his army across the stream if necessary. He constructed a pontoon bridge upstream, beyond range of the Yankee guns on the high ground. Through the morning of Sunday, May 15, Johnston held his position at Resaca and anxiously waited for news from General Walker about the apparent crisis to the south at Lay's Ferry.

While Johnston worried, Sherman prepared to attack. Again he struck with the left center of the Blue line, except that this day he used Hooker's corps to make the assault after shifting Schofield's forces to the extreme left of the Yankee flank. It was nearing noon when Hooker advanced with Williams's division on his left, Geary's in the center, and Major General Daniel Butterfield on his right. The attack went in against Hood once more, Stevenson's and Hindman's divisions.

Rugged terrain and confusion continued to hamper the Federals. In Butterfield's division, for example, the Second Brigade mistakenly fired a volley into the First Brigade, and in the ensuing chaos a mass of men ran through a portion of the Third Brigade, disorganizing some of its regiments. And in Geary's division, also plagued by "friendly fire" from the rear, some new troops broke and stampeded through the ranks of the One Hundred and Forty-ninth New York.

The main Confederate line, well entrenched, repulsed the Yankees without great difficulty. The Federals scrambled for whatever cover they could find and the two lines kept up a continual fire at one anther. In front of Stevenson's division stood a small, uncompleted dirt fort in which were posted four guns of Captain Max Van Den Corput's Georgia Battery, positioned to enfilade any Federal assault against Hindman's lines. Here the fight centered.

The Yankees made a concerted effort to take the fort. Going to ground as the artillery unleashed its violent discharge, the Federals quickly rose and raced to attack before the Rebels could load and fire again. Men from several Yankee regiments, led by Colonel Benjamin Harrison of the Seventieth Indiana (the same who later became president of the United States) broke over the works together. A hand-to-hand fight—inevitably vicious, brutal, and brief—raged as the Georgians refused to abandon their guns.

Hopelessly outnumbered and with no infantry support, the gunners were overwhelmed, dead and wounded men of both sides soon covering the ground with their bodies and blood. At once the triumphant Federals found the fort to be a death trap for them because it was badly exposed to fire from the main Rebel line. A murderous barrage forced them to evacuate immediately, scurrying for some semblance of cover. Alone and silent, the four cannon stood, neither side able to gain possession of them.

A member of the One Hundred and Forty-ninth New York, Captain George K. Collins, described the action from his perspective: "The men laid on their faces on the hillside, and when those in front were killed, wounded or out of ammunition, those in rear crawled forward and took their places. The enemy was not more than fifty yards away." Collins recalled a macabre episode of the struggle, writing that "occasionally a man, with undue curiosity, crawled too far forward. . . . One poor fellow, against the remonstrances of his comrades, crawled up where he could get a better view, and almost instantly was killed in his place. In falling his head was exposed and, during the afternoon, the enemy literally filled it with bullets."

MEANWHILE, Johnston, receiving a report from General Walker saying that the Federals had not forced a downstream crossing of the Oostanaula after all, renewed his original plan for Hood to strike again at the Yankee left flank. Supporting troops were sent from the Confederate left and center, and Hood's infantry was about to move forward to the attack when a second note was received from Walker. Now Walker reported that the Federal crossing of the river a half dozen miles to the south was definite.

Indeed it was. The Rebel confusion about the crossing resulted from the fact that Yankee troops under General Sweeny did cross on the previous day, only to pull back immediately to the northern bank, having themselves received a false report that a large body of Southerners was approaching, in position to cut them off from McPherson's corps. When Walker arrived at a point near Lay's Ferry the Federals were gone, of course. Leaving a small guard, Walker took up a position near Calhoun. But Sherman had ordered Sweeny to recross the river on May 15, which he succeeded in doing, driving off the Rebel pickets. Soon the news reached Walker, who relayed it to Johnston at once, before trying unsuccessfully to drive the Yankees back.

When Johnston received this second report from Walker, he countermanded his orders for Hood to attack and called for Hood, along with Polk and Hardee, to meet for a council of war that evening at his headquarters. It was obvious that Johnston could no longer hold Resaca and a retreat had to be made to the south bank of the Oostanaula. Unfortunately for the Southerners, Stewart's division did not receive Johnston's countermanding order in time to stop his attack. At 4:00 P.M. sharp, the division moved forward against the Union line of breastworks constructed from rail fences. The divisions of Brigadier Generals Marcus A. Stovall and Henry D. Clayton led the assault. Stewart reported that "the men moved forward with great spirit and determination and soon engaged the enemy . . . in heavy force and protected by breast-works of logs. The ground over which a portion of Stovall's brigade passed was covered with a dense undergrowth and brush. Regiments in consequence became separated, and the brigade soon began to fall back. Hastening to it and finding it impossible to reform it on the ground it occupied, it was suffered to fall back to its entrenched position." Clayton's brigade was thus left without support on either flank and facing a concentrated enemy fire. It too soon retreated.

Neither side attempted to launch another attack, but heavy firing swept over the field until long after dark, making the area, as a Confederate remarked, "most damnably dangerous." And after dark some of Hooker's Yankees finally managed to dig away the front of the dirt fort, where a number of soldiers on both sides had died, and drag off the four Rebel cannon with ropes. These were the only guns the Confederates lost in the entire campaign.

Perhaps this small Union success was symbolic of all the fighting to this point. From Dalton to Resaca, neither side seemed able to make anything work quite as the generals planned. Both had taken losses; both had been plagued by blunders and rough terrain. Yet, just as the Federals finally got the four guns, so too they ultimately forced the Rebels to fall back across the first of the rivers between Sherman and Atlanta.

Johnston met with the corps commanders at his headquarters, and orders were issued for the army to begin the retreat over the Oostanaula at midnight. Hood crossed on the pontoon bridge above Resaca, while Hardee and Polk used the turnpike and railroad spans, disregarding the threat of Federal long-range artillery fire. Strong details of skirmishers kept firing into the Yankee lines as the Gray columns trudged south toward a rendezvous below Calhoun. Rear guards took up the pontoons and loaded them into wagons for possible later use, and set fire to the railroad bridge; but in the rush to get away before the break of dawn they failed to destroy the turnpike bridge (an omission reminiscent of a similar failure to block the railroad tunnel at Ringgold).

When the Yankees moved forward in the morning, evidences of the carnage were all about. It is impossible to determine the losses suffered at Resaca, because Confederate reports are fragmentary and Federal casualties were compiled on a monthly basis. Ohioan Jacob Cox recorded in his diary that his division lost 500 men in the fighting on May 14. Judah's division lost even more. On May 15 the Seventieth Indiana took 156 casualties in the assault on the dirt fort in the front of Hood's position. One man who tramped over the battleground following the Rebel retreat said it was "thickly strewn with the dead and wounded. Inside and around the earthworks, rebel and Union officers and men lay piled together; some transfixed with bayonet wounds, their faces wearing that fierce, contorted look that marks those who have suffered agony. Others, who were shot dead, lay with their calm faces and glassy eyes turned to heaven. . . . Others had their skulls crushed in by the end of a musket while the owners of the muskets lay still beside them, with the death grip tightened on the pieces." Colonel Allen Fahnestock, Eighty-sixth Illinois, confided in his diary a ghastly moment: "As I got over their breastworks I picked up the top of a rebel soldier's head, a piece of skull as large as my hand, with long black hair; a piece of shell from our battery had cut it off clean." And Federals from the Third Wisconsin Infantry discovered the dead body of a Confederate chaplain in their front, shot, said some of the Confederate wounded, when he attempted to recover the body of his son, a captain who had just been killed. Father and son lay dead together, only a few yards from where the Third Wisconsin's own chaplain, who insisted upon going into the battle, had been mortally wounded.

Likely there were ample scenes of carnage to forever haunt the minds of Yank and Reb alike. But John C. Portis, a Confederate private in the Eighth Mississippi, whose wound of May 14 resulted in the amputation of his right arm at the shoulder (which he said was buried in a box by a comrade a mile south of Resaca), also would long remember vividly a wagon occupied by several women as it passed by north of the river and west of the railroad on Sunday, May 15. A Federal battery opened fire on the wagon, said Portis, and continued to fire until it had passed over the bridge, all the while a young woman standing erect in the wagon waving her hat, which had a red ribbon on it, in defiance of the Yankee gunners.

# 6

# I Lead You to Battle

FIVE hundred miles away as the crow flies, northeast across the rugged mountains of North Carolina and Virginia, the other major and differently developing Union offensive had been progressing under the direction of Lieutenant General U. S. Grant. Moving over the Rapidan River during the first days of May—while Sherman attempted to trap Johnston's Confederates north of the Oostanaula—Grant tried to steal a march and flank the Rebel Army of Northern Virginia to the east, never intending to fight in that tangled, timbered area called "the Wilderness." But Lee gave the Federal general no choice, striking the Army of the Potomac in flank as it moved through the Wilderness on May 5 and initiating a confused, sanguinary, two-day struggle that cost the Yankees 17,000 casualties.

From that time forward, Federals and Confederates in Virginia, just as in north Georgia, were never totally out of violent contact. For days following the Battle of the Wilderness, fighting swirled about a little crossroads to the southeast called Spotsylvania. The heaviest losses occurred on May 12, at a place known ever since as "the Bloody Angle." By May 16, when Sherman had compelled Joe Johnston to evacuate Resaca and retreat south of the Oostanaula, Grant's Federals had not pushed Lee's army back any farther than Sherman had forced Johnston. Also, Grant had suffered an average of more than 2,500 casualties per day, several times the losses of Sherman's command.

Even though taking heavy casualties, at least Grant was keeping the pressure on Lee's smaller forces, inflicting losses that the Southerners could not replace. Elsewhere, Union offensives were accomplishing nothing. Franz Sigel's small army of 5,500, hoping to devastate the granary of the Shenandoah Valley before assailing Richmond from the west, was badly beaten at the Battle of New Market on May 15. "I fights no more mit Sigel," chanted some of the defeated, retreating German-Americans. Sigel's replacement, however, was hardly an improvement. Beaten near Charlottesville, David Hunter conducted a retreat into the western Virginia mountains.

Another Union force, 35,000 strong, had moved up the James River from Norfolk, apparently with a good chance to take Petersburg and cut the railroad south of Richmond. But ineptness in top Union command was never more evident than in this campaign. Commanding was Benjamin F. Butler, known in the South as "Beast Butler" since the days of his administration in occupied New Orleans. By May 16, the incompetent Butler had been defeated by an inferior force and was falling back to Bermuda Hundred, there to be pinned between the James River on the north, the Appomattox on the south, and the Confederates in front— like being "corked in a bottle," to use Grant's words. Across the Mississippi, on the Red River, the Federal gunboats and Nathaniel Banks's infantry column continued to retreat; grim evidence that the Federal effort to establish a presence in Texas was also a failure.

Thus Sherman's north Georgia offensive, although not achieving what he had desired, appeared impressive when set against other Federal efforts. Even the Virginia campaign under Grant was actually a poor second in comparison. If the newspapers allotted more space for the struggle in Virginia, such was only to be expected for so it had been all through the war. Spurred by the aura associated with Lee, Jackson, and Stuart, enticed by the drama connected with Washington and Richmond, and fascinated by the politics and changes of Union high command, the majority of reporters "working the war" had found action abundant as they covered the scant seventy-five miles between the two capitals. Also the war in the West was perceived as more dangerous, as well as entailing a more spartan existence for reporters than life in the East. Maybe the war was being won (or lost) in the western theater, but certainly not everyone recognized that fact. Why journey five hundred or a thousand miles when there was excellent copy close at hand?

Now the blood bath of Virginia fighting that began with the Battle of the Wilderness served to insure a continued media focus on that theater. Besides, Sherman was never known to encourage newsmen. In fact, he despised the press corps and had banned reporters from his army.

At the present, however, Sherman's mind was on General Joseph E. Johnston and the Rebel Army of Tennessee. Indeed, the campaign demanded total concentration by both commanders because it was entering a new phase and neither general was adequately informed about the terrain over which the armies contended. Even the maps prepared by Johnston's engineers, presumably better situated to learn about the region in their rear than the Yankees, were sometimes misleading.

South of Resaca the nature of the country changes abruptly. The thickly wooded terrain, rugged ridges, and narrow gaps that characterize the area north of the Oostanaula River suddenly give way to land that, in the words of Federal Brigadier General Jacob D. Cox, "is much more open and less broken than any other portion of Northern Georgia." From Resaca, as Sherman's bluecoats faced south, the Western & Atlantic Railroad and the Oostanaula River steadily diverged, somewhat in the likeness of a roughly-shaped letter V. The left side of the V would represent the railroad, running nearly due south to Calhoun, Adairsville, and Kingston. The right side would represent the Oostanaula, winding southwestward to Rome where the Etowah, flowing almost due west from Kingston, joins it to form the Coosa.

Between Resaca and Kingston—a distance of some thirty miles—lay a sparsely settled farming region with only a handful of small towns, where gently rolling hills were lightly covered with vegetation. And the roads that connected these towns and farms, obviously of great interest to the leader of an invading army, provided several north-to-south routes.

Joseph E. Johnston had had no choice. He was forced to retreat across the Oostanaula. Did the Southern commander now sense that the campaign had taken a decided turn for the worse? Surely, as Richard M. McMurry, one of the students of the action, has written about the area between the Oostanaula and Etowah rivers: "The absence of defensible terrain and the presence of alternate roads made the region an ideal field of operations for a force like Sherman's that was campaigning against a smaller army."

Worse yet, Johnston's retreat could not cover both his railroad supply line from Atlanta and the Rome industrial complex with its factories and the Noble Iron Works. One or the other must be sacrificed and Johnston chose the latter, a heavy blow to the Confederacy's ability to manufacture military equipment. Perhaps his opponent in blue sensed as much, for Sherman sent only two divisions down the Oostanaula toward Rome, while the weight of the Union forces crossed in the vicinity of Resaca to march on Calhoun.

Drawing the Rome assignment were Brigadier Generals Jefferson C. Davis (infantry) and Kenner Garrard (cavalry). In addition to the choice plum, soon to be relished, of an irreplaceable Southern industrial complex, the movement on Rome protected Sherman's rail line to Chattanooga. as well as the right flank of the Yankee forces pursuing Johnston. Also, it would eliminate another Confederate railroad, the branch line from Alabama, which joins the Western & Atlantic at Kingston. Possibly too, this column just might discover a river crossing where it could get behind the Army of Tennessee and cut the railroad to Atlanta.

Still, the two divisions moving on Rome constituted only a sideshow. The main route south was the Western & Atlantic Railroad, down which General Thomas prepared to march with two corps of the Army of the Cumberland, hard after the withdrawing Rebels. Meanwhile, General McPherson's force proceeded to cross the Oostanaula farther to the southwest at Lay's Ferry, in position to take up the pursuit well on the right of Thomas. Schofield's Army of the Ohio, together with Hooker's Twentieth Corps of the Army of the Cumberland, moved several miles to the east, crossing upstream from Resaca at Field's Ferry for a march on the left of Thomas.

Thus the nervous, chain-smoking Sherman hoped soon to have all three columns of pursuit in the position he desired: Thomas's as the holding force applying pressure in the center, McPherson's and Schofield's ready to make a flanking movement. By detaching Hooker's command to advance with Schofield, the Union commander achieved a better balance of strength on his flanks and enabled the large Army of the Cumberland to push forward more rapidly.

Federal spirits were high. The enemy had fallen back from what seemed to be formidable positions north of the Oostanaula. The noisy iron horses, belching their black smoke, had been steaming close to the front lines with regularity, supplying the soldiers' food, coffee, clothing, medical supplies, and ammunition. Casualties did not seem alarmingly high. Some of the men were in a mood to frolic, if the conditions were conducive.

Schofield's column, which had no pontoons, was forced to cross two rivers. Marching to Fite's Ferry on the Connasauga, General Cox's division was in the advance. Halting and coming to a front face at the riverbank, the men stacked arms (which were to be ferried across with the artillery and wagons) and stripped to the skin. Carrying their clothes on head or shoulder, they prepared to wade the waist-deep stream when General Cox and his staff rode up. A soldier in the One Hundred and Twelfth Illinois, B. F. Thompson, wrote that "the boys greeted him with cheer after cheer, and made great sport of their ludicrous appearance." When the opposite bank of the river was reached, Thompson said that "the fun increased. The bank was steep and of a red clay soil. Every man carried out a little water on his person, which dripped to the ground, and the bank soon became as slippery as a sheet of ice, and as difficult to climb, barefooted. Many a man would get half-way up the bank and go sprawling into the mud and roll down the embankment to the water." Those who had reached high ground cheered and laughed, of course. Luckily there was a pond of clear water close at hand in which the men could wash off the mud before dressing. General Cox later confirmed the story in his book on the Atlanta campaign.

Meanwhile, the Confederate army had pulled up at Calhoun, some six miles down the rails from Resaca. Sherman thought it possible that here Johnston might make a stand. The Southern commander's mind is not easy to fathom. Even the record in his memoirs, where presumably he had time to fashion a consistent account, is contradictory. After stating that initially he would have preferred to establish his defensive line at Calhoun, except for the demoralizing effects of withdrawing from Dalton, the general wrote, and only a few pages later, that upon arriving at Calhoun, he discovered that no good defensive position could be established there.

Perhaps part of Johnston's problem was a defensive mind-set. If he had been thinking in aggressive terms—a true offensive-defensive strategy—he had, as Thomas L. Connelly well observed, a good opportunity to make a fight north of Calhoun, despite the absence of defensible terrain. Wrote Connelly of Johnston: "Actually he could have hoped for no better place. On May 16 with a portion of Sherman's army crossing the Oostanaula west of Calhoun, and part following the Confederates across at Resaca north of Calhoun, Johnston seemed in an excellent position to strike Sherman's army while it was crossing the Oostanaula. . . . Johnston might well have held that portion of Sherman's army at Resaca on the north bank while striking at that part isolated west of Calhoun."

But Johnston apparently no longer thought in terms of aggressive, offensive strategy—if he ever did—and determined to fall back a dozen more miles to Adairsville. There, he contended in his memoirs, he expected to find a good defensive position. Probably, however, the Southern commander's After Action Report, dated October 20, 1864, is more accurate. Indicating that he was already following a general retreat policy, Johnston wrote that he "determined to fall back slowly until circumstances should put the chances of battle in our favor." He commented further that he expected the Union army "to be materially reduced before the end of June by the expiration of the terms of service of many of the regiments which had not re-enlisted."

Such a general retreat policy is consistent with Johnston's strategic thinking before the Federal offensive ever began. It will be remembered that when Johnston earlier was urged to mount a campaign into Tennessee, he responded to the Richmond administration that the correct strategy was to lure the Federals into Georgia as the best means of defeating them, after which an offensive campaign might be waged successfully.

Johnston was also counting on assistance from Confederate cavalry in Mississippi and Alabama to disrupt Sherman's railroads in Tennessee, thus depriving the Federals of their supply line. In his report Johnston said that Lieutenant General Stephen D. Lee "gave me reason to hope that a competent force could be sent . . . to prevent the use of the railroad by the U.S. army," and in his *Narrative of Military Operations* Johnston is emphatic: "I was confident, too, that the Administration would see the expediency of employing Forrest and his cavalry to break the enemy's railroad communications, by which he could have been defeated."

Aside from these being after-the-fact statements, was Johnston exaggerating? Did Confederate cavalry have the potential, if used efficiently, to compel Sherman to retreat for lack of supplies? Certainly Sherman had feared that Rebel horse soldiers, operating against his railroad communications between Nashville and Chattanooga, would present a major problem; particularly the powerfully-built, colorful, and controversial Nathan Bedford Forrest, fresh from the alleged massacre of black Union soldiers at Fort Pillow on April 12. (Already the Joint Committee on the Conduct and Expenditures of the War had completed an investigation of Fort Pillow and the U.S. Congress, on May 6, authorized the printing of sixty thousand copies of the damning report for the use of the House and the Senate). "Forrest is the very devil," Sherman wrote during the course of the Atlanta campaign; and later in his memoirs the Federal commander stated: "There was great danger, always in my mind, that Forrest would collect a heavy cavalry command in Mississippi, cross the Tennessee River, and break up our railroad below Nashville."

Unlike most cavalry units, Forrest's men worked hard, driven by a seemingly tireless commander who was ready to thrash on the spot any of his soldiers found shirking their duty. His cavalry just might have been capable of wrecking a railroad as efficiently as Sherman's infantry would later prove to be. Thus Sherman devised a strategy to keep Forrest occupied by Yankee forays from Memphis into north Mississippi, while his own 100,000-man force made a decisive penetration of the deep southeastern heartland.

Furthermore, Sherman had accumulated in Nashville a six months' supply for his army before the campaign began, which meant that attacking the railroad between Louisville and Nashville would be a waste of time and effort. Sherman also had two separate railroads to use from Tennessee's capital as far as Stevenson, Alabama. The longer of the two was by way of the Nashville & Decatur line, running almost due south from Nashville to a junction at Decatur with the Memphis & Charleston

Nathan Bedford
Forrest.

line, and thence eastward to Stevenson. The more direct route was via
the Nashville & Chattanooga, which wound its way southeastward from
the capital and also joined the Memphis & Charleston road at Stevenson. From that northeastern Alabama town a single line carried Sherman's supplies into Chattanooga. To seriously effect the Georgia campaign,
Confederate cavalry obviously would have to either concentrate heavily
against Sherman's railroad between Stevenson and Chattanooga or destroy
vital links in both of the other routes. The Confederate government had
no guarantee that even the resourceful, determined Forrest could succeed
against Union railroad defenders and repairmen marshalled by the wiley
Sherman. But with many vulnerable points on both railroads and the
stakes so high, the disappointing fact, from the Southern viewpoint, is
that the Confederates never made an all-out assault on the iron lifeline
of General Sherman's army.

CONCERNS of the top Rebel command were unknown to the great mass
of the army, of course. But a commanding general's decision soon affected

all, one way or another. Johnston's decision to retreat from Calhoun translated into a very trying night for one Confederate physician. In fact, fifty-three years later Dr. A. G. Donoho recalled it as the longest night of his life.

Left at the field hospital with ten seriously wounded men for whom there was no transportation, the doctor expected to be captured the next morning and sent North unless he could find some help quickly. "I went to every wagon I heard passing," the doctor wrote, "but they were all loaded and could not help me. About midnight everything became still, and so still!—no more wagons, no more noise." Then the cavalry skirmish line fell back, about to leave Dr. Donoho and his wounded to await the arrival of the Yankees. Desperate, the doctor prevailed upon some of the troopers to watch his patients while he went to see their colonel, in hope of getting some ambulances. The colonel had none, but he agreed to send a courier to Major General William W. Loring, reported to be five miles to the south, and attempt to obtain ambulances from him.

Back to his patients went the doctor; back to wait for the ambulances which he hoped would come—and come in time, before the enemy arrived.

Trestle Bridge at Whiteside, Tennessee.

"Just as I could see the gray dawn in the east three ambulances came," he recalled. One of the cavalrymen who had remained "assisted me in getting the men loaded . . . , which occupied some time. Before we got them all in, we could see the enemy advancing, and just as we had the last one, they saw us and opened fire. . . . The last man in, I caught on the hind end of the ambulance (there was no room inside), waved my hand to the Yankees, and trotted until within our lines."

PERHAPS General Joseph E. Johnston was too often a wishful thinker. Like the position at Calhoun, the one at Adairsville did not meet his expectations. Army engineers had studied the valley of Oothcaloga Creek, assuring the general that north of the town the valley was narrow enough for both of the army's flanks to be solidly anchored on high ridges. On the night of May 17 Johnston held a council of war. His senior corps commander, William J. Hardee, advised Johnston to make a stand at Adairsville. Johnston, however, was convinced the valley was too wide for his army. Hardee replied that they should fight regardless of the unfavorable terrain.

There were considerations that seemed to make a fight at Adairsville feasible, maybe advisable. Johnston's army had been reinforced by Polk's cavalry division, while Brigadier General Samuel G. French's infantry

William J. Hardee.

division was close at hand. Word arrived from General Stephen Dill Lee in Alabama that Forrest, with 3,500 troopers and two artillery batteries, would soon attack Sherman's rail lines in middle Tennessee, as Johnston had been advocating. An intelligence report had come in that a Federal corps of McPherson's command was moving southwestward, evidence, if accurate, that the Yankee forces were not tightly grouped. Additionally, the question of how far an army defending its heartland can retreat without destroying morale must be considered.

Regarding the latter, Private George W. Hagan of the Twenty-ninth Georgia Volunteers, in a letter to his wife, reflected the doubts and confusion gnawing at the common soldier when he penned the following observations in crude form: "I can not give you any news that is good. The Yanks have flanked us from Dalton to Calhoun 25 miles our forces have fought them very hard & in some places whipped them our line of Battle now is about 30 miles long & we are compelled to fall back I do not know how far we will fall back, our forces have done some of the hardest fighting I ever heard." A Confederate chaplain, James H. M'Neilly, later recalled: "I heard this remark often when we abandoned a position and fell back: 'Well, I don't see why we have to fall back again; but Old Joe knows what he is doing. He will show them Yankees a thing or two when he gets 'em where he wants 'em.' "

Surely "Old Joe" can be credited with a sincere desire to "get 'em where he wants 'em." But writings of many Confederate soldiers prove that frustration and demoralization were growing factors. Nevertheless, Johnston overruled Hardee's advice to give battle at Adairsville. Besides, the Southern commander had another idea.

Again he would retreat, only this time armed with a specific plan to draw the Federals into a trap. The result would become famous in Confederate legend as "the Cassville Affair," probably the most controversial aspect of the campaign during Johnston's tenure as commander of the Army of Tennessee.

The general's concept was not complicated and did appear promising. It hinged on a simple divergence of the roads. South of Adairsville, the main Atlanta pike veered southeast toward the little college town of Cassville, a dozen miles distant. The Western & Atlantic Railroad, paralleled by another pike, continued directly south to Kingston before turning first east toward Cassville and finally southeast once more toward Atlanta. One might think of the three towns as forming a triangle: Adairsville as the apex, with the base, some seven or eight miles long, stretching from Kingston to Cassville.

Johnston hoped that Sherman would divide his forces, sending part on the road to Cassville and the remainder down the pike to Kingston.

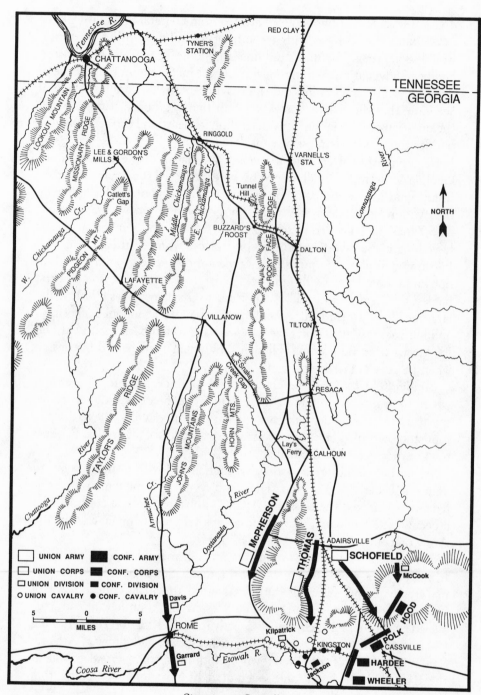

Situation at Cassville.

Then the Southern commander intended to attack one of the enemy columns while it was separated from the other. When the Confederates left Adairsville, Johnston would send Polk and Hood down the Cassville road, while Hardee was to take the road to Kingston. Hardee would also have the army's wagon trains with him, and continue skirmishing with the Federals as he fell back—factors which Johnston hoped would register in Sherman's mind as evidence that the entire Rebel army had gone to Kingston. If so, thought Johnston, Sherman would be all the more likely to divide his large command on the two diverging roads.

The plans for battle laid, Johnston and his corps commanders then proceeded to attend to matters of faith and the soul. Mrs. Johnston had just written to Bishop-General Polk: "General Johnston has never been baptised. It is the dearest wish of my heart that he should be, and that you should perform the ceremony." In front of an improvised altar at Johnston's tent, while Hardee and Hood looked on by candlelight, Polk in his religious vestments performed the rite of baptism, just as he had done for Hood only a week earlier. When the Christian ceremony was completed, the generals separated to resume the business of war. One wonders if any problems of reconciling Christian principles with military actions troubled their minds as they prepared to carry out Johnston's plan.

AND so the Confederates abandoned Adairsville without making a fight. That fact, however, would never have occurred to Private Sam Watkins and a bunch of his comrades in the First Tennessee Infantry. Doubtless they would have testified that there was a bloody hell-of-a-fight at the little town. Soon after arriving at Adairsville, Watkins recalled that, "All at once we saw our cavalry thundering along the road at full retreat and firing back towards the rear. An order came for us to go forward and occupy an old octagon house in our front. The Federals were advancing—were even then nearing the octagon house. The race commenced as to which would reach the house first."

The Rebels won the dash for the house, but quickly found themselves almost surrounded and, according to Watkins, would have fled had it not been for Colonel H. R. Field, "who seized a musket and threatened to shoot the first man that would try to get out of the house." Thus the Rebs were persuaded to stand their ground. What followed was a fierce, prolonged fire fight, in which "shot and shell would scream through the windows, while the plastering would fall upon the floor, and the solid shot from their cannon would penetrate the walls with a terrible, unearthly jar. . . . At length," continued Watkins, "a shell loaded with shrapnel

. . . exploded in the room, right in our very midst. When the smoke slightly cleared we saw eight men in that little band weltering in their life blood, and many others wounded. In other rooms similar scenes were being enacted." Watkins claimed thirty-four corpses eventually lay in the house.

Surrender was demanded by the Federals. When the Confederates refused, the Union soldiers tried to take the house by storm, but, said Watkins, "We had fought and held our position so long that we had lost all consciousness of fear, and every man determined to die before he would consent to surrender. Our blood was up and we held the house." Finally it was all over and the Yankees fell back. And so then did the Rebels. "When we came out [of the house]," concluded Watkins, "shattered wrecks of every kind of furniture were scattered all over the floors, and the walls looked . . . old and dilapidated. . . , begrimed with smoke and soot, the curtains all torn down and trodden under foot and bloody." Nothing, of course, was changed by it all—nothing beyond the hideous waste; the obvious fact that a host of men were dead, and to no avail. The Federals eventually continued their march into Adairsville, the Confederates retreating once more.

But now Johnston sought to spring his trap at Cassville. Sherman was proceeding as the Southern commander had hoped he would. The redhead really thought that Johnston was going to Kingston, although he did not understand why. "All signs continue of Johnston's having retreated to Kingston," he said in a communiqué to Schofield, "but why should he

Railroad Junction at Kingston, Georgia.

lead to Kingston, if he designs to cover his trains to Cartersville, I do not see." In the very next sentence, however, Sherman had devised an explanation. "But it is possible he has sent to Allatoona all he can by cars, and his wagons are escaping south of the Etowah by the bridge and fords near Kingston. In any hypothesis our plan is right," the Federal commander assured Schofield. "All of General Thomas's command will follow his trail straight, let it lead to the fords or toward Allatoona. . . . If we can bring Johnston to battle this side of the Etowah we must do it, even at the hazard of beginning battle with but a part of our forces."

Sherman's wish for battle seemed to be confirmed by deserters from the Confederate army who came into the Yankee lines on the morning of May 18. They reported that the Rebels were planning to dig in and make an all-out effort to whip Sherman. Convinced that the Confederates were headed toward, and possibly marshalling at, Kingston Sherman sent McPherson and the main portion of Thomas's army toward that town. Hooker's Twentieth Corps was to take the direct road to Cassville, while Schofield's small Army of the Ohio advanced on the east of Hooker, to rendezvous with him near Cassville.

It was about noon when the Confederates, 65,000 to 70,000 strong, began taking position to ambush the Union army. Two of their three corps were just north of Cassville, Polk's corps on the left, astride the Adairsville-Cassville road, with Hood's corps to Polk's right. Hardee's corps and most of the Rebel cavalry were off to the west, north of Kingston, and skirmishing with the advance elements of the Northern army. By nightfall the Southerners were ready. While Hardee conducted a holding action on the morrow, Hood and Polk would attack the smaller Federal force marching south along the Adairsville-Cassville Road.

On the morning of May 19 Johnston announced that the retreat had ended and the army would give battle to the Northern invader. At the head of each regiment the general's confident, inspiring words, adorned with references to the support of the Almighty, were read to the men:

Soldiers of the Army of Tennessee:

You have displayed the highest qualities of the soldier—firmness in combat, patience under toil. By your courage and skill you have repulsed every assault of the enemy. By marches by day and marches by night you have defeated every attempt upon your communications. Your communications are secured. You will now turn and march to meet his advancing columns. Fully confiding in the conduct of the officers, the courage of the soldiers, I lead you to battle. We may confidently trust that the Almighty Father will still reward the patriots' toils and the patriots' banners. Cheered by the success of our brothers in Virginia and beyond the Mississippi, our efforts will equal theirs. Strengthened by His support, these efforts will be crowned with the like glories.

J. E. Johnston,
General

These were the words the men wanted to hear. After retreating for more than forty miles without a major battle, when much of the land relinquished was highly defensible terrain, the Confederate soldiers were primed to fight. The Reverend Robert Q. Mallard, ex officio chaplain to the Army of Tennessee, testified that many a Southern soldier expected that a great battle would be fought at the Etowah. Now the army's back was to the Etowah, and Johnston was saying "I lead you to battle."

"You could see self-confidence in the features of every private," wrote Sam Watkins in his diary. "We were going to whip and rout the Yankees . . . The soldiers were jubilant . . . I believe a sort of fanaticism had entered our souls." Colonel Ellison Capers of the Twenty-fourth South Carolina Infantry reported that, "The greatest enthusiasm prevailed in our ranks as the men and officers saw the army formed for battle."

Likely it appeared to the Rebels that nothing could prevent the seemingly imminent clash. The Federals were tramping steadily toward Cassville, every moment bringing them closer to the point where the Confederates would attack. The Yankees were coming with confidence, and probably not anticipating an imminent, bloody confrontation. Apparently some of the Federals were enthralled that morning with the spectacle of the military. A member of the Fifty-fifth Ohio, in Hooker's corps, Captain Hartwell Osborn, later recalled the scene as the regiment's line "mounted a small elevation and found itself part of a long line of Union troops moving forward with banners waving and guns flashing as if on parade. It was a magnificent display of the pomp and pageantry of glorious war. . . . Rarely does such quick transition come even in war from imminent danger . . . to great beauty of landscape, enlivened by the panoply and circumstances of arms. The magnificent spectacle made so deep an impression upon all who took part in it that nearly every history of the Twentieth Corps and the writings of those who were witnesses, make mention of it."

Maybe these Federals *were* ripe for the Southern ambush. But the great battle was not to occur. May 19 turned out to be a day of frustration for the Rebels that had few equals in the course of the war. Right up to the decisive moment everything appeared to be unfolding favorably for the Confederates. In the morning shortly after ten o'clock, Johnston heard from Hardee that Thomas's army was moving in force on Kingston and soon would be too heavily engaged to effect a rapid transfer of troops to the east. Polk's corps, by ten-thirty, was skirmishing with the Federals who were advancing on the Adairsville-Cassville Road, while Hood was moving to strike the flank of the unsuspecting enemy. "It was expected," wrote Johnston in his memoirs, "that Hood's [corps] would be in position to fall upon the left flank of those troops as soon as Polk attacked them in front."

Then chance played the key role. After advancing only a short distance, Hood discovered a column of Federals approaching on a road to his right. If the Rebel corps commander had formed his soldiers to face the Adairsville-Cassville Road, these Yankees would have been in position to fall upon his flank or rear. "Hood was furious," wrote the general's most recent biographer, Richard McMurry, "because Rebel cavalrymen had given him no warning, but he prudently halted his column and threw out skirmishers who were soon exchanging shots with the Northerners." Hood felt compelled to drop back and rejoin Polk, giving up his advance toward the Yankee left flank.

The next day General Johnston wrote President Davis that he had ordered a general attack, but "while the officer charged with the lead was advancing he was deceived by a false report that a heavy column of the enemy had turned our right and was close upon him, and took a defensive position. When the mistake was discovered it was too late to resume the movement!" As long as he lived, Johnston maintained that no Union troops were in position to endanger Hood's rear and that Hood had disobeyed orders to attack. In his memoirs Johnston was cryptic: "The report upon which General Hood acted was manifestly untrue," wrote the Southern commander as he referred to Hood's "strange departure from the instructions he had received," and "erratic movement," which "caused such loss of time as to make the attack intended impracticable."

Naturally Hood resented Johnston's account of "the Cassville Affair." Johnston had attempted to saddle the tall, sad-eyed Kentuckian turned Texan with primary responsibility for one of the Confederacy's lost opportunities; a chance to administer a severe blow, perhaps a crippling blow, against a major Federal army. Whatever else he may have been, Hood was a fighter; and he battled back, seeking vengeance against "Old Joe." For years to come Hood and Johnston engaged in a bitter argument over whether or not there had been any Northern troops to the east of Hood on that fateful May day. Hood even claimed, in fact, that "he received no orders for battle as related by General Johnston." According to Hood's account, he requested and received permission to march his corps across the open fields to attack the enemy column advancing on the Adairsville-Cassville Road. Hood maintained that Johnston had not ordered an attack nor given instructions for Polk to cooperate with him.

Whatever the truth as to the precise plan of attack, Hood was correct about the Yankee threat to his flank and rear. The irony is that these Federals, probably a wandering segment from Major General Daniel Butterfield's division of Hooker's corps, had taken a wrong turn and, several miles east of where they should have been, blundered into the right wing of Hood's corps. Thus, purely by chance, these Union soldiers caused the Rebels to pull back from making an assault that otherwise might have dealt a severe blow to one of the Federal columns.

Because Hood would later prove a miserable failure as an army commander, and because his accounts to justify his actions frequently contained misrepresentations about both campaign conditions and officers and men under his command, historians were inclined to accept Johnston's version of the lost opportunity at Cassville. Yet the evidence presented in Hood's *Advance and Retreat,* quoting letters of men who testified to an enemy presence on Hood's flank, as well as reports in the war records of a nomadic column from Butterfield's division, make it reasonably certain that there were Yankees where Hood said there were. It is also known that Federal cavalrymen were operating in the vicinity, hoping to reach the railroad near Cartersville.

Furthermore, the published journal purportedly kept at army headquarters by Lieutenant T. B. Mackall, aide-de-camp to Brigadier General W. W. Mackall, chief of staff, and long regarded as a primary source of evidence that Johnston's critics (especially Hood) were in error, can no longer be regarded as a contemporary source, written during the campaign. It has been convincingly demonstrated, in a 1974 issue of *Civil War History,* that someone tampered with the journal—which, intriguingly, was furnished to the war department for publication by General Joseph Johnston. Certainly Hood was not above misrepresentation; perhaps neither was Johnston.

But the Cassville Affair was not over; far from it. Succeeding events would quickly add to the confusion and controversy. All hope of surprise gone, Johnston fell back a short distance. Once Johnston decided not to attack, he sought a good defensive position in the hope that Sherman would assail it. The Army of Tennessee was soon dug in, still north of the Etowah, along a wooded ridge immediately east and south of Cassville, and overlooking the town.

Later Johnston called the position "the best that I saw occupied during the war. . . , with a broad, open, elevated valley in front of it completely commanded by the fire of troops occupying its crest." Others also were impressed by the position. Brigadier General Arthur M. Manigault, commanding a brigade in Hindman's division of Hood's corps (and with a good record for military competency) wrote that "the ground upon which our army was drawn up, so far as I could see, seemed to me to possess great advantages, comparatively open and well adapted to a battle-ground. We occupied the brow of a high range of hills, the ground in our front level and cleared up, consisting mostly of open fields, Cassville lying about a half-mile in our front."

The new Confederate line ran generally north-south, from a point east of Cassville to the railroad about three miles south of the town. Polk was in the center, Hood was on Polk's right, and Hardee came up to take position on the left. Union forces were in close pursuit and soon occupied a ridge just north and west of Cassville. McPherson was deploying on the Federal right, Thomas in the center, with Hooker and Schofield on the left. Again battle loomed imminent.

But the Rebel position had a weak spot. This was the area where Polk's corps joined with Hood's, particularly a bare section of the ridge held by the newly arrived division of Major General Samuel G. French and by Captain James Hoskins's Mississippi artillery battery. As the Confederates were hurriedly fortifying their new line, Johnston rode along the ridge with his staff. When he passed French's division, Brigadier General Francis A. Shoup, the army's chief of artillery, pointed out the problem. Shoup told Johnston that part of French's line could be enfiladed by the Union rifled guns on Sherman's left flank.

Johnston was not particularly troubled: the opposing ridge lay a mile across the valley; Federal guns were too far away to be dangerous. Besides, he concluded in dismissing the threat, if the Yankee fire became too heavy, the soldiers could build traverses, or retreat behind the ridge until the bombardment ceased. Then the men could come forth in time to repulse any Yankee assault, which certainly would not take place while the gunners were still firing. The general rode on.

Later in the afternoon the Union artillerists raked the position, and General Hood, surveying his line from horseback, apparently became convinced that the line could not be held if the Federals attacked. General Polk sent his engineer officer, Captain Walter G. Morris, to evaluate French's position. After hearing Morris's report, who was convinced the line would become untenable, Polk too was very concerned. Also, General Manigault's account, written immediately after the war, is helpful—especially because he thought the position generally was a good one. "As our artillery opened on them," Manigault wrote that the enemy guns "came into action in beautiful style, and selecting their positions with great skill, opened fire on ours, and soon showed an almost overwhelming superiority. It must be remembered that they had two guns to our one, and a greater number of rifled pieces, which also gave a great advantage in range and accuracy. I saw one battery of ours knocked to pieces, and the gunners driven from their guns in less than fifteen minutes. I was told of another instance of the same kind that occurred in our division front, and I think it likely there may have been others."

Two of the Rebel batteries in French's division were badly mauled, and even before some of the guns could be unlimbered. Sherman, however, did not intend to bring on a general engagement that evening and as dark approached the firing gradually ceased. The Confederates continued to strengthen their defenses, preparing for battle on the following morning. It was then that the famous council of war, which involved the very highest stakes, took place. The drama of fleeting moments, in a little cabin belonging to the William McKelvey family (which had fled south), was soon to be obscured by confusion and contradiction.

Even how the council originated is unclear; and of no real consequence except to illustrate how muddled are all the facts, with Johnston contradicting himself by giving one version in a postwar conversation with Sherman; another in a letter to Polk's son-in-law, Colonel W. D. Gale; and still another in his memoirs.

Present at the council were Johnston, Polk, Hood, Hardee, French, and Morris, although Hardee arrived late and French left early. Hardee, just as at Adairsville, wanted to fight and argued that the line could be defended. When Captain Morris later alleged that General French claimed he could not hold his position, French not only denied that he had taken any such stance, but rather said that he left the meeting convinced Johnston would fight, only to be surprised an hour later by orders to retreat.

It seems reasonably certain that Hood and Polk thought they would be unable to hold their positions when Union artillery opened fire in the morning. Their evaluation, considering terrain, superiority of Yankee artillery, and the afternoon's experience, may well have been correct. The significant issue is the question of what they proposed to do. Johnston said both Hood and Polk urged him to fall back across the Etowah. The Rebel commander said that he yielded at last, in the belief that "the confidence of the commanders of two of the three corps of the army, of their inability to resist the enemy, would inevitably be communicated to their troops, and produce that inability." Thus Johnston said he issued orders for the army to retreat south of the Etowah.

Hood's version of the meeting was quite different from his commander's, maintaining that he and Polk, while contending they could not successfully defend their position, urged Johnston to *attack*. Hood became rather impassioned as he wrote in *Advance and Retreat*: "I do at this day and hour, in the name of truth, honor and justice, in the name of the departed soul of the Christian and noble Polk, and in the presence of my Creator, most solemnly deny that General Polk or I recommended General Johnston, at Cassville, to retreat when he intended to give battle; and affirm that the recommendation made by us to change his position, was throughout the discussion coupled with the proviso: *If he did not intend to force a pitched battle.*"

Polk did not live long enough to write his version of the council. But the bishop's son, Dr. A. M. Polk, who was an aide-de-camp to his father at Cassville, sent a letter to Hood in 1874, in which he essentially confirmed Hood's account. The younger Polk said conversations with his father shortly before his death revealed he was "not willing to stand there and wait for the enemy to attack us, but more than willing to take the initiative in bringing on a general engagement."

Although historians will probably never learn all they would like to know about that fateful war council meeting, two facts are certain: Johnston decided to retreat, and the seeds were sown to destroy the relationship between Johnston and Hood, which up to then seems to have been cordial.

SOON after the council broke up, Johnston sent out staff members with orders for another retreat. Sherman had not brought Johnston to battle as he hoped, but the Union commander was forcing the Confederates across another river. Clearly the momentum of the campaign was with the Yankees. Again the Rebels were disappointed at another withdrawal—and bitterly. "To our great surprise, and to the disgust of many," remembered General Manigault, "at midnight, we received the order to retire, and at two o'clock, our division drew out as noiselessly as possible, and, bringing up the rear of our corps, took up the line of march for the railroad crossing at the Etowah River."

Morale of the Federals seemed to reach a new high. All through the night the Yankees had been contemplating a hard fight on the morrow. Then unexpectedly, the Confederates were gone. Sergeant Henry C. Morhous, of the One Hundred and Twenty-third New York Infantry, was among the Union soldiers moving into Cassville at dawn of May 20.

The day was pleasant and the town "was a beautiful little village," he thought. But it was deserted. "The citizens had left their homes and fled on the approach of the Yankees," he wrote. Morhous thought the Rebels had been frightened out of "a very formidable position, and one they had evidently intended to hold. Indeed, they were so determined to make a strong line that they had not hesitated to run it through a beautiful cemetery, and the graves, in many cases, were shovelled open, to throw up the breastworks. Nearly every monument and headstone was broken to fragments, and the whole enclosure was little else than a rubbish heap."

# 7

# I Am Turning the Enemy's Right Flank, I Think

ONLY one more river to cross. Already Sherman's Yankees were over the Oostanaula and the Etowah, two of the three major rivers between Chattanooga and Atlanta. Only the Chattahoochee remained and the campaign was not yet three weeks old. On May 23 Sherman affirmed: "The Etowah is the Rubicon of Georgia." As his soldiers began crossing the river that day, the Union commander continued to write in his exuberant style: "We are now all in motion like a vast hive of bees, and expect to swarm over the Chattahoochee in a few days."

Besides the obvious triumph of forcing the enemy south of the Etowah, Sherman's troops had already secured the industrial town of Rome on May 18. Midmorning was nearing that day before General Jefferson C. Davis, handicapped by a heavy fog, realized that the Confederates, except for a handful of soldiers, had abandoned the town. The tiny band of Rebels was soon driven away and Davis's Yankee division triumphantly hoisted Old Glory above the Floyd County Courthouse. This small but significant victory meant not only that the Noble Iron Works were in Federal possession, but also Confederate options were eliminated. No longer might the grayclads possibly swing westward into Alabama and middle Tennessee. Now they could only move southward toward Atlanta.

The Confederates might have held the north bank of the Etowah River. About nine or ten miles south of Cassville the Western & Atlantic Railroad and the pike to Atlanta pass through a hamlet called Cartersville, shortly before crossing the Etowah. The terrain just south of Cartersville would have provided the Confederate commander with a good defensive

Defenses of the Etowah Bridge.

position along a steep ridge rising several hundred feet in elevation. Here Johnston could surely have delayed Sherman. Johnston could have accepted a Federal attack with confidence, or assailed the Yankee army while divided if the Northern commander tried to cross the river to flank him. Moreover, this would have been a better position than the one Johnston eventually assumed south of the Etowah.

But the Confederate commander's retreat across the river gave the Federals the valuable Etowah Iron Works southeast of Cartersville, meant the permanent loss of the Rome industrial complex with its railroad to Alabama, and delivered a blow to the morale of the Army of Tennessee. Probably most ominous for the future, Johnston's action demonstrated that he had little or no awareness of the importance of prolonging the war. Clearly the Confederate commander was aware of the superiority of Federal manpower, and logically he had sought to conduct the campaign from an offensive-defensive stance, but there is no evidence that Johnston's thinking ever progressed to a realization that Northern war weariness constituted the South's only realistic hope of establishing independence. And now Sherman was in control, gaining more sooner and easier than he should have; that he was filled with assurance is no wonder.

"I knew more of Georgia than the Rebels did," Sherman later blurted. He had reference to the new position of Johnston's army at Allatoona

Allatoona Pass, Looking North.

Pass and his statement was not altogether an exaggeration. Twenty years earlier, when a lieutenant of the Third Artillery on detached duty at Marietta, Sherman had explored the surrounding region. (He was also courting a young woman named Cecilia Stovall, who lived in a fine house called Etowah Heights; this the general did not mention in his memoirs, although it well may have been his primary interest in the area.) Sherman wrote: "I had stopped some days . . . to see some remarkable Indian mounds on the Etowah River, usually called the 'Hightower.' I therefore knew that the Allatoona Pass was very strong, would be hard to force, and resolved not even to attempt it." Instead, explained the Union commander, he decided "to turn the position, by moving from Kingston to Marietta *via* Dallas."

The line that Johnston occupied along the high range known as the Allatoona Mountains centered around the gap through which ran the railroad and the pike to Atlanta. The problems with the new Confederate position, aside from the fact it was south of the Etowah, were that it could be easily flanked and, ironically, was simply too strong if Johnston hoped to lure Sherman into a direct attack.

Johnston was somewhat aware of still another problem: the campaign as perceived in Richmond. Concerned about what Jefferson Davis thought of the continued retreat and seeking to reassure the president, Johnston pointed out that he had prevented Sherman from detaching any troops for service in Virginia, "repulsed every attack he has made," and "earnestly sought an opportunity to strike." Not Davis but Braxton Bragg responded, however, noting "the high condition" of Johnston's army and informing him that another brigade of infantry and a cavalry regiment were being sent for reinforcement. "We confidently rely on a brilliant success," wrote the former commander of the Army of Tennessee.

If Johnston did not feel increasing pressure after such correspondence with Richmond, he surely did from Sherman. The Union commander was on the move again. Deciding to cross the Etowah some miles west of Johnston's position at Allatoona, where the hills were farther back from the river and the country a little more open, Sherman initially would march for Dallas, a small town about fifteen miles south of the river and nearly twenty miles west of Marietta, the Rebels' new supply base. Thus Johnston would be compelled to give up his formidable line in the Allatoona vicinity or else Sherman would soon threaten his railroad from Atlanta.

Sherman's plan necessitated abandoning his own railroad supply line for several days. Accordingly he gave orders on May 20—the same day that a Confederate in Cleburne's division recorded in his diary, "for the first time since we left Resaca the Yanks did not shoot at us today"—to have twenty days' rations prepared by the troops. Marching orders soon followed, instructing General Thomas, as usual, to take his Army of the Cumberland by the direct middle route, south from Kingston through Stilesboro; Schofield would advance on his left, by way of Burnt Hickory; McPherson's hard-marching Army of the Tennessee, on Thomas's right, would loop wide again, through the little town of Van Wert, to approach Dallas from the west. The Federal cavalry would cover the flanks and protect the line of the Etowah.

Apprehensive of the future as the campaigning resumed on May 23, colorful Major General John "Black Jack" Logan, commanding the Fifteenth Corps in McPherson's army, wrote to his wife Mary. "I may fall," he told her, "and if so, I shall fall in a just cause and will be only one man added to the list. . . . I want you to know that if I do not survive, I have deposited with Colonel John C. Smith, chief of the 15th Corps, $10,000 that he will pay you on demand." Logan was quick to assure her that the money was "no false or improper gain," but that it came from a land deal. Logan's chances of surviving, along with many others in the Federal army, were improved, of course, by Sherman's decision to flank the Rebels. As an Ohio soldier expressed it: "It seems that we are turning the enemy's left. Allatoona Mountains held by Joe Johnston's army are not the thing to run squarely against!"

Another of Sherman's approving soldiers said of him: "He's all hell at flanking. . . . He'd flank God Almighty out of Heaven, and the Devil into Hell." And a soldier of the Eighty-sixth Indiana, passing one of the few cabins in the area, claimed to have heard the woman residing there say she knew Sherman was "flanking" again because she had seen "his flanking machines" go by just a few minutes earlier. She apparently referred to a battery of artillery that had passed the cabin. It seemed that "flanking" was on everybody's mind.

The Yankee march to Dallas was difficult due to heat and ragged terrain. The country between the Etowah and the Chattahoochee was desolate, with little sign of habitation. Unlike the piney hills north of the Etowah, growth here was scrubby and dense, and loose sand on hill slopes and quicksand-bordered streams slowed the marchers. An Illinois soldier who served with McPherson's army wrote that "distance, heat and dust have made it by far the hardest march we have made for a year. I never saw so many stragglers as today. For 12 miles no water was to be had; then we came to a spring. . . . All the officers in the army could not have kept the men in the ranks."

Maybe the hard marching would have been more palatable if the Federals could have taken the Rebels by surprise. But Confederate scouts soon discovered the Union plan, reporting an enemy crossing of the Etowah several miles to the west, and Johnston moved to meet the threat. Shifting his army to intercept Sherman, Johnston sent Hardee's corps toward Dallas late on May 23. Polk's corps would follow, with Hood the last to vacate the Allatoona line.

The Confederate march was a rigorous one too. Like the Federals, many a grayclad suffered from the heat and dust. "I never in my whole life saw more dust," said a Tennessean. "Eyes, noses and mouths were filled with dust," he testified. "Cavalry and artillery could not be seen at ten paces, being perfectly enveloped in dust." A Texan recorded in his diary: "We travel in a south west direction, but none of us have any idea where we are going. . . . There are a great many conjectures. . . . Some say we are going to Florida and put in a pontoon bridge over to Cuba. . . . Others contend that some Yankee would put a torpedo under it and blow it up."

The Rebels learned their destination quickly enough. "We did not expect to meet the enemy so soon," wrote General Manigault as he recalled the surprise when the fighting erupted once more. On the afternoon of May 24 the Army of Tennessee concentrated near Dallas, defending a line that generally faced northwest. Hardee's corps was on the left, and nearest to the town, while Polk's corps moved into position on Hardee's right flank to the northeast. Hood's corps lay to the right of Polk, and on the morning of May 25 moved to a crossroads about four miles north-

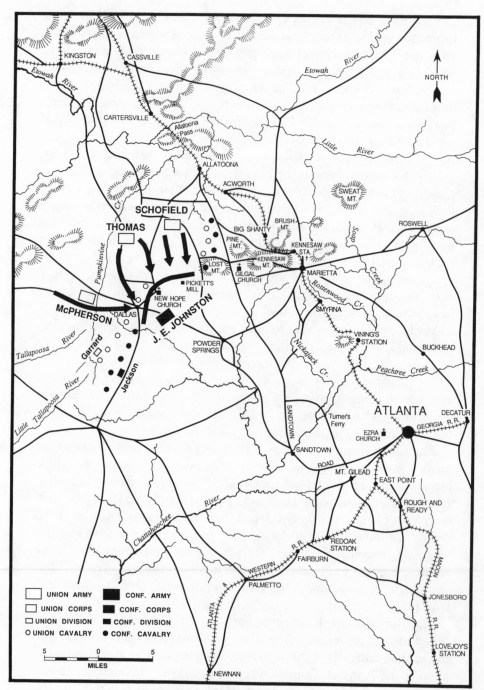

Dallas-New Hope Church-Pickett's Mill.

east of Dallas. The crossroads was the site of an ordinary log church building. This small Methodist meeting house was about to become a Civil War landmark. It was called New Hope Church, but many of the Yankees would soon refer to the place as "the Hell Hole."

Hood deployed his men with Major General Thomas C. Hindman's division on the left, Major General Alexander P. Stewart's division in the center at the church, and Major General Carter L. Stevenson's on the right. Hood's troops spent the late morning and early afternoon clearing the ground in their front and erecting breastworks along portions of the line. Logs were piled in front of some units and scotched in place by rocks and sticks. Trenches were dug behind the logs and in these the men waited.

In Stewart's division, holding the key crossroads at the church, guns were checked and surplus equipment placed under trees to the rear, while soldiers talked of the strengths and weaknesses of their position. Three brigades manned Stewart's front line. On the left was Marcellus A. Stovall's brigade, consisting of five regiments; Henry D. Clayton's brigade of four regiments occupied the center; and Alpheus Baker's three-regiment brigade held the right. Clayton's and Baker's units had logs piled in front of their line. Two brigades, under Randall Gibson and John C. Brown, were in reserve.

Occupying generally high ground (some reports referred to it as a ridge), Stewart's men held a favorable position for repelling an attack. These Rebels looked across a large expanse of open area, perhaps a hundred yards or more according to some witnesses, to the dense woods beyond.

By late afternoon the hot day had moderated and a pleasant coolness prevailed. Water boys gathered up canteens to be filled at a nearby spring. Then came a courier, dashing into Stewart's headquarters with news that the Federals were only a short distance away and advancing steadily.

THE savage fighting that soon characterized the Dallas–New Hope–Pickett's Mill line has been described by some historians, and popular writers as well, as merely a series of brief clashes amounting to little more than heavy skirmishing between enemy outposts. James Reston, Jr., for example, in *Sherman's March and Vietnam*, dismisses all action except Resaca, Kennesaw Mountain, and the three battles around Atlanta itself, as simply "maneuver, usually Johnston fortifying the high ridges and Sherman bypassing them to the west."

Actually, the intensity and casualties of the conflict along this line clearly raise it beyond the level of skirmishing and maneuvering. In many respects, the struggle is reminiscent of the Virginia fighting in the Wilderness. Much of the ground was worse than the Wilderness. Besides densely wooded terrain, traversed by a few narrow roads, the area was cut by creeks and deep ravines. These features contributed to a confusing struggle in which many participants were fighting blindly. That these encounters have never been generally recognized for the hard-fought clashes they were may be explained not only by the long overemphasis on the Virginia theater, but also in part by the fact that victors usually write the histories of war. Major participants in the Union army blundered and most likely would not have considered their efforts here particularly memorable.

On May 24, as Sherman continued his march on Dallas, "Fighting Joe" Hooker's Twentieth Corps of Thomas's Army of the Cumberland had the lead, tramping through Stilesboro and on to Burnt Hickory, where he camped for the night. Schofield was initially delayed in crossing the river by Hooker's men, but then made good time and came up on Thomas's left near Hooker's camp. McPherson, meanwhile, reached Van Wert and turned eastward toward Dallas. By the night of May 24 Sherman knew that the Confederates were marching to block his path. At all points the Yankees were meeting stiff resistance and a Rebel courier had been captured with dispatches revealing that the entire Confederate army was moving to intercept him.

On the morning of May 25 Hooker's Twentieth Corps advanced on three separate roads. Fighting Joe had controversial Major General Daniel "Little Dan" Butterfield, a thirty-two-year-old New Yorker who was the son of the founder of the Overland Mail Company and eventually to be awarded the Medal of Honor for service at Gaines' Mill, leading the division on the left of the corps. While serving in the Peninsular campaign he had written "Taps." Long after the war he would be placed in charge of the funeral services for General Sherman. Butterfield was also a good candidate for the dubious honor of being the most unpopular general in the Union army. Said to have had "enemies in every arm of the service," the general was dubbed "Dan the Magnificent" by one of his critics, and variously described by others in such terms as a snob, an intriguer, a demagogue, a blemished character, and a man lacking "practical common sense in all points." But whatever else he may have been, "Little Dan" Butterfield was loyal and faithful to Hooker. In fact, Butterfield had come to think of himself as Hooker's protector—protecting Hooker from Hooker, that is.

Major General Alpheus S. "Pop" Williams, habitually biting on a cigar, led the division on the right of the corps. Some soldiers in Williams's division claimed the general's manner with his cigars was like a weathervane in revealing whether or not action was imminent, the cigar twirling in Williams's mouth if fighting could be anticipated. In the center of the corps marched Major General John W. Geary's division. Geary's command, accompanied by both Hooker and Thomas, led the march.

A conspicuous man, Geary was six feet six inches tall and weighed three hundred pounds. Forty-four years old, he had served as a colonel in the Mexican War, as noted before. That morning, Geary began his advance before seven, moving southward along the direct road from Burnt Hickory to Dallas. After going three or four miles Geary's division reached a bridge over Pumpkinvine Creek. "The major general commanding corps and myself, with our staffs and escort, preceded the troops to the bridge at Owen's Mill, which we found burning, having just been fired," wrote Geary. "While engaged in extinguishing the flames and repairing the bridge we were fired upon from the hill opposite. . . . A portion of Major General Hooker's cavalry escort fording the creek, deployed and advanced. . . , driving before them . . . an outpost of . . . cavalrymen. My infantry soon came up, and the repairs to the bridge being finished. . . , the entire division crossed."

On the south side of Pumpkinvine Creek the road forked, one route continuing to Dallas while the other led to New Hope Church. Pursuing the retreating Rebel cavalry, Geary's division tramped about two miles along the branch to New Hope and struck advanced infantry elements from Hood's corps. A sharp battle ensued. Not until Geary had deployed all three of his brigades were the Yankees able to force the Rebels, about two regiments strong, back upon their main line at New Hope Church. From prisoners the Federals learned that Hood's entire corps was in their front, with Hardee's corps not far off, in the direction of Dallas.

Geary was worried. "My division was isolated, at least five miles from the nearest supporting troops," he later reported, "and had been sustaining a sharp conflict with the enemy for four hours. Close in my front was an overwhelming force." Hooker, who was with Geary's column still, also considered the situation critical. Notifying Thomas, Hooker ordered Geary to dig in on a ridge. A slight barricade of logs was hastily thrown up, while skirmish lines were shaken out, to a greater extent than normal, and ordered to keep up an aggressive fire in hope of misleading the Confederates to believe the Federals were stronger than they really were. General Thomas understood the situation and approved.

But then Sherman came up. His idea of the tactical situation was quite different—and wrong. Believing that he was on the left flank of Johnston's line and that no large body of the enemy was in his front, he studied a map, instantly recognized the importance of the crossroads at New Hope Church, and ordered Hooker to take it. Both Thomas and Hooker protested, urging Sherman at least to postpone an attack until the other two divisions of the Twentieth Corps came up to join Geary. Reluctantly Sherman consented, remarking to one of Thomas's staff officers: "Let Williams go in anywhere as soon as he gets up. I don't see what they are waiting for in front now. There haven't been twenty rebels there today."

Williams, incidentally, was having a hard march to "get up." The head of his column had come within a mile or so of Dallas before orders reached him to move as quickly as possible to the support of Geary's division. Rapidly countermarching the column, crossing and recrossing Pumpkinvine Creek, his men covered a number of miles and then assaulted, in Williams's words, "without sufficient halt to recover breath."

It was four o'clock when the three Union divisions, about 20,000 strong, advanced to the attack. Struggling through the dense woods and tangled undergrowth, they tramped toward the center of Hood's position at New Hope Church as dark clouds gathered in the sky, accompanied by the roll of thunder and the crackling of lightning. Geary's division was in the center, Williams's on the right, and Butterfield's on the left in reserve position. Unfortunately for the Union, the divisions were deployed in columns of brigades (that is, one brigade behind another), narrowing the front of each division to the width of a brigade. Thus the entire front of Hooker's corps was only about the width of the single Confederate division, under Major General Alexander P. Stewart, which took the brunt of the Federal attack.

The Yankees made a fierce, determined attempt to break the Rebel line. But the Union assault, in deeply packed columns, enabled the Confederates to concentrate their fire against the enemy's narrow front. General Stewart had sixteen pieces of artillery, some positioned for cross fire, massed along his relatively short section of the Rebel line. A forty-two-year-old Tennessean, Stewart was known as "Old Straight" from the days when he taught mathematics, first at West Point and later at Cumberland University in Lebanon, Tennessee. Stewart was a veteran of all the army's major battles. Well respected, his disciplined manner had developed a strong sense of esprit de corps in the division.

As the Yankees moved steadily toward the grayclad position, General Stewart mounted his horse and rode along the line. He shouted encouragement to the men, who responded with enthusiastic yells. "Stewart's old roan was seen all along the line," recalled Bromfield Ridley of Murfreesboro, Tennessee. Ridley said that Stewart's "quiet way" had won the admiration of the division. "They begged him to get back, fearing he might be killed, but he rode along as unconcerned as ever." And when Joe Johnston, realizing that the entire Yankee effort was concentrated on the New Hope crossroads in a desperate engagement, asked Stewart

Battlefield of New Hope Church, Georgia.

if he needed reinforcements, "Old Straight's" reply was: "My own troops will hold the position."

Indeed they did. Time and again Stewart's men unleashed a withering fire that first staggered the Federal advances, then sent the Yankees recoiling from the slaughter. A Confederate officer described the action: "As the advancing line would break, we could only greet their departure with a yell before another line would come." The intense fire mounted by the Southerners—a storm of bullets and shells tearing through the Union ranks—had a demoralizing effect upon some Federals, as is clear from the After Action Report of Lieutenant Colonel James C. Rogers, commanding the One Hundred and Twenty-third New York Infantry in "Pop" Williams's division.

Rogers said his unit had advanced "close under the enemy's guns, . . . so near that by lying on the ground nearly all [shots] passed over it harmlessly." There the regiment lay until a fresh regiment came up to relieve it, but the new unit "scarcely had formed in front when the enemy's battery, which had been silent for a few minutes, opened again." As a result the relief regiment, according to Rogers, "rushed in disorder to the rear, all attempts to stop them and force them back to their place, even with a line of bayonets, proving useless." Apparently Williams's division was hit the hardest at New Hope Church, subjected to "a most effective and murderous fire" that, reported General Williams, came "from all directions except the rear." More than 800 of his division would be casualties when the fight was over.

The Federals were in a terrible situation. Unable to bring up their own artillery because of the dense woods, they attacked in a manner that nullified their superior numbers while giving the Rebels an opportunity to rake them with artillery cross fire, as well as massed frontal fire from both artillery and infantry. Reported Yankee general Geary: "The discharges of canister and shell from the enemy were heavier than in any other battle of the campaign in which my command was engaged."

A Union soldier, Samuel Hurst, of the Seventy-third Ohio in Butterfield's Third Division, wrote bitterly of the engagement: "When the battle had raged at the front for some time, with a fierceness that told all too plainly how merciless and deadly was the strife, the Third Division was ordered forward." The Confederate line lay across the road, Hurst said, "with the extreme right and left pushed a little forward, forming a kind of semi-circle, into which our attacking force advanced. . . . It seemed a worse than useless sacrifice of life," continued Hurst, "to attempt thus to maintain an open fight against a fortified foe. . . . But brigade orders were imperative that this unequal fight should be continued; and so the regiment stood to the work, though with rapidly thinning ranks. . . . Most bitter to us was the belief that this great sacrifice had been unnecessarily made."

For the better part of three hours the violence continued. The ground over which they fought became a spectrum of keyed-up men, muddy and sweaty, struggling amidst the dead and dying and wounded that lay sprawled about, all intermingled with other hideous debris of war that littered the earth. The din of thousands of rifled muskets was joined by the roar of cannon, explosion of shells, and the sound of men yelling and shrieking.

In the midst of the fighting the black clouds above unleashed their fury, a violent thunderstorm blending its lightning and thunder into the man-made hell at New Hope Church. The rain fell harder and harder until it beat against the ground in torrents. A cold, chilling wind swept the battlefield. "The night was intensely dark," remarked General Geary, "and a very severe thunder-storm, with cold, pelting rain, added to the gloom."

When the Yankees continually fell back from the galling fire dealt out by the Confederates, somebody said that the spot was a Hell Hole, and the name stuck. "No more persistent attack or determined resistance was anywhere made," was the tribute to both sides paid by General Stewart in his report, while one of his front-line brigade commanders, Henry

Clayton, wrote that "the engagement lasted uninterruptedly until night, or more than two hours, and when the enemy finally withdrew, many of my men had their last cartridges in their guns."

A Northern officer, the one-armed General Oliver O. Howard, said that after the fighting had ended, "the nearest house to the field was filled with the wounded. Torch-lights and candles lighted up dimly the incoming stretchers and the surgeon's tables and instruments. The very woods seemed to moan and groan with the sufferers not yet brought in." Dawn of the following day revealed to the Confederates a disquieting scene of destruction which their weapons had wrought. A Rebel officer wrote of "the seething mass of quivering flesh, the dead piled upon each other and the groans of the dying."

Hooker stated his casualties were 1,665 killed or wounded, but the Confederates were convinced the true figure was much higher. It proba-

Joseph Hooker.

bly was. Already Hooker had developed a reputation for understating his own losses and exaggerating those of his enemy. No figures are available as to Confederate casualties, but undoubtedly they were relatively light, considering the good defensive position from which the Rebel's fought. Possibly the percentage of loss was higher in the artillery than the infantry. One report stated that artillery losses along Stewart's line were forty-three men and forty-four horses. Among the artillery casualties were two brothers who fought in Fenner's Louisiana Battery. Serving in the dangerous post of rammer at the muzzle of the gun, one brother was killed and his place taken by another who was severely wounded in the thigh. Then a third brother took the position and passed through the fight unharmed, according to Sergeant Robert Howe, who was in charge of the guns.

When the carnage was over Sherman blamed the Northern failure on the delay in attacking, which, he incorrectly believed, had given Johnston the chance to bring up reinforcements. Actually, of course, Stewart's Confederates were in position well before the fight. According to a rumor that went through the Yankee camp the evening of May 25, an angry Hooker retorted to Sherman that about fifty more Confederates might have joined the defensive line during the afternoon. Hooker did not care for Sherman anyway: after the Chattanooga campaign, in a letter to Secretary of the Treasury Salmon P. Chase, Hooker described Sherman as an officer "as infirm as Burnside," who "will never be successful."

Regardless, Sherman never changed his version of the New Hope debacle, writing in his memoirs that General Hooker asked for time to bring up his other two divisions, "but before these divisions had got up and were deployed, the enemy had also gained corresponding strength."

In the midst of the struggle and confusion, suffering and death, blame and recrimination, there were a few light moments for one Johnny Reb. Nelson Rainey wrote that he was sent with a message for an officer near New Hope Church. When the message was delivered, Rainey said the distance back being too great, he "begged shelter at a farm house within half a mile of the church. Cannon shot and bullets were flying thick over and about the house. The farmer, his wife and two pretty daughters were much alarmed. One of the girls ran to me and begged me to save her and threw her arms around me. I didn't object to that but it was embarrassing, especially as mammy and pappy were looking on."

THE morning after the fight at New Hope Church the Union army sought to pull itself closer together in the heavily timbered country north and east of Dallas. McPherson was on the right of the Federal line facing Hardee's corps, Thomas held the center confronting Hood's troops at New Hope Church, and Schofield's Army of the Ohio was on the left, although Brigadier General Jacob D. Cox commanded. During the night Schofield's horse had slipped and fallen with him into a gully, resulting in a rather painful injury that forced the relinquishment of his command for a couple of days.

On May 26 there was constant skirmishing all along the line, but no major fighting took place. The Confederates, realizing that the weight of the Northern army lay near New Hope Church, shifted troops in that general direction. Hood moved Hindman's division to his right and, most notable in view of coming events, Patrick R. Cleburne's division, which Johnston had sent from Hardee's corps to reinforce Hood, took position on the right of Hindman at Pickett's Mill, a tiny community about two miles northeast of New Hope Church. Polk's corps was moved up toward Hood's left flank, with Hardee's troops thus on Polk's left just as before the clash at the church. Wheeler's cavalry was stationed to protect the Southern army's right flank, while William B. Bate's division of Hardee's corps held the army's far left, positioned on the Dallas-Atlanta road, about a mile and a half distant from the rest of Hardee's troops.

Sherman mulled over the situation. From the day's skirmishing he knew the enemy line stretched for four or five miles. No significant gaps, which might have encouraged him to make an attack, had been revealed. By early morning of May 27, he decided instead to turn the right flank of the Rebel position. General Oliver O. Howard was Sherman's choice to make the march. And picked to lead the flanking movement with his division was Brigadier General Thomas J. Wood, a Kentuckian who had roomed with Grant at West Point. Wood had seen extensive service in Mexico, on the frontier, and in the Civil War, but his unfortunate withdrawal from the line at Chickamauga, due to a misunderstanding at army headquarters, had created a gap though which the Southerners charged to win that battle.

Richard W. Johnson's division of the Fourteenth corps would support Wood, and a brigade from the Twenty-third Corps would also cooperate in the attack. The total strength of the force would be about 18,000. An artillery barrage, unleashed from the batteries of Hooker, Howard, and Schofield, was to precede the flanking march, the firing beginning at dawn and continuing until nine in the morning. All along the front lines, Union troops, particularly those of Hooker and McPherson, would be making demonstrations in order to pin down the Rebel troops while Howard and Wood marched for the enemy's flank.

The fortunes of war had not been kind to either Wood or Howard;

but especially not to Howard, who had lost his right arm at the Battle of Seven Pines in 1862. Bad luck continued to stalk the general, just as it had at both Chancellorsville and Gettysburg, where his Eleventh Corps each time was struck in flank by a devastating assault. Now Howard himself was attempting to deliver a smashing blow to the enemy's flank, but the troops posted in his path were probably the best division in the Confederate army—the very same command which had stopped Sherman's far superior numbers at the northern end of Missionary Ridge a half year before. Pat Cleburne's 5,000-man division, composed of Arkansans, Texans, Mississippians, and Tennesseans, had already discovered Howard's march, thanks to a reconnaissance by Daniel C. Govan's brigade. Even if Govan had not spotted the Yankees, however, their bugle calls probably would have alerted the grayclads in ample time.

Alexis Cope, in the Fifteenth Ohio's regimental history, wrote: "Strange to relate, our brigade commander decided to have all orders given by the bugle. . . . More than one officer and man exclaimed: 'If we are expected to surprise the enemy, why don't they stop those damned bugles?' But on we went, our bugles blowing. Even when we halted for a short rest, the bugles sounded the long drawn out note which commanded us to stop."

General Howard did not know where he was—a fact that is hardly surprising to anyone who has seen the terrain, which apparently, to judge from photographs, appeared in 1864 much as it does now. "The march," he declared in his autobiography, "was over rough and poor roads, when we had any roads at all. The way at times was almost impassable for the 'mud forests' closed us in on either side, and the underbrush shut off all distant objects." Lieutenant Colonel Joseph S. Fullerton, assistant adjutant general at the headquarters of Howard's Fourth Corps, who kept a valuable journal throughout the Atlanta campaign, likewise testified to the difficult, perplexing terrain: "1 p.m., have advanced about one mile and a half, and country rolling and covered with timber and undergrowth; we can see nothing fifty yards in front."

The march was delayed by constant reconnoitering, followed by still farther tramping to the left. Shortly after three in the afternoon, Howard was standing in the edge of the woods, using his field glasses in an attempt to distinguish the enemy lines. The general's aide, Captain Henry M. Stinson, boldly advanced into an opening in the thickets, anxious to test his new field glasses. Hardly had Stinson raised the glasses to his eyes when a bullet passed through his body, penetrating the lungs, and the captain fell face forward to the ground. Stinson would recover from the wound, severe though it was, but General Howard was shocked; the incident contributing to the stunned condition that seemed to characterize the commander of the Fourth Corps for the rest of the day.

Uncertain of where the Confederate right flank was located, uncertain of his own position, and no longer in touch with the main body of Sherman's army (a sizable gap having developed between Nathaniel C. McLean's brigade and the rest of the Army of the Ohio), Howard continued his groping trek eastward. Already he was much farther to his left than Sherman had anticipated when he conceived the flanking march. At 3:35 P.M., Howard sent a note to Thomas stating his position as he understood it and telling the difficulties encountered in moving over the rugged terrain.

By late afternoon Howard's Yankees were near a settlement known as Pickett's Mill, located on the rolling hills along Little Pumpkinvine Creek, also called Pickett's Mill Creek. The stream took its name from a three-hundred-acre farm and mill that had belonged to Benjamin Pickett. A member of one of Wheeler's cavalry regiments, Pickett might well have fought across his own farm on this date, but he had been killed at the Battle of Chickamauga, leaving a twenty-seven-year-old widow and four children.

In the general vicinity of Pickett's Mill, Howard completed preparations for his attack—an attack which he delayed for the better part of two hours, yet never getting all the troops together. Neither Johnson's division on the Federal left nor McLean's brigade on the right would provide the support expected and needed.

"I am now turning the enemy's right flank, I think," reported Howard to General Thomas's army headquarters at 4:35 P.M. Actually Howard was no more turning the Confederate's right flank than Sherman had been their left flank when he ordered Hooker to take the crossroads at New Hope Church. A statement of bitter humor in retrospect, Howard's words might well have been applied on a broader scale, because they are indicative of the blind groping and fighting that characterized so much of the struggle along the Dallas–New Hope–Pickett's Mill line.

Howard and Wood decided upon an assault formation in column of brigades, a plan that essentially nullified their manpower advantage. This type of attack formation had contributed to the failure at New Hope Church two days before. Feeling the move would succeed this time, Wood formed his three brigades in column, one behind the other. The Second Brigade, commanded by Brigadier General William B. Hazen, was chosen to take the lead. "We will put in Hazen and see what success he has," remarked Wood. Another intriguing statement, like Howard's just quoted, Wood's words proved, as Phillip L. Secrist remarked in a *Civil War Times Illustrated* article, "an accurate forecast of the piecemeal character of the attack which was soon to take place."

The novelist-to-be, Ambrose Bierce, serving as a topographical lieutenant, who later would write a scathing account of this action which he entitled "The Crime at Pickett's Mill," observed Hazen's response when he heard Wood's plans to place him in the forefront of the attack: "When he (Hazen) heard Wood say they would get him in and see what success he would have in defeating an army—when he saw Howard assent—he uttered never a word, rode to the head of his . . . brigade and patiently awaited the command to go. Only by a look which I knew how to read did he betray his sense of the criminal blunder."

There was nothing wrong with the choice of Hazen to spearhead an assault. At Stones River (Murfreesboro) his reputation as a fighter had been confirmed when he successfully defended the key salient at the center of the Federal line that protected the railroad and the Nashville Pike. Just as at New Hope Church, however, the Yankee front was too narrow.

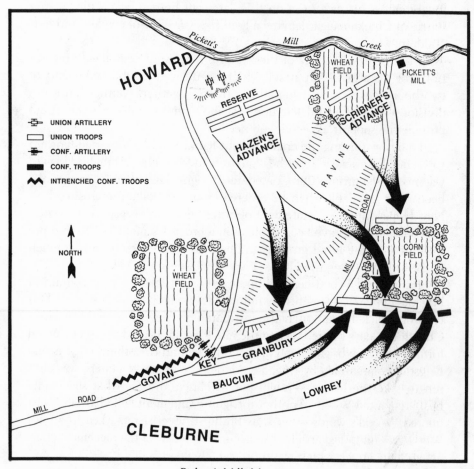

Pickett's Mill, May 27.

Hazen's brigade, in column of battalions, covered a front of hardly more than two hundred yards. Hazen's unit was to be followed closely by the First and Third brigades of Wood's division, commanded respectively by Colonel William H. Gibson and Colonel Frederick Knefler. Johnson's division of the Fourteenth Corps, unknown to Hazen, had still not come up on the left flank and Nathaniel C. McLean's brigade of the Twenty-third Corps had lost connection on the right long before, and in the words of Colonel Knefler, "was not again met with the remainder of the day."

The signal for the Federal advance came about five o'clock. With battle flags floating in a brisk breeze, the men moved forward across rough ground, cut by ravines and filled with dense undergrowth, hoping they were about to assault an unsuspecting and unprotected flank of the Confederate army. Instead, the Yankees' own left flank and front was harassed by enfilading fire from Brigadier General John H. Kelly's dismounted troopers, posted in the woods to guard the extreme right of the Confederate line. Despite this severe annoyance, Hazen's men pressed on with determination. Thus began a fight whose development is still today one of the most confusing and difficult to unravel of all Civil War engagements.

Stumbling down the side of a steep ravine that is some 100 to 120 feet deep and struggling to ascend the even more precipitous far slope, the Yankees suddenly were swept by a galling musketry fire as they ran against a solid line of Confederate infantry. Much of the Rebel position lay concealed in a dense covering of underbrush. But at the top of the slope the distinctive blue flags that always marked Cleburne's division could be seen clearly.

Cleburne's brigades were ensconced on a low ridge above the valley of little Pumpkinvine Creek, where they had been posted the day before to protect the Confederate right flank. Govan's brigade was entrenched on the right of Major T. R. Hotchkiss's battery of twelve guns, which first had been sited to fire across a wheat field to their front, but later, thanks to Cleburne's foresight, had also been prepared for a flanking fire to the right. This was fortunate because their oblique fire had a deadly effect on the Yankee assault. Cleburne had placed two other brigades, under command of Hiram B. Granbury and Mark P. Lowrey, in a supporting line where they could be quickly moved to any threatened point. The nature of the terrain, along with the Irishman's well-drilled emphasis on rapid-fire technique, provided more than an adequate advantage to halt the reckless charge of the Federals.

Granbury was ordered at once from the second line to prolong Govan's right, and according to Captain Irving A. Buck's account, "so sud-

Hiram B. Granbury.

den and vigorous was the rush of the Federals that Granbury was barely in time to prevent Govan's flank from being turned—his men firing by file as they came into line." Hazen's brigade, climbing over the rocks that lined the face of the ravine, was devastated by the point-blank fire of Granbury's right front, at many points hardly forty paces away. "Displaying a courage worthy of an honorable cause," to quote Cleburne's sarcastic words, the Union soldiers charged, some shouting as they came: "Ah! damn you, we have caught you without your logs now!"

Logs or no logs, the Confederates held an impregnable position for repelling a direct assault on a narrow front, and once more it was proved that courage is never a match for the sickening thwack of a well-placed bullet as it smashes into flesh and bone. Awaiting the Union soldiers, "with calm determination," according to Cleburne's After Action Report, the Confederates "slaughtered them with deliberate aim" as they appeared upon the slope. Some of the Rebels, having been apprised of news reports circulating in the North, stating that the Confederate soldiers were demoralized, had their own special taunt for the Federals charging their line. From time to time, various ones would cry out at the Yankees: "Come on, we are *demoralized!*"

The Confederate fire was so effective that the Federals shifted farther to their left in the ravine, still probing for the enemy flank. As Hazen's right regiments struggled desperately with Granbury's Texans along the ravine, the left portion of his line charged across a cornfield and threatened the right rear of the Confederate position. The Rebels were fully equal to the challenge.

General Granbury sent an aide galloping to Cleburne for help. Immediately Cleburne ordered two regiments of Govan's brigade—which was not challenged since McLean's Federals had failed to support Hazen's right flank—to meet the Yankee threat. Coming on the run, the Eighth and Nineteenth Arkansas regiments, led by G. F. Baucom, stormed into Hazen's men at the edge of the cornfield. Soon the Arkansans were joined by General Lowrey's brigade, also hastened from the rear by Cleburne, and the Federals were forced back across the cornfield where, reforming, the weary Yankees then repulsed a Rebel counterattack.

Meanwhile, on Hazen's left flank and to the rear, Colonel Benjamin F. Scribner's lead brigade of Johnson's division was experiencing a rough time moving along Pickett's Mill Creek and was never able to provide the support for Hazen that was expected. General Kelly's cavalry did an excellent job of blocking the advance of Scribner's infantry. The twenty-four-year-old Kelly, a native of Alabama who was attending West Point when the war broke out, had become the youngest general officer in the Confederacy when he was commissioned in 1863. Kelly had his dismounted troopers on both sides of the stream near the mill, where the rugged ground rises abruptly from the creek banks. Scribner was ultimately forced to put three regiments across the creek to clear out the Rebel cavalry holding the bluff on the east bank before he could continue his advance. The result was that neither Hazen's brigade nor Gibson's (which was to follow) had any support on their left flank.

Within a few minutes—thirty to forty-five, depending on whose account one reads—Hazen had suffered an admitted 500 casualties and the survivors of his brigade fell back from the forefront of the action. Ambrose Bierce was near the right of Hazen's line and described a "dead line" beyond which no Yankee soldier advanced. "Of the hundreds of corpses within twenty paces of the Confederate line, I venture to say that a third were within fifteen paces and not one within ten."

Actually, bad as it was, Hazen's repulse constituted only the beginning of a terrible affair for the Yankees. Next came Colonel William H. Gibson's brigade, and the slaughter grew worse. General Wood hoped that Gibson's men would find the Rebels weakened by Hazen's attack. It was not to be. Charging past the right of Hazen's broken brigade into the ravine, and clambering up the steep slope of the ridge, Gibson's soldiers were subjected not only to the enfilading fire from the left flank that had punished Hazen, as well as the murderous barrage from the front; but now the Southerners had an even more effective artillery fire, supported by infantry fire, raking the Union soldiers from their right flank. Two howitzers of Captain Thomas J. Key's battery, and a rifled battery, had been wrestled through the mud to a position near the junction of Govan's and Granbury's brigades at the head of the ravine where, with some of Govan's infantry, their fire enfiladed the Federals who were pinned down on the slope of the ravine.

"I regretted I did not have more guns for this service," reported Cleburne, explaining that he had sent his Napoleon guns to the right of the line where they were useless, being unable to find a suitable position from which to fire.

Making the hellish situation still worse for the Union, as becomes evident from the reports and recollections of those who actively participated in the struggle, was the fact that the Northern troops lost their formations. Confessing to "a momentary fit of complete demoralization," caused by the disorganized condition of his regiment, Alexis Cope graphically described the events: "We were thrown into dire confusion by conflicting or misunderstood orders. . . . Before the disorders were corrected, the bugler, Wilson S. Iler [who was to die in the assault], with quick-sharp, clear notes, sounded the advance and we charged . . . into the woods and . . . pressed forward up the side of a ravine, found the enemy on its further edge, in a position too strong to be successfully attacked, and held on. . . . We suffered from a severe cross and enfilading fire from both the enemy's right and left. This fire did little damage to the men closest to the enemy's line. . . ," remarked Cope, "but was killing the wounded who were lying in the ravine and on its slope to our rear."

Another survivor of the Union assault, Sergeant Major J. A. Gleason, testified in his diary that "[n]early every regiment seemed to have lost all formation in the mad and futile charge into the angle of the enemy's works." Most men could find no place to hide. Crouching behind what he described as a medium-sized tree on the brink of the ravine, Gleason shared his meager shelter with another soldier. Gleason's unknown companion, hugging the tree, was shot squarely in the temple. "It killed him so suddenly that he never changed his position, and had I not heard the shot strike and been spattered by his blood and brains, I might have believed him still untouched."

Gibson's brigade had stormed into a slaughter pen. Taking about 700 casualties, the brigade had losses in some units that exceeded any battle during their entire war service. Piled into the ravine, line upon line, it was as bad to fall back as it had been to advance, until darkness covered the scene. At approximately six o'clock a brigade bugle sounded the recall but, not surprisingly, was generally ignored since the day was not yet dark.

Confusion and near panic prevailed at General Howard's headquarters. In their frustration, Howard and Wood lashed out at others for the bungled attack, focusing upon McLean and Johnson for failing to support the flanks of Wood's division. Wood was still calling for his fellow Kentuckian Johnson to bring up his division on the left, when one of his aides was shot and killed near his side. General Wood lost control of himself, and Howard later recalled: "For a few minutes, sitting beside his dying friend, he was completely overcome."

Then it was Howard's turn. A bursting shell blew fragments in all directions and Howard felt something strike his left foot. In horror he imagined that he had lost part of his leg. To his great relief, after first crying out that he was afraid to look down, he saw he still had his leg, although it was badly bruised. Disoriented, Howard seemed unable to do anything except watch the results of his disastrous assault, as the wounded were transported to the rear.

At about six o'clock Howard received a dispatch, written from Thomas's headquarters at 5:15 P.M., which had it come earlier, could have prevented the tragic affair that sacrificed so much of Howard's command. Thomas instructed Howard to connect his right with the left of General Schofield's Twenty-third Corps and take up a strong position that he could hold until reinforcements were sent. Thomas told Howard not to place his men in a position which would risk their being turned by the enemy. Further, Johnson's division was to form in a manner that would prevent Howard's left from being flanked and, in the words of Colonel Fullerton's journal, "if necessary to do this our left must be refused."

But the orders had arrived too late to save Hazen and Gibson from the ill-advised attack. Following the failure of Gibson's assault, General Wood sent forward Colonel Frederick Knefler's Third Brigade with orders to relieve Gibson, who, like Hazen, was running out of ammunition, because the division's munitions wagons did not reach the battle area until after dark. Knefler was to hold the ground without renewing the assault so that as many of the dead and wounded as possible could be brought off the field. While not suffering like the units of Hazen and Gibson, Knefler also sustained many casualties, both in moving to the front and from heavy skirmish firing that continued long after darkness had covered the "scenes of awful carnage"—to borrow the words of Ambrose Bierce. By dark many of Knefler's soldiers were out of ammunition and taking cartridges from the dead and wounded.

Colonel Knefler summed up his attack briefly, stating that in the advance "the first line was completely enfiladed by the enemy's artillery, suffering severely. The advance was made rapidly and in good order. After sustaining a murderous fire, I regret to say, it was thrown into disorder."

About this time General Scribner's Federal brigade had finally driven back Kelly's cavalry and reached the edge of the cornfield where they joined Knefler's left flank. Scribner was repeatedly assaulted by Confederates of Lowrey's and William A. Quarles's brigades. Scribner's soldiers held firm, however, and were the last to retreat from the battlefield.

As always in battle, individual exploits of heroism were evident, but none exceeded those of the Yankee color bearers. Sergeant Ambrose D. Norton, color bearer of the Fifteenth Ohio, was killed and his flag fell into the open area in front of the Confederate line. Several Ohioans were shot down in succession as they sought to recover their banner. Finally, Sergeant David D. Hart managed to bring it back safely. Another color bearer was struck by a hail of bullets as he came to within a few feet of the Rebel line. Dying, he placed the flag against a tree so that it would not touch the ground.

Such stubborn determination symbolized what General Wood later called "altogether the fiercest and most vigorous assault that was made on the enemy's intrenched positions during the entire campaign." Then, in appalling understatement, the Federal general added: "The attack was made under circumstances well calculated to task the courage and prove the manhood of the troops."

Years later, in a more subdued state, General Howard reflected upon the carnage at Pickett's Mill, which he compared to Antietam and Gettysburg. He wrote of "faint fires here and there revealing men wounded, armless, legless, or eyeless; some with heads bound up with cotton strips, some standing and walking nervously around, some sitting with bended forms, and some prone upon the earth—who can picture it? A few men, in despair, had resorted to drink for relief. The sad sounds from those in pain were mingled with the oaths of the drunken and more heartless."

From the time the Rebels of Govan's brigade discovered the march of the Yankee column, it is highly unlikely that there was any chance of success for the movement as conceived and executed by Howard and Wood. Not only had the Federals assaulted across unreconnoitered ground, which proved to be broken, rugged, and dense; against an enemy whose position and strength were unknown; and in columns on a narrow front enabling Cleburne's single division to overlap their lines with flanking fire. Also the Union's superior numbers were wasted, because the supporting troops were either never brought into the action, as on the Federal right, or delayed until any chance of success was gone, as with Scribner on the left. General Sherman, having blamed the New Hope Church fiasco on the delay in attacking, did not even mention Pickett's Mill, either in his report or his memoirs.

With sporadic firing, the fighting at Pickett's Mill continued until well past the onset of darkness. As the time moved toward ten o'clock Cleburne agreed to Granbury's request for permission to clear his front of "the enemy lying up against it." Rebel captain Samuel Foster later confided to his diary the feelings he experienced just before he charged with Granbury's line: "While waiting (all this time none had spoken above a whisper) we could hear the Yanks just in front of us moving among the dead leaves on the ground, like hogs rooting for acorns; but not speaking a word above a whisper. To make that charge in the dark, and go in front at that; and knowing that the enemy were just in front of us, was the most trying time I experienced during the whole war."

Punctuated by what one Federal called "demoniac yells and shouts" that pierced the black night, Granbury charged with his whole line. Startled and then panic-stricken, many Yankees fled, while others surrendered or were killed, and at last the battle of Pickett's Mill came to an end.

Lieutenant Thomas J. Stokes, Tenth Texas Infantry, participated in the night charge into the ravine, inadvertently wandered away from the main body of soldiers and became lost between the lines of the two armies. He later described the experience, alone in "the darkness of midnight," with the wounded, the dying, and the dead. "The moon at this time was just rising," he wrote, "and casting her pale silvery rays through the dense woods, made every tree and shrub look like a spectre. I saw a tall, muscular Federal lying dead and the moonlight shining in his face. His eyes were open and seemed riveted on me. I could not help but shudder."

Only with the break of dawn could the full extent of the destruction be grasped. A Texas lieutenant, R. M. Collins, wrote: "When the sun had chased the shades of night away . . . , it revealed a sight on that hill side that was sickening to look upon. All along in the front of the center and left of our brigade the ground was literally covered with dead men." A correspondent of the *Memphis Appeal* recorded that the "spectacle [was] the most bloody mine eyes ever beheld. . . . Along a line of about one hundred yards, . . . and over a broken woodland, lie the dead bodies of seven hundred Yankees, heaped in confused piles of two, three and half a dozen. . . . The sight is horrible." And Captain Foster vividly recorded, in gory description, that it seemed like the Federal dead "have nearly all been shot in the head, and a great number of them have their skulls bursted open and their brains running out, quite a number that way. I have seen many dead men, . . . but I never saw anything before that made me sick." According to Foster, Generals Johnston, Hardee, Cleburne, and Granbury "all say that the dead are strewn thicker on the ground than at any battle of the war."

Cleburne, who was usually accurate, reported that his men "took upward of 1,200 small arms," and thought the Federals could not have lost less than 3,000 killed and wounded. The dead piled in front of the Confederate line, Cleburne said, were "pronounced by the officers in this army

who have seen most service to be greater than they had ever seen before."
Texan Thomas Stokes described the dead as "hundreds upon hundreds,
in every conceivable position; some with contorted features, showing the
agony of death, others as if quietly sleeping."An Alabama Rebel recorded
that "such piles of dead men were seldom or never seen before on such a
small space of ground." Whenever possible burial details did their work
the night following the fight, but circumstances sometimes delayed them
in performing their grisly task.

The Federal division led by Wood reported almost 1,500 casualties.
Johnson's division, which had failed to protect Wood's left flank, did not
make a separate report of its losses. Johnson himself, being wounded,
had relinquished command of his division. What McLean had been doing
while he was to support Wood's right flank is not clear, but he suffered
no losses of consequence. Whatever the precise figure on Federal casualties—and it seems reasonable to place it between 2,000 and 3,000—
Cleburne's division had experienced one of its most successful days of the
war. Good as that division was, it could never have meted out such
destruction to the Federals apart from the Yankee blunders. Well did
Ambrose Bierce remark that Pickett's Mill was an engagement "fore-
doomed to oblivion" because "the vanquished have not thought it expe-
dient to relate it. . . . Whether it was so trifling an affair as to justify this
inattention let the reader judge."

There were obvious similarities between New Hope Church and Pickett's Mill. In both instances, the grayclad infantry had beaten far-supe-
rior numbers because of position, fortification, and Yankee blunders. In
both cases, the Federals had charged in column covering only a narrow
front.


CLATTERING rifle fire ushered in May 28 and the scorching Georgia sun
climbed high to hover over two sweating, bleeding armies. Early in the
day, Sherman decided to move his army eastward, back toward the railroad, and McPherson was told to withdraw and march toward the Union
center near New Hope Church. Hot skirmish action made it impossible
for McPherson to pull out, and he spent the morning and early afternoon
fending off Rebel forays. Johnston seems to have guessed that Sherman
would attempt such a maneuver and directed Hardee to make a reconnaissance to determine if the Yankees were still in force in front of the
Confederate left.

Hardee selected Bate's division to make the reconnaissance and that
officer formed his command in three columns in order to strike at separate points. The cavalry of Brigadier General Frank C. Armstrong's bri-

gade was to play a key role, forming on Bate's left and advancing first. If the Yankees were gone, Armstrong's men were to fire their guns as a signal for Bate's infantry to charge and attack the Federals as they marched. But, as Richard McMurry observed, "Nobody seems to have asked what would happen if the Federals were still in their trenches!"

Thus the scene was set for another of those terrible blunders that so often contributed to making the war the most costly in American history. At about three-thirty the grayclads advanced. McPherson's Army of the Tennessee was still behind its works on the Federal right and naturally fired upon the advancing Confederate cavalry. Naturally the resulting fight led Bate's men to assume that the shots heard were the signal to advance. And so they charged, directly into the fortified lines of the Fifteenth and Sixteenth corps. The engagement was vicious, and even though the outcome was never in doubt, Bate's men, fighting valiantly, gave the Federals some anxious moments.

The first blow came on Brigadier General William Harrow, at the weakest point in the line of Logan's Fifteenth Corps. Harrow was a forty-one-year-old former Illinois attorney who had ridden the Eighth Circuit with Lincoln. His regiment had been decimated at Antietam, and after Gettysburg he came west to a new command. Harrow's division lay across the Villa Rica Road where the road wound down the backbone of a ridge in terrain difficult to fortify. The Southern assault struck this point, sweeping in skirmishers from Colonel Charles Walcutt's Second Brigade and overrunning three guns of the First Iowa Battery. With the enemy only eighty yards from their works, Walcutt's men fired volley after volley across the plateau, the deadly fire preventing the Confederates from turning the Iowa guns on the Union works. The fighting in front of Walcutt was murderous. His four regiments "stood unflinchingly at their guns," led by Walcutt, "who stood on the parapet amid the storm of bullets, ruling the fight."

Seeing the battle storm on the right, Logan, who had been primed "like a horse ready for battle" the previous day only to be disappointed, galloped to Walcutt waving his sword in the air, his red undershirt showing beneath his torn uniform tunic. Disorganized groups converged on Logan asking for their regiments and officers. Logan thundered at them, "Damn your regiments! Damn your officers! Forward and yell like hell!" With the First Iowa's guns still in Rebel possession, Logan mounted a counterattack by rallying Harrow's division to retake the battery. He jumped his horse over the works, followed by shouting troops racing into a hail of enemy fire. Logan, struck in the left forearm by a Rebel ball, saw the men claim their guns and hurl the enemy back.

His arm supported in a hastily torn sling, Logan rode back to the line

John A. Logan.

followed by the cry, "Black Jack's wounded." He continued to ride along the front urging his men to repel new assaults. Several times Bate's men rallied against Harrow, but each time he was turned back. Shortly after the Confederates first struck Harrow, they swept in on Morgan L. Smith and Peter J. Osterhaus, but the ground in front of the latter two was more favorable for defense and the attackers could gain no successes. In the brief, costly action, the heaviest assaults had been made by the Kentucky "Orphan Brigade" of Brigadier General J. H. Lewis and Brigadier General J. J. Finley's Florida Brigade. Lewis lost 51 percent of his men, killed, wounded, or missing. On the Northern side, Logan reported a loss of 379 in the Fifteenth Corps. Casualty figures for the Sixteenth Corps are not available. Logan estimated Confederate losses at 2,000, but judging from Bate's reported loss of 450, they could not have been nearly that high.

Following the battle McPherson reported to Sherman that the Rebels were "handsomely repulsed." Logan, his wound troubling him only slightly, exultantly reported to his wife Mary, "Since the fight of Saturday, the men are all enthusiasm and think I am all they want to command them."

Despite Confederate efforts, McPherson was able gradually to disengage the Union troops and shift eastward. Sending details to the rear to prepare another line of trenches, he would post a strong skirmish line when these were completed, and quickly and quietly move the mass of the Army of the Tennessee to the new position. There was no other general engagement in the area of Dallas–New Hope Church–Pickett's Mill. Instead the Federal forces accomplished a gradual shift toward the Western & Atlantic Railroad on the east, with Joe Johnston moving the Rebels in the same direction to keep constantly in front of Sherman.

Actually, the Confederates did attempt to initiate another engagement. Either Johnston or Hood (both later claimed to have suggested the movement) proposed to attack the Federal left flank. On the morning of May 29, Hood began a march with the intention of assailing Howard's corps. Learning that the Federal position had been fortified, and acting upon orders to assault only if conditions were favorable, Hood again failed to attack. For the third consecutive time, Joe Johnston called off a planned assault on Sherman because of the advice of Hood. But Howard's corps was strongly fortified in their position; furthermore, the Federals were aware of Hood's movement and prepared for an attack. A Confederate foray could well have been a replay of Pickett's Mill, only with the attackers and defenders reversed.

"The Hell Hole" was an appropriate description, not only of the battle at New Hope Church, but all the fighting in the region from Dallas to Pickett's Mill. One Yankee soldier described it as "probably the most wretched week" of the campaign. Besides the murderous assaults and the sharpshooting of pickets, rain, heat, and shortages of food contributed to the general misery of both Yank and Reb. And the nature of the campaign was changing. Gradually the war in the West was becoming one of entrenching, with elaborate systems of ditches, earthen parapets, headlogs, and abatis. Probably no engagement contributed more to this change than the New Hope Church fight, where only three of Stewart's brigades had thrown back an entire Union corps, administering sizable losses. After the experiences of "the Hell Hole," both sides followed the practice of throwing up entrenchments wherever they stopped long enough to do so. Obviously the fighting at New Hope Church, and at Pickett's Mill, was considerably more than heavy skirmishing between enemy outposts.

# 8

# At Times Assaults Are Necessary

STEADILY drumming June rains turned Georgia clay slippery and made life uncomfortable for Sherman's bluecoats. The rain also covered Joe Johnston's first withdrawal of the campaign's second month. On June 4 he slipped southward into a new position, one that Sherman viewed with apprehension and frustration. Hardee was on the Confederate left on 500-foot-tall Lost Mountain and at Gilgal Church, bishop-general Polk held the center from Pine Mountain's 300-foot brow to the Western & Atlantic south of Acworth, and Hood's troops were on the right. Hood's lines crossed the railroad and ran along Brush Mountain, a 300-foot ridge. Johnston's flanks were covered by Joe Wheeler's cavalry to the east and Red Jackson's horsemen to the west. Two miles in Johnston's rear loomed Kennesaw Mountain, a higher point and one to which the Confederate commander could easily withdraw. The entire region was covered with thick vegetation and appeared to Fourth Corps commander Oliver O. Howard as "our interminable wilderness."

Nasty weather and an elusive foe caused Sherman problems but there was also good news in June's first days. By the eleventh the efficient Union engineers and their track crews had the railroad running all the way to Big Shanty. Trains arrived, eagerly awaited mail was delivered, and, while Union troops might be damp, their stomachs were full. An Indiana infantryman wrote, "Our profoundest admiration goes to the way Sherman keeps up his railroad and our rations." He thought he heard the locomotives whistle, "How-do-you-doo-oo General Sherman!" when they arrived. The rains and Johnston's withdrawal had also slowed combat so Yankee veterans were well rested. An Indiana lieutenant had time to write in his diary, "Idle today, save bathing, changing clothes, writing letters and so fourth," while an Illinois soldier "slept, talked, and smoked."

Another heartening development for Sherman was the arrival of Frank Blair's Seventeenth Corps. By June 9 Blair's 10,000 men, who had gone north to reenlist, had rejoined the Army of the Tennessee. Blair's welcome reinforcement made up for many of Sherman's casualties in the campaign's first month. The Missouri corps commander brought with him wagons of iced champagne and gave a party for Schofield and McPherson that was "damned elegant."

When Blair rejoined McPherson he found the Army of the Tennessee once again in close contact with the Rebels. McPherson held the left across the railroad at Big Shanty, while Thomas's Cumberlanders held the center with Schofield's Army of the Ohio positioned on the right. The Union invaders were about four miles from Marietta and less than twenty from Atlanta.

Along this new line Sherman's men had quickly erected parapets. They had become skillful in throwing up these four-to six-foot-high protective structures. In time Sherman developed pioneer units, attached to each division, composed of two hundred freedmen who had fled Confederate control. In return for food and ten dollars a month these blacks labored at night on the Union works.

In spite of Johnston's obvious terrain advantage around Marietta, Sherman thought his opponent would not give battle there. He told Schofield on June 5 that Johnston "will oppose us lightly all the way to the Chattahoochee and defend that line with all his ability."

By June 9 that optimism had tarnished a bit and Sherman revealed his misgivings about his next move to his brother John.

> My long and single line of railroad to my rear, of limited capacity, is the delicate point of my game, as also the fact that all of Georgia, except the cleared bottoms, is densely wooded, with few roads, and at any point an enterprising enemy can, in a few hours with axes and spades, make across our path formidable works. . . . It is a big Indian war, still thus far I have won four strong positions, advanced a hundred miles. . . . Johnston's army is still in my front and can fight or fall back, as he pleases. The future is uncertain, but I will do all that is possible.

What general was better fit to lead a "big Indian war" than one named Tecumseh? Confederate general Samuel French, a Yankee Quaker who had moved south before Sumter and commanded a division under Johnston, saw something in the name when he wrote in his diary: "It does seem strange that we cannot have one quiet Sabbath. Sherman has no regard for the Fourth Commandment. I wish a Bible society would send him a prayer book instead of shipping them all to a more remote heathen, but it would be the same in either class. The one is uncivilized by nature—the other, I fear, becoming so from habit. Perhaps 'Tecumseh' has something to do with it."

The uncertain future he wrote of to his brother had Sherman engaged in some hard thinking. His last flanking movement, following New Hope Church and Pickett's Mill, had succeeded in forcing the Confederates to give up impregnable Allatoona Pass, but he had hoped to sweep to the Chattahoochee River on Atlanta's northern edge. Instead, he was well north of the stream and facing the Rebels situated on high ground able to watch his every move. A frontal attack on Johnston's line was filled with peril but another flanking sweep would move Sherman away from the railroad, the "delicate point of his game." The slippery roads and swollen creeks also made a flanking movement questionable.

During this pause, as throughout the campaign, their commander was a source of fascination for Union soldiers. At night, while the rain fell, they watched him by candlelight pacing back and forth in his headquarters-house. "When Uncle Billy can't march by day, he marches all night," they said.

The weather brought hard times to men in both armies. From the Seventieth Indiana a lieutenant wrote, "For three days and nights we were wet to the skin, not a dry article of clothing on us; each night our beds were the wet and muddy ground." A Union soldier wrote day after day of rain and soggy roads, but added philosophically, "I consoled myself with the idea that a wetting was better than a killing." Even generals found conditions unpleasant. John W. Geary told his wife Mary, "I am now seated on some wet leaves in the woods, writing a note to you by candlelight."

Johnston's army was also uncomfortable and disgusted with the weather. One soldier found the roads "the worst I ever saw," and the "clay and mud . . . haf a leg deepe, stickest mud you ever saw." Private Moses Kirkland from sandy southwestern Georgia found his new camp "very nasty" because "hit is a clay land." An officer in the First Georgia State Troops was "disagreeably wet," had dysentery, huddled in his tent, "a rail pen covered over," and was convinced "war is a troublesome thing sure."

The rain did drop the level of combat, and enterprising soldiers could find something to do in spite of the deluge. A member of the Fifth Connecticut reported, "Our pickets are about ¾ of a mile from us, having gay times trading papers with the rebel pickets." He talked to some Tennesseans who said that although the Yankees might win in Georgia, "Lee is licking Grant terribly at Richmond." "Their accounts are somewhat different from ours, for we learn that Grant has begun the siege of Richmond," he commented. One other piece of information received by Sherman's army on June 11 was "the cheering news of Uncle Abe's nomination. . . . Three cheers for that. It did heeps of good. I want to cast one more vote for him next fall."

There were other amusements as well. Michigan soldiers played poker with gun caps for chips and Thomas Taylor of the Twelfth Ohio found the "female portion of the population friendly disposed." One night Union soldiers struck up the plaintive words of "Tenting Tonight On the Old Camp Ground." As they sang,

> Many are the hearts that are weary tonight,
> Wishing for the war to cease;
> Many are the hearts looking for the right,
> To see the dawn of peace.

they heard, faintly from above, another song about rights,

> Hurrah! Hurrah! for Southern Rights, Hurrah!
> Hurrah! for the Bonnie Blue Flag,
> That bears a single Star!

So into June's second week through the drizzle, Sherman kept the pressure on, straight ahead with no hint of a swing left or right. The Rebel response was to pull back slightly, a move that shortened and strengthed their line. Hardee, on the left, was concentrated at Gilgal Church; Hood, on the right, was behind Noonday Creek covering the railroad; and Polk was in the center ready to move in any direction.

One wonders what Johnston thought of the letter he received from Braxton Bragg about this time. Doubtless Bragg intended to encourage and inform him about the war in the East, although the communiqué, in historical retrospect, was obviously misleading: "Grant has been so much crippled by his constant repulses, of which he sustained a very severe one yesterday [Cold Harbor] that I apprehend but little damage from him now." Nevertheless, Grant was less than ten miles from Richmond and able to replace his losses much more effectively than Lee could the Confederate casualties. Whatever Johnston thought, he had little time to ponder the military contest in Virginia.

When Johnston set his new line he left a brigade from Bate's division on Pine Mountain, an excellent spot from which to observe Sherman's movements. The position, called a less majestic "Pine Top" by local citizens, gave Johnston a splendid view but it was so far in advance of the Confederate line as to be vulnerable to a quick Union strike. To

Pine Mountain.

defend the salient Johnston put two batteries on its crest, one commanded by Lieutenant René Beauregard, son of the hero of Sumter and
Manassas.

General William Hardee believed the new Rebel line was "strong enough
to resist any attack of the yankees," but he was edgy about the security
of his troops on Pine Mountain. On June 14 he persuaded the commanding general to ride forward with him to calculate the risk. Johnston and
Hardee, trailed by their staff officers, rode forward as did General Polk,
who wanted to take a look at Sherman's position. The morning was cool
and overcast as the party climbed the hill. Almost at once Johnston
agreed with Hardee that the position was precarious and he ordered all
Confederate forces off the hill after nightfall. Having made the decision,
Johnston stopped for another look at the enemy's flags, tents, and white
wagon tops in the distance. The generals disregarded warnings that Sherman's artillery had the exact range of the hill.

In the valley below, Captain Hubert Dilger and his rifled Parrotts of
Battery I, First Ohio Light Artillery, waited. Dilger, well known in Sherman's army as "Leatherbreeches," was dressed as usual in a white shirt,

highly polished boots, and doeskin trousers. An officer in the Prussian army, the captain had been on leave and had arrived in New York at the outbreak of the war. He joined the Army of the Potomac in 1861 and fought in all of its battles through Gettysburg before coming west with Hooker to serve at Chattanooga.

Dilger's reputation for the accuracy of his guns as well as his audacity in combat more than matched his background and appearance. His battery was so effective that he was permitted to move about independently, bringing his guns to bear where he thought they would provide the best support. That was often so close to the foe that two generals suggested that Dilger equip his pieces with bayonets. The Prussian loved to talk about his guns. To a fascinated Cord Foote, fifteen-year-old drummer in the Tenth Michigan, he said: "A gun, she shust like a gut dog. Be kind to her, feed her, luf her, and she do shust vat you say, efry time." Rather than give orders in his German-accented English, he clapped his hands as the order to fire. On the fourteenth his guns were well in advance below Pine Mountain when he sighted the group of Rebel horsemen.

Sherman had also seen them. "How saucy they are," he said and he told Howard to fire to "make 'em take cover." The order passed to Dilger and the Prussian sighted down a rifled Parrott, said "Shust teeckle them fellers," to his Ohio gunner and clapped his hands. The first shot struck close to the knot of Confederate officers and a second landed even closer.

Johnston and Hardee had seen enough and moved quickly out of sight. The more portly Polk, with all the dignity he had shown as Episcopal bishop of Louisiana, walked slowly away. Dilger's third shell found its target, striking Polk in the side and passing through his body before exiting to strike a tree. The barrage continued and Johnston and Hardee were persuaded to go to a nearby tent and wait while soldiers brought Polk to them. They saw at once that the general was dead. "My dear, dear friend," cried Hardee. Johnston, also in tears, touched Polk's head and said, "We have lost much. I would rather anything but this."

While waiting for the ambulance to reach Pine Mountain, the dead general's friends found a copy of Dr. Charles Quintard's book of poems, *Balm for the Weary and Wounded,* in his bloodstained tunic. The book fell open to a marked stanza:

> There is an unseen battlefield
> In every human breast
> Where two opposing forces meet
> And where they seldom rest

That afternoon Polk's body was hauled down the hill and that night Bate's grieving division followed. Johnston's army mourned its dead leader.

Leonidas Polk.

He had commanded in the Army of Tennessee since 1861 and, although his military abilities were sometimes questioned, he was widely believed to be a strong moral force in the army, one that Shelby Foote said, "enabled it to survive hardships, defeats, retreats, and Bragg." On hearing of Polk's death one Rebel soldier said, "he was a very nice man, but of not much use to the army."

The Army of Tennessee's historian, Thomas L. Connelly, has estimated the impact of Polk's loss:

> His deficiencies as a commander and his personal traits of stubbornness and childishness had played no small role in several of the army's disasters in earlier times. The loss was one of morale and experience. Polk was the army's most beloved general, a representative of that intangible identification of the army with Tennessee. The army's first actual commander in the early days of 1861, Polk seemed a link with better times. Now this link seemed to be fading, and with it went Polk's vast experience.

Leading the Confederate mourning for Polk was his old friend, Jefferson Davis. The president called the death "an irreparable loss" and equated its effect with the deaths of Albert Sidney Johnston and Stonewall Jackson.

Sherman's army discovered quickly what Dilger's guns had wrought. Union observers, who had broken the enemy code, read a wigwag signal as "Send an ambulance for General Polk's body." Both during and after the war Confederates, who had turned Sherman into their personal devil, spread the story that the commander himself had sighted the gun and fired the shot that killed Polk. Sherman, who had ridden away before Dilger fired, denied the charge. Yet Polk's death pleased him and he telegraphed Halleck, "We killed Bishop Polk yesterday, and made good progress today."

The "good progress" was his order to move forward to the abandoned Pine Mountain. When his men reached the hill's crest they found a sign that read, "You damned Yankee sons of bitches have killed our old Gen. Polk." The rain had started again and the mud was a hindrance, but Thomas, McPherson, and Schofield pressed Johnston all along his impressive line as the campaign's sixth week ended. One of Schofield's divisions captured a hill, which allowed his artillery to enfilade Hardee's lines. The Rebels pulled back, but Johnston's most vulnerable point remained there on his left.

In addition to the killed and wounded, prisoners, some of them deserters, were being picked up by both Blue and Gray. To one Union soldier, captured Rebs seemed "quite despondent over their continuous retreats." One evening a Confederate officer came into the lines of the Seventy-sixth Ohio, "stuck his sword in the ground and said he was not going to use it anymore in the rebel army." There was nothing despondent about one Union prisoner who told his captors Sherman would soon drive them into the Gulf of Mexico. "He was pretty saucy chap and no doubt meant to bully us a little," concluded one of his guards.

By June's second week time for another important decision was at hand for Sherman. On the thirteenth he had told Halleck, "We cannot risk the heavy loss of an assault at this distance from our base." But three days later he completely reversed himself and his wire to Washington told Halleck, "I am now inclined to feign on both flanks and assault the center. It may cost us dear, but the results would surpass any attempt to pass around."

This reversal was not the decision of an instant; for some time Sherman had been weighing his continued dance with Johnston against the prospect of a frontal assault. He had even come to the conclusion that his movements thus far had blunted his troops' aggressiveness and made them timid in the face of enemy fortifications. He was critical of his army commanders, who he felt reinforced this timidity. To Grant he wired, "My chief source of trouble is with the Army of the Cumberland. A fresh furrow in a plowed field will stop the whole column and all begin to intrench. I have again and again tried to impress on Thomas that we must assail and not defend; we are on the offensive." Sherman was also scornful of the extensive tent city surrounding "Old Tom's" headquar-

The Front of Kennesaw Mountain.

ters. Even the men in the ranks called it "Tom Town" and "Thomas' Circus."

Sherman was even critical of McPherson, his favorite. The commander urged the Army of the Tennessee on and complained about delays. His third army chief, Schofield, also felt the sting of Sherman's words about the loss of the army's fighting spirit. The Army of the Ohio's young leader saw no reason to fault his troops and found their behavior in uniform merely a continuation of their actions in civilian life. "The veteran American soldier fights very much as he had been accustomed to work on his farm or run his sawmill. He wants to see a fair prospect that it is going to pay."

Three days after Sherman wired Halleck about his inclination to strike the Rebel center Johnston waited for dark and slid backwards again. This withdrawal placed the Confederate center on Kennesaw Mountain, two miles south of Pine Mountain, a considerably more formidable situation. Facing this elevated Southern position an Illinois officer wrote, "If the Rebs can not hold such a country as this, they can not hold anything."

Polk's division, temporarily led by Major General W. W. Loring, dug in along Kennesaw's northern rim, with Hood on the right blocking the railroad and Hardee on the left. Hardee's line began at the western edge of Kennesaw and then turned south across the Dallas-Marietta road, lying at right angles to the remainder of the Confederate position. That center that Sherman had talked of hitting had become Johnston's citadel. Indeed, the Confederate army had held no position during the Georgia campaign that was any stronger than this one. Those Yankee veterans must have wondered if an attack here was a "fair prospect."

The Union army was impressed with Kennesaw's bulk, defiantly standing in its path. Blueclad troops watched the enemy felling trees and erecting fortifications and noted as did Sherman that Kennesaw was "crowned with batteries," and that Rebel signalmen seemed very busy passing Johnston's orders along the line. Sherman called this new obstacle "the bold and striking twin mountain." Illinois Major James A. Connolly was more descriptive when he wrote, "Kennesaw Mountain is I should think about 700 feet high and consists of two points or peaks, separated by a narrow gorge running across the top. The mountain swells up like a great bulb from the plain." Big Kennesaw was 700 feet high with the second of the "twin" peaks, Little Kennesaw, rising to a height of 400 feet.

In Johnston's first days on Kennesaw, ladies and gentlemen from Atlanta rode up the mountain to observe the scene below. Their presence was galling to Union soldiers who felt it showed "disdain for the legions of the North." It brought a mixed reaction from their own soldiers. Albert Quincy Porter saw Atlanta belles looking at the enemy through spyglasses and heard "their voices ringing out in merry laughter." "It seems strange they can laugh where there is so much misery and destruction all around," he confided to his diary. After a few civilians were killed the excursions to Kennesaw were halted.

When Johnston pulled back on June 19 Sherman had at first believed he was retreating to the Chattahoochee but, as he recalled, "we were soon undeceived." Aware that his adversary was dug in on his Kennesaw line, he weighed his old policy of dodging Johnston against a more recent urge to strike straight ahead. Sherman ordered Thomas to mass his 130 guns and open on the enemy above. Union soldiers stopped their ears against the roar and watched the projectiles sail overhead. A member of the Seventy-sixth Ohio "laughed" as he watched Rebels dodge the shells, while another Ohio infantryman watched "sheets of white flame" rise at night "like so many sky rockets," creating "weird, unearthly reflections on the clouds." Word passed around a Wisconsin unit's rifle pits that Sherman was either going to take the mountain or "fill it full of old iron."

The Rebels had a bird's eye view of the shells, which "roared, hissed and howled" up the mountain and were intermingled with the incessant "pop-pop-pop of musketry." Andy Neal, of Florida's Marion Light Infantry, counted thirty-one holes in his unit's flag, riddled because it would not be lowered as long as the Union's "striped rag" remained unfurled. A member of the Eighteenth Arkansas complained that the shells clipped trees and rained their tops down on their heads. W. B. Corbitt of the Fourth Tennessee Cavalry was disdainful of the flying shells and believed their only effect was the "consternation which it produced among the teamsters in the rear." When Confederate artillery fired back it cheered a Georgia soldier who boasted, "Old Kennesaw thundered in reply from his summit to his base. Oh, it was terribly sublime."

While the Cumberlanders' guns wailed away, Sherman sent McPherson to nibble at Johnston's right flank urged on by a hope that he might cut the railroad and force the Rebels off Kennesaw. From June 19 to June 21 McPherson's men fought a series of skirmishes, some of them fierce, but accomplished little.

On the other and more vulnerable end Sherman sent Schofield, supported by Hooker's corps, in an attempt to slide by Johnston and take either Marietta or Smyrna—a strike that, if successful, would be even more menacing to the graybacks on the peak. Starting on the nineteenth, Schofield moved to the southwest. He had shoved back Jackson's cavalry and crossed Nose's Creek when on June 22, at Kolb's Farm, he ran into John Bell Hood.

Kolb's Farm was on the Powder Springs–Marietta road. In the early afternoon of the twenty-second Hood, ordered by Johnston to march to the left to protect Hardee's flank from Union probing, bumped into the Fourteenth Kentucky and the One Hundred and Twenty-third New York of Schofield's advance. He attacked immediately. Hood's impulsive charge was launched without reconnaissance and his troops slowly shoved the Yanks back. Emboldened by this success the reckless Kentuckian ordered a pursuit, which quickly found the bulk of Schofield's force protected by hastily constructed rail works. That morning Schofield had sent out scouts to discover the enemy's location so that he might move into Smyrna and seize the railroad, and while this intelligence was being gathered he and Hooker had their men erect works facing a cleared field.

Rather than pull back in the face of this well-placed foe, and without informing Johnston, Hood pressed the thrust. The Rebels came "shouting and yelling . . . moved forward on a run." "It was a splendid sight," thought one of Hooker's soldiers. When that first charge failed Hood hurled his men forward again just before dusk. The Southerners moved uphill under penetrating artillery and rifle fire: an Alabama soldier shot in the charge wrote that "shell and shot and miney balls flew thick as hale." For an army already badly outnumbered such an attack was madness. Hood lost 1,000 men, mostly from General Stevenson's division.

The Fifty-fourth Virginia sent 450 men into action but reported only 150 fit for duty that night. The Union loss was less than 300.

The Kolb's Farm affray accomplished little. When dawn of June 23 revealed a strong Confederate line blocking Schofield from further thoughts of a march into Smyrna, it became obvious that there would be no easy way to bypass Kennesaw in that quarter with the force available. Also that morning Hooker's fanciful report of the enemy he faced had Sherman raging against the general from the East. On the previous day Hooker had informed his chief that he had "repulsed two heavy attacks" and had asked for reinforcements since "three corps are in front of us." Sherman observed cynically "Hooker must be mistaken; Johnston's army has only three corps," and went to Hooker's command on the twenty-third to "reprove him more gently than the occasion demanded" for his inaccuracies.

It was drizzling when Sherman found Hooker and Schofield. The trio went inside a small church to talk about the action of the twenty-second. Sherman later remembered that Schofield was "very angry" with "Fighting Joe"; after the war the Army of the Ohio's commander did not recall being "very angry" himself, but remembered that Sherman certainly had been. Sherman and Hooker both had prickly personalities; relations between the two men, already tense, became impossible in the one month Hooker had remaining in Georgia. "From that he began to sulk," wrote Sherman. He thought Hooker "seemed jealous of all the army commanders, because in years, former rank, and experience, he thought he was our superior."

By June 23 Sherman's thoughts had returned to the idea of frontal assault. Never very patient, Sherman was quick to anger these days. He ran his fingers through his hair, rubbed his beard, smoked cigars constantly, and paced back and forth as the rain splashed down and Rebel bullets whizzed by. "The whole country is one vast fort. Our lines are now in close contact and the fighting incessant, with a good deal of artillery," Sherman wired Halleck on the twenty-third. He added in dismay, "as fast as we gain one position, the enemy has another all ready."

Perhaps the old concern about his army's loss of its combat edge was still in his mind, but there were other reasons for Sherman's shift of strategy. McPherson's scouts' latest appreciation of Johnston's adjustments to his line made the bristling mountain fortress appear a little less awesome. When Hood was sent to check Schofield, Loring's corps was shifted eastward to help cover for the departed troops. The Rebel line, still undeniably strong, stretched out for eight to ten miles and must be thin somewhere. An aggressive attack pressed home with the element of

William Tecumseh Sherman.

surprise might succeed. Sherman met with Thomas, McPherson, and Schofield: in his *Memoirs* he wrote that "we all agreed that we could not with prudence stretch out any more, and therefore there was no alternative but to attack 'fortified lines,' a thing carefully avoided up to that time." Schofield, writing later, remembered opposing the idea, and there is evidence that Thomas balked at the change.

Also on Sherman's mind was a fear that had marched with him since Chattanooga—that his failure to press Johnston strongly enough might make it possible for the Army of Tennessee to send reinforcements to the Army of Northern Virginia. A standoff or lengthy delay at Kennesaw might mean failure for both Sherman *and* Grant.

There were other thoughts crowding Sherman's mind as he considered a decision that might be the most important of his military career. He was afraid of appearing too predictable to his opponent; afraid Johnston would believe that Tecumseh Sherman would never attack a stoutly fortified Rebel position. An attack here would jar Johnston's complacency, if he had any, and not permit the luxury of a predictable foe.

Then too, there was Sherman's knowledge that some in his own army thought he was a general who would not fight. In the days just before this campaign began, such whispers had angered him. No one would dare make such charges after an attack on this citadel.

Another force driving Sherman to hurl his men at Kennesaw was mentioned after the conflict by Cincinnati journalist Don Piatt. Piatt's source was John A. Logan. (The newspaperman's dislike for Sherman, coupled with Logan's bitter postwar relations with his old chieftian, place some doubt on the account.) Logan, according to Piatt, reported a scene in McPherson's tent on the night of June 26. The Union commander was reading a newspaper filled with accounts of Grant's war in Virginia when he looked up and said:

> the whole attention of the country was fixed on the Army of the Potomac and that his army was entirely forgotten. Now it would fight. Tomorrow he would order the assault. McPherson quietly said that there was no necessity for the step since Johnston could be outflanked and that the assault would be too dear.

Sherman replied to McPherson, saying "it was necessary to show that his men could fight as well as Grant's." One problem with the Piatt-Logan story is that it makes it appear that Sherman made the decision to attack on the twenty-sixth. The attack order was given on June 24, when Special Field Order 28 told his lieutenants to "make full reconnaissances and preparations to attack the enemy in force on the 27th instant, at 8 a.m. precisely."

It was inevitable that men facing Kennesaw's slopes would compare this objective with experience in past battles. Oliver Howard, a veteran of Gettysburg, thought Johnston's line was far tougher than the one Lee had assaulted in Pennsylvania. Conversely, Sherman remembered Missionary Ridge. Bragg's lines had seemed more defensible and yet many of Thomas's troops slated to strike Kennesaw on the twenty-seventh had stormed up the ridge and routed Bragg. A victory of the same magnitude might collapse Johnston into the Chattahoochee and bring complete victory.

On June 25 and 26 attack plans were decided upon. McPherson would send two Fifteenth Corps divisions against Little Kennesaw, and use the Sixteenth and Seventeenth corps to demonstrate toward Big Kennesaw.

Two of George Thomas's divisions would move up the Dallas road one mile south of McPherson, while Hooker's corps would demonstrate along its front. Schofield, on Thomas's right, would feint as would Kenner Garrard's cavalry well to the north.

When Sherman discussed the Army of the Tennessee's attack with McPherson he said "about half way up the mountain you will find a plateau where there is a peach orchard; it will be a good place to stop and let your men get breath for the assault." He went on to tell his lieutenant about riding up Kennesaw in 1844 and discussing peach growing with a Georgia farmer.

Sherman's attack plan called for only about 20 percent of his force to move forward; the remainder were to be a ready reserve set to support a successful onslaught. Surprise was important, and an early-morning bombardment just before the attack would surely awaken Johnston. The hope was that the two attacks and two feints would keep the Rebel chief guess-

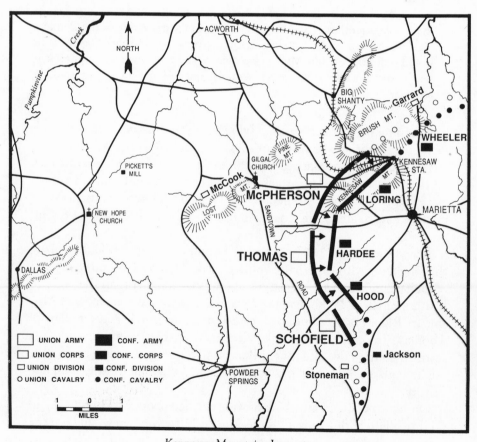

Kennesaw Mountain, June 27.

ing until Thomas's spearhead and possibly McPherson's advance were successful. Sherman's order read, "Each attacking column will endeavor to break a single point in the enemy's line, and make a secure lodgement beyond, and be prepared for following it up toward Marietta and the railroad in case of success."

Word of the impending assault was kept from all of the men and most officers. The twenty-fifth and twenty-sixth passed with occasional skirmish action and sporadic artillery exchanges. Men died even in this random firing. On the twenty-fifth the lieutenant colonel of the Thirty-first Indiana, reading a paper behind the lines, was shot dead by a sniper. The next day a Georgia soldier, well behind the lines, was killed as he kneeled to drink cooling water from a spring. There were few safe places, and carelessness brought sudden death.

The defenders along Kennesaw's heights watched this random action and wondered when and where Sherman's stymied army would launch its next slide around them. It was about time, they thought, for the dance to begin again.

When the sun rose on Monday the twenty-seventh the opposing lines were calm. To Tennessee's Sam Watkins the "heavens seemed made of brass, and the earth of iron. . . . It seemed that the arch-angel of Death stood and looked on with outstretched wings, while all the earth was

View from Kennesaw Mountain.

silent." Then the silence ended and the music of battle began. Two hundred Union guns slammed shells into Johnston's line as one defender shouted, "Hell has broke loose in Georgia, sure enough!" Poised to charge, Theodore Upson of the One Hundredth Indiana watched the white puffs dot the hillside and hoped everything had "been smashed to smithereens."

At about eight o'clock the artillery growled and muttered into silence, and the infantry stepped forward. The rain had ended the previous day and a clear, very warm day greeted the Blue attackers. Of his men's objective "Black Jack" Logan had written the day before, "We have to climb . . . and assault earth works of a very formidable character. The men are in good heart, though they have a bloody road before them." The road was to be bloody indeed. For a time the Union soldiers were covered by woods and spurs of the mountain, but well in front of Johnston's lines they came out into clear view.

Sam French's Confederate division, on Loring's left, exploded into action, pouring a deadly fire into Morgan Smith's division of Logan's Fifteenth Corps, which, supported by C. C. Walcutt's brigade, was making its way up Little Kennesaw. Smith had raised the tough Eighth Missouri Infantry along the St. Louis riverfront, and fought in most of the Army of the Tennessee's battles, rising to division command—and developing a reputation for profanity that equalled Jeff C. Davis. Surely he must have reinforced that reputation on this day. The 5,500 men following Smith and Walcutt had to deal with Rebel fire and also with the rocky, uneven terrain. Between the Rebel rifle pits and the main line a bloody struggle raged with the combatants using clubbed muskets, bayonets, and even fists. The defenders also rolled large stones and threw rocks, often with telling effect, at their attackers. Smith's men got to "within about thirty feet of the enemy's main line," he later reported, but there they "staggered and sought cover as best they could behind logs and rocks." A few men from the Fifty-fifth and One Hundred and Eleventh Illinois reached French's trenches but were killed climbing the parapets. Logan, who had ridden his horse "Old John" up the slope, urging his men on, reported that "after vainly attempting to carry the works . . . and finding that so many gallant men were being uselessly slain, I ordered them to retire to the last line of works captured, and placed them in a defensible condition."

French had his foe pinned down and most of the Northerners were unable either to go forward or back down the hill. The Yankee survivors counted themselves lucky and did not forget this day. "It was almost sure death to take your face out of the dust," recalled one, while another added, "It was only necessary to expose a hand to procure a furlough."

To kill the enemy, observed a Tennessean up the hill, "all that was necessary was to load and shoot." Of Smith's 4,000 veterans, 563 fell before Confederate guns.

One mile to the south the divisions of Jeff C. Davis and John Newton, from Thomas's army, moved forward. This was Sherman's main thrust, and it aimed up the Dallas road at Benjamin Cheatham's outnumbered division. Although he had a force only one-half the size of his attackers, Cheatham's men could fire from behind head logs and were aided by French's gunners who, having stopped McPherson, could swing their fire to the left.

The point at which the men of the Fourth and Fourteenth corps struck, soon to be known as "Dead Angle," was a salient where Hardee's line veered sharply southward. Cheatham's soldiers, aided by French and Pat Cleburne—whose men also poured fire into the attackers—littered the hill with dead and wounded. An Ohio soldier remembered "the air seemed filled with bullets, gave one the sensation experienced when moving swiftly against a heavy rain or sleet storm." Another saw Rebel trenches as "veritable volcanoes . . . vomiting forth fire and smoke."

There were acts of heroism on both sides as the armies merged. The color bearer of the Fifty-second Ohio climbed on the enemy parapet and was challenged by a Southern officer. In the deadly struggle the bearer killed his adversary only to be shot by the Confederates. Fourth Corps brigadier Charles G. Harker led his men forward yelling "Forward and take those works!" He was mortally wounded as he closed on the Rebel lines. Also a casualty of this attack was Colonel Dan McCook, one of Davis's brigade commanders and in those long-ago days before the war, Sherman's law partner. A member of the "Fighting McCooks of Ohio," a family which sent fourteen men to wear the blue, Dan McCook's father and two brothers had already been killed in action. Before the charge the prophetic McCook recited Horatius' speech: "Then how can men die better than facing fearful odds." McCook went down, yelling to his men, "come on boys, the day is won." Before the day was over he was dead.

In front of Cleburne's works the exchange started a brush fire and wounded Cumberlanders in its path were about to burn to death when Arkansas lieutenant colonel William H. Martin leaped up on his works waving a white handkerchief. His truce brought a cease-fire, and Federal and Confederate soldiers dragged the wounded away from the flames. That done, fighting began again. For this act a Federal officer presented Martin with a brace of pistols.

Hard hit, Jeff C. Davis lost 824 men, John Newton, 654. By eleven o'clock it was evident that further advance was impossible.

On his army's left at Signal Hill, Sherman could see McPherson halted.

He knew that Schofield, on the far right, who had made the day's most significant advance, could provide no relief for Thomas. In the early afternoon, evidently still hoping Thomas could spring a miracle, Sherman asked "the Rock of Chickamauga," "Do you think you can carry any part of the enemy's line today?" He told Thomas that McPherson had been stopped, but said to Pap, "I will order the assault if you think you can succeed at any point." The answer came back, "We have already lost heavily today without gaining any material advantage. One or two more such assaults would use up this army."

Of the 12,000 men Sherman had thrown at Kennesaw, about 3,000 were casualties. The entire Confederate toll was between 750 and 1,000 men.

Thomas was right. Sherman would not use up his army, and for the last three days of June he worked on the resumption of his flanking strategy. He made the decision after dark on the twenty-seventh and spent the next few days waiting for the roads to dry and deciding which direction to arc around Kennesaw.

McPherson's "whiplash" Army of the Tennessee would swing behind Thomas and link up with Schofield for a push toward Fulton just beyond Smyrna and three miles north of the Chattahoochee. In moving the Army of the Tennessee, Sherman risked losing his slender thread with the North, the Western & Atlantic. He believed the risk was small since Johnston, who could observe his every move, would surely withdraw in the face of McPherson's encirclement rather than lunging northward to take the railroad. Yet just to make his rail line more secure, Sherman dismounted Garrard's cavalrymen and put them into McPherson's abandoned trenches near the tracks. The decision to flank was welcomed by Thomas, who told his commander, "I think it decidedly better than butting against breastworks twelve feet thick."

While the new plans were in the making, a truce was negotiated with the Confederates. The object was the burial of the dead, primarily Union dead, lying in the summer heat on Kennesaw's slopes. On June 30 men from both armies joined in the grisly task of handling bodies exposed to the Georgia sun for three days. Trenches were dug, and officers and troops were dragged into common graves. The men were forbidden to rifle the dead. For some Kennesaw veterans this was the most vivid memory of the struggle there. A Rebel wrote long after the conflict, "I get sick now when I happen to think about it." No wonder. Alexander Ayers, of the One Hundred and Twenty-fifth Illinois, reported being able to identify only a few Union dead and those only by their uniforms since "their bodies and especially their faces were a moving mass of maggots."

When they finished the burial details, Gray and Blue soldiers chatted,

Benjamin Franklin Cheatham.

exchanged newspapers, and traded coffee for tobacco. Some Confederate officers were present and drew particular attention. Lyman Widney of the Thirty-fourth Illinois recorded in his diary that General Cheatham, whose soldiers held the "Dead Angle" in front of which many Federals died, was there and noted that Cheatham's "looks did not belie his reputation as a rough and ready fighter, dressed as he was in coarse gray pants, tucked into rough unpolished boots, blue flannel shirt and a battered gray hat, no coat, vest or mark of rank. He looked as if he had made his headquarters in the ditch with his men." One Federal talked to Southern officers who "were certain of success," and believed "the North and South could never be again united." Alexander Ayers joined Rebel officers and they "drank and smoked together like brothers." Their fraternization over, they turned in opposite directions, and said as they departed, "I hope to miss you, Yank, if I happen to shoot in your direction," or, "May I never hit you Johnny if we fight again."

The carnage, and his decision to attack, was on Sherman's mind. He wrote his wife Ellen on June 29, "I begin to regard the death and mangling of a couple of thousand men as a small affair, a kind of morning dash." "It may be well that we become hardened," he wrote, and concluded ominously, "The worst of the war is not yet begun." The western commander told Halleck, "The assault I made was no mistake, I had to do it," and defended his move by saying that both his army and the

Rebels "had settled down into the condition that the assault of lines formed no part of my game." He felt there was a significant advantage in proving a point and wrote in his campaign report, "I yet claim it produced good fruit, as it demonstrated to General Johnston that I would assault, and that boldly." He also found it a defense of his actions to compare his losses with Grant's much larger totals in Virginia and wrote Thomas, "At times assaults are necessary and inevitable." In his report he did call Kennesaw a "failure . . . for which I assume the entire responsibility."

In his postwar reminiscences General Joseph E. Johnston saluted the courage of those who attacked on the twenty-seventh: "the characteristic fortitude of the northwestern soldiers held them under a close and destructive fire long after reasonable hope of success was gone."

Sherman was right. Kennesaw was a failure and his attack had squandered the courage of those northwestern soldiers and had handed Johnston one of the most clear cut victories of the Atlanta campaign. Yet the triumph brought little real advantage to the Southern cause. Sherman's smoothly rolling rail line kept his army well supplied, and his larger force could absorb the Kennesaw losses and move southward with hardly a hitch in stride.

On July 2 McPherson's army, together with Schofield's force—which had moved forward smartly since the twenty-seventh and had taken a strong position south of Olley's Creek—began the push toward the Chattahoochee and around Johnston's left. Observing this latest movement, a Confederate, taken prisoner by the One Hundred and Third Illinois, drawled in exasperation, "Sherman'll never go to hell. He will flank the devil and make heaven in spite of the guards."

The next afternoon, as McPherson's army took the lead from Schofield, the two young generals sat on their horses and talked about old times back home. McPherson told his friend he was engaged to be married and asked when he thought he might be free to go north for the ceremony. "After the capture of Atlanta, I guess," said Schofield.

When Sherman started McPherson, he also ordered Thomas's army and Garrard's men to probe toward Kennesaw at dawn on July 3 to discover if the Rebels had withdrawn. Up early, Sherman borrowed a large tripod-mounted spyglass from Colonel Orlando Poe, his chief engineer; through it, from his vantage on Signal Hill, he saw his pickets on the crest of Kennesaw.

With the collapse of the Kennesaw line the civilians who had not already fled southward from Marietta and Smyrna joined the refugee tide to Atlanta and beyond. Mary Mallard, one of Robert Manson Myers's "Children of Pride," had remained in Atlanta and expressed "unbounded confidence" in Johnston and the army. Nevertheless, she added "It would be a great relief . . . could we be assured General Johnston would not fall back to the Chattahoochee." After listing a number of items that her family had already sent out of the city, Mrs. Mallard added bitingly, "Some of the Jews have removed their possessions."

On the day Sherman struck Kennesaw, Lavender Ray, in Atlanta, wrote his father in Newnan, warning him of the mounting danger and urging him to prepare to refugee. "I would by no means let the girls stay exposed to the insults of the excorable Yankees," he advised. "It is possible that a bloody dutchman or puritan may be in command and harass you continually with his insults," warned Ray.

The Stars and Stripes flew over Kennesaw, but where was Johnston? Could the Rebels be caught north of the Chattahoochee and uncovered by fortifications? The Union chief had his staff scurrying in all directions organizing "a pursuit by every possible road, hoping to catch Johnston in the confusion of retreat, especially at the crossing of the Chattahoochee River." The infantry would keep the pressure up, but the cavalry was what was needed to locate the Rebels and provoke them to turn and stand with the river at their backs.

But Kenner Garrard, who had learned his trade in the East, was not aggressive enough for an impatient commander who could taste a quick end to his campaign. When Tecumseh Sherman reached Marietta on the morning of the third he found the Rebs gone and the town in the hands of Thomas's advance. His cavalry was nowhere to be seen and Sherman, furious with the leader of his mounted arm, roared, "Where's Gar'd? Where in hell's Gar'd?" After a time Garrard rode up, told Sherman that organizing his column had delayed him, and heard the general say, "Get out of here quick!" When Garrard asked, "What shall I do?" all he got was "Don't make a damned bit of difference so you get out of here and go for the rebs."

There would be no attack and no quick victory north of the Chattahoochee. Johnston, more impressed than ever by his opponent who quickly flanked rather than launching another frontal assault, was in Smyrna, firmly established in strong works he had earlier ordered constructed for just such a situation. Rottenwood and Nickajack creeks further covered his flanks and Sherman was not ready to repeat Kennesaw.

Sherman did tell Thomas on the third that "We will never have such a chance again," and emphasized in almost hysterically aggressive language, "the importance of the most intense energy of attack tonight and in the morning." "Press with vehemence at any cost of life and material," he told "Old Slow Trot," but on neither the third nor fourth was there such an attack. One year ago Independence Day had been a great day for the Union cause, but this July 4 would pass without a repeat performance. Thomas's army did fire all day long sounding like an extraordinarily large July 4 celebration.

In spite of his talk of a strike "at any cost of life and material," General Sherman once again relied on McPherson. The Army of the Tennessee, led by Grenville M. Dodge's Sixteenth Corps, swung around the Confederate left and by dawn on July 5 found that Johnston had once again slipped away. The opposing armies were both within five miles of the river. Sherman, his thoughts ever on delivering a crushing blow on the Chattahoochee's northern bank, pressed forward. Near Vining's Station he found Johnston again, and again he was well posted in what the frustrated but impressed Ohio West Pointer called "the best line of field intrenchments I have ever seen."

When he wrote *Advance and Retreat* after the Civil War, General Hood did not portray Johnston's withdrawal from Kennesaw to the river as an orderly movement from one strong line to another in the face of a large enemy flanking force. He said that McPherson and Schofield led "a few troops to make a rumbling sound in our rear," and implied Johnston's cowardice and stupidity when "we folded up our tents, as usual, and retreated."

The two armies had reached the last major natural barrier shielding Atlanta. Joe Johnston's next move might still give Sherman his chance to crush the Rebels, but Sherman had learned that his enemy was not likely to be too careless. Nevertheless, the Rebel retreat, as well handled as it had been, had allowed the general from Ohio to march his army to the gates of Atlanta.

Sherman's troops agreed with a member of the Twentieth Corps who believed "our army has been very successful." He added that the men were in the "best of spirits," feasting on "black-berries and green apples for the sauce, so we live good again."

On the other side, a Tennessee lieutenant reported on July 5 that "the people around here are beginning to fear that Sherman will get Atlanta." He disagreed and added, "Our army is in the best of spirits." A Rebel captain felt, "Our confidence in ourselves and Gen. Johnston is unshaken notwithstanding we have retreated eighty miles." But Confederate soldier James Watkins disagreed. On July 4 he told his wife Frankey, "I think the Yankees will have Atlanta in a few days," and added the next week, "I think our Confederacy is about to go up the spout." He missed Frankey so much he was not sure he cared: "Frankey, I had rather Sea you than to have the Southern Confederacy," he wrote her.

Near Vining's Station the Federal commander could at last actually see the gates of Atlanta or at least, as Illinois major Connolly, serving in the Fourteenth Corps, wrote to his wife, "The 'domes and minarets and spires' of Atlanta . . . glittering in the sunlight before us, only eight miles distant." When Union troops heard that the "Gate City" was in sight some climbed trees to improve their view, and "such a cheer went up as must have been heard even in the entrenchments of the doomed city itself." Connolly and his men were soon joined by Sherman and Thomas who "for a moment, gazed at the glittering prize in silence." Then the major saw Sherman "stepping nervously about, his eyes sparkling and his face all aglow." The excited Illinoisan, and perhaps Sherman and Thomas as well, seemed to see Samarkand rise in the distance instead of an important but small city in Georgia. Atlanta did have domes and an occasional church spire but not a single minaret. The Union officer might be forgiven the excesses of his description. After nine weeks, more than one hundred miles, and the loss of more than 17,000 of his comrades, his army's objective was in sight; Major Connolly could say, "Mine eyes have beheld the promised land."

# 9

# Feel Down Strong on Atlanta

John McAllister Schofield stood on the north bank of the Chattahoochee River, reconnoitering on a hot day in early July, 1864. The native
of Gerry, New York, was not yet thirty-three years old, a little less than
average in height, and balding noticeably. Ordered by Sherman to make
a crossing upstream from the formidable Rebel fortifications, Schofield
looked across a swift and deep river, swollen by incessant rain until few
fords could be found. The Chattahoochee was 150 yards wide, with an
uneven bottom and muddy banks. It presented a tough challenge, but
Schofield thought he had found the right spot.

It was where the stream known as Soap's Creek flowed into the river.
After winding generally south for several miles, the creek cut through a
deep ravine, paralleling the Chattahoochee for a considerable distance
before making a short curve to empty into it. Just below the mouth of
the creek, near Phillip's Ferry, the South bank of the Chattahoochee
appeared to be held by only a light force of Confederate cavalry. To cross
in the face of strong enemy resistance would be difficult, but the situation
seemed favorable for a surprise attack. Schofield thought he might get
across the river before the Rebels knew what had happened.

Sherman, too, thought this looked like the opportunity for which he
had been searching. Schofield wanted to reconnoiter more fully the next
day, but Sherman had learned that the main body of the Gray cavalry
was several miles downstream, on the left flank of Johnston's army. The
time to act was at hand. Schofield was instructed to cross as soon as
possible and entrench on the far bank.

At daylight on July 8 Schofield marched, Jacob Cox's division in the

John M. Schofield.

lead—ready to cross by surprise if possible, by force if necessary. From Colonel Simon Cameron's brigade fifty "tall and strong" men were selected, constituting an advance column. Schofield planned to put them across the Chattahoochee at an old fish dam, about half a mile above the mouth of Soap's Creek. The water would be up to their mouths at times, and their footing on the piled-up stones would be slippery. If they made it across, the rest of the brigade—except one reserve regiment—would follow immediately by the same means, and push down the river on the opposite side, attacking and driving off any Rebel force encountered. This would place Cameron's men in position to cover the second phase of the operation: a wooden pontoon bridge, launched in Soap's Creek well above its mouth, far enough to be concealed from any graycoat lookouts. Loaded with the Twelfth Kentucky Infantry, under Lieutenant Colonel Laurence H. Rousseau of Robert K. Byrd's brigade, the pontoon floats were to emerge into the main stream thirty minutes after Cameron's men began crossing at the fish dam. Within a matter of minutes the pontoons should be in place across the Chattahoochee.

The rest of Byrd's brigade, advancing simultaneously to the river's

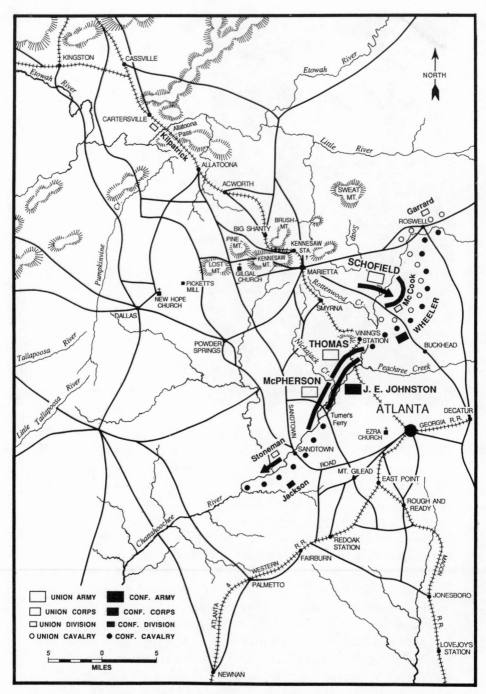

Crossing the Chattahoochee.

edge, would provide covering fire for the pontoons if necessary, and be ready to cross as soon as the bridge was in position. Artillery was brought up, screened by brush along the crest of the ridge at the river, where it could be wheeled into position for firing at the instant the crossing began. Along the Chattahoochee's north bank, the land was heavily wooded right down to the water's edge. The bank on the south appeared to be eight or ten feet high. Beyond lay open, level bottom, less than a hundred yards wide; and beyond that, a rather steep hill, rising perhaps two hundred feet, and covered with timber.

The crossing was set for half past three in the afternoon. Schofield, atop the ridge, could still see nothing on the opposite side except a cavalry outpost with a single piece of artillery. He gave the signal to advance. The fifty-man assault column emerged from the woods and started scrambling along the broken rocks in the swift current at the fish dam, holding their guns and ammunition over their heads. Some did not expect to get across alive. A few slipped and went under the water, but were helped up and pushed onward. In a few minutes the fifty were clambering safely up on the Confederate side and others were following. Deploying in a skirmish line, the advance made for the timbered area. "They met with no opposition," General Cox later reported, "the enemy being taken completely by surprise. The whole brigade, except the Twenty-fourth Kentucky Volunteers, was crossed within the half hour and gained the ridge after exchanging only a few shots with the enemy's pickets, which fled."

Then, about four o'clock, twenty-five pontoon floats emerged from the mouth of Soap's Creek, infantry teams perched atop, oarsmen pulling for the other side as fast as possible. "The enemy opened with his single piece of artillery, which was, however, silenced by the simultaneous fire of a battery on the ridge on our side and of the infantry along the river," continued Cox in his report, "the latter keeping up so well-directed a fire of rifles upon the piece that the cannoneers, after firing two shots and running the piece forward from cover to fire again, were driven from the gun without discharging it." General Schofield, differing with Cox only in the number of times the enemy fired, wrote of the action: "The astonished rebels fired a single shot from their single gun, delivered a few random discharges of musketry, and fled, leaving their piece of artillery in our possession. The crossing was secured without the loss of a man." By night a bridge had been laid, and General Cox's entire division was entrenched on the Chattahoochee's south bank.

Many Federal troops were soon crossing the river at several places above Johnston's fortified position. Some incidents, although of minor consequence in the total operation, are remarkable. On July 6, Garrard's cavalry division had captured the village of Roswell on the north bank of the river, the site of several cotton mills that manufactured cloth for the Confederacy. About four hundred young women worked in these factories, as the Yankee troopers quickly discovered. One soldier proposed, presumably tongue in cheek, that factory girls be issued to officers on " 'Special Requisitions' certifying they are for their own use." Many of the soldiers, having had no opportunity for female companionship in weeks or even months, were delighted with any chance for association with the opposite sex, and a dance was soon organized—according to some sources.

Others painted a darker picture. In one story, whiskey was passed around, the resulting delirium of a number of soldiers taking the form of aggression upon several of the women. There is no doubt that once captured, the sheltering, feeding, and safeguarding of hundreds of females in the midst of the diverse sorts found in a field army presented a major discipline problem.

Sherman quickly ordered a program of mass deportation. He wrote to General Joseph D. Webster, a member of his staff at the army's rear in Nashville, instructing that "when they reach Nashville have them sent across the Ohio River and turned loose to earn a living where they won't do us any harm." He concluded: "The women were simply laborers that must be removed from this district." When General Thomas commented that "it seems hard to turn them adrift," Sherman replied that he had ordered General Webster "to dispose of them. They will be sent to Indiana."

The women, joined by others from Sweetwater, were placed in empty supply trains bound for Nashville, from there transported across the Ohio River where they could no longer aid the Confederacy. Some were never able to return to Georgia, as General Thomas had anticipated. An 1896 *Confederate Veteran* article claimed: "Very few if any of these poor women ever saw their native soil again." Meanwhile, the mills were torched. Despite the display of a French flag above one mill, Sherman said the mill should suffer the same fate as the others. In fact, Sherman authorized Garrard specifically in dealing with the alleged French owner: "Should you, under the impulse of natural anger, natural at contemplating such perfidy [to claim immunity from destruction because of foreign allegiance] hang the wretch," he wrote Garrard, "I approve the act beforehand." To Garrard's credit, he let the Frenchman live. According to some accounts the "Frenchman" was only an employee who hoisted the French flag in an attempt to save the property and, presumably, his job.

Sherman's main concern, of course, was for Garrard to get across the river. He wanted him to cross on July 8, but the cavalry leader delayed his attempt until early the next morning. The Northern troopers faced a heavy skirmish fire from the Confederate shore, but with covering fire from the Federal bank, a detachment of Yankees waded into the river and started for the opposite side. Armed with Spencer repeating rifles that fired seven metallic waterproof cartridges, the troopers crouched in the water with only their heads exposed while they worked the lever arm of the weapon. A man would quickly rise from the river, drain the water from the gun's barrel, take a shot, and sink down again with only his head exposed. As soon as he worked the lever, the operation would be repeated. The much-admired Spencer was a weapon that, one Federal officer wrote, "our men adore as the heathen do their idols."

The Rebels, still armed with single-shot, muzzle-loading weapons, watched in astonishment as the Federals bobbed their way across the river. "Look at them Yankee———— —— ————, loading their guns under water!" the amazed Confederates called out to one another. According to a Union soldier, some Rebels were so enthralled that they ceased firing and instead of fleeing remained on the south bank to surren-der, "anxious only to see the guns that could be loaded . . . underwater."

Also on July 9, a detachment from Brigadier General Edward M. McCook's cavalry division, led by Colonel James P. Brownlow (the son of noted east Tennessee Unionist William G. "Parson" Brownlow) was ordered across the Chattahoochee at Cochran's Ford, where the water was deep. In an intriguing demonstration of "raw courage," Brownlow's men crossed the river in the nude, equipped only with guns, cartridge boxes and, of all things, hats—according to McCook's report. Once on the south bank, an attack by the naked men drove off the Confederates, several of whom were captured. "They would have got more," declared McCook, "but the rebels had the advantage in running through the bushes with clothes on. It was certainly one of the funniest sights of the war, and a very successful raid for naked men to make. Everything is quiet along the line, and citizens on the other side say the enemy were totally unprepared for a crossing on this flank."

Indeed, during the evening of July 9, because of the Yankee threat to the Rebel right flank, General Joseph Johnston decided to withdraw the Confederate army to the south bank of the Chattahoochee. Sherman's plan had worked well. Taking advantage of his numerical superiority, Sherman had gradually extended his lines to threaten the Confederate right flank, all the time feinting against their left with Stoneman's cav-alry division, which supposedly was searching for a ford below Turner's Ferry several miles to the south.

Yet the bluecoat's victory had come too easily. Sherman even later asserted, in a rare criticism of Johnston, that the Confederate commander had neglected a great opportunity during this operation and "had lain comparatively idle while we got control of both banks of the river above him." Sherman also called the Rebel fortifications at the Chatta-hoochee "the best line of field intrenchments I have ever seen." Quite possibly the Union victory at the Chattahoochee—the last of the major rivers between Chattanooga and Atlanta—is more accurately explained by Rebel blundering than Yankee brilliance.

WHAT had been happening in the Confederate high command? To begin with, the formidable Rebel line on the north bank of the Chattahoochee was not Joe Johnston's conception, but had originated with his chief of artillery, Brigadier General Francis A. Shoup. Some two weeks earlier, while at Marietta, Shoup realized that the army would soon be forced to retreat again. Thus he approached Johnston with a plan for making a fight at the Chattahoochee. Shoup's proposal dealt with key factors. Faced with the problem of defending a river whose low south bank was domi-nated for some distance by high ground on the north side (both above and below the railroad bridge) Shoup advocated that the Confederates make their stand on the north bank; and in a somewhat novel system of fortifications that would enable a small portion of the army to hold the railroad span and five other bridges at their back, while the main body of the army would be freed to attack a portion of Sherman's army when-ever the Yankee commander made a move to cross the river.

"The General was at once taken with the project," recalled Shoup "and began eagerly to discuss it with me." Even if Shoup exaggerated Johnston's interest in the plan, it is a fact that Johnston ordered the line prepared. By the last days of June a thousand slaves were at work on the fortification. By early July heavy guns from Mobile had been brought to strength the position.

While the generals contemplated the dreary prospect of falling back once more, some of the Rebel privates, in the time-honored fashion of all armies, depended on whiskey to relieve the unpleasantness of reality. At Marietta, "an amicable and lovable fellow" who was called "Henry B.," went into town and rapidly absorbed far too much of a potent brand of Georgia whiskey. Soon, Henry's condition began to show its conse-quences. He leaned against a tree and soliloquized: "Drunk! Here I am drunk! No doubt my poor girl is at home now praying for my poor soul and here I am drunk like a fool on Sunday!"

Meanwhile, as "Henry B." and, no doubt, some of his peers consumed their liquor, work progressed at the Chattahoochee. When completed, the Rebel line began a quarter of a mile above the railway bridge, swept in a rough semicircle until distant about a mile from the river, then returned to it approximately three miles below the bridge. The nature of the line was not a system of earth works, but a string of detached log redoubts, packed in with earth, and placed about 240 feet apart, so that they mutually supported each other. Manned by a company of 80 soldiers, the redoubts were positioned so that each would be protected by cross fire from half a dozen others within easy range. In an interesting 1895 article published in the *Confederate Veteran,* Shoup recorded many construction details, including connecting lines for rapid transfer of troops to threatened points and reinforcement against artillery bombardment.

Within Shoup's line was ample room for maneuver, so that the army could be massed to attack a weak point of the enemy line. Or if Sherman attempted to cross the river with part of his force, the Confederates, with several bridges at their back, could quickly move to contest the attempt on either the north or south bank, with good prospect of success. Shoup later wrote that such people as Hardee, Cleburne, and many general officers expressed their confidence in the position. Also Shoup declared that he considered it "the only remaining position [before Atlanta] which offered any decided advantage for defense."

Obviously General Johnston was not as impressed with the Chattahoochee line of fortifications as Shoup—or Sherman. One wonders what Johnston was thinking. As the last possible chances to thwart a decisive Union military campaign (and that in the midst of a critical Northern political campaign) were rapidly slipping beneath the sea of Confederate "might-have-beens," the Rebel commander seemed strangely complacent. He appeared, considering both his lack of action and his few, laconic communications with the government (marked by a touch of aloofness), to be almost out of touch with reality. Sherman's words describing Johnston—"idle while we got control of both banks of the river above him"—are not exaggerated.

The Confederate commander, from all evidence, was totally deceived about where Sherman would cross the Chattahoochee. Apparently the Federal feint against the downstream crossings confirmed in Johnston's mind what he already expected. Earlier he had instructed Shoup to extend regular entrenchments three miles farther downstream, to cover Mason and Turner's ferry—an order which Shoup said he found disturbing, both because it would consume precious time and seemed to indicate that Johnston did not really understand his plan after all; or was not fully committed to it.

Convinced that the Federal threat would be on his left flank, Johnston did not take precautions to anticipate or prevent a crossing upstream. Yet the decided advantages to the Federals of an upstream crossing were unmistakable. Confederate defenses extended only a quarter of a mile above the Western & Atlantic railroad bridge but more than six miles below it, meaning the Yankees could remain much closer to their railroad supply line with an upstream crossing. Also, they would have both a more direct route to Atlanta and be in excellent position to cut the Georgia Railroad coming in to Atlanta through Decatur, thus severing Johnston's army from its line of contact with Richmond.

Nevertheless, Johnston deployed most of his cavalry to watch the downstream crossings, leaving little more than scouting parties to observe possible upstream crossings at such places as Powers' Ferry, Isham's Ford, Johnson's Ferry, Phillip's Ferry, and Roswell Ford, all within easy striking distance of the Union forces. And even after Johnston knew that the Yankees had appeared in force northeast of his defensive line on July 5 and 6, he still made no attempt to determine if they might be about to force a crossing of the river. When he finally learned that the Federals were over the Chattahoochee, Johnston's decision was to retire his entire army to the south bank, simply abandoning the laboriously wrought works on the opposite side.

Still he had a great opportunity: a chance to strike with overwhelming force, and smash a relatively small, isolated segment of Federals on the south bank of the river. But unfortunately for the Rebels, Johnston had no idea how many Federals were across the river, having failed to deploy the troops that might have provided such vital information. His decision

South Bank of the Chattahoochee River.

was to withdraw still farther, retiring the mass of his infantry another three miles to high ground overlooking Peachtree Creek, while Sherman crossed the river unmolested.

Opportunity still stared Johnston in the face. For several days while crossing the Chattahoochee, Sherman's forces were badly divided—and this time Johnston knew it. At one point the Yankees were divided by the river and scattered over a twenty-mile front. Yet Johnston did not attack.

Perhaps a statement made by General Shoup years later, as he described his conversation with Johnston at Marietta, points to the most likely explanation of Johnston's lethargic and puzzling conduct of operations. Shoup said he asked Johnston, before suggesting the Chattahoochee fortifications, if the commander had any specific plans as to his movement after leaving Marietta. Wrote Shoup: "He replied that he had not—that he should be compelled to make the best of his way across the river." Shoup's account, although written years afterward, reveals Johnston in a manner consistent with the general's own 1864 words during the latter stages of the campaign. When Jefferson Davis pressed Johnston about the details of his plans for holding Atlanta, an inquiry dated July 16, Johnston's brief reply said he must remain on the defensive and that his plan would "depend upon that of the enemy." His purpose, he declared, was "mainly to watch for an opportunity to fight to advantage."

Throughout the entire campaign, basically, Johnston seems to have been reacting to what Sherman did. He does not appear to have had any overall, carefully conceived strategy. This is the only answer that makes sense when one examines what the Southern commander actually did—or more accurately, failed to do—and compares it with his later contradictory explanations.

In his report to Richmond in late 1864, Johnston declared that he never intended to fight north of the Chattahoochee; rather, he meant to draw Sherman as deep into Georgia as possible before turning to fall upon the Yankee invader. On the other hand, in a telegram to Jefferson Davis in May, while heavily involved in the struggle with Sherman, Johnston maintained he would have fought north of the Oostanaula River had he not been outflanked by Sherman at Calhoun. When set against his later campaign report, that communiqué could be interpreted as evidence that Johnston was willfully misleading Richmond about his intentions.

Also, in his memoirs, Johnston indicated that he would have preferred an initial line at Calhoun rather than Dalton. But what difference did it really make whether the first line was at Dalton or Calhoun if Johnston originally intended to retreat all the way to the south bank of the Chattahoochee, regardless? Again in his memoirs, and elsewhere, Johnston talked about a Peachtree Creek strategy—that he meant to ambush Sherman, not immediately south of the Chattahoochee, but three or four miles still farther south at Peachtree Creek, when Sherman presumably would have to divide his army to cross that stream. Yet, clearly contradicting both the Chattahoochee and the Peachtree strategy, Johnston (for once at least) had seemed on the verge of launching an attack at Cassville when he delivered his "I lead you to battle" speech. Even his plan to attack at Cassville, however, was projected on the basis that Sherman would divide the Federal army to march on separate roads. Johnston's plan of attack was simply a reaction to an expected move by Sherman.

Taking the campaign as a whole, another major trouble with Johnston was that he was not very aggressive. In fact, the only time in his military career that Johnston launched an attack was in Virginia, on the peninsula between the James and the York rivers a few miles from Richmond, at Seven Pines (Fair Oaks) in the late spring of 1862. There he had been twice wounded, once in the right shoulder by a musket ball and, a few minutes later, severely in the chest by a heavy fragment of shell. Now, during the long retreat from Dalton to Atlanta, the situation for making an attack never had appeared quite right to Johnston.

Time and again he had held strong positions. Time and again he made statements of intention to fight, only to revise his plans and eventually retreat. Granting that more than once he had good reason not to attack, or not to stand and fight, it is the cumulative factor that forms the ultimate blotch on the Virginian's banner. Johnston was of a conservative, cautious nature, which seemed to keep him from battle unless convinced that every advantage was his. Yet one can never hope to "cross every t and dot every i" when writing a plan for battle. Johnston let too many opportunities pass him by that an aggressive commander would have seized upon.

Not only does Johnston seem to have lacked both an overall plan for coping with Sherman and an aggressive temperament; he was his own worst enemy in still another sense. He refused, for whatever reason, to communicate adequately with Richmond. Perhaps he was troubled by how readily military information leaked out at the Confederate capital. Maybe he was piqued by past injustices, as he perceived them, perpetrated by President Davis. Or possibly Johnston's laconic, inadequate communications return to the first criticism, that the general had never devised a specific strategy for coping with Sherman.

In his discussion in *Autumn of Glory*, Thomas L. Connelly observed that Johnston's lack of communication with Richmond "almost approached condescension." Stating that secrecy was "not necessarily evidence of a great strategic mind at work," Connelly suggests that, to the contrary, Johnston may have been so uncommunicative "because he lacked any overall plan for dealing with Sherman. A disturbing looseness to Johnston's planning belies a cautious, crafty general employing Fabian tactics to draw Sherman deep within Georgia for destruction."

Whatever the reason, Johnston could not afford the luxury, as criticism mounted against him at Richmond and he retreated to the suburbs of Atlanta, of not keeping the president fully informed about the military situation and his own intentions. Yet Johnston not only told Davis very little, and that in general terms; he also misrepresented the facts when he did send estimates of Federal strength and casualties. These he exaggerated—the former apparently to prove his need for more soldiers; the latter to indicate his successful management of an outnumbered army in continual retreat. For instance, as late as July 16 he told Davis that he could not take offensive action because Sherman outnumbered him two to one. By this time, however, some of the Richmond authorities were skeptical about Johnston's statistics and therefore doubtful of anything he said—when indeed he said anything. (While Sherman did have a decided advantage, it was not as great as two to one.) To make matters still worse, Johnston seemed oblivious of the political implications of his retreat to the outskirts of Atlanta.

John Bell Hood, seeing the possibility of getting command of Johnston's army, might send damaging information to Richmond. Braxton Bragg might channel uncomplimentary reports to Davis about Johnston's plans for the defense of Atlanta. A number of politicians might urge Davis to remove Johnston. Regardless of all these factors, Johnston was his own worst enemy and handled the campaign in such a manner as to eventually compel Davis to remove him. This the president did on July 17, convinced that Johnston could neither be depended upon to attack Sherman nor to hold Atlanta.

And now Hood, the army's newly appointed commander, must try to halt Sherman. What manner of man was this young general, charged with defending Atlanta? And why had Jefferson Davis chosen him for the position?

No Civil War officer on either side had experienced a more rapid rise in rank than Hood. The Kentuckian advanced from a lieutenant in 1861 to a division commander by 1862, distinguishing himself time and again on the eastern battlefields where he developed a widespread reputation for aggressive leadership. He also became a prominent figure in social life when he visited Richmond. Mary Chesnut detected a "fierce light" in Hood's eyes, which she thought was "the light of battle." Perhaps what she thought she saw was the light of amour, for in Richmond Hood met

John Bell Hood.

and pursued a vivacious young woman, Sally Preston, popularly known as "Buck," with the same degree of passion he displayed on the battlefield.

Yet neither his love for "Buck," nor the severe wound at Gettysburg that left his left arm useless, dampened Hood's ardor for war. As a corps commander at bloody Chickamauga Hood led the assault column that broke through the Union line, only to be knocked from his horse at the height of the triumph by a rifle shot in his thigh, which necessitated amputation of his right leg. Afterward, as he recovered strength, Hood yearned to return to the battlefield, to repeat the same aggressive tactics that had won him fame.

It was the pattern of a life. From a childhood adulation of power, weaponry, and horsemanship on a Kentucky slave farm through a careless military academy career (he was on the verge of expulsion from West

Point); to the reckless conduct in 1856 that cost a quarter of his Second Cavalry in a fight with Comanches at Devil's River, Texas, through Second Manassas, Sharpsburg, and other Civil War engagements; Hood was always a gambler and a bold, headlong fighter. And, it should be noted, recklessness had proven the key to his success.

Indeed, although Hood's commands were consistent in suffering high rates of killed and wounded, and although General Lee chided him for carelessness and once characterized him as "all lion, none of the fox," Hood's aggressive reputation had won his extremely rapid promotion—from an obscure second lieutenant to the prestigious level of lieutenant general within three years. And now Hood commanded the Army of Tennessee.

But certainly Jefferson Davis had not picked Hood for the position because the crippled Kentuckian was a clear and outstanding choice to lead an army. Even though the president's friend Braxton Bragg had assured him that "if any change [of command] is made," the selection of Hood would give "unlimited satisfaction," Davis was at once placed on guard as Bragg quickly and pertinently added that he did not propose Hood "as a man of genius, or a great general, but as far better in the present emergency than any one we have available."

Why had Davis selected Hood? Not because Hood had any obvious ability to command an army. Not because Hood had continually fawned over Davis while recovering from his wounds at Richmond. Not merely because of Hood's disparaging judgments upon Joe Johnston. And certainly not because, as some critics later claimed, Davis had long wanted to remove Johnston for personal reasons—if that were so, he could have done it long before Johnston reached Atlanta.

Basically, Davis was disappointed with Johnston's strategy of retreat during the campaign from Dalton to the outskirts of Atlanta. The president was convinced that he could not count upon Johnston either to attack Sherman or defend Atlanta. Johnston's last response to Davis while still in command, previously noted, was hardly reassuring. His conduct of the campaign had been even less so. (Johnston's statements that he would not have given up Atlanta without a fight are all after the fact and, therefore, meaningless.) John Bell Hood had the reputation of being an aggressive warrior. At least Davis felt he could depend on Hood to fight—and, as Bragg had indicated, there really were not many officers from whom a choice might be made.

Robert E. Lee could not be sent to Georgia, tied up as he was in the struggle with the Army of the Potomac at Petersburg. Besides, Lee had declined the western command on earlier occasions. Longstreet had been far from satisfactory as an independent commander in Tennessee during the previous year. Bragg, who had left the command after the miserable debacle at Chattanooga, could hardly be returned to command without risking open rebellion by many of the army's generals. Between Beauregard and the president there was personal animosity, and too, the Creole was fighting in Virginia. Kirby-Smith was commanding the Trans-Mississippi department. Polk was dead. People like Stewart, Cheatham, or Stephen Lee did not have as much experience in command as Hood.

There had been one other possibility, however. When Robert E. Lee expressed to Davis his misgivings about Hood, saying he was "a good fighter," but "careless" off the battlefield, he added, pointedly, "General Hardee has more experience in managing an army." Certainly he did.

But Hardee was also one of the group who had opposed Bragg, the problem going all the way back to the Kentucky campaign of 1862. Bragg never forgot such matters. Bragg, of course, was close to the president and advised Davis against Hardee, apparently depicting him as an unaggressive general. It was a like canvas on which Hood portrayed Hardee for the president.

It is ironic that Hardee was the one corps commander who clearly wanted to fight upon at least two occasions early in the campaign: at Adairsville and again at Cassville. But unfortunately for the Confederates, Jefferson Davis evidently accepted the Bragg-Hood interpretation of Hardee as a passive officer. Concluding that he must have an army commander who would fight, and not blessed with an abundance of choice, Davis placed the mantle on Hood.

While no one doubted Hood's courage, which had been demonstrated many times, ominous clouds now darkened his horizon. The young general drank too much, as well as sometimes using laudanum—partly to relieve the pain in his maimed body; perhaps also to ease his mind, because the love he offered "Buck" Preston had been rejected. Worse, General Hardee resented Hood's appointment and made no effort to conceal his dissatisfaction. Hardee was Hood's senior in rank and considered it a personal insult for Hood to be appointed over him. In a moment of intense bitterness Hardee would submit his resignation only to reconsider when President Davis appealed to his patriotism. But worst of all was the fact that, just as some feared, Hood's capacity for command would prove to be limited.

When the news came to Sherman that Hood was now facing him, the Federal commander immediately asked General Schofield, who had been Hood's classmate at West Point, what the man was like. Schofield replied that Hood was bold, rash, and "courageous in the extreme." McPherson, a member of the same West Point class, agreed with Schofield's assessment, as did George Thomas, who had been one of Hood's instructors at the Point and later served with him in the United States Army in Texas. General Howard knew Hood, too. His evaluation, penned in a letter to his wife on July 23, was blunt: "*Hood* was a classmate of McPherson. He is a stupid fellow, but a hard fighter, does very unexpected things."

Howard was wrong about the last comment, at least in this part of the campaign. Hood did exactly what the Union officers expected him to do: attack. Also, and as they expected, he did not wait long to do it.

SHERMAN had decided upon a general right wheel of his army as the Yankees drew near the Gate City. On July 18 he had written General Thomas, "I would like you to . . . feel down strong on Atlanta. General Howard has already started and Generals Schofield and McPherson; I am on the point of starting and will be near General Schofield. . . . I want that railroad as quick as possible." Swinging wide to come in from the east along the Georgia Railroad, McPherson's Army of the Tennessee was closely supported on the right flank by Schofield's Army of the Ohio, while Thomas's big Army of the Cumberland moved directly across Peachtree Creek to close down on Atlanta from the north. As the troops moved, a gap of more than two miles developed between Thomas and Schofield.

It was July 20. "God defends the right," declared the Atlanta *Appeal* on this day. "His hand is the buckler and shield of the soldier who bravely maintains such a cause as ours." Whatever one may wish to make of God's part in it all, the horrors of war, unfortunately, are never limited to soldiers. The Fifteenth Army Corps, under "Black Jack" Logan, led the march of McPherson's army, tramping on the main road from Decatur to Atlanta. About one o'clock that afternoon Captain Francis DeGress posted Battery H of the First Illinois Light Artillery and opened fire with his 20-pounder Parrott guns, "the first shots . . . which entered the city of Atlanta," according to Logan. The very first shell, said a witness, exploded at the intersection of Ivy and East Ellis streets, killing a small girl who had been walking with her mother and father. When the smoke had cleared the child lay in a pool of her blood.

One o'clock was also the time General Hood had set for his attack. To his headquarters on the morning of July 20 Hood had called the corps commanders: "Old Reliable" Hardee (as he had been known since Shiloh), the Tennessean Stewart, and the newly appointed Benjamin Franklin Cheatham. A native of Nashville, Cheatham had been in most of the Army of Tennessee's major battles, earning a reputation as a fierce fighter, whose drinking and cursing became legendary.

Hood's plan of attack seemed simple enough—on the map. The

Atlanta and Its Railroads.

Southern commander intended to take advantage of the two-mile gap that had developed in the Union army between Schofield and Thomas. Cheatham's corps, supported by Wheeler's cavalry and General G. W. Smith's 5,000-man Georgia Militia, with artillery massed on Cheatham's left flank, would provide a screen to the east against Schofield and McPherson, insuring that the Yankee army would remain divided. Meanwhile, the weight of the Confederate army—the two corps of Hardee and Stewart—would strike Thomas's Army of the Cumberland while it was still crossing Peachtree Creek and before it could prepare defensive positions on the south bank.

It was to be an oblique order attack from right to left (a maneuver massing steadily increasing strength against one wing of the enemy's battle line until it buckles, while using smaller forces on other sectors to fasten the enemy's attention and prevent the transfer of troops to the threatened wing). Hardee was to begin the attack at one o'clock, starting with Bate's division on his right. Walker's and Maney's divisions were to take up the assault in order, east to west, while Cleburne was held in reserve to exploit any advantage that might develop. Next, Stewart's corps would follow, the divisions of Loring and Walthall extending the strike still farther to the left, with French in reserve.

Hood's objective was to drive Thomas's army against Peachtree Creek, turning it toward the west and the Chattahoochee River, separating it still farther from the rest of the Yankee forces and trapping it in the narrow space between the confluence of the two streams. "Everything on our side of the creek was to be taken at all hazards," wrote Hood.

The jump-off line for the Confederate attack was hardly more than four miles north of Atlanta. Many of the Southern soldiers, as well as civilians, especially citizens of Atlanta, had hoped for an end to the long retreat from Dalton—that the army would stand and fight; that the city would not be abandoned without a struggle. Now Atlanta had its wish. At last, on a steaming July afternoon, the Confederate army was about to strike.

Among the Rebel soldiers who likely welcomed the impending attack, in hope that it might prove decisive, was Morgan Leatherman of Murfreesboro, Tennessee. Leatherman had just written a letter to his parents saying that he had experienced "quite a heavy time for the last two or three months. We have not the whole time been two or three days out

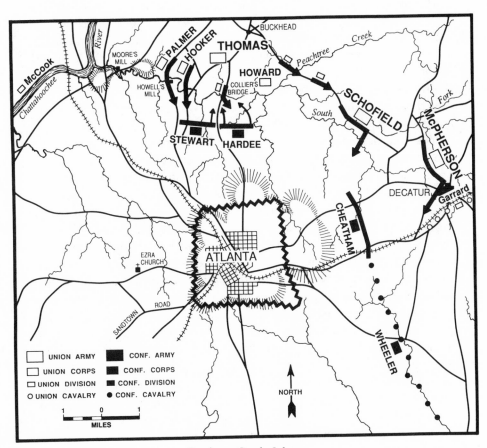

Peachtree Creek, July 20.

of the hearing of cannon and small arms and the most of the time have been in range of them. . . . Although I am not very fond of fighting," the young man readily admitted, "I am anxious to see the decisive battle of this campaign come off. . . . I have no fears as to the results when it does take place such soldiers as compose our army can not be whiped no matter what the odds may be." One wonders if Leatherman, who would be killed in Hood's attack, might have felt some special sense of anxiety as he contemplated a "decisive battle" and then penned the question: "Though we may never meet no more below can we not try to meet in a better world?"

THE situation at Peachtree Creek seemed somewhat favorable for the Rebels—if they had attacked at one o'clock as planned. At that time many of Thomas's units were still crossing the creek. Also, although Sherman had warned his commanders to be alert, the Union forces had picked up no signs that an attack was imminent. "The bloc was sudden and somewhat unexpected," admitted Sherman in his After Action Report. General John Geary's division was fated to be in the heat of the fight and Geary later reported that moments before the attack, "Not a man of theirs was to be seen or heard in any direction." Enos Fourat, commanding the Thirty-third New Jersey Infantry, and occupying an advanced position, recalled: "General Geary was with me, and from the feeble opposition made to our skirmishers and the statements of prisoners he was led to believe that no large force of the enemy was in close proximity."

But unfortunately for the Confederates their attack plan began to break down at midmorning, when Cheatham sent word that he would have to shift his line farther to the south in order to prevent McPherson's army from overlapping his right flank beyond the Georgia Railroad. Of course Hood approved, instructing Cheatham to extend his line a division's length to his right. A major problem developed however when Cheatham, apparently very fearful for his right flank, continued the sidling movement, eventually moving his line about two miles to the right. This was a much greater distance than Hood, who was not on the field, (having taken up a headquarters post in Atlanta) had anticipated. Cheatham's movement indirectly resulted in delaying the Rebel attack for three hours.

To prevent a gap from developing in the Confederate line when Cheatham moved to the right, Hood ordered both Hardee and Stewart to shift to the right one-half of a division's front. Hardee soon discovered that half a division front brought him nowhere close to Cheatham, and continued sidestepping to the right for approximately two miles, despite the long delay in launching his attack that the movement obviously entailed. Stewart's corps, naturally enough, followed Hardee's sidling movement. Apparently Hardee, whose attitude throughout the day was a bit sulky, did not dispatch a courier to Atlanta to inform Hood of the situation.

Not only was the Rebel attack delayed for three hours by this side-stepping movement; it also contributed to a badly coordinated assault effort in which, contrary to plan, Stewart's right-wing division (Loring's) attacked before Hardee's left-wing division (Maney's). In fact, Stewart's main effort preceded Hardee's. General Hardee sent word to Stewart before three o'clock that he was ready to attack, but actually (the reason is not clear) Hardee did not go forward for another hour. Obviously too, the sidling movement to the east largely invalidated the information which Hardee's scouts had earlier gleaned from reconnoitering the rough, thickly wooded terrain in their front. When the attack finally did go forward, one of Hardee's divisions—Bate's, on the right flank—failed to find the Yankees on the immediate front. Probing then for the Federals' left flank, Bate's advance was hindered by "an almost impenetrable thicket," through which his troops eventually struggled to within seventy-five yards of the Union position, only to be raked with a blazing artillery fire hurling canister into the gray mass of soldiers.

Meanwhile, thanks to the Confederate delay, George H. Thomas's Army of the Cumberland had gotten nearly all of its combat elements across Peachtree Creek, and some were partially entrenched. Facing southward toward Atlanta, Howard's Fourth Corps was on the left, Hooker's Twentieth Corps in the center, and Palmer's Fourteenth Corps held the right of the line. The Yankees who would bear the brunt of the Confederate strike were, east to west, John Newton's division of Howard's corps; all three divisions (William T. Ward's, John W. Geary's, and Alpheus S. Williams's) of Hooker's corps; and, to a lesser extent, Richard W. Johnson's division of Palmer's corps.

These Federals occupied extremely rough, heavily timbered ground. Cut by deep ravines, it also presented the formidable obstacle of entangling undergrowth. Shrubs, saplings, and vines laced the rugged, sometimes swampy, often radically undulating terrain. A regimental commander in the Third Brigade of Geary's division, Lieutenant Colonel Harvey Chatfield, wrote of his unit's advance on the south bank of Peachtree Creek: "The regiment moved forward, but owing to the dense undergrowth and rough nature of the ground, the advance was rendered very difficult and the line irregular, besides an almost utter inability to keep in view the other regiments of the brigade."

Despite major difficulties presented by the ragged terrain, on the whole the Yankee line proved well positioned for throwing back an attack. Not only had the Federals located a few open areas, and thus established portions of their line with a clear field of fire to the front—notably at places along the line of Hooker's corps—but the irregular nature of the Union line (due in great part to the terrain) also proved advantageous.

When, in uncoordinated fashion, the Confederate attack at last went forward in mid- to late afternoon, William Ward's Federal division was just coming into position a few hundred yards to the rear of John Newton's right flank; while farther to the west, Alpheus Williams's division was already located a few hundred yards to the rear of John Geary's right flank. The Confederate charge, in each instance, was blunted by a recessed division—the commands of Ward and Williams, respectively—and then harshly thrown back by both frontal and enfilading fire which swept the angle formed by the Union divisions.

Ward gave an interesting and revealing, albeit somewhat pompous, account of the action on his front where Hardee's corps made the attack. "Meeting my line of battle seemed to completely addle their brains," he reported of the Rebels. "Their first line broke, mixing up with the second line; they were now in the wildest confusion, firing in all directions, some endeavoring to get away, some undecided what to do, others rushing into our lines." Colonel Benjamin Harrison, the future president of the United States, was commanding Ward's First Brigade. At the beginning of the Confederate attack, Harrison ordered to the front a detail of 100 men equipped with seven-shot Spencer repeating rifles, which "punished the enemy severely." Colonel Harrison said he observed many Confederates "lying down and a few even turning back, while the officers with drawn swords, were trying to steady their lines and push them forward."

General Ward's whole division then met the Rebel offensive with a counterattack, forcing the Confederates to retreat. Maintaining a steady fire, the three Federal brigades moved relentlessly forward. "Our advance, though desperately resisted by the enemy, was steady and unfaltering," reported Benjamin Harrison; "the fighting was hand to hand, and step by step; the enemy was pushed back . . . and the keypoint of the battlefield won."

Ward's division was one of those fortunate to come upon an opening in the dense countryside. "I still advanced my men," wrote Ward, "keeping up a steady fire, crossed a deep ravine to gain the next hill to make good my connections with General Newton on my left and General Geary on my right, and also to gain a position which commanded the open country for 600 yards in advance. Once [the enemy] made a feeble effort to rally, but they were too badly broken."

Farther to the west, the fight on General Geary's right flank seems to have presented the Federals with their toughest challenge. This was due, in part, to the advance position of the Thirty-third New Jersey regiment, isolated on a small hill some three hundred to five hundred yards or more (depending on which officer's account is accepted) in front of Geary's main line. It was also due to the Southerners' determination to smash the Northern forces. These attackers were the men of Stewart's corps, Loring's division going in first against Geary's division, while Walthall's division (on Loring's left, with reasonably good timing) moved in against the Yankee division of Williams shortly after Geary had been struck.

William W. "Blizzards" Loring had two brigades of infantry in his division front (the third brigade was unavailable, having been detailed for picket duty) as he emerged from a thick forest to a large open field, the opposite side of which lay Geary's Yankees.

At the edge of the field, Loring's troops were halted and their lines rectified. Weapons loaded and bayonets fixed, they grimly moved, 2,700 strong, at double-quick time toward the Union position eight or nine hundred yards away. Orders were to fire one volley and then give the Yankees the bayonet. The Federals waited and watched; the tension mounted. On came the Confederates. Firing a volley soon after entering the field, the grayclads tramped relentlessly forward: six hundred yards to the Union line; five hundred yards to the Union line.

Then the Federal field batteries opened fire and some of the grayclads began to fall. But the forward movement of the Rebels did not falter. The cracking report of Yankee musketry sounded up and down the line. The Confederates broke into a charge, emitting the shrill, wild Rebel yell. Closing with a rush, coming directly against the front and around the flanks of the Thirty-third New Jersey's unlucky soldiers, was the weight of the Confederate charge. The Thirty-third's commander reported: "Under these circumstances, with such an overwhelming force against us and on three sides of us, with such a withering fire from front, right and left, and the enemy rapidly gaining our rear, to stand longer was madness, and I reluctantly gave the order to retire fighting."

The result, in some cases, was a footrace with the Rebels to the Federal line, the pursuing Southerners clubbing and shooting the Yankees as they fled. "As the enemy fled," General Loring reported, "the steady aim of the Mississippi, Alabama, and Louisiana marksmen of my command produced great slaughter in his ranks."

Surging through the advance position held by the Thirty-third New Jersey, Loring's men swept on to Geary's main line. Geary's right flank received the full fury of the Rebel onslaught, and part of his line, not entrenched, simply could not, or at least did not, hold its ground. Three regiments fell back, and Colonel Ario Pardee, commanding the One

Hundred and Forty-seventh Pennsylvania, which maintained its ground with heavy losses, was very critical of the retiring units. The colonel said that "the disorganized masses of men as they rushed by the right of my line told a fearful tale. The men seemed to be panic-stricken, and I regret to say that there was manifested a lack of energy, coolness, and determination on the part of the officers which was truly deplorable. It was impossible to stop any organized body of men."

Perhaps the colonel was overly critical. The Confederates had launched a devastating attack, which hit Geary's right flank with smashing force. Geary himself, who had seen a lot of fighting by this stage of the war, thought the grayclads charged "with more than customary nerve and heartiness in the attack." Adding that he had "never seen more heroic fighting," Geary said that "the fury of the battle . . . could not be surpassed," and that "the field everywhere bore marks of the extreme severity of the contest." In fact, the general said the appearance of the field "recalled to my mind . . . the scene of conflict where the same unit fought at Gettysburg."

The solution for Geary, of course, was to change front to the right with a portion of his command, eventually linking up to his right rear with the left flank of Williams's division. That division, as previously noted, had come under attack by the Rebel division of Walthall about the same time that Loring hit Geary. When the change of front to the right was accomplished, Geary's division was then able not only to hold its line effectively, but also to direct an enfilade fire against those Confederates who advanced against Williams's division. Thus, in the end, Stewart's corps, although elated by the initial success of its attack, was to be hurled back with terrible losses. Rebel brigadier general Winfield S. Featherston, commanding one of the brigades that stormed Geary's division, reported his unit's casualties at 50 percent. Every regimental commander, except one, was either killed or wounded, said Featherston. Loring's other brigade, led by Brigadier General Thomas M. Scott, took leavy losses also, though not as many as Featherston's command.

The smoke of battle had hardly settled along the south bank of Peachtree Creek when the placing of blame for the failure of the Confederate attack began to abound, along with recriminations. Loring and his brigade commanders blamed their repulse on the delay in attacking of Hardee's left-wing division under Maney, which they said enabled unengaged Federals to direct an enfilading fire into their ranks from the right. Hardee blamed the ultimate failure on the necessity, in the critical last stages of the battle, to send his crack reserve division under Cleburne, with which he was ready to launch a final assault, to reinforce Cheatham's corps, lest the Yankees drive into Atlanta from the east.

Peachtree Creek Battlefield.

Hood blamed Hardee for the failure at Peachtree Creek. Warmly praising Stewart, who "carried out his instructions to the letter," Hood charged Hardee with being the first to delay attack and also with failing to push the assault as ordered. Although commanding "the best troops in the army," Hood charged that Hardee "virtually accomplished nothing."

Clearly the Rebel attack had suffered from delay and lack of coordination. But equally, if not more, important in explaining the Confederate failure were three other factors. One was certainly the stubborn resistance of the infantry in Thomas's Army of the Cumberland, assisted by well-positioned artillery fire. (Thomas himself urged the guns forward, using the point of his sword on the rumps of laggard battery horses.) A second factor was the pressure of McPherson's Army of the Tennessee to the east, which originally caused the delay in the Confederate attack, and necessitated the withdrawal of Cleburne's division late in the afternoon. Finally, the accidents of terrain had a major impact, contributing enormously to the Yankee ability to direct enfilading fire against the assaulting grayclads. Northern general Jacob Cox stated the matter succinctly: "The direction of all the ridges and ravines from Newton to Williams was such as to throw forward the right of each command as it rested upon them, and the division commanders . . . found their right flank receiving the brunt of the first attack." As the attacking Confederate columns surged past these flanks in their leftward oriented drive they were shattered by an enfilade fire unleashed by Yankee reserve, and reformed units rushed to these critical positions. This largely chance occurrence perhaps explains more about why the Union won the fight at Peachtree Creek than any other single factor.

Sherman, who was with the left of his army on the northeast side of Atlanta, learned from Thomas in the late afternoon that the Confederates were still in strength north of Atlanta. The Union commander had hoped his advance on the city from the east would cause Hood to shift his main force in that direction, thus allowing Thomas to "feel down strong on Atlanta" against slight opposition. It was not so happening, and Sherman's reply to Thomas at 6:10 P.M. evidences a touch of frustration: "I have been with Howard and Schofield today, and one of my staff is just back from General McPherson," the commander explained to Thomas. "All report the enemy in front so strong that I was in hopes none were left for you, but I see it is the same old game . . . , each division commander insists he has to fight two corps. . . . I will push Schofield and McPherson all I know how."

Soon after, Sherman received Thomas's general report, without details, of the action along Peachtree Creek. Realizing the extent of fighting in that sector, Sherman informed Thomas that he would send the report, but expressed his opinion that "the opportunity of operating on that flank, if it did exist, is now past."

One of the century's foremost military historians, the late Basil H. Liddell Hart, in a biography of Sherman, expresses an insightful perspective, suggesting that the "real clue" to the day's developments was to be found in the fact that McPherson graduated from West Point ranked first in the class of 1853, while Hood had ranked forty-fourth in the same class. Thus McPherson was "too technical in mind to be dashing" while Hood was "too limited in mind to be caught." Perceiving the danger from the direction of Decatur, a sharper Confederate commander might have shifted his forces to deal with it, as Sherman had hoped. Or—the other side of the picture—a bolder, less academic commander than McPherson might have probed harder and found the opportunity to drive into Atlanta. Perhaps that is an oversimplification. And then again, perhaps not.

# 10

# McPherson and Revenge

FOR most of the men in the two armies locked in deadly embrace at Atlanta, July 21 was a day without combat. In Civil War almanacs the twenty-first seems to be a day of peace between the twentieth and twenty-second, two of the bloodiest days of the campaign. But for the grayclad men of Pat Cleburne's division and for Mortimer Leggett's division of McPherson's army, the twenty-first brought no respite from shot and shell. Along the Georgia Railroad's tracks between Decatur and Atlanta and around an important rise of ground called Bald Hill, these troops fought a sanguinary struggle that Cleburne called "the bitterest" of his military career. McPherson's rifled guns took a terrible toll in the Gray ranks, once wiping out an entire company of the Eighteenth Texas Cavalry in a single shot. Casualties were also heavy on the Union side. Manning Force's brigade of Leggett's division lost 40 percent of its strength and yet it "swept over the works precise as on parade." By late afternoon Cleburne had been shoved away from the hill and forced to fall back on Atlanta.

As combat swirled around the hill that afternoon, Francis R. Baker of the Seventy-eighth Ohio held fire momentarily, startled to see "a woman bareheaded, with her hair flying over her shoulders, and carrying a little child in her arms . . . running towards our lines." The orphans of the storm reached safety from their house, which stood between the battle lines.

The capture of Bald Hill was important. Seventeenth Corps commander Frank Blair wrote: "If the enemy had been allowed to retain it and fortify himself securely upon it, he could not only have prevented our advance, but would have made the positions previously held by the Seventeenth and Fifteenth Corps exceedingly insecure and dangerous."

As the sun went down on the twenty-first, McPherson told Blair to communicate to his unit commanders "the importance of being on the alert at all times to repel an attack, especially about daybreak." McPherson also informed Sherman that he had made his left as strong as possible, but warned that no cavalry was on hand to watch for Rebel movements on that flank. He closed with the pointed remark: "the whole rebel army . . . is not in front of the Army of the Cumberland."

Looking forward to July 22, Sherman did not expect an attack from Hood. The victory at Bald Hill strengthened that opinion, and Sherman talked about a slow advance by all three armies that would end in a massive bombardment of the Rebel lines. The action of the twenty-first, coupled with the Confederate repulse at Peachtree Creek, led him, on

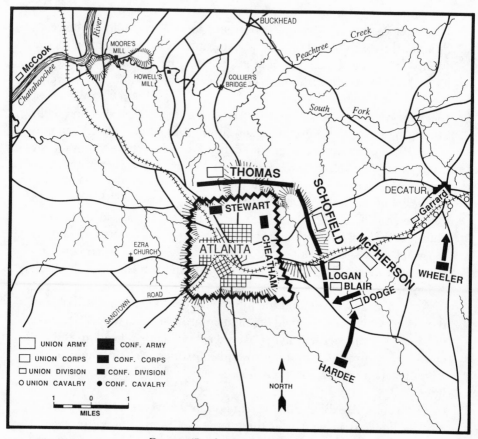

Decatur (Battle of Atlanta), July 22.

James B. McPherson.

the morning of the twenty-second, to exclaim of Hood, "I would not be astonished to find him off in the morning."

The twenty-first was a day of savage thinking for John B. Hood. His "first sortie" had failed, but he was determined to challenge Sherman again, and quickly. The loss at Peachtree Creek was on Hood's mind. The initiative must be seized, and the Army of Tennessee must not become demoralized. Hood was thinking only of attack and he intended to be "off in the morning," but in a way not imagined by his Union opponent. His first thought seems to have been a strike at Sherman's center, but the action of the twenty-first, together with intelligence provided by Wheeler's cavalry, caused a change.

Most of the fighting on the twenty-first had been to the east, and evidence that McPherson was moving in from Decatur in strength concerned the Southern chief. He was afraid that an unchallenged Army of the Tennessee might slice on toward the south and turn west, imperiling Confederate hold on Atlanta by cutting the railroad to Macon.

Hood also seems to have discovered on the morning of the twenty-first that, in spite of McPherson's strong position, the Union general appeared to have committed a grave military blunder. While he struggled with Cleburne in his center he seemed to have neglected his left. Wheeler's horsemen found McPherson's left "in the air," unprotected by cavalry and an open invitation to his enemy. To Hood it appeared that the

Union had given him an opportunity always sought but rarely found. Robert E. Lee, using his able lieutenant Stonewall Jackson, had exploited such an opportunity at Chancellorsville and had crushed Hooker's Army of the Potomac. Could Hood repeat Chancellorsville, crush McPherson's army, drive Sherman back, and save Atlanta?

By the afternoon of the twenty-first the Rebel commander's plan was complete, and he brought his three corps commanders to headquarters to give them their orders. All three would break off contact with the enemy at nightfall and retire to the well-constructed Atlanta lines. This withdrawal was intended to disguise Hood's plan for a renewed attack. Alexander P. Stewart's corps would hold the city's northern face against Thomas's army. On Stewart's right, bending to the east, Benjamin Cheatham's corps would hold position in front of Schofield's army and the right end of McPherson's force. These two corps were supported by G. W. Smith's small force of state militia. Hood's remaining corps, led by William Hardee, would be his "whip lash," the spearhead of his "second sortie."

Amazingly—since he had complained of Hardee's action (or lack of action, on July 20)—it was the Georgian he decided would play Jackson to his Lee on the twenty-second. According to Hood, one reason for his choice was that Hardee had "taken but little part in the action of the Twentieth," and his corps was "comparatively fresh." This ignored Cleburne's wearing combat of the twenty-first.

Hardee was ordered to pull his corps, the army's largest, out of line and move southeastward down the McDonough Road to Cobb's Mill. From that point he would hook to the northeast on the Fayetteville Road and march to the Widow Parker's Farm, south of the Georgia Railroad's Decatur-Atlanta line. Hardee's three divisions, led by George Maney, W. H. T. Walker, and William B. Bate, would begin the movement and would be joined by Pat Cleburne, who was still in contact with the enemy. Hood's timetable called for a vigorous night march of about eighteen miles that would set Hardee's men in position to strike McPherson's exposed left rear at dawn. An entire day (which promised to be broiling hot) should be enough to whip the Federals.

To assist Hardee, Joe Wheeler's riders would be sent to attack McPherson's wagon train, parked in the Decatur town square. Furthermore, once Hardee attacked, Hood would send Cheatham forward to occupy Schofield, while Stewart would engage Thomas so that Sherman could not send reinforcements to the Army of the Tennessee.

After dark on July 21 General Hood called his corps commanders together for a final parlay. As he later recalled in *Advance and Retreat*: "To transfer after dark our entire line from the immediate presence of the enemy to another line around Atlanta, and to throw Hardee, the same night, entirely to the rear and flank of McPherson—as Jackson was thrown, in a similar movement, at Chancellorsville and Second Manassas—and to initiate the offensive at daylight, required no small effort on the part of the men and officers." To make certain the kind of effort he wanted was clearly in their minds, he got his commanders together.

After the battle Hood and Hardee argued about the precise nature of the orders given to the flanking corps. In his report written in 1865, as well as in his postwar memoirs, Hood asserted that the reason for the failure of Hardee's sweep was the corps commander's negligence in not marching *"completely"* around McPherson and coming in on his rear near Decatur. Hardee, in response, pointed out that on the night of the twenty-first Hood's plan was altered so that the corps would have a shorter route to cover, one that would allow him to strike McPherson's left flank. His attack, therefore, obeyed Hood's latest orders. On April 5, 1865, Hardee wrote in his own defense: "In proof that General Hood's instructions were obeyed I have only to mention that when my dispatch informing him of the position I had taken and the dispositions I had made for the attack was received he exclaimed to Brigadier-General Mackall, his chief-of-staff, with his finger on the map, 'Hardee is just where I wanted him.' "

One source of misunderstanding about the flank movement of the twenty-second may have been Hood's vagueness about the distance to be covered. Twice in his memoirs the Rebel commander wrote that the distance from Atlanta to Decatur was "only six miles." It may have been six miles by arrow flight, but Hardee's men had anything but a direct line to follow. All of this confusion and wrangling bears out Thomas L. Connelly's assessment of Hood's most basic problem: "Hood's planning, fashioned after a well-oiled command structure in Virginia, simply was too sophisticated for the new western command."

In spite of Hood's efforts at coordination, problems plagued his second sortie from its inception. One of the most obvious was the weariness of his army, especially Hardee's men, heavily engaged on the right throughout the day. Even those not in combat on the twenty-first had been baked by the sun and were worn out. Many had not slept for two days. At the very least Hood's tired troops were being asked to drop back to a new line, begin improving it at once, and stand ready to push forward on the twenty-second. At most they were being asked to march hard all night and be in position to attack at dawn.

When night fell and the army started to move, the timetable began immediately to crack apart. Cleburne's division, near Bald Hill, found it difficult to break off contact with the Federals. To do so abruptly might reveal that a flank march was underway. It might even bring forth an advance by McPherson that would alter his entire line, thus changing the possible target of the twenty-second. At seven-thirty Hardee told Cleburne to break off skirmishing, but more than three hours later Cleburne remained in contact with McPherson. It was almost midnight before Hardee told Cleburne to leave his skirmishers in place while moving the bulk of his force into line behind Walker who was following Bate and Maney. It was not until three o'clock on the morning of the twenty-second that all of Hardee's corps was on the move. This was not a very auspicious start for an attack slated to begin at dawn.

With the Confederate army on the move, Atlanta civilians were confused and alarmed. One businessman reported "a complete hub-bub with army wagons and soldiers and marauders as though the whole army was passing through." Many people stood on rooftops watching their army move out and waiting for the Union invaders to occupy the city. Atlanta's populace was not safe even from its defenders, and "a lot of cavalry robbers broke into the stores and stole everything that they took a fancy to." Fears prompted an increase in the refugee exodus southward and the Gate City's last newspaper, the *Appeal,* prepared to evacuate.

In an attempt to maintain the secrecy of Hardee's objective, regimental commanders had received oral rather than written orders. Fear that prisoners or deserters might reveal the target led to the unusual precautions. But no general has ever devised a way to prevent rumors from racing through an army, so as the tired Confederates trudged through the dark they talked about what was ahead. Before daybreak, men in Bate's division knew "that we are to attack the enemy at day light at a point near a little village called Decatur."

Even after Hardee's corps reached the McDonough Road, delay followed delay. The unmapped country was a wilderness of woods, thickets, gulleys, and swamps. The dark, narrow road was jammed with weary, marching troops and occasionally with Wheeler's cavalrymen jogging on toward Decatur. Some graybacks were so exhausted that they fell by the roadside and went to sleep. When the dawn lightened the piney woods the column's advance had just reached Cobb's Mill and still stood six miles from its objective. The sun rose quickly and the marching men sweated through the morning as they approached the Parker Farm. It was around noon before Hardee's corps was set to attack. Maney held the left, Cleburne's division straddled Flat Shoals Road, Walker was on Cleburne's right between the road and Sugar Creek where the line swung northeastward, and Bate stood ready on the northern end of the line. Hardee's corps was in position to give what Hood hoped would be a "signal victory to our army," but half of the day was gone.

In addition to the loss of time, the men were worn out by the night march. Kentucky sergeant major Johnny Green felt "It has been a terribly tedious march," and one of Cleburne's brigadiers, James A. Smith, reported his troops believed "the loss of another night's rest," after the fierce action of the twentieth and twenty-first, "was a heavy tax upon their powers of endurance."

And there were other problems. Friction between Confederate generals, a crippling problem throughout the campaign, appeared on the twenty-second. Hood, still seething over Hardee's actions on the twentieth, felt his anger rise as he waited past dawn and through the morning for the sound of Hardee's guns. He would find it difficult to credit Hardee's nickname "Old Reliable" that morning.

Neither general labored hard enough to maintain the kind of communications necessary to carry such an operation to success. Hardee was fifteen miles away from Hood's headquarters, well behind schedule and out of touch with his commander. The corps commander made little effort to inform Hood of his problems, and Hood made no effort to fill his own information void. Had he known that Hardee's attack would be hours late, Hood might have employed Cheatham and Stewart to draw attention away from Hardee and occupy Sherman north of the city.

There was also command friction within Hardee's corps. A face-to-face flare-up occurred that morning between the corps commander and his fellow Georgian W. H. T. Walker. The division commander, who had attended West Point with Hardee, came to the corps commander to request a change of front. A treacherous briar patch lay in his path and he wanted to move around it. Already far behind schedule and touchy about the delay, Hardee snapped at the veteran, "No sir! This movement has been delayed too long already. Go and obey my orders."

Furious at this curt dismissal, Walker asked a staff officer, "Major did you hear that?" The aide attempted to soften the effect of Hardee's words but Walker vowed, "I shall make him remember this insult. If I survive this battle he shall answer me for it." After Walker rode away, Hardee, realizing his words' effect, sent a staff officer galloping after him. He caught Walker and told him Hardee regretted "his hasty and discourteous language," adding that he would have apologized in person "but that his presence was required elsewhere, and would do so at the first opportunity." The apology did not placate Walker. As he prepared to attack he said to his aide, "He must answer me for this."

By noon Walker and his fellow division commanders were ready to turn their attention to McPherson. Maney, just south of Bald Hill, charged Mortimer Leggett's division of Blair's Seventeenth Corps and Cleburne threw his hardened but fatigued veterans against John W. Fuller's division of Grenville M. Dodge's Sixteenth Corps. Walker's men scrambled through the briar patch toward Fuller, and Bate's attack struck Thomas W. Sweeny's division of Dodge's corps. Hood's perception from his distant headquarters led him to believe that Hardee had struck McPherson's strength along Leggett's front, rather than the left which was "in the air" and vulnerable.

What Hood could not see, did not know—and evidently did not bother to learn when he wrote *Advance and Retreat* in 1880—was what Hardee's men were suddenly learning as they moved forward under the scorching sun. McPherson's left was not "in the air." Luck, that weapon all generals hope ride with them into battle, had mounted with Sherman that morning. The luck that rode with Bragg, Longstreet, and Hood ten months earlier on the left at Chickamauga had changed uniforms. Hood had once been its beneficiary; on July 22, 1864, he would be its victim.

On the twentieth and twenty-first McPherson's Army of the Tennessee had established firm control east of Atlanta along the Georgia Railroad. On the twenty-first Sherman ordered the young Ohio army commander to use one of his corps to "destroy every rail and tie of the railroad, from Decatur up to your skirmish line." McPherson sent Dodge's Sixteenth Corps to do the job. The observation that the Army of the Tennessee's left was "in the air" was made while Dodge worked on the railroad. Before noon on July 22 Dodge halted his destruction and was about to take up position on Frank Blair's left. As his men marched south from the railroad, along a wagon track, Dodge learned that Confederates were advancing toward him along Sugar Creek. The Sixteenth Corps' two divisions were simply ordered to face to the left and they quickly established a formidable triple line of defense. If Hardee's force had launched its attack at any time between dawn and around eleven-thirty that morning, it would have found Blair and Logan uncovered and been able to take those two corps in the rear. As it was they missed their chance by about thirty minutes.

Instead of "air," Walker and Bate ran through thick underbrush, into the pines and straight into Dodge's corps. Kentucky Rebel Johnny Green who, like his commanders, expected no prepared Union resistance, wrote in amazement, "we now discover that the yanks have two lines of battle in front of us." The hotheaded Walker, urging his men on, was one of the earliest casualties of Hood's second sortie. This former commandant of West Point had been wounded three times in the Seminole War and once severely in Mexico, but this time a Yankee soldier's rifle shot killed him. Walker would never make Hardee answer for the imagined insult. Hugh Mercer took command of Walker's division.

Surprise was with the defense this time and Bate and Mercer were unable to make any progress on the right. Both divisions encountered a mill pond which could not be crossed, forcing each to swing to the left, losing time and mingling units in the tangled brush. As the Confederates finally "burst forth from the woods in truly magnificent style . . . with battle-flags proudly flaunting in the breeze," a Missouri battery ripped their line, slowing the advance. When Union fire forced Rebel withdrawal, Dodge counterattacked with three regiments, which swept the field, causing heavy losses and seizing 226 prisoners.

On the left Maney, laboring through undergrowth and marshes, struck Leggett's entrenchments, was driven back, and charged again only to be repulsed again.

As Tennesseean Sam Watkins charged with Maney's division, a fellow soldier cried out over and over, "God have mercy on my soul!" even stopping to kneel and pray. Watkins's demand, "Quit that nonsense!" had no effect. Union artillery began tearing through the Tennesseeans and Watkins heard "O, God have mercy on my soul!" one last time. Turning, he saw "the ball had cut his body nearly in two. Poor fellow, he had gone to his reward."

The only one of Hardee's divisions able to gain ground was that of Patrick Cleburne. The Arkansans hit the point at which Blair and Dodge joined and where the Union line veered northeastward. They forced the bluecoats out of their lines and up Flat Shoals Road toward Bald Hill. Cleburne's advance was slowed somewhat by the concentrated fire of Fuller's troops as well as by the effective bombardment of the Fourteenth Ohio Battery. Although the Union line generally held firm, Cleburne's advance was a cause for concern.

Sherman had moved Thomas and Schofield forward on the morning of the twenty-second and for a time Union skirmishers failed to make contact with the Rebels, leading Sherman to believe that Hood had evacuated the city. Soon strong Confederate parapets were visible which grayclad soldiers worked hard to strengthen.

McPherson rode to Sherman's headquarters that morning to ask his commander for permission to bombard a foundry whose smokestack was visible from his battery of 32-pounders being positioned on Bald Hill. Sherman's command post was the two-story Augustus Hurt House in Schofield's rear, about one-half mile north of the railroad. McPherson felt that a bombardment would bring Atlanta's fall, and Sherman agreed that the Army of the Tennessee's cannoneers could begin at once.

Sherman later remembered sitting on the front steps with McPherson discussing the "general character" of their new opponent. "We agreed that we ought to be unusually cautious and prepared at all times for sallies and for hard fighting," he wrote, "because Hood, though not deemed much of a scholar, or of great mental capacity, was undoubtedly a brave, determined and rash man."

While McPherson was at the Hurt House Sherman led him to his map of the Atlanta area and detailed the strategy he hoped would finally claim his objective. He planned to shift all three armies to the west, severing Hood's rail lines with Macon and Alabama. Sherman warned McPherson not to slip his force too far to the left, in view of these future plans. He cautioned the army commander, "I would let Stoneman try it, but I hate to base any calculations on the cavalry." At around twelve-thirty that afternoon, while McPherson listened to his commander and friend, gunfire suddenly rose away to the south.

Sherman located the musketry with his compass, and a concerned McPherson gathered his staff and rode toward the unexpected sound. The Union commander watched him go and recalled eleven years later:

> McPherson was then in his prime (about thirty-four years old), over six feet high, and a very handsome man in every way, was universally liked, and had many noble qualities. He had on his boots outside his pantaloons, gauntlets on his hands, had on his major-general's uniform, and wore a sword-belt but no sword.

The army commander rode up a ridge in Dodge's rear and saw the Sixteenth Corps holding its ground. The greatest threat was clearly on the right where Blair's men were retiring. Then a roar far off to the east, also audible to Sherman at his command post, indicated an attack in progress against the wagon train at Decatur. McPherson sent staff officers toward Decatur—to Dodge to urge him to hold his position, and to Logan to send Hugo Wangelin's brigade into the hard-pressed area between the Sixteenth and Seventeenth corps. Then, accompanied only by an orderly, he rode through the trees toward the Seventeenth Corps.

Riding across the rear of Bald Hill the general and his orderly suddenly encountered a group of Southerners from Cleburne's command. An Arkansas captain raised his sword as a signal to surrender. He remembered that McPherson "checked his horse slightly, raised his hat as if he were saluting a lady, wheeled his horse's head directly to the right, and dashed off to the rear in a full gallop." The captain ordered "Shoot him!" and a corporal fired.

In his flight McPherson rode bending low to avoid the forest's low-hanging limbs. The corporal's bullet struck the general in the lower back and tore upward close to his heart. McPherson's orderly was knocked to the ground, stunned by a branch, and recovered to find himself in the

Scene of McPherson's Death.

dust lying next to the general. The soldier bent to ask if he was hurt and McPherson replied weakly, "Oh, orderly, I am." His body quivered, his face fell to his side, and he died. The Union soldier's grief was momentarily replaced by fear as he was grabbed by a Rebel who yelled, "Git to the rear, you Yankee son of a bitch." The Arkansas captain rode up, saw the major general's stars and asked, "Who is lying here?" With tears in his eyes, the orderly choked out, "Sir it is General McPherson. You have killed the best man in our army."

Word reached Sherman that McPherson's horse had come back riderless. For a time McPherson's body was in Confederate hands, but soon the general's body was brought to Union headquarters. The Sixty-fourth Illinois, moving forward to hurl back Cleburne's advance, failed to accomplish that mission but succeeded in securing McPherson's remains. The dead general's pockets had been emptied by the Rebels but, to Sherman's relief, a notebook detailing future Union strategy was found on one of the forty prisoners taken by the Illinoisans. At the Hurt House the thirty-four-year-old commander of the Army of the Tennessee was stretched out on a door supported by two chairs.

The orderly's words, "You have killed the best man in our army," would have been echoed by many. Sherman's feelings for McPherson were very special. He regarded the young Ohio West Pointer as a protégé and also exhibited the kind of affection he might have shown a younger brother. But his regard for McPherson transcended that of either protégé or brother. He still believed the war would be a long one and he saw a special role in it for his handsome lieutenant. "I expected something to happen to Grant and me; either the rebels or the newspapers would kill us both, and I looked to McPherson as the man to follow us and finish the war." Now tears for his friend ran down his red beard.

Sherman's grief was great for the loss of a friend, a brilliant fellow officer, and the man he felt would carry the Union cause to victory. But there was another deep personal tragedy in McPherson's death, one of which Sherman was well aware. Earlier in the war, the young general had become engaged to Emily Hoffman of Baltimore. He asked to get away to be married, but the western force was being reorganized and leave had to wait. The campaign began and McPherson was put off again.

Emily Hoffman's wait ended with a telegram telling her the general was dead. She loved McPherson in spite of the strong pro-Southern attitude of her family and had agreed to marry him in the face of their disapproval. General O. O. Howard had been told by McPherson that Miss Hoffman's "mother is secesh, her brother in the rebel army. She keeps the Union flag over the mantel in her room." To compound her grief, when the telegram reached Baltimore Emily Hoffman overheard a member of her family say: "I have the most wonderful news—McPherson is dead." The young woman went to her room, closed the curtains, and spoke to no one for a year.

The grieving Miss Hoffman received a letter from her dead fiancé's commander. "I yield to no one on earth but yourself the right to exceed me in lamentations for our dead hero," wrote Sherman. "I see him now, so handsome, so smiling, on his fine black horse, booted and spurred, with his easy seat, the impersonation of the gallant knight." In final salute, Sherman wrote: "Though the cannon booms now, and the angry rattle of musketry tells me that I also will likely pay the same penalty, yet while life lasts I will delight in the memory of that bright particular star."

News of McPherson's death spread through the Union army by night-fall. Almost every diary entry or letter from the twenty-second mentioned the sad fact. The underground telegraph in Sherman's army was swift and, although rumors sometimes clogged the lines, it was usually accurate. Swift dissemination of word of McPherson's death is an excellent example. George Metz of the Ninety-ninth Indiana wrote, "Horrowable was this day . . . Gen. McPherson was killed." Lyman Widney of the Thirty-fourth Illinois called the army commander "a valuable officer and very popular with the whole army." Another Indianan, William Miller, reported that the death "casts a gloom over the entire army," while Lysander Wheeler of the One Hundred and Fifth Illinois remarked philosophically, "generals as well as others are not exempted from bullets." John D. Lowman of Indiana's Fortieth Infantry was more balanced: "Gen. McFurson was cilled but the rebels got defeated."

As the Ohio general's body moved northward by rail it produced "a very great sensation at his loss," according to a Hoosier soldier in Marietta. Will Pepper, a pessimistic Illinoisan attached to a hospital unit in Marietta, was shaken by McPherson's death and believed "our men got badly whacked yesterday. This is an excitable time here in the rear and everybody uneasy." Edward P. Stanfield, a railroad guard in the Forty-eighth Indiana at Chattanooga, mourned as the general's body passed. He concluded, "When the news . . . reaches Gen. Grant, I think that the 'Mississippi River horse' will shed tears over the dispatch."

With "that bright particular star's" body laid out before him, Sherman went about hurling back Hood's sortie. He immediately ordered John A. Logan—the Illinois Democratic congressman turned soldier, and the senior corps commander—to take command of the army. And it would be the Army of the Tennessee's fight. With the exception of one of Schofield's

General Logan Rides to Rally the Troops. (*From the* Atlanta Cyclorama.)

brigades sent to Decatur to help hold the wagon train and one of Dodge's brigades called in late in the day, together with some of the Army of the Ohio's artillery, McPherson's army would fight its battle. In his *Memoirs* Sherman wrote: "I purposely allowed the Army of the Tennessee to fight this battle almost unaided." He added, "If any assistance were rendered by either of the other armies, the Army of the Tennessee would be jealous."

John A. Logan led the army into its battle with the vigor and style he had shown on the stump in southern Illinois and in combat from Donelson through Vicksburg. Waving his floppy hat, his dark hair streaming behind him, "Black Jack" rode to the retreating Seventeenth Corps and roared: "Will you hold this line with me? Will you hold this line?" Shouting "McPherson and Revenge!" and chanting "Black Jack! Black Jack!" over and over, they began to turn back the grayclads.

The greatest pressure Logan faced was just south of Bald Hill where Maney and Cleburne had struck Giles Smith's division of the Seventeenth Corps. Rebel attackers benefitted from strong artillery support and from the gap between Smith and the Sixteenth Corps. Smith's front held against Maney but the flanking attack of Govan's Arkansans from Cleburne's command broke the Yankee line. Two batteries and major elements of two Iowa regiments were forced to surrender. The remainder of Smith's division, faced by the collapsing flank, quickly took cover on the reverse side of their own works and succeeded in halting the yelling Rebels. Suddenly the Southerners attacked that reverse side, sending the Federals back over their works. Because Smith's position appeared in danger of complete collapse, Logan ordered General Charles C. Walcutt and his left brigade of the Fifteenth Corps to turn to face Cleburne's attackers. Walcutt's fire was so effective that the Rebels wavered, halted, and then turned to the left against the rear of Leggett's division holding Bald Hill.

One of the oddest pieces of this struggle around Bald Hill involved Govan's Arkansans. These Rebels crawled up the hill on hands and knees and leaped into enemy trenches. Union defenders surrendered to what they believed were superior numbers, but on counting the Rebels they realized their mistake and demanded that the Rebels surrender. While the parlaying went on, it became evident that the forces were equal, so both capitulations were cancelled and furious combat was renewed.

The struggle was particularly intense around Bald Hill—already called Leggett's Hill by the Yankees—where Mortimer Leggett's Third Division fought against Hardee's charging lines. Leggett was a prewar law partner of Jacob Cox and had fought at Fort Donelson, Shiloh, and Vicksburg. Logan was with Leggett's division, rallying the men in the army he knew best. Holding the hill's most hotly contested sector was Leggett's First Brigade, commanded by Ohio brigadier Manning F. Force. Among Force's regiments was the Thirty-first Illinois—Logan's old "Dirty First," the unit he had organized in what seemed like long-ago days in politically divided southern Illinois. Indeed, Force's entire brigade had fought at Logan's side in many of the conflict's battles. (Logan would name his son born in 1866 after Force.)

Force's brigade was pressed from front and rear and changed sides of its breastworks to hurl back the enemy, which charged with "demoniac yells." Union captain Henry Dwight saw Force's men change sides, thinking that they looked "like a long line of those toy-monkeys you see which jump over the end of a stick . . . firing front and rear, and to either flank as they held their works." Once, when fire swirled in torrents about his position, Force asked for a flag. A young officer assumed his commander was ready to surrender and looked for something white to raise over the lines. "Damn you sir!" Force roared when he realized the lieutenant's intention, "I don't want a flag of truce; I want the *American* flag!" Soon Force was shot in the face and, even though he lost his voice, the brigadier continued to lead his men with gestures.

Bald Hill was the pivot of action on the twenty-second. Of great assistance in holding the elevated position was Walcutt's brigade and two 24-pound howitzers. His enfilade fire tore holes in the attack line and Walcutt reported, "We slaughtered the Rebels by the hundreds." Alonzo Miller of the Twelfth Wisconsin cheered, "The Rebs got it," and boasted, "I could stand up on the breastworks and count 50 dead Rebs, some dressed in fine cloths as if they came out to fight for the day."

When Cleburne was hurled back in the early afternoon Logan hastened to shore up the gaps in his line. Dodge and Blair were ordered to alter their positions so as to create an unbroken front, and one Fifteenth Corps brigade was sent to reinforce Dodge. Logan told Blair to hold Bald Hill "at whatever cost."

Before the repairs to the line could be completed Cleburne and Maney rushed forward again. Giles Smith's Fourth Division was the principal target and Frank Blair was certain, "If the enemy had concerted his attacks front, flank and rear . . . it would have been extremely difficult, if not impossible, to hold our ground." For two hours savage, but uncoordinated, strikes were hurled at the Union line.

The confused night movements had left Atlanta's population uneasy as the sun rose on the twenty-second. They did not know if Hood was retreating or attacking, and as one man wrote, "it was impossible . . . to obtain trustworthy information." "Furthermore," he added, "the non-combatant who dared to question . . . ran considerable risk of being hustled off to the trenches." As the sound of fighting rose east of the city in the sweltering afternoon, remembered by an Atlanta eleven year old as "the hottest day I believe I ever saw," people clambered up to their rooftops again to try to obtain early news of a change in Confederate fortunes. At about three-thirty they heard the roar swing slightly to the north.

After delaying for hours, General Hood finally decided to send Cheatham forward to create a diversion in support of Hardee. The attack was launched toward the Fifteenth Corps, holding the Army of the Tennessee's right. This corps, led by Morgan Smith after Logan's elevation to army command, joined Blair's corps on the left and the Army of the Ohio on the right. The most vulnerable point in the Fifteenth Corps' front lay along the railroad cut in its center.

The tragedy for Hardee's bleeding corps in Hood's delay in sending Cheatham forward was compounded by a further delay in executing the order. By the time a new thrust was mounted, between three-thirty and four o'clock, Hardee's assault was wavering and the value of the supporting "diversion" was minimal and too late.

Cheatham's fresh troops surged through the pines and drove a gap in the Union line. Colonel Wells S. Jones, in command of two regiments and two guns of the First Illinois Artillery that served as an advanced skirmish line, held the Rebels off as long as possible and retired in order to the main Federal position. The first Confederate wave, Manigault's brigade, was slowed by heavy Union fire, but a second force of graybacks penetrated the railroad cut and hurled the enemy back seizing a Union battery.

Rebel attackers also captured Captain Francis DeGress's battery of four 20-pound howitzers. His enfilade fire tore holes in the attack line and men of the Second Division, commanded by General Joseph A. J. Lightburn, fell back to a line of works they had held that morning. R. M. Gill, of the Forty-first Mississippi, was exhilirated by the Southern success. "I never enjoyed a thing better in my life," he wrote, "we had the pleasure of shooting at Yankees as they ran without being shot at much." When Gill and the Mississippians reached the abandoned Union trenches they were amazed by the great variety of supplies hastily left behind, and paused to haul off all they could carry.

When Lightburn's division fell back, the Fourth, led by William Harrow, on Lightburn's left, also slowly retreated to the second line of "ditches." On Lightburn's right, Charles R. Woods, leading the First Division, dropped his left back about four hundred yards and assumed a key role in the Fifteenth Corps' defensive struggle. Woods's unit held position on the flank of Cheatham's assault force. Sherman met with

Woods and ordered the brigadier "to wheel his brigades to the left, to advance in echelon, and to catch the enemy in flank."

Schofield's army was nearby but Sherman, for the most part, stuck to his intention of letting the Army of the Tennessee fight its battle. He did tell Schofield to use twenty guns to aid Logan. Sherman himself sighted the first of Schofield's guns, an action Schofield remembered as "Sherman's splendid conduct as a simple soldier, the occasion for which occurs so rarely to the general-in-chief of a great army."

Sherman's presence in the midst of action was in marked contrast to the distance at which Hood held himself from the battlefield. The Union commander was in position to respond quickly to changes in the flow of combat, while the more remote Confederate leader was unclear as to troop movements and largely out of control of his army.

As he looked down the barrel a bullet struck close to Sherman's head. "Ha!" he exclaimed, "close shaving—we'll pay back that compliment. Fire! Very good, very good; that kicked up the dust and some of their heels, too." The Army of the Ohio's guns tore through Rebel ranks, helping the Fifteenth Corps, urged on by Morgan Smith, a former Indiana schoolmaster, to shove its assailants back. Logan, summoned by a staff officer who told him of "the disaster to the Fifteenth Corps," galloped back accompanied by the Fifteenth Corps brigade sent earlier to Dodge. He also took with him a Sixteenth Corps brigade led by General August Mersey, called "the *funny* German revolutionist of '48," by an officer in the Fifty-second Illinois. Mersey lost his horse that afternoon and said disconsolately, "Mine Gott! Poor Billy ist dead—he fights no more mit me."

Logan and Smith rode forward to lead the Federal counterattack. The three divisions of the Fifteenth Corps, supported by Mersey's men, rolled forward to the accompaniment of withering artillery fire from their own guns as well as from those of Schofield's army. Major Clemens Landgraeber, chief of the First Division's guns, and another of those brilliant German gunners in Sherman's force, covered the field with canister and spherical caseshot—"Canned Friut," according to one Illinoisan—from his six-gun battery. He killed DeGress's battery horses so that the Rebels could not move the guns and when the infantry retook their lost trenches, DeGress unlimbered and unspiked his retaken pieces and fired on the retreating foe. By five o'clock that afternoon Cheatham's men had been driven back into the trees out of which they had surged a little more than an hour earlier.

As the two armies battled back and forth, one Fifteenth Corps soldier charged "almost against a white horse on which rode some rebel officer with a flag in one hand and a revolver in the other. I got within four or five feet of him—he ordered me to halt. I said, 'Hell stranger, this is no place for me to halt!' and dodged in the bushes, he shot and I called to some men near me to shoot the son of a bitch."

At Hood's headquarters in Atlanta, it was a day of hope and overconfidence mixed with confusion. The intense heat forced the Rebel commander and his staff to drag tables and chairs out of doors. Hood sent and received couriers, and several times rode to high spots where he could see the smoke of battle to the east. Couriers brought reports of Confederate successes announcing: "We've got 'em . . . Whipping them like hell . . . we'll capture Sherman's whole army."

As the sun fell combat still raged in spots along the line. Intense rifle fire and occasional, desperate hand-to-hand fighting continued, especially around Bald Hill. Between five and seven o'clock Cleburne and Maney threw three separate assaults against the Seventeenth Corps' tired but undaunted defenders around the hill. Giles Smith was amazed at the repeated Confederate charges: "In the impetuosity, splendid abandon, and reckless disregard of danger with which the rebel masses rushed against our line of fire, of iron and cold steel, there has been no parallel during the war." With each pause between assaults the Union position was strengthened, but Hardee's men continued to charge as the bloody, torrid Georgia afternoon came to an end. Once, Colonel W. W. Belknap of the Fifteenth Iowa seized Colonel H. D. Lampley of the Forty-fifth Alabama, dragged him into the Union works, and screamed, "Look at your men! They are dead!" Here and there fighting could be heard after nightfall, but the issue had been decided.

Belknap's words to Lampley seemed to echo across Confederate lines to Hood's headquarters that night. The new Rebel commander had lost his second battle in three days. This time the results were far more devastating than had been those of Peachtree Creek. The Confederate loss stood at about 8,000 killed, wounded, and missing as compared to 3,722 for Sherman. In return for his 8,000 casualties Hood had gained little. Against Dodge's corps Hardee had gained no ground, and even around Bald Hill and the railroad tracks the gains were insignificant by day's end. In Decatur, Wheeler's thrust at the army's wagon train had been hurled aside. The teams were harnessed and moved to Schofield's rear with little loss. Eight thousand casualties had been the price for taking a dozen guns, a few battle flags, and a thousand prisoners.

July 22 had been a long day for William Tecumseh Sherman. In his report to Halleck he admitted that his casualties were high but added that his men had "made sad havoc with the enemy." As he sat in the Hurt House that night the satisfaction of having stopped Hood's second sortie was mingled with the grief of McPherson's death. That grief had followed him all afternoon, but it was mixed with the joy he felt as his old army stopped every attack Hood could muster.

Late that afternoon Southern artillery had been crashing around his command post, and the general and his staff found shelter in the woods. There Sherman saw a terrified soldier hiding behind a tree. "Lord, Lord, if I once get home," and "Oh, I'll be killed," he moaned. The redhead began throwing stones at the tree, increasing the man's fear and bringing more agonized cries of terror. Finally Sherman yelled, "That's hard firing, my man." His eyes tightly closed, the soldier quaked, "Hard? It's fearful! I think thirty shells have hit this tree while I was here." When the barrage ceased the general said, "It's all over now; come out." The soldier left his tree, opened his eyes, saw scraggly, bearded "Uncle Billy" and bolted into the timber as Sherman roared with laughter.

When men later examined the Battle of Atlanta some faulted Sherman for failing to use Thomas and Schofield on the twenty-second. What might have happened had the Federal chief thrown his two largely idle armies forward against Hood's center and left, which had been weakened by the Rebel strike east of the city?

Sherman's statement that reinforcements from Thomas or Schofield would have made the Army of the Tennessee "jealous" is peculiar. Erroll Clauss, in a detailed account of the battle, has written perceptively:

> In one sense, this attitude represented a pandering to the intense rivalry that existed in his armies, especially between the Army of the Tennessee and the Army of the Cumberland. In another sense, it was a manifestation of the *mystique* or unique relationship that exists between a great captain and his men, an attitude that can lead to great accomplishments and exertions in the name of military pride and honor.

In 1897 General Schofield's memoirs denied that jealousy would have been created by detaching troops from one army to aid another. He believed that Sherman "lost a great opportunity" by his failure to call for reinforcements on the twenty-second.

While there is no denying that Sherman's responses to the surprise attack east of Atlanta and to McPherson's death were quick and decisive, the failure to use the Army of the Cumberland looms as one of the major lost opportunities of the Atlanta campaign. This was especially true after Cheatham was sent against the Army of the Tennessee. By four o'clock in the afternoon more than two-thirds of the Confederate army was fighting just over one-third of the Union army. Pressure from Thomas might have turned a Confederate repulse into a crushing rout.

But Sherman had little patience with second-guessing, either in 1864 or after the war. The failure of Hood's second sortie, accompanied as it was by such bloodshed, had paved the way for Sherman's next move. He could shift his entire army to the west with greater certainty that Hood's depleted ranks could not stop him.

As for Hood, the twenty-second was a disaster. Luck rode with his enemy, but the Confederate failure cannot be attributed to chance alone. The long flank movement on which Hood pinned his hopes needed rested troops, vigorous action from his subordinates, and close coordination from the commander himself. The worn-out men jostled each other down crowded roads and were not handled well by Hardee. The half-day delay allowed the Union army better to prepare itself and permitted the fortunate placement of Dodge's men. When the attack came, Hardee's divisions were flung into action piecemeal. Virtually every Union general who commented on the battle mentioned lack of coordination as a reason for Confederate defeat.

Yet the most costly Confederate command failure was Hood's delay in sending Cheatham to Hardee's support. Hood's biographer, Richard McMurry, calls it "the most serious flaw of the day." "For over three hours Hood held Cheatham out of battle, while Hardee's men fought," wrote McMurry, continuing, "When Cheatham was finally committed, Hood, so far as the record shows, made no attempt to coordinate his effort with Hardee's." "The only rational explanation for this failure is that Hood expected Hardee alone to rout McPherson's men and to use Cheatham to complete the victory," concluded the Kentuckian's biographer.

In early 1865, when Hood reported to Richmond on the battle, he admitted that "the grand results desired were not accomplished," but he believed that "the movements of McPherson upon my communications were entirely defeated, and no further effort was made in that direction at any time." The reason for no further Union pressure southeast of Atlanta was Sherman's prior decision to march to the west, not a Confederate "victory" on the twenty-second.

Sixteen years after the battle the words of *Advance and Retreat* reveal much about John Bell Hood. His problems on the twentieth and twenty-second "arose from the unfortunate policy pursued from Dalton to Atlanta, and which had wrought such demoralization amid rank and file as to render the men unreliable in battle." In spite of Johnston's "unreliable" army, which Hood had inherited, he was still convinced that the struggle of the twenty-second was a "partial success," and brought "much benefit to the Army." The benefits cited by the Kentuckian were: improved morale; and infusion of "new life and fresh hopes;" a decline in desertions; and a demonstration "to the foe of our determination to abandon no more territory without, at least, a manful effort to retain it." There is little evidence of Hood's "benefits"; there is much evidence that his "manful effort," further crippled an army already badly outnumbered by a determined enemy.

Two deaths saddened the Rebel army chieftain. Walker, Hood recalled, had ridden to the Confederate command post to say that "he was with me in heart and purpose, and intended to abide with me through all emergencies," just before riding off to his death. News of McPherson's death led Hood to write, "No soldier fell in the enemy's ranks whose death caused me equal regret." The two men had graduated from West Point in 1853, as previously noted, McPherson first in a class of fifty-two while the Southerner trailed in forty-fourth place.

Although Hood should have had enough information to enable him to evaluate the day's results, junior officers, men in the ranks, and civilians were often confused after a battle. They drew mistaken conclusions, influenced by their enthusiasm for the cause and hope that dead friends had not been lost in a defeat.

Confederates were saddened by their heavy losses but encouraged by their new and aggressive commander's "victory." A Confederate commissary officer called it a "partial victory," but Columbus Sykes of the Forty-third Mississippi wrote of Hardee's "successful demonstration," and Elijah Hawkins of the Forty-sixth Georgia told his sister that "we . . . came out victorious." J. C. C. Black, of the Rebel Ninth Kentucky, believed "Hardee and Wheeler attacked the enemy with brilliant success."

In the city, young Wallace Reed reported "the people had a very confused idea of what had occurred." The city remained in Rebel hands, Union prisoners marched by, and citizens were told that McPherson was dead. Reed wrote: "It is little wonder that they jumped to the conclusion that the Confederates had won a big victory, and some of the most sanguine predicted that Sherman would beat a retreat." "Perhaps for the first time since Johnston's removal," Reed continued, "the non-combatants felt thoroughly satisfied with Hood."

On July 23 Hood kept his army in the position it held at the end of the previous day's fighting. The following day he ordered Hardee back inside the Atlanta defenses. Two defeats, heavy losses, and this retirement inside the well-built lines covering the city's perimeter did not mean John Hood had lost his aggressive spirit. If Sherman gave him an opening he was determined to lunge again.

Sherman watched his foe pull back and continued to think out his grand counterclockwise sweep around Atlanta. Before that movement could be launched, the Ohioan had to decide on a permanent com-

Confederate Works in Front of Atlanta.

Confederate Works in Front of Atlanta.

mander for the Army of the Tennessee. It would prove to be a difficult decision and one that would spark anger, disappointment, and hostility that would last long after the guns fell silent. The decision would also reveal deep personal friction between Sherman's lieutenants and a fundamental clash between professional and amateur soldiers.

On July 23 George H. Thomas went to see Sherman about McPherson's successor. Thomas opposed Logan, admitting that he was "brave enough and a good officer," but adding, "if he had an army I am afraid he would edge over both sides and annoy Schofield and me." His hostility toward Logan stemmed from a difference of opinion over the use of railroads at Chattanooga. In March 1864, while temporary commander of the Army of the Tennessee, Logan had protested to Sherman about what he felt was Thomas's unfair domination of railroads. The commander tried to satisfy Logan and appease Thomas, but his actions were "not as soothing to Thomas as Sherman believed."

Recalling that contretemps, Thomas proposed that General Oliver O. Howard be given the post. Howard had led the Fourth Corps in Thomas's army throughout the Georgia campaign. Sherman argued that Howard, having come from the East, might be opposed by his western soldiers, but Thomas insisted.

"If you give it to Logan," said the solemn Thomas, "I should feel like asking to be relieved."

"Why Thomas," exclaimed Sherman, "you would not do that?" "No," said "Old Tom" slowly, "I would not, but I feel that army commanders should be on friendly terms and Logan and I cannot. Let the President decide it."

Sherman snapped, "No it is my duty and I'll perform it." The discussion continued. General Joe Hooker, senior corps commander in Sherman's army, was mentioned; "but his chances were not even considered," wrote Sherman. Few could get along with the ambitious, quarrelsome former commander of Union forces in Virginia. Sherman, in particular, disliked Hooker. Rumor had it that differences between the two dated back to the 1850s. In any event, while Hooker commanded in Virginia, Sherman had written: "I know Hooker well and tremble to think of his handling 100,000 men in the presence of Lee."

Clashes had occurred during the Atlanta campaign. Schofield thought he saw hostility between the two at Resaca. At Kulp's Farm the two clashed again. The latter embroglio brought the feud into the open. Even men in the ranks observed what one called a "spirited interview" between the two generals. Then, on July 22, Sherman received another complaint against Hooker. General John Newton of the Fourth Corps wrote that he was unable to advance because Hooker had "cut in ahead" of him. Complaints of this kind reminded Sherman that Hooker too "edged over the sides."

Talk returned to Howard, a West Pointer, who had served in the East from First Manassas to Gettysburg, and commanded with distinction at Antietam. At Chancellorsville, as previously noted, his Eleventh Corps was surprised and routed by Stonewall Jackson. In the fall of 1863 Howard had come west and served at Chattanooga. Sherman thought him "very honest, sincere and moral even to piety, but brave." Sherman wanted harmony between his army commanders, and he regarded Thomas's advice highly. The day following the interview with Thomas, he wrote Halleck: "After thinking over the whole matter I prefer that Maj. Gen. O. O. Howard be ordered to command the Army and Department of the Tennessee." He later wrote:

> General Logan had taken command of the Army of the Tennessee by virtue of his seniority, and had done well; but I did not consider him equal to the command of three corps. Between him and General Blair there existed a natural rivalry. Both were men of great experience, courage, and talent. Both were politicians by nature and experience, and it may be that for this reason they were mistrusted by regular officers like Generals Schofield, Thomas and myself.

Sherman considered Logan more than adequate in a fight, but was not certain of the amateur's ability to run all of the technical aspects of departmental command through a long campaign. He was about to wheel the Army of the Tennessee over to the right and was unsure of Logan's ability to carry off this intricate movement.

Howard's name, sent in on the twenty-fourth, was approved on the twenty-sixth. The following day he relieved Logan. "Black Jack" had commanded the army for four days; in that time he had received little warning that he would not be sustained in command. Howard's appointment stirred up a hornet's nest in Sherman's force. Hooker was furious and resigned in a huff. He told Logan in a letter on the twenty-seventh: "I asked to be relieved from duty with the army, it being an insult to my rank and service. Had you retained the command I could have remained on duty without the sacrifice of honor or principle." To Thomas he wrote: "I have just learned that Major General Howard my junior, has been assigned to the command of the Army of the Tennessee. If this is the case I request that I may be relieved from duty with this army. Justice and self-respect alike require my removal from an army in which rank and service are ignored." Hooker's resignation encountered no opposition from Thomas and Sherman. Thomas sent Sherman his application "approved and *heartily* recommended."

Having resigned, Hooker revealed his decision to his staff. He told them that the entire corps had been insulted and degraded by Sherman. The resignation brought deep regret from the Twentieth Corps. General A. S. Williams, Hooker's temporary successor, felt "Fighting Joe" had been a "superior corps commander" and "it was a blue day when he left us so suddenly." The men in the ranks were also upset. "Bully for Joseph," wrote a Massachusetts soldier, "it is hard to blame him for this step. By the rules which govern military men, he could not do otherwise." While others were disappointed at Hooker's departure and felt him justified, their disappointment was tempered by a feeling that he should have remained on duty and "made such a record that 'Uncle Billy' would have no longer distrusted him." On the twenty-ninth Hooker rode along his lines for the last time. As he left for the rear, "Fighting Joe" was cheered wildly by the men who had followed him through many of the war's bloodiest battles.

Sherman commented pointedly on Hooker's decision to leave the army: "General Hooker is offended because he thinks he is entitled to the command. I must be honest and say he is not qualified or suited to it. He talks of quitting. I shall not object. He is not indespensible to our success." By September Sherman was bluntly writing Halleck: "Hooker was a fool. Had he stayed a couple of weeks he could have marched into Atlanta and claimed all the honors." In his *Memoirs*, Sherman at first indicated near contempt for Hooker's "fighting qualities." In his second edition, Sherman was willing to admit that Hooker was an able fighter. Yet, he added, "I did feel a sense of relief when he left us."

When he reached the North, Hooker unleashed attacks on Sherman. He told anyone who would listen that Sherman would fail in Georgia and that the army was split by dissension. Secretary of the Navy Gideon Welles reported that "Hooker has arrived . . . in a pet. . . . He is vain, has some good and fighting qualities, and thinks highly and too much of himself." "Fighting Joe" carried his assault into the postwar period by calling Sherman "crazy," with "no more judgement than a child."

Hooker's letter to Logan on the twenty-seventh was probably sent in hope that Logan would join in asking to be relieved. Logan, though disappointed, refused to follow Hooker. He had asked Sherman to retain him in command until the campaign ended, but Sherman declined. Logan's disappointment was shared by many in the Army of the Tennessee. Dodge felt that the army "had in it material to command itself." Shortly after Logan's removal, Dodge went to Sherman's headquarters and found Logan sitting on the porch.

> He hardly recognized me as I walked in, and I saw a great change in him. I asked General Sherman what the change in commanders meant. . . . As

everyone knows, Logan's independence and criticism in the army was very severe, but they all knew what he was in a fight, and whenever we sent to Logan for aid, he would not only send his forces but come himself; so, as Blair said, we only knew Logan as we saw him in battle. Logan could hear every word that was said between Sherman and myself. Sherman did not feel at liberty to say anything in explanation of this change. He simply put me off very firmly, but as nicely as he could, and spoke highly of General Howard. . . . I went away . . . without any satisfaction, and when I met Logan on the outside I expressed to him my regrets, and I said to him 'There is something here that none of us understand,' and he said: 'It makes no difference; it will all come right in the end.'

The "something" Dodge could not understand Logan felt he understood completely. Logan believed until he died that he was replaced because he was not a West Pointer. On July 14 he had written his wife: "My command was first on Kennesaw and in Marietta, but that will make no difference unless I was a West Point Officer." Illinois general John M. Palmer (also soon to leave the army after a clash with Sherman) main-

Sherman with His Generals, Howard and Logan Farthest to Left.

tained that the "real reason" Logan was not sustained was Sherman's antipathy toward volunteers. Sherman's *Memoirs* did little to convince Logan otherwise; indeed his words seemed to substantiate Logan's opinion. "I regarded both Generals Logan and Blair as 'volunteers,'" wrote Sherman, "that looked to personal fame and glory as auxiliary and secondary to their political ambition, and not as professional soldiers." Though Sherman insisted that he had not been partial to any class, his words read differently. Sherman was particularly distressed by his political generals' periodic visits to the North for political purposes and preferred to have commanders he could depend upon to stay with the army.

Logan seemed to bear little ill will toward Howard personally. After the war he called Howard, then head of the Freedmen's Bureau, a "noble officer." Howard in turn was impressed by Logan's diligent return to duty as corps commander and took every opportunity to praise his ability and courage.

Sherman's decision was a difficult one, since his "heart prompted him to name Logan, whose battle conduct entitled him to command the army that was already his in spirit." But his uncertainty as to Logan's command capabilities, and his unwillingness to offend Thomas, led him to his decision. That he felt uneasy about Logan was obvious from the tributes he paid him during the rest of the campaign. On the day Howard was named, Sherman wrote Logan:

> I fear you will be disappointed at not succeeding permanently to the command of the army. I assure you in giving prejudice to Gen. Howard I will not fail to give you every credit for having done so well. . . . No one could have a higher appreciation of the responsibility that devolved on you so unexpectedly and the noble manner in which you met it.

In mid-August Sherman confided to Halleck: "I meant no disrespect to any officer, and hereby declare that General Logan submitted with the grace and dignity of a soldier, gentleman and patriot, resumed command of his corps, and enjoys the love and respect of his army and his commanders."

Although Logan took his disappointment into postwar politics, his 1864 actions won high admiration. He had vowed to leave the army only when the rebellion had been suppressed, and on July 27 Hood's plainly audible picket fire told Logan that time had not yet come. Moreover, Logan had a budding political career to nurture, and a rash decision to follow Hooker might not be popular with his Illinois constituents.

There is some inconsistency in Sherman's handling of the Army of the Tennessee in late July. On the twenty-second he refused to send outside assistance to the army lest it be "jealous." Yet a few days later he went outside the army when he chose its new commander. In spite of the inconsistency Sherman's appointment of Howard proved generally popular. Though some troops grumbled initially, they soon warmed to their new commander. "I think we'll like Howard first rate," an Illinois soldier wrote. "If he is as good as McPherson he'll do." Other soldiers spoke of Howard's bravery and his diligence in looking after his new command. The troops in the army from Howard's old Eleventh Corps who had followed him from Virginia were particularly interested in his elevation and called him an "ideal choice." The same soldier-authors criticized Hooker's retirement and praised Logan's devotion to duty.

Sherman was immensely satisfied with Howard. Soon he wrote home that "the Christian Soldier" had "elicited the shouts of my old corps, and he at once stepped into the shoes of McPherson and myself." The Union commander added, "I have now Thomas, Schofield and Howard, all three tried and approved soldiers."

The question of who would lead the Army of the Tennessee was not the only Union command controversy to follow the Battle of Atlanta. On July 25 an explosion erupted in the Sixteenth Corps. Thomas W. Sweeny, an Irish native who had lost his right arm in the Mexican War, then developed a reputation as an Indian fighter before the Civil War, and now commanded Dodge's Second Division, accused John W. Fuller's Fourth Division of cowardice on the twenty-second. Dodge angrily denied the charge and defended the English-born Fuller. Sweeny swung his attack to the corps commander, berating Dodge for mismanagement. When Dodge defended himself Sweeny roared: "You are a God-damned liar, sir," added, "You are a cowardly son of a bitch, sir," and "You are a God-damned inefficient son of a bitch, sir." The slight Dodge then slapped the much larger Sweeny, who fought back, striking Dodge in the nose and splattering blood across his face. Fuller joined the fracas, wrestling Sweeny to the ground and attempting to choke him. When the three principals were finally separated Dodge put Sweeny under arrest, and as the division commander was led off he fired a final salvo, calling Dodge, "a God-damned inefficient political general," and challenging him to a duel.

Outside of the tent where the struggle took place, one of Sweeny's officers listened to the ten-minute melee, which ended when the brigadier "acknowledged the order of arrest, but refused to give up his sword." He wrote in his diary in amazement of the "scuffle *between two stars or more.*" It seemed that not only could generals be shot like privates, they could behave like privates as well.

Thomas Sweeny was court-martialed, but the officers who heard the evidence refused to rule against him and the charges were dismissed. His career in ruins, the Irishman resigned and became active in the Fenian movement.

As Sherman began his swing westward, he could take heart in his "three tried and approved army commanders." He also knew that he led a confident army, one that believed almost to a man that the Battle of Atlanta had been a great victory. *"Remember this day . . . Bully!"* wrote a member of the Seventieth Ohio, while Elias Prichard of the Twenty-second Wisconsin wrote home in Welsh that the battle "proved very disastrous for the rebs." Captain Augustus Van Dyke, of the Fifteenth Corps, felt "the Rebs came pretty near using up their army" on the twenty-second.

Union soldiers seemed fascinated by the new Confederate commander, his tactics, strategy, and the change his elevation to command had brought to the campaign. Colonel Allen Fahnestock of the Eighty-sixth Illinois explained Hood's tactics on the twenty-second and gloated that he "got badly whipped for his smartness." William Baugh reported that Rebel prisoners cursed "their general for making them charge. They say they have lost more men in these two fights, since Hood commands, than they did the whole campaign before when Johnston was commanding." Illinoisan James Snell boasted, "we have given Hood a lesson he will not soon forget."

Josiah Cotton, a surgeon in the Ninety-second Ohio, wrote, "Hood is a hard fighter but was not regarded as good an officer as Genl. Johnston." The perceptive doctor analyzed Confederate strategy for his wife: "The rebs may hold out until after the election in hopes that some Democratic candidate may be elected. When they see old 'Abe' elected (which will most certainly be the case) they will have to give up. I think they have more hopes of dissension in the north then they have of success in fighting."

Orlando Poe, Sherman's brilliant chief engineer, lectured his wife: "The rebel tactics seem to have been changed so that they now fight all the time. From a strictly defensive policy they have changed to what is known in military parlance as the 'offensive-defensive.' " He added, somewhat scornfully, that the change had cost the Confederates 15,000 men.

When Sherman marched his three armies westward in a giant flanking movement, his men were impressed that their general's tactics would not butcher his army. They were content to allow Hood's offensive-defensive to hurl the graybacks at their lines. Sherman's grand flanking strategy also impressed at least one Rebel. A prisoner of the One Hundred and Fifth Illinois told his captors, "Sherman ought to get on a high hill and command, 'Attention! Kingdoms by right wheel!' " In the world that was his army, Tecumseh Sherman was about to do just that.

# 11

## Hood Is Not the Man to Manage Sherman

BEFORE Kennesaw, Sherman told his brother John that the Atlanta campaign had turned into "a big Indian war." His words implied the most primitive kind of war: guerrilla warfare, reminiscent of Washington and Braddock and James Fenimore Cooper. The phrase reflected Sherman's frustration with Johnston's dodging from one line to another in heavily wooded country, always seeming to present a shadow target.

There was no further talk of "a big Indian war" once Hood assumed Confederate command. John Bell Hood was no elusive specter of the woods. With the failure of his second sortie Sherman again saw clearly what the campaign had always been—a big railroad war. Far from the preindustrial implications of the general's earlier words, the Atlanta campaign was very much a military campaign of the nineteenth century, involving one of that century's most important innovations, the railroad.

The blue tide had rolled southward, always aware of the two steel lines that made up the Western & Atlantic. Federal engineers kept locomotives and rolling stock operating while track crews attended to rails, ties, roadbed, tunnels, and bridges. By July 25, Sherman's crews had completed a railroad bridge over the Chattahoochee, replacing the span destroyed when Johnston retreated. The 760-foot bridge hung 90 feet over the stream and allowed trains to deliver supplies to a base just north of the Army of the Cumberland.

Four rail lines ran into Atlanta, "the turntable of the Confederacy," and by July 25 the use of two had been denied the Rebels. The Western & Atlantic was Sherman's, and the Georgia Railroad, running eastward from the city, had been ripped apart by Dodge's Sixteenth Corps shortly

249

before the Battle of Atlanta. Hood's two remaining roads ran southwest, sharing the same rails from the city to East Point, five miles down the line. At that junction the Atlanta & West Point ran southwest, connecting with such vital centers of production as Montgomery, Selma, and Mobile. The region served by the West Point Road had hardly been touched by the war and its farms and factories were needed not only by Hood but by the Army of Northern Virginia as well. The second road, the Macon & Western, turned to the southeast and ran to Macon and on to Savannah. It, too, linked Atlanta with a region largely untouched by the war and able to supply the Army of Tennessee with valuable resources, especially food. On July 27 Sherman began his swing westward, determined to cut these two lines, win his railroad war, and capture Atlanta.

When Sherman launched his flanking sweep, one of Hood's remaining rail lines was not operating along its entire course. The previous week Major General Lovell Rousseau had ridden southward into Alabama and wrecked thirty miles of track on the Atlanta & West Point between Montgomery and Opelika.

While Sherman prepared to destroy Hood's railroads, the Rebel leader struggled with his army's growing problems. After the Battle of Atlanta he had only 30,000 effective infantry, and pulling Hardee inside the city's defenses was made necessary by this Confederate manpower shortage. Hood did have G. W. Smith's Georgia Militia, but it was untested and the commander was reluctant to rely too heavily on these men.

Hood also wrestled with serious command deficiencies. The Kentuckian's old corps passed through four commanders in eight days, falling to the young South Carolinian Stephen D. Lee, who arrived from Alabama on July 27 to replace Cheatham. Lee, only thirty-one and the youngest lieutenant general in the Confederate army, had not seen major combat in two years. Some in the Army of Tennessee resented his replacement of Cheatham. After W. H. T. Walker was killed on the twenty-second, Hood searched for a replacement, found not a single experienced division leader in his force, and split the unit up among Cheatham's, Cleburne's, and Bate's divisions. There were other problems with division commanders and staff officers. T. C. Hindman, too ill to go on, was replaced by Patton Anderson, called up from Florida. Hood's chief of staff, General W. W. Mackall, resigned, taking all of his records with him, leaving a state of confusion for General Francis Shoup, his successor.

But hostility between the army commander and his senior corps commander, General William Hardee, was the most corrosive problem facing Hood. That he held Hardee responsible for the defeats of his two sorties was clear, and when General Braxton Bragg came to Atlanta from Richmond on July 25 Hardee asked to be transferred. His request was denied. Any future Rebel strike must depend on Hardee's resolve and Hood's trust in his subordinate, and this smoldering enmity gnawed at the Southern army's unity of purpose.

On July 27 the Union Army of the Tennessee, led by its new commander, General Oliver O. Howard, with wagon wheels muffled in hay and grain sacks, marched north and then turned west along the south bank of the Chattahoochee. To occupy the Rebels while these Federals were on the move, Sherman ordered Thomas and Schofield to advance their skirmishers and feel the enemy. The Armies of the Ohio and the Cumberland were to keep Atlanta's defenders occupied all day on the twenty-seventh by being, as Sherman wrote, "as bold and provoking to the enemy as possible." Sherman sent Jeff C. Davis, who led the division on Thomas's right at the point soon to be occupied by the westward-moving Army of the Tennessee, on an even bolder move forward. Davis was ordered to drive the Rebels out of their rifle pits into their main line to cover the arrival of the Army of the Tennessee. The plan then called for Schofield and Thomas to pull back and to follow Howard along the same route. This Federal concentration southwest of the Gate City would deny Hood contact with the south and west and force Atlanta's surrender.

There was more to Sherman's plan of encirclement than massing his infantry against Hood's left. The Union general had found his cavalry of little use in the first two and a half months of the campaign, but Rousseau's successful raid may have awakened him to the possibilities of a well-handled cavalry campaign. At any rate, columns of horsemen appearing both southeast and southwest of Atlanta would force the Rebels to respond and might even accomplish their objective, which was the destruction of track.

Brigadier General Edward McCook with 3,500 troopers, one brigade a recent addition from Rousseau's force, would ride down the north bank of the Chattahoochee, cross at Campbelltown, and strike the Macon & Western near Jonesboro. If McCook could smash the railroad in the manner Rousseau had demonstrated in Alabama, Hood might be forced out of Atlanta without another major battle.

If one cavalry raid could not accomplish this goal, perhaps two might succeed. Sherman, therefore, ordered General George Stoneman, with 6,500 men, including Kenner Garrard's division, to ride out of Decatur on July 27, link up with McCook at Lovejoy's Station and destroy the Macon & Western.

Originally, Sherman wanted both of his mounted missions to begin on the twenty-seventh, complete their raids within three days, and rejoin the army. But Stoneman proposed to sweep beyond the railroad—once it had been ripped up—and drive for Macon and the infamous Andersonville prison, to free the more than 30,000 Union prisoners held there. Sherman, who wrote that he found Stoneman's proposal "most captivating," agreed to the plan but ordered him to ride toward Macon only after destroying the railroad, and only after sending Garrard to join McCook in supporting the army's general flanking movement. Stoneman seemed to see in his projected ride to Macon and Andersonville the kind of raid to make Stuart's and Grierson's exploits pale by comparison. Even though he consented to the raid on the prison compounds, Sherman remained skeptical of his mounted arm. "This is probably more than he can accomplish," he told Halleck, "but it is worthy of a determined effort."

McCook's troopers rode down the Chattachoochee and found the railroad at Lovejoy's Station, seven miles below Jonesboro. Stoneman's force was nowhere to be seen so McCook waited a while and then set his men to work. They burned the depot, wrecked a large wagon train, and were ripping up track when Red Jackson's grayclad cavalrymen, reinforced by a brigade from Wheeler, rode up. The Yankees had destroyed two and

Edward M. McCook.

one-half miles of the railroad but with Jackson's appearance they quickly dropped their wrecking bars and galloped toward the river. The Rebels chased McCook all the way to Newnan, on the Atlanta & West Point, and in the running battle the Union general lost 950 troopers, his supply train, and his guns. On July 30 the column crossed the river and turned northward to rejoin Sherman's army. When McCook recrossed the Chattahoochee, volunteers from the Second and Eighth Indiana Cavalry regiments covered the crossing, fighting until their ammunition was gone. "History contains no nobler example of devotion," wrote the general of his Hoosier rear guard.

McCook had lost almost one-third of his force and had accomplished little. Yet the general reported that his raid was a "brilliant success" since "the injury inflicted on the rebels is much greater than any we suffered." Two days after the destruction at Lovejoy's Station the Rebels had patched up the Macon & Western, and supplies chugged into Atlanta once again.

Meanwhile, Stoneman divided his 6,500-man force when he rode out of Decatur. At the head of 2,200 troopers Stoneman moved east for Covington while he ordered Garrard with 4,300 horsemen to strike south to lure Wheeler in that direction. Stoneman's plans were not completely revealed to Sherman, probably because he had no interest in his assignment of wrecking railroads and was determined to race for Macon, Andersonville, and fame.

Ten miles south of Decatur at Snapfinger Creek, Wheeler's men found Garrard. By the twenty-eighth the Confederates appeared to be so strong that Garrard halted his advance at Flatrock Bridge and rode for Decatur to avert a disaster. He won the race back into the protective embrace of the Union army, but he had destroyed no track and was no longer of any assistance to Stoneman. If young Joe Wheeler had not been forced to split his force of 6,000 to chase McCook and Stoneman, Garrard might have been soundly thrashed.

Stoneman reached Covington without drawing Wheeler's attention and turned south along the east bank of the Ocmulgee River. According to Dolly Lunt Burge, "They robbed every house on the road of its provisions." The angry Georgia woman reported that the Yankees took more than food: "They would take silk dresses and put them under their saddles, and many other things for which they had no use." "Is this the way to make us love them and their Union?" she asked.

Stoneman approached Macon, still largely unopposed, and looked for a ford while his troopers exchanged shots across the stream with a small unit of local militia. The militiamen battling Stoneman were led by Howell Cobb, one of Georgia's most prominent citizens, who still played host in Macon to retired army commander Joseph E. Johnston. Suddenly, three of Wheeler's brigades dashed up in the Union rear. He had herded McCook and Garrard northward and was about to smash the third Union cavalry threat. Abandoning all thought of freeing prisoners, Stoneman turned and streaked northward. The Rebs kept up a stinging fire for twenty-five miles. Near Hillsboro, at Sunshine Church, Stoneman realized that he was virtually surrounded. The New Yorker, a veteran of Indian wars, recognized his desperate situation and decided to send two of his brigades riding for Decatur and stand and fight at the head of the third. Some troopers of his 700-man rear guard were killed; most, including Stone-man, were taken prisoner.

The general and his officers wound up in Macon after all, and the enlisted men were sent on to Andersonville. It was a different kind of fame. In addition, only one of the two units that fled Sunshine Church returned to the Union army intact. At Jug Tavern, well north of Covington, the second was smashed on July 30. The rout of Sherman's three raiding forces was judged Wheeler's "finest hour as head of the army's cavalry" by Thomas L. Connelly, the army's historian.

Both armies were well aware of the cavalry raids. Union soldiers hoped they would succeed, while men in the Gray ranks knew they were a threat and prayed for their destruction. Confederate soldier Tom Key "hoped that the whole raiding party will be brought to repentence for its attempt to destroy our communications." On July 31 Key reported that the raiders, near Macon, had been repulsed by an army led by Joe Johnston. Another Rebel soldier told of "excitement" among Georgia troops who feared Union raiders would endanger their homes and families. Andrew Rose, of the One Hundred and Twenty-fourth Ohio, learned from prisoners of short rations in Hood's army and eagerly grasped at the rumor that Stoneman had cut all of Atlanta's rail lines. Ultimately, news of the cavalry debacle brought concern to men in the Union trenches. A member of the Twenty-second Wisconsin feared the disaster would be followed by Confederate raids on Union lines of communication. After expressing the same fear and complaining, "we can hardly spare 2,000 cavalry," Rufus Mead of the Fifth Connecticut concluded that the raids were "the worst accident we have had so far in this campaign."

Stoneman's raid was poorly conceived and had little chance of success from its inception. Sherman had labeled it "a bold and rash gesture," and realized the problems involved in freeing thousands of Union prisoners. He believed "the difficulty will then commence for them to reach me" after Stoneman's horsemen reached the two compounds. Stoneman proposed arming the prisoners, but the source of the weapons was never revealed. The possibility of marching thousand of prisoners, many in

George Stoneman.

weakened condition, across one hundred miles into Sherman's lines, without a serious challenge from Confederate soldiers was remote indeed. While Stoneman was chiefly responsible for the fiasco, Sherman also bears some responsibility for feeding his cavalryman's flight of fancy and for failing to exert adequate control over his mounted arm. On August 7, when Sherman knew at last that Stoneman was in Rebel hands, he wrote Halleck that the hope of freeing the captives was "so inviting to one's feelings," that it alone "would have drawn me to command a military mistake . . . as that of dividing and risking my cavalry, so necessary to the success of my campaign."

Cavalry raids would not run Hood out of Atlanta. Sherman wrote later, "I now became satisfied that cavalry could not, or would not, make a sufficient lodgment on the railroad below Atlanta, and that nothing would suffice but for us to reach it with the main army." He reported to Washington, "On the whole, the cavalry raid is not deemed a success," an understatement given the loss of 4,200 troopers, almost one-half of his mounted force. Following the failures of McCook, Stoneman, and

Garrard, Sherman dismounted Garrard's division and sent it into Schofield's trenches when the Army of the Ohio swung westward. The rest of his mounted force was divided into two small units.

On the day the ill-fated cavalry raids moved off, July 27, the men of the Army of the Tennessee filed out of their trenches and marched to the northwest in Schofield's rear. South of Peachtree Creek the army veered due west behind Thomas, crossed the Western & Atlantic, and turned to the southwest. Dodge's Sixteenth Corps took the lead, followed by Blair's Seventeenth and Logan's Fifteenth. They moved without opposition all day long on the twenty-seventh. By nightfall Dodge was in line along a ridge that ran due south from the end of Thomas's line. Blair was to extend the line on to the south but his deployment was stopped by darkness. At dawn on the twenty-eighth Blair completed his movement while Logan marched the Fifteenth Corps on to the south. When Logan's divisions were positioned, the Army of the Tennessee's line, using high ground, ran south and then turned almost due west near Ezra Church. Dodge and Blair faced east while the bulk of Logan's corps faced south.

Concerned that his right might be "in the air" and that Hood might attempt the "game of the 22nd," Sherman dispatched Jeff C. Davis's division of the Army of the Cumberland to support Logan's right flank. Poor maps and tangled terrain so confused Davis that he never found his assigned position.

On the twenty-seventh Sherman had written Logan, "Act with confidence . . . act offensively to show him [Hood] that you dare him to the encounter." On the morning of the twenty-eighth as Logan approached Lick Skillet Road, west of Atlanta, a masked battery opened on his lead unit. In the rear of the Fifteenth Corps Howard and Sherman heard the cannon fire and the latter said, "Logan is feeling them, and I guess he has found them." Listening to the gunfire, "the Christian Soldier" had a feeling: "General Hood will attack me here." Sherman instantly disagreed, saying, "I guess not. He will hardly try it again," before riding to the rear to hasten Davis's march to Logan's right. The general from Maine knew Hood much better than did Sherman and he believed he would attack again. Howard had been at the military academy with the Kentuckian and later related, "I said that I had known Hood at West Point and that he was indomitable."

Indomitable? Perhaps. Excessively rash? Surely. Sam Hood, undeterred by two failed and costly sorties, ordered a third for July 28. Early on the twenty-seventh Hood had discovered Sherman on the move, informed his commanders "the indications are that the enemy will attack our left," and that afternoon told Lee and Stewart to have their men ready to march "at a moment's notice." When the men of the two corps ordered westward began to move they were urged toward the foe by vintage words from their commander. "Soldiers:" said Hood. "Experience has proved to you that safety in time of battle consists in getting into close quarters with the enemy—guns and colors are the only unerring indication of victory." He told his men that they must stop the Federal attempt to flank or "our course is in peril." But, Hood added, in words that must have been puzzling to some Southern veterans, "Your recent brilliant successes prove your ability to prevent it."

Sherman's wheeling movement had given the Rebel leader another chance to wreck part of the invading army. In spite of the failure of Hood and his corps commanders to coordinate their movements on the twentieth and twenty-second, the image of Lee and Jackson and Chancellorsville would not go away. This time Hood would send his old corps, whose command had been assumed just the day before by Stephen D. Lee, to

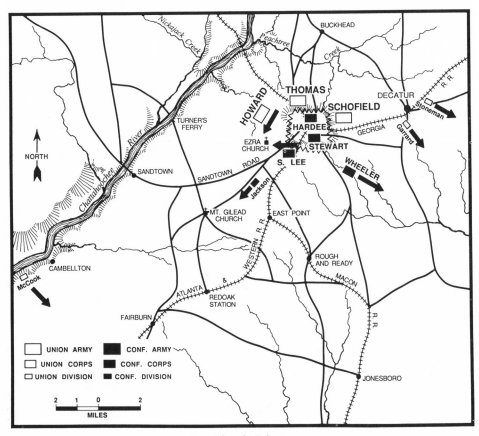

Ezra Church, July 27.

intrench in a line facing north at Ezra Church, the point at which Lick Skillet Road was crossed by an important north-south road that connected with the Marietta Pike. Control of this junction might stop Sherman's westward movement. Lee, fresh from a much smaller command in Alabama, was to stop the Army of the Tennessee's westward march so that Alexander Stewart's corps, moving out the Sandtown Road after dark, could march around Lee's left and assault Howard's right flank and rear the following morning. While these two corps struck Howard, Hardee's corps would remain in Atlanta's trenches to keep Schofield and Thomas out of the city.

The Methodist meeting house called Ezra Church was on Lick Skillet Road three miles west of Atlanta. Here Lee fired on Howard's advance and discovered Logan's corps was in position, prepared to fight, and already in control of the intersection he had been ordered to seize. Without informing Hood of the changed situation and without waiting for Stewart's men to come up in support on his left, Lee attacked. He did not even have all of his own corps on the field, and sent his divisions forward one by one. Logan was ready for him.

The fiery Illinoisan, disappointed with Sherman's refusal to give him the army command, was aching to prove something to his commander. He would soon have his opportunity, for Lee, in a manner much like Hood at Kolb's Farm, hurled his men at the Blue line.

Howard, like Lee in a new command, had that slight advantage provided by his intuitive feeling that Hood would attack again. He had followed that hunch with an order to the Fifteenth Corps to halt, prepare to meet an attack, and quickly throw up works made of logs, rails, and anything at hand. Hugo Wangelin's brigade, near Ezra Church, dragged benches out of the meeting house and covered them with knapsacks. The Union troops had little opportunity to raise much of a barrier before the first Confederate wave roared out of the thick brush at eleven-thirty. Logan's line lay along a ridge and the slightly elevated terrain aided the defending Federals.

Long after the battle Howard recalled the "terrifying yell" of Lee's men as they closed on Logan's position. The Confederate corps commander sent John C. Brown's division against Morgan Smith, holding Logan's left. The charge unnerved a few Union soldiers who broke for the rear only to meet Logan "greatly animated . . . with drawn saber," who turned them back to their units. Brown's onslaught repulsed Smith's skirmishers in what an Illinois defender called "a brilliant charge" that left "perfect clouds of smoke in the air." "Hold 'em! Hold 'em!" roared Logan, and the Fifteenth Corps poured volley after volley into the Gray attackers, throwing Lee back. Brown lost three brigade commanders and reported "my troops were driven back with great slaughter." Clayton's division, on Lee's right, struck Harrow's "with great desperation" and was also repelled by the concentrated Federal fire. When the fire slackened, "Black Jack" had his men bustling about strengthening their position.

At one in the afternoon Lee charged again, absorbed heavy casualties, and retreated, only to move forward a third time. Most of the Rebel pressure came against the Union center and right, held by the divisions of Generals William Harrow and Morgan Smith. As the July afternoon wore on the tyro corps commander launched three more hopeless charges against the reinforced Union position, each turned back with heavy loss. Again and again the Southerners charged until finally some broke under the pounding. "What are you running for?" cried a Georgia officer after his men. "Bekase I kaint fly!" shouted a Rebel who had tired of attack and die. Union general Jacob D. Cox reported that his troops saw Confederate soldiers refuse to advance "and line officers with their drawn swords . . . march to the front of the troops that would not follow them."

All afternoon Howard worried that the Rebels would decide his front was too strong for a successful assault and slide their attacks westward against his weak right flank. He looked for Davis, who Sherman had said was on his way to reinforce the Fifteenth Corps. But the Cumberlanders blindly struggled to find their way and failed to arrive. It was the Fifteenth Iowa and Thirty-second Ohio from Dodge, and the Sixty-fourth Illinois and Thirty-fifth New Jersey from Blair, as well as twenty-six massed field guns that finally reinforced Morgan Smith on Logan's right. Colonel W. W. Belknap, leading the Iowans, found Smith's hard-pressed troops, "Their faces . . . begrimed with powder and covered with perspiration and their muskets so hot from repeated firing they could scarcely handle them." Belknap also found the profane General Smith who "could outswear the army in Flanders," hurling curses at the attacking Confederates. Somehow neither General Lee nor General Brown ever realized that Logan's most vulnerable spot was his extreme right.

Neither did Stewart when his corps moved toward the firing at about two o'clock. Major General E. C. Walthall's division struck the right end of Logan's line, a position which the division commander found "of great natural strength." Colonel Belknap watched Walthall's men move forward in a "grand display as they took up their line of march down the hill, marching as cooly and as deliberately as if they were going out on battalion or grand review." The fire from Logan's men as well as from the reinforcements sent by Dodge and Blair scythed through the Southerners. Hurled back, Walthall, sword in hand, led his men forward again, supported by Clayton's division to the east, hammering once more against Harrow.

When Sherman learned that Hood was attacking in force he cried: "Good! That's fine! Just what I wanted, just what I wanted. Tell Howard to invite them to attack, it will save us trouble, save us trouble, they'll only beat their brains out, beat their brains out." He also sent Thomas and Schofield forward in case Hood had weakened his Atlanta defenses to support his latest sortie. The Army of the Ohio probed forward, was quickly checked, and Schofield reported the Rebels still in Atlanta "in sufficient force to resist an assault."

By three o'clock the Confederates flailed about in confusion. Hood, in Atlanta far from the field, did not realize that the enemy already controlled the road junction and he ordered Lee to "hold the enemy in check . . . to prevent him from gaining Lick Skillet road." This dispatch seems to indicate that, more than three hours after the battle began, Hood was completely unaware that his old corps was on the offensive. There was also confusion in Stewart's action. Instead of striking Logan in flank and rear, as ordered, he marched toward the firing and, like Lee, assaulted Logan's fortified front.

It was all to no avail. Walthall told his commander that a force twice his size could not have overrun the enemy position, and at four o'clock the battered Confederates fell back nearly to Lick Skillet Road. Stewart's reinforcement did nothing to reverse the results of Hood's third disastrous sortie, except add to the casualty totals.

That afternoon Hood learned that both Lee and Stewart had been wounded and he ordered Hardee to Ezra Church to take command of the two corps battling Howard. Given Hood's relations with Hardee, it was a peculiar decision. Time was lost in sending couriers to find Hardee and still more time was lost as the corps commander talked to Hood. When Hardee reached the scene of battle he decided further attack was useless and, as night fell, the firing stopped. In spite of evidence that the struggle at Ezra Church was not going well for the Confederates, Hood made little effort to improve his understanding of the situation and no effort to go to the battlefield. According to his most recent biographer, Richard McMurry, the Southern commander "remained at his headquarters where he neither knew what was happening nor issued any helpful instructions."

After the Battle of Ezra Church the already divided Confederate command engaged in further recriminations. In his report, Hardee commented on Hood's decision to order him to leave his own corps, in front of Atlanta, and take command of Lee's and Stewart's corps: "If I failed of my duty in any respect on the 20th and 22nd of July, it is a little singular that on the 28th General Hood, remaining at his headquarters in Atlanta, should have sent me to take a command on a field where there was no portion of my own corps, and where nearly two-thirds of his army were engaged." "Old Reliable" clearly inferred that Hood intended to use him as a scapegoat "to cover up any want of success on the part of others."

In a more absurd and tragic controversy, Hood and Lee both reported that Confederate failure was due to what the army commander called a "lack of spirit" on the part of Southern troops. Stephen Lee was even more pointed in maligning the men who charged the Fifteenth Corps time after time. "If all the troops had displayed equal spirit we would have been successful, as the enemy's works were slight," wrote the young corps chief. In words that charged his men with cowardice, he added that they "were so impressed with the idea of their inability to carry even temporary breastworks . . . that they did not generally move to the attack with that spirit which nearly always ensures success." The testimony of the enemy did not bear out these charges. Neither did the reports of combat leaders such as Walthall, and neither did the list of 5,000 casualties.

Eight days after the battle President Davis wrote Hood "the loss consequent upon attacking [the enemy] in his intrenchments requires you to

Entrenchments Near Atlanta.

avoid that if practicable." Davis added a suggestion that must have galled the Kentuckian: "General Hardee's minute knowledge of the country, and his extensive acquaintance with the officers and men of the command, must render his large professional knowledge and experience particularly valuable in such a campaign as I hope is before you."

On the Union side, General Oliver O. Howard had purposely remained in the rear during the battle so that General Logan might garner credit for the victory. Both the army commander and Sherman were lavish in their praise of the way Logan handled his corps at Ezra Church. Howard said of the corps, "I never saw better conduct in battle," and wrote in his report: "The general commanding the Fifteenth Corps . . . was indefatigable, and the success of the day is as much attributable to him as to any one man." Sherman hailed Logan's "conspicuous" leadership.

Despite the accolades, Logan continued to brood. To his wife Mary he revealed his deep anger. After Ezra Church he wrote: "On the 28th I had the hardest fight of the campaign with my corps alone and gained a great and complete victory, but will get no credit for it, West Point must have all under Sherman who is an infernal *brute.*" Two weeks later Logan wrote directly of the army command controversy. "You speak of my treatment by Sherman. He asked for Howard. . . . I feel it as sensitively as any one can and so does the whole army and they speak of it in very severe terms, but the good sense of it is for me to say not a word but go on and do my duty to my country."

Sherman had asked for Howard, and was well pleased with his choice after Ezra Church. So were the men in the ranks—even Westerners. Illinois sergeant-major Lyman Widney wrote: "We were glad to see Gen. Howard directing these operations. . . . The hardest sinner in our ranks respected him." On the evening of the twenty-eighth, when the firing died away, the men of the Fifteenth Corps saw Howard and gathered around him, cheering their new leader. Sherman later recalled, "To this fact I . . . attached much importance, for it put me at ease as to the future conduct of that most important army."

Ezra Church was the Fifteenth Corps' finest hour. An Ohio soldier reminded himself in his diary that night: *"Do not forget the 28th,"* and ended his entry calling Ezra Church "the hardest fighting I ever saw." One prisoner of the Fifty-fifth Illinois told his captors, "Our generals told us that the Fifteenth Corps had bragged long enough that they had never been whipped and today we'd drive you to the river or hell before supper." In front of their works the Fifty-fifth found dead Rebels "in windrows, sometimes two or three deep." Illinois Major Connolly called the Confederate tactics "butchery." He believed the graybacks "fought manfully, like Americans," and he saluted the enemy "for their valor, even though they fought in a bad cause." Connolly angrily continued, "Why it was perfect murder. We slaughter them by the thousands but Hood continues to hurl his broken, bleeding, battalions against our immovable lines with all the fury of a maniac. Reason seems dethroned and Despair alone seems to rule the counsels within the walls of Atlanta." Not as well written, but no less graphic, was the report of George Metz, a private in the Ninety-ninth Indiana. "This was discidedly the hardess fighting I ever saw. Our men helt their position with a small loss. The Rebs suffered terable. The ground is covered with dead Rebs. Oh such sites. . . . I never saw the beat of killed Rebs in my life." One Illinois soldier, looking over the gory battlefield, said to a friend, "This pays for Kenesaw."

On the heels of Peachtree Creek and the Battle of Atlanta, Ezra Church was a Confederate disaster, perhaps an even greater disaster than the first two. Again the objective had not been accomplished and the coordination of the Confederate attack had been poorly managed. Lee and Stewart had lost 5,000 men while the Yankees had suffered less than 600 casualties. If the ratio of losses was not serious enough, the effect on morale was. Hardee said later: "No action of the campaign probably did so much to demoralize and dishearten the troops engaged in it."

That night a Fifteenth Corps soldier found out about Confederate morale when he yelled into the darkness, "Say, Johnny. How many of you are there left?"

"Oh, about enough for another killing," replied one of Hood's beaten graybacks.

There had been a great deal of killing in Hood's army that bloody July. The Rebels had lost about 15,000 men while the killed, wounded, missing, and captured in Sherman's army stood at about 8,000. After three months the total loss in the smaller Confederate army was approaching 30,000. Sherman's loss since the campaign's beginning had not quite reached 25,000.

It is clear to historians that Hood's three sorties were strategic and tactical defeats. But were these battles viewed as defeats by the Confederates in 1864? Southerners, from generals to men in the ranks, wrote home of their "victories" that had kept Sherman out of Atlanta. On August 2 a Confederate defender told his family: "For eight or ten days Sherman has been fighting and flanking . . . but having been tolerably well used up in two pitched battles. . . . Now and then he will make a bold attempt to drive our pickets in and advance his lines . . . his 'blue coats' have the mortification of being driven back in disorder to their ditches." His picture of Atlanta to the home folks was almost exactly the reverse of reality.

Marcus Blakemore, serving in the Confederate army in Virginia, hailed Hood's "victory" on July 22 and believed "Sherman can go no further, and if he is not already retreating, he will soon." A family friend in Georgia agreed that "the enemy decidedly got the worse of it." After Ezra Church a Mississippian serving at Atlanta boasted that Sherman had "attempted to flank us," but the Yankees "were driven back to their works." With no hint of defeat he wrote proudly, "This is the third time in eight days we have assaulted their works. Hood does not permit the army to be idle, lively times are looked for under his management." At the Confederate capital J. B. Jones, a war department clerk, believed Hood had been victorious. "The enemy's account of our loss in the battle before Atlanta is exaggerated greatly," he wrote. "Sherman's army is *doomed*, I think," added Jones.

After Peachtree Creek, Atlanta, and Ezra Church, Sherman slowed his movements, further evidence in the minds of Rebel defenders that they had not been beaten in July's clashes around the Gate City. Even one Union soldier, George Cadman of the Thirty-ninth Ohio, believed that Hood's aggressive tactics had kept the Union army out of Atlanta. He wrote home: "Had it not been for Johnston's removal I believe we should have had it some time ago."

There were Confederates who knew the sorties had not brought victory. A member of the Fifty-third Tennessee described charge after charge on the twenty-eighth and a retreat leaving their dead and wounded on the field, for which "we are all very grieved." Rebel private W. P. Archer lamented for his unit: "their colors were shot to ribbons, and not more than one-half of that fine brigade that left that morning returned." A Kentuckian, who also charged Logan's works, wrote in his diary, "This day to be remembered with shame and sorrow." One Southerner, with a clear grip on reality, summed up the day's results simply: "Our forces did not accomplish there objection [objective] as they found the Yankees to strong for them and had to draw off." After the three sorties, A. T. Holliday, who had left his plantation and was serving in the Georgia Militia, was critical of his commander's frontal assaults: "Hood is not the man to manage Sherman," he told his wife on July 31. "Sherman has more sense; his whole plan is to flank."

In early August Schofield followed Howard around to the west, and by the second his army was in position along the north branch of Utoy Creek. Hood, aware of the potential threat to his rail hub at East Point, strengthened his line of intrenchments facing the Army of the Ohio. Two days later Sherman sent John M. Palmer's Fourteenth Corps, from the Army of the Cumberland, to reinforce Schofield, and ordered the Ohio army commander to drive on the railroad until he gained its "absolute control." "If necessary to secure this end ordinary parapets must be charged and carried," ordered an impatient Sherman. The remainder of the Union army would support Schofield by demonstrating against the Rebels all along the line.

Sherman was in a hurry to move on Hood's railroad and, "under the impression" that Schofield outranked Palmer, he ordered the Fourteenth Corps' commander to "report to and receive orders" from the leader of the Army of the Ohio. Citing a technicality, Palmer immediately shot back: "I am General Schofield's senior. We may co-operate but I respectfully decline to report or take orders from him." In an attempt to soothe Palmer's ruffled epaulettes, Sherman replied: "I was under the impression that General Schofield ranked you. I had not thought of the relative rank. Co-operate heartily and the same result will be obtained. . . . I assure you that I have no disposition to qualify your true rank."

The Union commander's attempt to jolly Palmer into quick action for a move that Sherman felt should begin at once made no impression on the proud Illinoisan (who would be governor of the Prairie State after the war). Palmer informed Schofield: "You are my junior. . . . I will not obey either General Sherman's orders or yours, as they violate my self-respect." But was Palmer really Schofield's senior? That afternoon and evening both Schofield and Sherman said "no." Schofield told the angry Palmer, "You are my junior for two reasons, first, because I have the senior commission, and, second, because I am by the President's order commander of a separate army." Sherman agreed and told Palmer, "my decision is that he ranks," and went on—his patience wearing thin—to leave little doubt as to both his rising anger and his expectation that his decision would be obeyed with alacrity: "The movements for tomorrow are so important that the orders of the superior on that flank should be minutely followed. General Schofield's orders for movement tomorrow must be regarded as military orders and not in the nature of co-operation. I did hope that there was no necessity of making this decision, but it is better for all parties interested that no question of rank should occur during active battle. The Sandtown road and the railroad, if possible, must be gained tomorrow if it costs half your command. I regard the loss of time this afternoon as equal to the loss of 2,000 men."

These pointed words had no effect on Palmer. Sitting in his tent just before midnight on the fourth he wrote Sherman, "I am unable to acquiesce in the correctness of the decision that Major-General Schofield legally ranks me," and went on to cite dates of promotion and appointment. Palmer ended with a request that he be allowed to resign corps command. There seems to have been no personal animosity toward Schofield on Palmer's part. He wrote later that he barely knew the Army of the

Ohio's commander and was unaware of any ill feeling between the two men. But Palmer always believed he had stood on principle and that he was Schofield's senior in rank. In his *Autobiography*, published thirty-five years later, he wrote angrily, "It was the idea of the regular army men that they ranked all volunteer officers."

The frustration of the command controversy and the stalled army was best caught in a dispatch from Sherman's chief telegrapher J. C. Van Duzer at eleven o'clock that evening: "Nothing accomplished today, movements having been brought to deadlock by squabble about rank between Schofield and Palmer, which at this hour is unsettled. Hope to do something tomorrow but cannot say exactly what."

On August 5 Palmer suggested a resolution by having Schofield issue orders to Brigadier General R. W. Johnson, the Fourteenth Corps' senior division commander. Palmer also asked Sherman to relieve him from corps command at the day's end. Johnson did command on the fifth and Schofield reported to Sherman that he "totally failed to make any aggressive movement with the Fourteenth Corps." Sherman turned to Thomas, in whose army Palmer and Johnson served, with complaints about the Fourteenth Corps. "I would prefer to move a rock than to move that corps," he said, continuing, "on the defensive it would be splendid, but for offensives it is of no use." Looking ahead, the frustrated redhead told Thomas, "It must have a head that will give it life and impulse." Thomas expressed surprise for he had found the corps "always . . . prompt in executing any work given to it." But, he concluded, "if General Palmer is an obstacle to its efficiency, I would let him go." On the sixth Palmer was "let go." His resignation was approved and Sherman elevated to corps leadership one of his favorite division commanders—General Jeff C. Davis. Perhaps the aggressive Hoosier could inject the needed "life and impulse."

All of this furor over military protocol in the face of the enemy was too much ado about nothing for Major James Connolly of the One Hundred and Twenty-third Illinois. He felt Atlanta might be taken "if our generals hadn't fallen to quarreling among themselves." "I'm glad I'm not a general," he wrote to his wife, "to be quarreling with my companions about questions of rank, like a bunch of children quarreling about their painted toys." Connolly knew the army won the battles not the generals, and wrote of his feuding superiors, "if they had happened to be killed the army would go along just the same."

On August 6, Schofield sent Jacob D. Cox's division southward toward the Sandtown road and Hood's left. Milo S. Hascall's division was to support Cox on his right while two Fourteenth Corps divisions were to occupy the Rebels with a skirmish line and artillery fire. At ten o'clock that morning James W. Reilly's brigade of Cox's division shoved back Gray skirmishers and the Union troops closed on Bate's division, well intrenched along a ridge east of Utoy Creek and near the Sandtown road about two miles from the railroad at East Point. Bate's men had erected a tangle of felled trees and thick underbrush about a hundred yards in front of their works, and the attacking Federals, slowly feeling their way through the obstructions, were easy targets. From behind their well-built works, the Southerners opened a withering fire, which stopped Reilly with heavy loss. The brigade commander—a long way from the Ohio legislature in which he had once served—attacked a second time, withdrew again in the face of enemy fire, and held his ground until it became obvious that a successful assault over that ground was impossible. The brigade had lost 306 men while the protected Rebels suffered only about 20 casualties.

After Reilly's repulse it was Hascall's turn. In the late afternoon Schofield sent his Second Division against Hood's extreme left. Hascall moved toward the point at which Sandtown Road crossed Utoy Creek and had pushed Confederate skirmishers back into their works only to have nightfall stop the advance.

The exchange of dispatches between Sherman and Schofield on the night of the sixth reveals continued hope for a successful attack on Hood's left, but also shows growing concern for renewed action in the tangled country along Utoy Creek. "There is no alternative but for you to continue to work on that flank with as much caution as possible, and it is possible the enemy may attack us, or draw us out," advised Sherman, emphasizing, "He must defend that road." Schofield replied: "We are working hard for the big road. The ground is very rough. I am confident of getting the road, but doubt my ability to either reach the enemy's left or break his lines, but will give it a fair trial."

At dawn, Hascall's men discovered that Bate's division had withdrawn to the main line of Confederate breastworks covering the railroad between Atlanta and East Point. Schofield ordered an advance on the seventh over the rough terrain in what Sherman told Halleck was "a noisy but not a bloody battle." This second day of fighting along Utoy Creek had not brought Sherman "absolute control" of the railroad. Schofield received orders to suspend his offensive and "dig in." The general heard one of his volunteers respond to the new order with, "Well, if digging is the way to put down the rebellion, I guess we will have to do it."

Utoy Creek, following the three failed sorties, meant that the Confederate army's aggressive spirit had not been broken, and caused an alteration in Sherman's strategic game. In mid-June he had stopped flanking and hit Johnston head on at Kennesaw. When that failed he began flanking again. This time Sherman decided that his counterclockwise swing around Atlanta should be halted. "I do not deem it prudent to extend any more to the right," he informed Halleck on August 7. Sherman did not propose to hurl another frontal attack against the Confederates, nor did he propose to give Hood another semi-isolated target such as Howard at Ezra Church or Schofield at Utoy Creek. His army would "push forward daily by parallels, and make the inside of Atlanta too hot to be endured." His words meant only one thing—siege!

The Confederate army, and the civilians who had chosen to remain in the Gate City, would be pounded by Union guns which Sherman would inch forward at every opportunity. He would take Atlanta, "the turntable of the Confederacy," by hammering it into submission. He would break the spirit of Atlanta's defenders, and make its civilians refugees, choking roads and railroads to the south and east. He would show the people of Atlanta, of Georgia, and of the Confederacy that their government was powerless to protect them. His long guns would bring the war to the city's streets, businesses, and living rooms—to its men, women, and children. They would share the peril of the men in the trenches and know the reality of war. And they would surrender. It would be a victory gained without inflicting heavy casualties on his three armies. In a very real sense the total war of the March to the Sea and the March through the Carolinas began with Sherman's decision of early August.

# 12

## Let Us Destroy Atlanta

WHAT Sherman had in mind for Atlanta was made abundantly clear in the days following his decision to bombard the Gate City. He told Halleck, "We can pick out almost any house in town," and threatened, "whether we get inside of Atlanta or not, it will be a used-up community when we are done with it." On August 10 he proposed to General Howard, "Let us destroy Atlanta and make it a desolation."

The Federals hauled new long-range guns down the railroad from Chattanooga and soon were able to fire 223 cannon toward Atlanta. Hood's line had been pushed back to the edge of the city and artillery pieces aimed at the Rebel army were bound to take their toll of civilians and their property. In addition, the Union commander was determined to wreck the railroad station, arsenals, and supply depots in the city's center. Sherman's words and Union practice showed little concern for nonmilitary destruction as the earth shook day and night for almost three weeks through the sizzling August of 1864.

While Sherman bombarded Atlanta he never intended to invest the city with regular siege approaches. He still thought of severing Hood's communications and, although the bombardment would weaken Atlanta's defenders, the Federal commander never accompanied the artillery attack with an attempt to push saps forward to puncture their lines. Vicksburg had been truly besieged, but Atlanta, according to Sherman, "was not . . . and could not be, completely invested." From August 9 to August 25 there was little change in the Union position. Schofield slid on a bit to the left, but as a Wisconsin soldier wrote, "Both armies are laying still for the present, watching one another to see how and where the other will jump, just like two great savage dogs." On the thirteenth Hood made clear to his men "the absolute necessity of holding the lines they occupy, to the very last."

Sherman's line of works, about twelve miles long, ran parallel to Rebel lines around Atlanta, ending at East Point. Schofield held the right with Howard's Army of the Tennessee on his left and Thomas east of Howard covering Sherman's rail connections. In the Rebel army Hardee's corps was moved to the western end of the line at East Point. Lee held the center around Ezra Church, while Stewart, reinforced by the Georgia Militia, stretched across the Marietta Road and faced Thomas north of the city. The opposing works were rarely more than two or three hundred yards apart and the area between them had been cleared. Often at night burning pine cones or kerosene-soaked cotton balls were thrown into the cleared area to make certain opponents were not attempting surprise attacks or trying to infiltrate.

Before long-range guns arrived from the North, some of Sherman's cannons dropped shells perilously close to Yankee lines. Soldiers of the Twelfth Wisconsin, after such near misses, yelled back at their artillery-men, "She slobbers at the mouth—take 'er away." The Badger State volunteers and their fellow bluecoats hailed the advent of more powerful

Confederate Works in Front of Atlanta.

weapons and cheered "There goes the Atlanta express," as missiles arched overhead.

Shortly after Sherman unlimbered his long guns he wrote his wife of the targeted city, "Most of the people are gone; it is simply a big fort." If Sherman believed these words he was badly mistaken. Although many Atlantans had begun their refugee treks southward prior to August 1, there were still many civilians in the city when the bombardment began. A Southern journalist wrote of "the excitement in Atlanta," adding, "Everybody seems to be hurrying off, especially the women. Wagons loaded with household furniture and everything else that can be packed upon them crowd every street. . . . Every train of cars is loaded to the utmost capacity. The excitement beats everything I ever saw, and I hope may never witness such again."

Although the exodus continued throughout the siege, civilians remained in the city through August and into September. Confederate military authorities never ordered a complete evacuation of Atlanta's citizens. While Hood did not say as much, perhaps he had the same idea that led Joseph Stalin to refuse to evacuate Stalingrad in World War II: "The army will fight better for a live city than a dead one." After three weeks of day-and-night bombardment the civilians that remained were saluted by the Confederate commander in his memoirs. Hood never heard "one word from their lips expressive of dissatisfaction or willingness to surrender."

Undaunted by the "Atlanta Express," Atlantans who could not or would not leave went about their business. They developed instincts about the pattern of the shelling and became skilled at avoiding the plunging missiles. The flaming fuses of Union bombshells provided an early warning, but shells with percussion caps gave only a brief, shrill whistle. Fortunately, the latter were highly unreliable, often thudding into the ground and failing to explode. The Georgians also learned how to build "bombproofs," and took shelter in these burrows in the red clay.

Sherman's shells brought death and destruction in the indiscriminate manner of modern long-range warfare. Yankee gunners never saw Solomon Luckie, a popular Negro barber, who stood outside his shop on Alabama Street listening to the distant thunder of the guns. Their shell hit the sidewalk and ricocheted off a lamppost. Fragments ripped through Luckie's body. He was taken to a hospital where he died two hours later. Near the railroad station an aged refugee, bending over to pick up something from the street, was killed instantly. In the front yard of her house on Forsyth Street, a woman said good-bye to a Confederate officer when a shell burst nearby, wounding the officer and her young son. The two were laid on the grass under the trees and both bled to death.

Some were more fortunate. A shell tore through the roof of an Atlanta market where thirty women were shopping. They clawed out of the dust and rubble to discover that no one had been seriously injured. At the Confederate telegraph office on Alabama Street, Major Charles Hubner and his telegraphers were sleeping on a row of cots when a shell roared into their basement room; it failed to explode, but tore the legs from the cots throwing the men on the floor. Once a Yankee missile exploded behind a wagonload of Confederate dead. The wagon's mules stampeded, scattering bodies along the road for blocks.

As the bombardment progressed and the city's houses, factories, and stores burned and exploded, one Rebel soldier found "the place looks like it was haunted." Across the city stone flues remained where houses had once stood. "Sherman's chimneys," as both armies called them, were mute testimony to the destructiveness of the big Union guns. In 1863 those civilians trapped in Vicksburg faced famine. With one railroad line still open, Atlanta's citizens were on short rations, but the Gate City's food problems never reached that of "the Gibraltar of the Mississippi." Atlantans did have to improvise, and "Confederate fricassee," and "Sherman hash," stews made of anything on hand, appeared on most menus.

Railroads at Atlanta.

Since the Atlanta campaign had always been a railroad campaign, its trains were a special target for Federal gunners. Shells rained on the car shed and were hurled at every train that appeared. In early August Hood ordered his locomotive engineers to blow their whistles to give the impression that reinforcements were arriving from the south. The whistles brought an instant Union barrage, leading citizens to ask Hood to quiet the trains. Whistles stopped but coal smoke puffing above the city still traced these strategic targets.

Those living near the station were in constant danger, and yet for some there was little choice. The Huff family fled its home near Peachtree Creek and took refuge in a borrowed house on Railroad Street. Young Sarah Huff lay in her bed and watched the shells arching over the city. Since the house was not theirs, the Huffs would not build a bombproof. Instead, they took shelter in the cellar of a flour mill across the tracks. Sarah Huff's memories of refuge in the mill's basement are reminiscent of the London blitz: "The more furious the firing the bigger the crowd in the basement. There was no such thing as a stranger, there never was in war-time." Eventually, Lieutenant Jeremiah Huff, serving in Virginia, got a furlough and came to Georgia to assure himself of his family's safety. Slipping through Union lines, Huff found his family in danger and moved them ten miles south of the city out of the range of Union gunners.

While many citizens fled Atlanta, some came into the city during the siege; often for the reason that brought Fanny Beers from Newnan. Her husband was one of the Confederate defenders and she came by rail, reaching the depot as Federal guns opened up. "Before I could think twice, an awful explosion followed; the windows were all shivered, and the earth seemed to me to be thrown in cart-loads into the car." Nor was that the end. As Fanny looked for a house, the barrage continued: "For a few hours I was so utterly demoralized that my only thought was how to escape. It seemed to me *impossible* that any body of soldiers could voluntarily expose themselves to such horrible danger. I thought if *I* had been a soldier I must have deserted from my first battlefield." She eventually found an abandoned house and sent word to her husband. That night her husband and several fellow soldiers arrived. "They were all ragged, mud-stained and altogether unlovely," Fanny recalled, "but seemed to me the most desirable and welcome visitors, I could imagine."

Early in the siege one of Georgia's first citizens, Robert Toombs, former United States senator and general of militia by 1864, came to the beleaguered city. Captain Thomas Key watched as the militia cheered Toombs, "an aged man of corpulent dimensions," after he told them to "stand by the artillerists and you will whip the Yankees like the devil."

When Sherman brought the war to Atlanta's doorstep, there were several men of Northern birth in the city. A few were dealt with harshly although they had served the Confederacy and there was little evidence of treason. James L. Dunning, superintendent of the Atlanta Machine Company, was from Connecticut and was forced to give up his business. He was jailed on suspicion of treason. William Markham, also from New England, and owner of the Atlanta Rolling Mill, was attacked by a man with a knife but managed to escape. On one occasion a Rebel soldier invented the charge that a bookstore had a copy of *Uncle Tom's Cabin* in stock. A mob attacked the store and the owner only avoided being tarred and feathered when the assailants failed to find Mrs. Stowe's hated book.

Fortunately for historians, there were several excellent diarists in Atlanta during the siege. Bookstore owner Samuel Pierce Richards, who edited the *Soldier's Friend* for the men in gray, traced the weeks of terror in his diary. He dug his bombproof or "pit" for his family, later deepening it for safety. Some days Richards tended his vegetable garden and some nights "the shells flew about all night on the other side of town, but we slept pretty well." He listened to a sermon at the Methodist Church by the Reverend Atticus Haygood and attended a "serenade" by an army band.

But the war was never far away. Richards was in the militia and hated the duty. He stood guard every other night and complained, "If they go on making us do *active service* at 'the ditches' or 'the front' I shall try to get off from it." He disliked even his limited service and wrote, "this being ordered about by others as though we were niggers is not much to my mind." On August 18 Richards and his brother Jabez started to move their business out of the city, then changed their minds. Samuel wrote with resignation, "the future is very dark and uncertain, truly a *sealed book* in our finite minds." Three days later, when a shell struck his store, Richards wrote, "It is like living in the midst of a pestilence, no one can tell but he may be the next victim."

A very different observer of Atlanta's days under fire was Carrie Berry, who began her diary on August 1 and wrote two days later: "This was my birthday. I was ten years old. But I did not have a cake, times were too hard. I celebrated with ironing. I hope my next birthday we will have peace in our land and I can have a nice dinner." Day by day she reported the bombardment, writing on the eleventh, "How I wish the Federals would quit shelling us and we could get out of the cellar and get some fresh air." But three days later the ten year old thought, "I dislike to stay in the cellar so close, but our soldiers have to stay in the ditches."

On August 15 and 16 shell fragments struck Carrie's house and the next week her father moved the family to Alabama Street where they could use a much larger cellar under the Express Company. It was a "nice large cellar . . . where we can run as much as we please and enjoy it. Mama says that we make so much noise that she can't hear the shells."

Joseph B. Semmes was chief of the Confederate commissary depot in the city. This cousin of Raphael Semmes, captain of the commerce raider *Alabama*, regularly wrote his wife during the siege. He spent a sleepless night "disturbed by clouds of mosquitoes and . . . the murderous and vindictive Yankee guns," on August 11. Ten days later he reported that "2000 shells were thrown into the city and it was really a beautiful sight . . . like meteors or shooting stars." Some shells, thought Semmes, sounded like flying locomotives while others sang " 'flibberty, gibbety' in a very loud and fearful manner." On the twenty-fifth, the post surgeon told the commissary officer that he had performed 107 amputations on men, women, and children since the siege began. The previous month Semmes had called Atlanta "this all important city—a city destined to become celebrated for either our glorious success or defeat." By August's third week the city seemed to be crumbling around him.

No one in the besieged Gate City observed more than the journalist Wallace Reed, who chronicled the bloody weeks of 1864. He seemed omnipresent. Reed watched the comings and goings at Hood's headquarters on July 22, moved about the city to watch its citizens under fire, and was on hand for the city's surrender. The day fixed most vividly in Reed's memory was August 9. After twenty days of sporadic firing into the city, Union artillerists threw an estimated five thousand shells into Atlanta on the ninth. To General Hood "the 9th was made memorable by the most furious cannonade which the city sustained during the siege." No American city has ever sustained such a one-day bombardment.

Atlantans were used to dodging shells but suddenly there was no place to hide. Fires started all over the city, buildings exploded, and "the very air was loathsome with the odor of burned powder, while a pall of dust and smoke overhung the city." A family of six scrambled into their shelter. It was struck by a direct hit and all were killed. A woman who had fled Rome ahead of Sherman was struck by a fragment and killed while ironing in her house on Pryor Street. Nelson Warner and his six-year-old daughter lay asleep in their house at the corner of Elliott and Rhodes streets. A shell tore through the ceiling and ripped the girl's body in half. The same shell cut off both of Warner's legs at the thighs. He bled to death.

Reed called Tuesday the ninth "that red day in August, when all the fires of hell, and all the thunders of the universe seemed to be blazing and roaring over Atlanta." Looking up, Reed saw that "great volume of sulphurous smoke rolled over the town, trailing down to the ground, and through this stifling gloom the sun glared down like a great red eye peering through a bronze colored sky."

In the "ditches" around Atlanta Hood's troops, battered by three failed sorties, held on grimly. The Confederate command change was still hotly debated in the ranks. Johnston's partisans condemned Hood's aggressiveness and believed the Kentuckian had "found out that 'charging' does not pay." By August's second week, while Sherman's army was strong and united, Hood's force was divided and growing weaker. His army had 35,371 men, and morale among his officers was poor; they talked of removing Hood. Some Rebels had always resented Johnston's removal and resentment of Hood grew with the failures and casualties of July. Hood's intimation that the army was cowardly did not help the situation.

The Hood-Hardee confrontation also continued into August. "Old Reliable" asked President Davis if he could exchange commands with General Richard Taylor. Davis refused and wrote Hardee that his government needed him in Georgia. Another Hood-hater, General Samuel French, elevated to temporary corps command after Stewart and Loring were wounded, was replaced by Cheatham in late July. French protested to Hood, and on August 16 his request to be relieved was granted.

For many grayback defenders morale was good and hope of saving Atlanta and winning the war remained alive. A Georgia regimental surgeon said confidently, "We will hold Atlanta in spite of all the enemy can do." Doctor G. W. Peddy found the men of the Fifty-sixth Georgia "in fine spirits" willing to "fight indefinitely [rather] than sacrifice any of the principles for which we are contending." W. B. Honnoll of the Twenty-fourth Mississippi reported his comrades "still think we can whip them." He found it "very disagreeable to be under fire of the enemy," but was consoled because "they are in the same fix."

But there were those who felt differently. Lieutenant R. M. Gill of the Forty-first Mississippi found the Federals "almost invincible." "Our soldiers are brave and true, yet they cannot accomplish impossibilities. I am endeavoring to prepare my mind for the worst. The enemy are making fearful inroads upon us," wrote the Mississippian. Gill looked beyond Atlanta's ditches to the possibility of the war's end if Lincoln was defeated in November. But he concluded there was "no hope" for a Democratic victory since Union prisoners told him their army was solidly for Lincoln. "I believe them. Their army is as well united as ours today and better disciplined," he admitted.

Desertions were a further example of declining morale. Gill wrote that "desertions are numerous" since "there is such demoralization in the army." James W. Watkins's observations confirmed Gill's report. "Tha is a grate many of ours men a running a way every nite," wrote Watkins.

One factor contributing to declining morale was the state of medical care. J. S. Speir, sick with "feever," was taken "to a place they call hospitle." He wrote his wife, "I had rather be here with my friends, then be in such abomable place as they have here for the sick for they give the sick nothing suitable for a sick man." Tennessee's Sam Watkins decided to visit an army hospital and came away depressed. "Great God! I get sick when I think of the agony, and suffering, and sickening stench and odor of dead and dying . . . of the groaning and wailing . . . in the rear of the building I saw a pile of arms and legs, rotting and decomposing; and although I saw thousands of horrifying scenes during the war. . . . I recollect nothing with more horror than that pile of legs and arms that had been cut off our soldiers."

Civilian and army doctors worked together, battling a scarcity of drugs and anesthetics and terrible overcrowding. Gangrene was solved by amputation, and both civilians and soldiers were operated on without anesthetic.

Routine life in the Confederate lines, while boring and dangerous, was a relief from the bloody battles of July. The constant skirmish fire, called "woodchopping" in the Rebel army, took its toll. Georgian W. H. Tucker saw "the balls fly so thick that we had to lay very close in the ditches to keep from being killed." Food was in short supply, steadily rising in price. Occasional showers made "the ditches very unpleasant," but "stray minies, and . . . shells from the Yankees make it unsafe to be out on open ground."

There were pleasant moments. W. J. Walker, marching with the Fifty-third Tennessee, seemed just as happy when "we drawed whisky last knight," as when "we had preaching here every knight." On August 19, Ellison Capers told his wife that a shell had recently burst overhead, its fragments narrowly missing him, then he observed "what sweet moonlight nights we are having."

With the campaign suddenly stationary, Hood's army experienced a religious revival. On duty after dark, the Sixth Iowa heard services "carried on until a late hour at night, when the shouting and singing could be distinctly heard in the Union lines." A Mississippian wanted soldiers to be Christians "as they would not fear the consequences after death as others do."

This religious spirit reached to the top of the Confederate army. Hood told Dr. Charles Quintard, Polk's old friend and minister of St. Luke's Episcopal Church, that he wished to be confirmed. With Bishop Henry Lay presiding, the general and nine other officers were confirmed. The crippled Hood could not kneel, so, leaning on his crutch, he bowed while the bishop performed the laying on of hands. Lay recalled, "The praying was good, the service animated. Shells exploded nearby all the time."

One unit in John B. Hood's defense force that stood out anywhere it went was the Georgia Militia, dubbed "Joe Brown's Pets," by Rebel veterans. Some resented the militia's long service in reserve, but Artillery Captain Tom Key thought they were "ready to do their duty," adding, "it is laughable to see their awkward motions and blunders at simply military evolutions." Sam Watkins left a vivid description of "Joe Brown's Pets:"

> Every one was dressed in citizens' clothes. . . . A few had double-barreled shot-guns, but the majority had umbrellas and walking-sticks, and nearly everyone had on a duster, a flat-bosomed 'biled' shirt, and a plug hat; and, to make the thing more ridiculous, the dwarf and the giant were marching side by side; the knock-kneed with the bow-legged' the driven-in by the side of the drawn-out; the pale and sallow dyspeptic, who looked like Alex Stephens, and who seemed to have just been taken out of a chimney that smoked very badly, and whose diet was goobers and sweet potatoes, was placed beside the three hundred pounder who was dressed up to kill.

Early in the siege the militia went into action, conducting itself so well that the laughter and resentment subsided.

Serving in Company A, First Regiment of the Georgia Militia, was A. T. Holliday, a planter from Wilkes County, who left his wife and five children in May and marched off to defend his state from the Yankee hordes. This instant soldier mirrored the bewilderment and frustration of "Joe Brown's Pets," but Holliday's sense of humor carried him along as he told his wife Lizzie and the children of papa's life in the army.

In early August, Holliday vowed "I have a plenty of war to do me and my family and my children's great grand children's children. I have lived in the ground until I have turned to be nothing more than a gopher or a mole." Four days later he wished "the Yanks would quit their foolishness and let us have some rest. It is very annoying to anyone that has been raised better."

The militiaman fought lice and red bugs—his "body guards"—and admitted, "I can't love corn bread. It won't get good any way I can fix it." On the twelfth he paid $10.00 for a watermelon and $3.50 for a dozen peaches. When Holliday's back hurt he wrote, "If I can get a horse this morning I intend to go over to see our doctor, or rather our quacks." As the siege became routine the Georgian found, with amazement, "It is strange how reckless men will get."

By mid-August Holliday yearned for his farm in Wilkes County. On the seventeenth when rumors circulated that Confederate cavalry might force a Union withdrawal, the three months' soldier wrote, "I expect Brown will want us to follow them but here is one that won't do it." A week later Holliday's box from home disappeared. He found it empty the next day and convinced that Rebel veterans had stolen it, he lashed out at them and the city he was defending: "It was no doubt done by some old soldiers, and some of them say it was carried to Atlanta to feed harlots on. It would be a good blessing if the whole city was burned up and all the devils with it. There was a large fire there this morning. I had not a tear to shed over its destruction." The siege was taking its toll on Hood's men in gray.

WHEN General Sherman halted his swing to the west he wrote Halleck that he was by nature "too impatient for a siege." Through the siege the signs of nervousness he had shown in the weeks before Kennesaw appeared again. He slept little, talking to major generals and privates alike as he moved through his three armies. He smoked constantly and ate very little. One of his officers reported: "He ate hardtack, sweet potatoes, bacon, black coffee on a rough table, sitting on a cracker box, wearing a gray flannel shirt, a faded old blue blouse, and trousers he had worn since long before Chattanooga." But this observer found the general remained "bright and chipper." David Conyngham, a reporter, one of that breed that Sherman disliked so intensely, saw him with "no symptoms of heavy cares—his nose high, thin and planted with a curve as vehement as the curl of a Malay cutlass-tall, slender, his quick movements denoting good muscle, added to absolute leanness, not thinness."

The bluecoats who served in his armies came to love and respect the general from Ohio. They shared their rations with him, talked with him of the war and home, and affectionately called him "Uncle Billy." Everywhere the general appeared his men cheered him and told him they were "willing to go wherever he led." Indianan John D. Lowman expressed an attitude almost universal in the Federal force: "it will take a smarter man than General Hood" to hold Atlanta against "Old Tecumseh." Rarely have the soldiers of any army had such a strong feeling for their commander's concern for their daily welfare and for his determination not to waste their lives needlessly, as well as for his superior generalship.

Like its commander, the Union army besieging Atlanta was confident and determined. An Ohio artillerist believed "everything is working with satisfaction at the front." Illinoisan Lysander Wheeler told his brother: "We will never be discouraged for that word has become obsolete, as there is no use for it in this war." John Finton, a forty-year-old private in the Eighty-fifth Indiana, after telling his daughter, "I am pretty well used up with the rheumatism," hastened to add, "but I intend to follow the regiment as long as I am able to walk. I want to be at the taking of Atlanta."

These confident Yankees watched with awe, amazement, and hope as their guns rained death on Atlanta. If the guns did their work, there would be no need for the army to attack Hood's defenses. Day after day diaries and letters were filled with news of the bombardment. Wheeler saw Illinois guns use the city's spires to guide their fire. Ohioan Andrew Rose counted five thousand "cannon shots that we fired into Atlanta in a short time," in August's second week. On August 8 John Wilkens of the Thirty-third Indiana was pleased that the big guns from Chattanooga had arrived and would "talk with thunder tones to the rebels of Atlanta." Nine days later an Illinois lieutenant watched a battery "fire all day and throw hot shot all night."

The damage meted out to the beleaguered city was obvious to the Federals. Alpheus Bloomfield saw shells "burst in the streets," making "the citizens hurry to and fro." He observed, on August 21, "scarcely a night passes but what the town is set on fire." James Nourse noted "great fires" in Atlanta every day from August 9 through August 14, the peak of Sherman's bombardment. On the latter date Nourse saw Union gunners fire toward buildings from which dense black smoke already poured, so as to harass Confederate fire fighters. In spite of the danger, Atlanta's firemen did their best and, although many were injured, none was killed. After dark on the fourteenth John Wesley Marshall of the Ninety-seventh Ohio heard Atlanta's bells through the night, adding a soft yet urgent tone to the exploding shells.

Sherman's bluecoats spent much of their time avoiding the shells hurled out of Atlanta by Hood's gunners. These Rebel projectiles, variously called "Hospital Kegs," and "Camp Kettles," often passed harmlessly overhead but, wrote the Thirty-fourth Illinois' William Robinson, "they will make a fellow 'juke.'" Usually Union guns fired first, but on August 18, "at early dawn," the Southerners "opened the *ball.*" In one Michigan artillery unit, Marshall Miller reported that a lookout was on constant duty "and as soon as he could see the smoke of their guns we would all lie down so most of the shots passed over us." Lyman Widney became an expert on the different sounds of Rebel shells and balls. Some had a short "whisp" as if "well greased and sliding through the air," while others sounded "like a young thrashing machine, wheeling end over end."

Death came suddenly to men in Union trenches and even to those in the rear. Andrew Jackson Johnson's duty sergeant was killed by a stray ball while lying in bed. A member of the Twelfth Wisconsin went to tend the beans he was cooking when a shell fragment "struck him just above the mouth, cut off both jaws and killed him instantly." Others were more fortunate. New Yorker William K. Watson, carrying dinner forward to the skirmish line, was struck by a bullet. Spent, it fell harmlessly to the ground. Kentuckian George Gist told his sister "the only place of safety is in the ditches."

After the months of marching and fighting between Resaca and Atlanta, many Union soldiers were happy to be stationary. An Indiana surgeon reported that, in spite of the continuing danger, his unit was "enjoying itself after such hard and fatiguing work." A bluecoat from Michigan agreed: "No . . . Fighting at close quarters . . . all artillery fighting and that is what we like." Some of Sherman's soldiers had become inured to the incessant roar of the guns. John Platt of the Twentieth Connecticut wrote, "I don't know as we could sleep if they did not keep up the firing," and the Twelfth Wisconsin's Alonzo Miller realized, "I am getting so used to the noise I think no more of it than I would of the flies buzzing." But as the torrid August days passed, many agreed with a Wisconsin infantryman that "time in the trenches hangs rather heavily on our hands," and with Illinoisan James Suiter who told his mother, "It requires patience as well as perseverance to soldier."

One foe that required perseverance and often proved just as deadly as Rebel shells was disease. Nausea, diarrhea, "remitting fever and the Piles," as well as the "Bloody Flux," were widespread, with the latter fatal to one of Lysander Wheeler's friends in the One Hundred and Fifth Illinois. And there were other perils. Michigan artillerist Marshall Miller reported "most all of the men are lousey."

Many Federals reported trips to hospitals or regimental doctors who prescribed an array of salves, oils, and opium. But Alva Grist, who was "sick and vomiting" on August 9, had another solution. "I must keep up my spirits and control my thoughts for this is the only way to avoid sickness," believed this son of Indiana.

In addition to the dangers of Rebel fire and illness, Union soldiers faced a terror that increasingly preyed on their minds—capture. During the siege General Grant ordered a halt to prisoner exchange on the grounds that it prolonged the war. There was not enough food in Atlanta for Rebel soldiers and civilians, so Yankee captives were sent on to Macon or to the new compound southwest of Macon at Andersonville. There, with insufficient food and water, 34,000 Union soldiers, packed into thirty acres, died by the thousands. Many were men who marched with Sherman into Georgia.

There were pleasant moments for Union soldiers. On August 25, Lysander Wheeler sat in the rear, smoking on a "morning that is most too pleasant for a country infested with Rebels and might be enjoyed hugely if the inhabitants were what they ought to be." Entertainment ran the spectrum from joy at a good ration of whisky to the "worship of God seated around on the ground behind the breast works." Music was also welcome, and one Illinois regiment's band played away "while the balls whistled overhead." On the still evening of August 22 that same band traded songs with distant Rebel musicians.

Chaplain George Compton of the Sixty-third Illinois led his charges in singing from the *Hymn Book for the Army and Navy*. Among tunes included in this hymn book, and sung to the tune of "Dixie," was "Dixie for the Union." the first stanza ended with:

> Go meet those Southern traitors
> with iron will.
> And should your courage falter, boys,
> Remember Bunker Hill.
> Hurra! hurra! hurra! the Stars and Stripes Forever
> Hurra! hurra! Our Union shall not sever.

The most widely practiced form of recreation was sending and receiving letters. On a quiet August Sunday the troops of the Ninety-seventh Ohio broke out pen and paper "and the whole camp presents one vast writing school." Sherman was well aware of the effect on morale of news from home, and each train hauled mail as well as food and ammunition. His men marveled: "the mail comes in every evening regularly and goes out every morning at six." They praised a commander who they knew looked out for their personal concerns.

Sherman's regular mail service allowed John Lowman to tell his wife Cleary, "I resieved yor picture and you better believe it don me good to see yor fase a gain." It also allowed another Hoosier, Benjamin Mabrey, to respond sharply to his wife Lou's request to come to Atlanta to see him: "It is not a fit plais for wimen, home is the plais for wimen and not out in the front. . . . It is bad enough for men." Letters penned in the trenches of north Georgia even crossed the Atlantic. Joseph Lester, born in England but serving in a Wisconsin Infantry regiment, told his father and sisters that north Georgia resembled Derbyshire and added: "You in England can form no idea of our struggle; of the *vast* extent of country we have overrun."

Mail kept the Union army in touch with news of other military theaters as well as with news of politics in this presidential election year. Early in the siege, Sherman's men rejoiced at word that the Federal fleet had been victorious at Mobile. Many hoped aid for their campaign might come from that quarter.

They had little hope of aid from Virginia. Western soldiers scoffed at the Union effort in the East, many convinced that Sherman's army was the only real hope for Northern victory. One Indiana private was certain that Sherman's delay in taking Atlanta was contrived so that "the longer we can keep this army here the better it will be for Grant."

While Confederate soldiers rarely wrote about politics, their Federal foes tended to be far more concerned with political news. This was especially true in 1864. They seemed to be aware that their actions might effect the presidential struggle and were proud of their contribution. Almost all hailed Lincoln's renomination and indicated support for the commander-in-chief. William Robinson, serving in the Thirty-fourth Illinois, wrote with concern: "The soldiers are looking with some anxiety as to what course the opposition [the Democrats] propose taking in the Presidential election. The question seems to be narrowed to that of Peace or war, and though we have faith in the loyalty of the masses at home, yet there appears great danger of counter revolution in some parts of the North. Then and now is the time for us to show the world that we have a government, let the Draft be enforced and all home traitors be *put down.*" Major James A. Connolly was angry at the "faint hearts at home" that "begin to whisper the craven words of *compromise.*" He vowed "*Atlanta must fall*" and wrote, "we do not look to the croakers and demagogues at home for strength, our reliance is in God and a just cause and 'by that sign we conquer.' "

The draft was a matter of concern to the bluecoats. The wanted "stay-at-homes" sent to the front "now." "I suppose they begin to squirm some for fear of the draft. I want to see some of those copperheads out here," wrote John Platt of the Twentieth Connecticut. A Michigan cannoneer suggested that soldiers be sent home to hunt down Copperheads, concluding that the Peace Democrats had "better be in hell than in their fingers." Lysander Wheeler, serving in the Twentieth Corps, took the issue of wartime loyalty and active service into his image of post–Civil War America. In words that presaged the "Bloody Shirt," Wheeler wrote: "Those who have been in the Army will rule when the war closes, and a man might as well be dead as not be true blue."

Sherman's ability to control the rail line north to Chattanooga, Nashville, and the fertile prairies of the Northwest meant that his army was well fed. Army rations, supplemented by what was available from the Sanitary Commission and through foraging, provided a varied and usually ample diet for the Federals. One member of the One Hundred and Twenty-fifth Illinois listed beef, pork, bread, coffee, tea, sugar, flour, beans, and potatoes as "full rations from the government," augmented by green corn, apples, and sweet potatoes picked up by foragers. "We have no room to quibble on account of rations, there never was an army as well fed and clothed as we are," believed this infantryman. Wheeler's August cavalry raid northward caused a decline in the army's supplies, but on August 24 John Finton boasted that "trains all now running regularly [again] bring our mails and grub."

Foraging was not only a way of gathering food, it was also a time to vary the routine life of the siege lines. Most of Sherman's soldiers did not hesitate to seize produce from "secesh" farms. To defend his actions, one Indiana farmboy reported, in jest, that his company had killed several hogs "which attempted to bite our boys and were slain merely in self defense." C. B. Welton, an Ohioan, only approved of foraging when Confederate raiders reduced the regular supply of rations, but most Northerners did not make that distinction and Georgia green corn and potatoes filled blue haversacks.

Union commanders tried to prevent indiscriminate plundering, issuing orders against entering houses without permission from owners. Violators were to be punished "with the severest penalty of the law," but the practice went on in spite of the threat.

Confederate troops, especially cavalrymen, were also guilty of stealing from civilians around Atlanta. Hood issued an order on August 14 that "the lawless seizure and destruction of private property by straggling soldiers . . . has become intolerable. It must come to an end." This practice was demoralizing to Rebels defending Atlanta whose families remained at home in north Georgia and were victimized by their own troops. W. H. Tucker, from Newton County, was furious when he heard about Rebel cavalry destroying corn on his farm. Georgians came to fear Wheeler's horsemen almost as much as Yankees.

After three months in Georgia facing the Army of Tennessee and living among the state's citizens, the Yankees had ample opportunity to meet and observe their brothers and sisters turned enemy. Georgia women were called upon in their homes and welcomed into camp for a Sunday visit by one soldier, and dismissed with contempt as "*hard* looking" by another. John D. Lowman had a chance to visit some Southern women and reported: "As we was a coming a long we stopped at a house and some of the boys got to braging on Indiana and a yong lady spoke up and wanted to know what part of Tennessee Indiana was in . . . so you see how sharp the fare secks of Georgia is."

George Cadman of the Thirty-ninth Ohio had praise for the people of the invaded state. "From what I have seen of Georgia," he told his wife, "I must say that the people are more civilized than in any Southern state I have been in yet." "There is not the rabid feeling against the Federal soldiers here that I have witnessed in other states and the men are manly enough to acknowledge they have brought their punishment on themselves. They own up they are whipped," wrote the Ohioan.

From the Georgia campaign's inception, fraternization between the armies had gone on in spite of orders on both sides condemning the practice. During the siege, fraternization increased. A Wisconsin soldier picked blackberries with Rebels and felt "we fight for fun, or rather because we can't help ourselves." Men in the two armies met between the lines to exchange newspapers, coffee, and tobacco. Unfortunately they sometimes exchanged information; one reason commanders condemned fraternization was the transfer of information to the enemy. Occasionally pickets agreed to truces and even to fire over their foes. Confederate headquarters was forced to issue an order for the immediate arrest of anyone firing too high on purpose. For the most part, men in blue and gray met, exchanged talk and goods, and went back to the war. On August 11 Charles Pomeroy of the Thirty-third Ohio watched "Johnnies and Yanks talking together and trading." The following day, when firing "quit for a time," he walked out between the lines and talked pleasantly with Rebel soldiers. On August 13, Pomeroy raised his head to fire into the Rebel works and was killed by a sharpshooter.

Since the lines were so close together, the Johnnies and Yanks often taunted each other, singing political songs to goad the enemy. "Bonny Blue Flag" was certain to provoke a torrent of shot and shell from the Union side while "John Brown's Body" enraged the men in gray. On the night of August 23 the Ninety-eighth Ohio began singing of the hero of Harpers Ferry because it "would rile" the Rebels. When the Yanks "commenced to sing the rebs commenced to shoot."

As in most of the war's campaigns, old friends found themselves on opposite sides. This was especially true in Kentucky and Missouri units. George W. Gist, serving in the Union Seventeenth Kentucky Infantry, found himself facing an old Bluegrass friend in Rebel gray—John Bell Hood. "He was before the war the most intimate friend I ever had," wrote Gist, adding, "I should like to see him, not as a prisoner, however."

Four days after Utoy Creek seemed to have stopped the Federal thrust southward, John B. Hood decided to send Joe Wheeler northward to wreck Sherman's rail line. Jefferson Davis, with the actions of July 20, 22, and 28 fresh in his mind, warned Hood on August 5: "The loss consequent upon attacking him in his intrenchments requires you to avoid that if practicable." The president was telling his general, no fourth sortie! The raid on Sherman's railroad might bring a Union withdrawal and at least did not run the risk of another major bloodletting for the Army of Tennessee. Davis gave it his blessing.

Wheeler's troops had drubbed Stoneman, Garrard, and McCook so badly that the cavalry's absence, Hood felt, would create no peril for his army. If the three sorties could not run Sherman out of Georgia perhaps a successful cavalry raid might. If the Yankees did not retreat they might launch their own desperate attack, which Hood could hope to parry, and inflict heavy losses upon Sherman.

Hood's object in launching Wheeler's raid—as it had been in the three sorties—was not just to save Atlanta, but to force Sherman out of Georgia as well. Even if the Union army was delayed in taking the city, its guns could make Atlanta useless to the Southern cause. Furthermore, if Sherman did not retreat northward, he might throw his large army toward Selma, Montgomery, Columbus, Macon, or Savannah, wrecking the South's industrial heartland.

To assist Wheeler's column, Hood asked for support from Confederate cavalry in Alabama and Mississippi. This request revived the controversy over the mounted arm in the West that went back to Johnston's assumption of command months earlier. There had not been effective coordination of Rebel cavalry in the West earlier in the campaign, nor would there be in August.

With about 4,500 men, Wheeler rode out of Atlanta on August 10. Red Jackson, with about the same number, remained with Hood to cover Rebel flanks. Hood ordered Wheeler to destroy the Western & Atlantic and then cross into Tennessee west of Chattanooga where he would wreck the two railroads running into Alabama. That destruction completed, Wheeler was to leave 1,200 men in Tennessee to continue operations against rail lines there. He was then to return to Georgia with the rest of his force. The order sent Wheeler farther than was necessary.

"Fighting Joe" moved along the Western & Atlantic from Marietta to Cassville, Calhoun, and Resaca. In their first five days on the move, the raiders tore up some track and seized Union trains and supplies, including more than one thousand head of beef cattle. Rumors swept both Union and Confederate armies that Wheeler had wrecked that monument of Union engineering skill, the bridge over the Etowah, and later the railroad tunnel at Tunnel Hill, but the Rebel raiders achieved no such success. Union prisoners helped spread the story of Wheeler's effectiveness, and soldiers and civilians in the Gate City looked daily for a Union withdrawal. Most were elated with the first reports. Mississippi cavalryman Sid Champion thought the enemy would have to retreat within twenty days because of lack of food. On the other hand, while Joel Murphree of the Fifty-seventh Alabama Infantry believed Nathan Bedford

Forrest might sever Sherman's communications, he had "little confidence in Wheeler's ability to accomplish much."

On August 23 the Georgia Militia's A. T. Holliday reported "all rumors say Sherman's RR cut. How can this be so when the Yankee trains can be heard every day?" Always on guard against unfounded rumors, the cynical Holliday wrote his wife: "Wheeler made a mistake and went down to the Ga. road, captured Conyers or burnt it up, recaptured Stone Mountain and burnt up the mountain, captured 6 head of beef cattle, killing one blind yearling, and returned to Hood and told him that the Yanks were ruined forever." Holliday had learned much about the cavalry in his three months in the army.

On the fourteenth and fifteenth Wheeler's troopers struck near Dalton, threatening the isolated Union garrison before being chased away by bluecoat reinforcements. The Rebel horsemen then swung east of Chattanooga and went riding up the Tennessee River valley to Loudon. The river was impossible to ford there, and Wheeler almost reached Knoxville before turning back to the southwest. He had the Nashville & Chattanooga Railroad in mind and his troopers ripped up its track in several places before moving southward and recrossing the Tennessee River at Tuscumbia in the northwestern corner of Alabama on September 10.

Hood's original orders sent Wheeler too far, and the cavalry commander's violation of those orders in rambling even farther north—first to Knoxville and then to near Nashville—magnified the mistake. In addition, he failed to leave 1,200 troopers in Tennessee to continue wrecking the Nashville & Chattanooga. Furthermore, reports from Wheeler and talk of Union prisoners misled Hood as to the damage done to Sherman's lifeline.

Sherman was well aware that Hood might order a raid against his railroad. With the failures at Peachtree Creek, Atlanta, and Ezra Church, that strategy became almost inevitable. On August 1 Sherman had written, "the enemy will surely be on our railroad very soon." He was prepared for such a strike: he had established strong blockhouses at his bridges and tunnels and his mobile repair units were ready to race to damaged points. Sherman's strongpoints were so well established that on one occasion, a division of enemy infantry and three artillery batteries could not seize a strong point from thirty Yankee defenders. His repair units moved so swiftly and their engineering magic was so effective that the Rebels accorded Sherman the compliment of tall overstatement. One Confederate soldier, so a widely repeated story went, told a fellow Reb that Wheeler had blown up the Tunnel Hill tunnel and their enemy would have to retreat. "Oh hell!" replied the soldier, "Don't you know that old Sherman carries a duplicate tunnel along with him?"

One month had passed between Wheeler's departure from Atlanta and his fording of the Tennessee at Tuscumbia. His riders had averaged twenty-five miles a day and crossed twenty-seven rivers. Wheeler proudly reported that he had suffered only 150 casualities while seizing "1000 horses and mules, 200 wagons, 600 prisoners, and 1700 head of beef cattle," in addition to the damage done to track and bridges. By September 10, of course, Sherman had been in Atlanta for a week.

Wheeler's raid was the kind of campaign all too common in the Civil War. Reading the reports it seems a remarkable accomplishment, all those miles and rivers and all that destruction. Wheeler engaged in an orgy of statistical self-congratulation, failing to note at the end that all the track wrecked, rivers crossed, and cattle seized had no significant effect on Sherman. Wheeler was gone too long, ranged too far afield, and Sherman's clever and hard-working track gangs had the repairs completed almost before the dust stirred up by the grayback cavalry had settled in the distance. Wheeler's absence deprived Hood of adequate cavalry when Sherman launched his last attack and so the raid, like the three sorties, failed to deter Tecumseh Sherman in his drive to conquer the Gate City.

When Hood wrote *Advance and Retreat* fifteen years later the failed raid became a victory. He described Wheeler's success: "burning the bridge over the Etowah," retaking Dalton and Resaca, and wrecking eighty-five miles of track. The statement is almost completely untrue; the general could not admit the raid had been a failure.

The July disaster to Sherman's horsemen did not stop the Union commander from mounting his own cavalry effort in mid-August. Reports reaching the general from north Georgia indicated the absence of a large part of Hood's mounted arm, and the time seemed propituous for a Union raid. The hope still lingered that an effective raid might destroy the last Rebel line, end the siege, and make a major battle unnecessary. McCook had failed in July, and Stoneman was a Confederate prisoner. Kenner Garrard was available and was defended by Thomas since he "has preserved to us his fine division." Sherman thrust Pap's arguments aside, saying Garrard's unit was "as useless as so many sticks," and adding, "I am . . . thoroughly convinced that if he can see a horseman in the distance with a spy-glass he will turn back."

"Little Kil," Hugh Judson Kilpatrick, had returned to the army. General Kilpatrick, a twenty-eight year old from the academy class of 1861, had been transferred to the western theater at Sherman's request. A slight man with a pointed nose and long red sideburns, he was the first regular army officer wounded in the war. Kilpatrick also had been wounded more recently at Resaca, and his return to action—along with Wheeler's

Judson Kilpatrick.

absence—prompted Sherman to reinforce Kilpatrick's division with two of Garrard's brigades and to send him riding for the Macon railroad. "I know that Kilpatrick is a hell of a damned fool," he said of his choice, "but I want just that sort of man to command the cavalry on this expedition." On August 17 the self-confident Kilpatrick told his commander that a destructive raid on Hood's rail lines was "not only possible but comparatively easy."

The troopers' task was solely destruction and Sherman, weary of cavalrymen who forgot their orders once they were out of sight, was specific when he told Kilpatrick "not to fight but to work." He made his orders so clear there could be no mistake in the mind of another overly ambitious cavalry general: "It is not a raid, but a deliberate attack for the purpose of so disabling that road that the enemy will be unable to supply his army in Atlanta." He also instructed Schofield: "Tell Kilpatrick he cannot tear up too much track nor twist too much iron. It may save this army the necessity of making a long, hazardous flank march." While Kilpatrick rode to the southwest toward Jonesboro the main army would occupy Hood so that no Rebel infantry could be detached to strike the Federal horsemen.

After dark on August 18 Kilpatrick's column—4,500 sabers and two artillery batteries—rode out of Sandtown, aiming for the railroad near Jonesboro, about twelve miles away. That night the Yankee troopers shoved Sul Ross's Confederate cavalry toward East Point and early the following morning the Texan reported to Hood that he was "convinced the enemy I have been fighting is Kilpatrick's division on a raid." The Third Texas Cavalry was sent to help halt the Federals.

On the morning of the nineteenth, Kilpatrick reached the West Point Railroad near Fairburn and began wrecking track. Ross tried to drive the Yankees away but was repulsed. Following the scrap Kilpatrick's division, Eli Long's brigade leading the way, moved on toward Jonesboro and crossed the Flint River in spite of Rebel efforts to burn the bridge. Through the afternoon sporadic contact continued, but by five o'clock Kilpatrick had taken Jonesboro.

The troops labored for six hours—burning the depot and piles of cross-ties, and destroying three miles of track—when some of Jackson's cavalry attacked. The Blue horsemen dropped their tools, grabbed their weapons, and rode off to the south. Jackson, aided by D. H. Reynolds's infantry brigade, kept the pressure on Kilpatrick, blocking the Union attempt to seize Lovejoy's Station and virtually surrounding "Little Kil's" men. With drawn sabers, the Union cavalrymen charged through the Rebels, circled south of the city, and reappeared at Decatur on August 22. Kilpatrick told Sherman that his wreckers had shut off Hood's supply line for at least ten days. It was another empty cavalry boast and Sherman recalled in his memoirs, "On the 23rd, however we saw trains coming into Atlanta from the south, when I became more than ever convinced that cavalry could not or would not work hard enough to destroy a railroad properly, and therefore resolved at once to proceed to the execution of my original plan." There would have to be a "grand left wheel around Atlanta" after all.

# 13

# Atlanta Is Ours, and Fairly Won

AUGUST was almost gone when Sherman began his "grand left wheel." Since neither the cavalry strikes nor his artillery blasts could dislodge the Rebels, he called on his infantry. On August 23 the Union commander asked General Howard, "How soon can you be ready to execute the former plan of swinging our whole army by the right across by Fayetteville or Jonesborough?" The "former plan" had been drawn up one week earlier but postponed while Kilpatrick attacked the railroad. By the twenty-third Sherman had decided to activate his infantry sweep and begin moving his army after dark on August 25.

The general emphasized secrecy and the necessity of loading wagons with adequate, but not excessive, supplies in the orders delivered to each Union army, corps, and division. Kilpatrick had found fields of corn southwest of Atlanta and Sherman's men could forage liberally in the direction they were marching. The Union telegraph was dismantled on the twenty-fifth; couriers would maintain the link between the army on the march and the corps guarding the Chattahoochee Bridge.

To cover the army's movement, Sherman dismounted Garrard's troopers who, leaving their horses out of sight, filed into the vacated trenches to deceive the Rebels. Early in the day all artillery and wagon trains that could be moved without alerting the enemy were sent westward. After dark the guns from the front, with muffled wheels, began rolling and "silently stole away." James A. Congleton, a Yankee on rearguard picket duty, listened to the ghostlike movement: "The army is moving with the utmost care and very quietly. All we pickets can hear is occasionally the clink of a bayonet against a canteen."

On the twenty-fifth, Hooker's old corps, commanded by General Alpheus S. Williams (who would give way two days later to General Henry W. Slocum) moved to the Chattahoochee Bridge and began strengthening the works it found there. The Twentieth Corps was to hold railroad and pontoon bridges across the stream and keep a wary eye on Hood. Yankee cavalry also began riding, to screen the movements of Sherman's force, guard wagon trains, and secure the bridges at Sandtown over which the army would march.

When night fell on August 26 the Army of the Tennessee, designated to make the widest sweep westward, filed out of its trenches. Logan's and Blair's corps were trailed by the Sixteenth Corps, led since Dodge's wounding on the nineteenth by General T. E. G. Ransom. As Howard's army abandoned its works the enemy's bombardment increased. When the last Union pickets withdrew early on the following morning, Rebel skirmishers rushed into the Yankee ditches cheering wildly. They rummaged through the army's abandoned refuse, snatching food and supplies and marveling at the mess. They took particular delight in reading letters left behind, including some written especially for their benefit.

By the early hours of the twenty-seventh the Army of the Tennessee had crossed Utoy and Camp creeks and was moving on Fairburn. At that spot it was to hit the Atlanta & West Point Railroad—of limited use to Hood since Rousseau's earlier raid—cross the Flint River, and strike the Macon & Western at Jonesboro.

Thomas's Cumberlanders, moving in the center, crossed the two tributaries of the Chattahoochee and aimed for Red Oak on the West Point between Fairburn and East Point. Orders then called for Thomas to cross the Flint River before hitting the Macon road's tracks halfway between Howard and Schofield. On the left, John Schofield's Army of the Ohio had the smallest arc and would start last. Schofield would hold position on the Utoy until the two larger armies were well underway. He would then move close to Atlanta's outskirts, cross the West Point just south of the East Point junction, and make for Rough and Ready on the Macon & Western.

For two days, the twenty-sixth and twenty-seventh, the three Union armies encountered some driving rain but little Confederate opposition. Kilpatrick's horsemen shoved graycoat cavalrymen aside, seizing the West Point near Shadnor Church, between Fairburn and Red Oak. Although the road had been destroyed in Alabama, Howard's army joined Kilpatrick and the infantrymen began work to keep it out of commission. Logan, "as wide awake by night as by day," pushed the Fifteenth Corps on toward the railroad.

Sherman expected total destruction, so "that not a rail or tie can be used again." Instructed by Sherman's brilliant chief engineer, Colonel Orlando Poe, the bluecoat infantrymen did their job far more effectively than did the hit, miss, and ride-away cavalry. They heated rails on cross-tie fires and then wrapped them around trees or telegraph poles to make what the army happily called "Sherman's neckties." Then they worked on the roadbed. A proud Sherman wrote: "To be still more certain, we filled up many deep cuts with trees, brush and earth, and commingled with them loaded shells, so arranged that they would explode on an attempt to haul out the bushes. The explosion of one such shell would have demoralized a gang of negroes, and thus would have prevented even the attempt to clear the road."

On the afternoon of August 28, Jeff C. Davis's Fourteenth Corps of the Army of the Cumberland reached the tracks at Red Oak and began to destroy them. All night long on the twenty-eighth and into the following day, the men of Howard's army as well as the Army of the Cumberland ripped, twisted, pried, and burned. As Sherman's wreckers fired piles of crossties, a smoky haze settled over the countryside. The soldiers also ripped down fence rails and built smaller fires to roast the plentiful ears of corn that lined the right-of-way. On the twenty-eighth Sherman encouraged Howard to keep his wreckers working with, "You can't do too much of it." He added, "I don't think the enemy yet understand our movement. They have made no effort to stop us, only cavalry holding the road."

Sherman spent the day "which was hot but otherwise very pleasant," riding with Thomas. "The Rock of Chickamauga" said he thought the movement was "extra hazardous" since it took the army so far away from its railroad. But Sherman remained confident. As they rode along he told Thomas: "I have Atlanta as certainly as if it were in my hand!" No enemy appeared to disturb the troops' labors as they marched southwestward and wrecked the Confederate railroad. For five weeks Hood had countered Sherman's every move with force. Where was the Rebel army?

Perhaps no issue in the long and often controversial Atlanta campaign is more widely disputed than Hood's response to Sherman's "grand left wheel." Participants and historians alike have disagreed. Some have presented a confused and badly fooled Confederate commander certain that the invader was in headlong retreat toward Tennessee. Others counter that although Hood might have misinterpreted events initially, so did every other Confederate leader in Georgia.

Hood was informed on the twenty-sixth that the Yankees were on the move, and he telegraphed Richmond the news. He sent Jackson's troopers after the Federals, and reports came in that Sherman was falling back to the Chattahoochee. The few Union prisoners taken refused to say what their army was doing, but the siege guns had suddenly fallen silent on the twenty-fifth and the skies over the city were still peaceful on the twenty-sixth.

One possible interpretation for Hood was that Wheeler's destruction of Sherman's railroad had forced a retreat. The general was about to become the victim of his own cavalry strategy: rumors had Wheeler successful to the north when he had actually failed; and when Hood needed horsemen to provide accurate information as to Sherman's movements, he had too few to break through the Federal cavalry screen and discover the truth. For the rest of his life Hood insisted that "we had still a sufficient number, with Jackson, to protect not only the flanks of the Army, but likewise our communications against raids." The general could not admit his cavalry strategy had failed.

Hood's overestimate of Wheeler's effect on Sherman came from Union prisoners and from "Fighting Joe" himself. Wheeler's report went far beyond the true state of affairs, and Union prisoners told their Rebel captors that their mounted force had burned the Etowah Bridge and wrecked the tunnel at Tunnel Hill. A report of an Atlanta woman confirmed this information. The woman asked one of Schofield's officers for food. "No," he replied, "I would like to draw myself. I have been living on short rations for several days, and now that you people have torn up our railroad and stolen our beef cattle, we must live a damned sight shorter." And there was one other piece of evidence: no trains had been heard behind Federal lines for several days.

No sooner had word of Wheeler's successes arrived than Hood's scouts reported a major change in Sherman's position. Union lines northeast of the city had been abandoned. The Federals still held ferries up to the Chattahoochee Railroad Bridge, but by the twenty-eighth Hood was informed that Sherman's left was at Sandtown and that his line ran to the southeast to the West Point Railroad beyond East Point.

On August 26 Hood ordered Jackson to find out "what is going on." From the twenty-sixth to the twenty-eighth the Confederate command was confused. Information about Wheeler's raid, stories of food shortages in the Union camp, and reports that large numbers of Yankee soldiers were ending their terms of service and being mustered out helped convince Confederate headquarters that a withdrawal was underway. On August 26 Hood's chief of staff General Francis Shoup wrote that "the prevailing impression of the scout reports thus far indicated the enemy were falling back across the Chattahoochee." Lieutenant W. T. Trask wrote, "Hood and . . . Shoup are in high glee at the flattering prospect (to them) of Sherman's speedy destruction." The Confederate officer added,

"My own private notion is that instead of retreat, Sherman means to flank again—'Quien Sabe?'"

How badly fooled was Hood? Thomas L. Connelly, the Army of Tennessee's foremost historian, believes that Hood's old enemy, Hardee, is chiefly responsible for the image of the befuddled commander. Connelly points out that in his dispatches of August 26 through August 28 Hood "merely reported a change in Sherman's line. Nor was Hood so blind to Sherman's shifting of troops toward the West Point & Macon railroads as Hardee and others later maintained." Connelly continues, "A combination of prejudice and mythology has presented Hood as a much greater dupe during the last days of August than he actually was. . . . Hardee, Lee, and Stewart, on August 26–28, seemed to have no better idea than Hood as to what Sherman was doing." Hood's recent biographer Richard McMurry agrees: "All the Confederates seem to have misunderstood the situation. While alert to the danger of a raid against the railroad, the Rebels did not realize the magnitude of the disaster moving upon them. Hardee . . . Lee . . . and Hood . . . were equally ignorant of the situation."

The people of Atlanta were amazed by the quiet on the twenty-fifth. There had been other days in the past three weeks with little firing, however, so no one immediately assumed that Sherman was gone. When more eerie silence followed the next day—eerie after all the thunderous days—and when no smoke arose from the long line of Union works, the amazement turned to exhaltation. Relief from the bombardment alone would have caused rejoicing, but with word of Sherman's "retreat," "Men, women and children thronged the hitherto silent thoroughfares and exchanged congratulations." Bands played "Dixie," and on Sunday churches were packed. Thanks were offered from pulpits all over Atlanta and civilians heaped praise on the officers and men who were present. People came out of bombproofs, and Rebel soldiers climbed out of the ditches and cheered.

When it became clear that Sherman was gone many Southerners went into the ditches—Yankee ditches. Souvenir hunters picked over the quiet battlefields and trenches occupied by the Federals since mid-July. Braving crows, rats, and clouds of flies, they hauled letters, caps, canteens, and abandoned weapons home to be displayed as mementoes of Confederate victory.

When Carrie Berry's family came blinking into the sun, the girl's young heart was light. "I feel so glad to get home and have no shells around us." With September only a few days away, Carrie's thoughts turned to school and she went in search of her teacher. The Berrys believed the

Battle Area of Atlanta.

Yankees "were on their way back to Tennessee." For almost a week the girl's diary returned to the childlike events of peace.

As Atlantans moved about their city many realized for the first time how extensively it had been damaged. Samuel Richards walked out Marietta Street and found that section "badly cut up." Carrie Berry found her own home intact, but the town looked dirty and used up.

The initial reaction was relief with little concern for Sherman's whereabouts. Captain Tom Key believed "the scales have turned in favor of the South and the Abolitionists are moving to the rear toward their own homes." Just to make certain he lobbed some shells into Union lines to provoke a response. There was none.

Not everyone was so sanguine. In addition to the rumor that Sherman was in full retreat, other reports had him moving into Alabama to attack Montgomery and Mobile and still others said he was massing to attack the Confederate left, west of Atlanta. Businessman Richards feared, "We have not yet got rid of them finally, but they have some other plan in view to molest and injure us." And Alabama sergeant Joel Murphree observed that "where they have gone appears to be a mistery to all outsiders and I think Shermans move puzzles our high officials."

Through August 27 and 28 the Confederate high command was "puzzled." While his men searched for Sherman's army, Hood kept his own council. Journalists and the populace had to subsist on rumors. There were no official communiqués to spread across the Confederacy or to inform the people of Atlanta. Hood ordered the cavalry to find Sherman, and corps commanders were told to stand ready "for any emergency."

By the afternoon of the twenty-eighth the commanding general was able to telegraph Richmond that his enemy had changed position and was approaching the West Point Railroad between East Point and Fairburn. Hood's chief of staff General Shoup was informed that a large force of Union infantry, cavalry, and artillery had reached Fairburn. Besides sending his cavalry toward Jonesboro, the Rebel chief sent two infantry brigades to that town to aid the horsemen "in repelling raids." Over on the Macon railroad, John C. Brown's division was sent to Rough and Ready also "to repel raids." By the twenty-ninth these three units were in position to defend Jonesboro and Rough and Ready. Ten miles up the railroad from Jonesboro, William Hardee's entire corps was in camp at East Point.

On August 29 Hood's scouts reported that Sherman had columns marching toward both Jonesboro and Rough and Ready. On that same day Hardee, also unclear as to the Union position, asked General Stephen Lee to find out where the enemy was going. By August 30 Hood had moved Hardee down the road to Rough and Ready and brought Lee's corps to East Point. Two-thirds of the army lay within ten miles of Jonesboro. Thomas L. Connelly asks, "Why should Hood have thrown most of his force to Jonesboro as Hardee by hindsight argued that he should have done?" Confederate cavalry had still not fixed Jonesboro as Sherman's ultimate target, and "to stretch three slim corps the complete distance from Atlanta to Jonesboro would have been impossible. Hood did the next best thing by placing two-thirds of his infantry on the left flank at East Point and Rough and Ready," Connelly concludes, "Hood seemed to do all that he possibly could do by August 30."

By the early hours of the thirtieth, after two days of wrecking the West Point road, the Army of the Tennessee and the Army of the Cumberland were ready to push toward the Macon & Western. Logan's Fifteenth Corps marched straight toward Jonesboro with Ransom's Sixteenth, followed by Blair's Seventeenth moving on Logan's right. Kilpatrick's men scouted ahead of the army and covered its right. Among the horsemen was Captain Hibert Cunningham, General Logan's brother-in-law. Cunningham had worn both blue and gray in this war. An impetuous young man in a pro-Confederate portion of southern Illinois, he had joined a Tennessee regiment in 1861 to the distress of his sister and the embarrassment of Logan, then an Illinois Democratic congressman. After two years in gray he was persuaded to join the Union army, and in 1864 he rode into Georgia wearing blue. Cunningham's change of side was not common during the Civil War, but no suspicion of continuing Confederate sympathy followed him, because of his relationship to General Logan.

As Howard moved forward, Thomas's army left Red Oak and pushed for the Macon & Western. Jeff C. Davis's Fourteenth Corps with David Stanley's Fourth Corps led the way, and Garrard's mounted force screened the army's left and rear. Schofield's army brought up the rear, covering the army's wheeling movement, guarding the wagon trains and menacing the East Point junction.

As the Army of the Tennessee marched toward Jonesboro it faced what Howard called an "endless plague" of Rebel cavalry and artillery. Kilpatrick's force and two infantry regiments moved ahead to convince the Southerners that they should "keep traveling." By midday Confederate resistance had become even more persistent, appearing behind every timber line to harass Federals moving across cleared fields. Time after time a short artillery barrage and the rattle of muskets brought the Army of the Tennessee to a halt. "Every half mile the operation was repeated," Howard wrote, "till everybody became weary and impatient."

That morning as Logan rode forward at the head of his corps he heard his soldiers ask for a chaplain. He asked why a chaplain was needed and was told that, in a nearby cabin, the men had found a woman who had just given birth. Logan rode off with the clergyman. When they arrived at the clearing a Union doctor told him, "General you are just the man we're after." Logan asked, "For what?" "For a Godfather," replied the doctor. The baby, whose father had been killed fighting in Virginia, was christened "Shell-Anna" and Logan presented a gold coin as a gift. "Black Jack" also ordered that rations be left behind.

By three-thirty that afternoon General Howard had reached the Renfroe Place, his objective for the day. Sherman had told Howard that he could push on to Jonesboro if he had time, and since there was no water for men or animals where they were, the army commander decided to march on to the Flint River. His scouts informed him that the Rebels were entrenched at Jonesboro, but Howard believed he could establish a hold on the stream's eastern bank and stand ready to seize the Macon & Western on August 31. Continuing the advance would also solve their water problem.

For six miles Logan's infantry moved through the blistering heat down a rough road. At five o'clock they reached the river. The bridge was defended by Rebels on the eastern bank, but still intact. Howard sent his men forward at once and saw Logan's infantrymen "so excited that they almost kept up with the cavalry." Spearheading the rush for the bridge were infantrymen from William Hazen's division together with Kilpatrick's dismounted troopers. The Ninety-second Illinois Mounted Infantry, using seven-shot Spencer repeating carbines, "fired so fast that the rebels could with difficulty reply." By dusk the Fifteenth corps had secured a position east of the Flint while Kilpatrick, who rode into Jonesboro (a town his forces had battered in its August raid), was driven back to the main Union army. As the bluecoats approached, Kentuckian Johnny Green, serving in the Jonesboro defense force, wished, "Oh! that Hardee or night would come."

Night arrived and Logan had his corps busily building breastworks. Well after dark the Sixteenth Corps reached the river, remaining on the west bank. Behind Ransom, Blair's corps went into camp a few miles short of the Flint.

A lack of information continued to plague Hood throughout the thirtieth. He still could not be sure of Sherman's objective; was it East Point, Rough and Ready, or Jonesboro? He had shifted his army westward and waited for more definitive information before concentrating his force.

Controversy surrounds the Confederate leader's dispatches of August 30. At 1:00 P.M. Hood told Hardee he saw no need to send reinforcements to Jonesboro "today." One hour later he telegraphed Hardee that he did not think Sherman would attack Jonesboro on the thirtieth. These telegrams have been used to illustrate Hood's confusion. But who in the Confederate high command knew any more? There are no dispatches from Hardee, Lee, or the cavalry which pinpoint Jonesboro as the Union objective. On the contrary, that afternoon Hardee reported that Sherman was moving toward his unit at Rough and Ready. Furthermore, the Kentuckian did remain alert to the enemy threat, even issuing orders to Hardee. In the early afternoon Hardee, at Rough and Ready, received a dispatch advising him that reinforcements might have to be ordered to Jonesboro before the day's end. Even though in Hood's 2:00 P.M. message to Hardee he said he did not expect an attack, he did tell the corps commander "to take whatever measures you may think necessary to hold Rough and Ready and Jonesboro." That afternoon Hood gave Hardee command of all forces from East Point to Jonesboro, with instructions to respond in strength to any threat. "Yet throughout the afternoon," writes Connelly, "though later he claimed he knew the enemy was approaching Jonesboro in massive strength, Hardee kept his own infantry corps aligned between East Point and Rough and Ready." The historian follows with the inevitable question: "If he knew what he later claimed he knew, why had he not shifted his corps southward?"

Finally, on the evening of August 30, Hood was informed by Confederates at Jonesboro that the enemy had reached the Flint River. The commander immediately summoned Hardee and Lee by locomotive to his Atlanta headquarters on Whitehall Street and outlined his plan. He ordered Hardee's two corps to Jonesboro, to strike Logan at dawn on the thirty-first.

Hood's dispatches to Hardee about this planned attack reveal deep anxiety, reflecting not only a growing awareness of the danger to his rail lines, but also the memory of delay and poor coordination in the July sorties. At 3:10 A.M. on August 31 he urged, "You must not fail to attack the enemy so soon as you can get your troops up." Ten minutes later: "General Hood desires you to say to your officers and men that the necessity is imperative. The enemy must be driven into and across the river." And at 10.00 A.M.: "General Hood desires the men to go at the enemy with bayonets fixed, determined to drive every thing they may come against."

When the first day's attack succeeded, Stewart would join Lee at Rough and Ready and the two corps would drive down the west bank of the Flint, completing the destruction of the Army of the Tennessee. To hold Atlanta while his army assaulted Howard, the Georgia Militia and Red Jackson's dismounted cavalrymen, led by Hood, would remain in the Atlanta defenses.

From the start there was disturbing similarity between this sortie and its three predecessors, which Hardee must have realized in the early hours of the thirty-first. He rode an engine to Jonesboro and arrived ready to lead his corps against Howard at first light. No one was there. Neither his corps nor Lee's, also supposed to be nearby, was anywhere to be found. Hardee could not even find anyone who knew where they were. This dawn attack was beginning to look like the one Hardee was supposed to make against the same Union army on July 22. Hardee later claimed that he was aware of the Union threat. If so, why were his troops so tardy in arriving?

What did happen to the Confederate army on the road to Jonesboro? Hardee's corps, led by General Patrick Cleburne, in its commander's absence, bumped into sizable enemy forces and had to march around them. Stephen D. Lee also encountered blueclad troops and was even slower in reaching Jonesboro. There were also the problems of poor roads, poor maps, and a lack of shoes for many Rebel soldiers. The latter led to what General Patton Anderson called "a degree of straggling which I do not remember to have been exceeded in any former march of the kind." Anderson added that the night march was especially exhausting "to troops who had not been out of the trenches for thirty days."

By nine o'clock Hardee had his corps in line, but the bulk of Lee's force did not reach Jonesboro until eleven and some did not arrive until that afternoon at one-thirty. When the Rebels reached Jonesboro they used what tools were available to work on their lines. They were issued sixty rounds of ammunition and told "that General Hood expected them to go at the enemy with fixed bayonets, and drive them across the river." At two o'clock Hardee's force was in position to attack, yet "Old Reliable" delayed and not until three did the Southerners move forward. By the time they charged Logan, Hood's plan had fallen nine hours behind schedule.

While the Rebels slowly gathered at Jonesboro, Logan's Fifteenth Corps, together with John M. Corse's Second Division, Sixteenth Corps, waited, lying just east of the Flint. That morning units from Hazen's division seized high ground overlooking the entire Confederate position. Logan's commander, Oliver O. Howard, held the balance of his army west of the river. He anticipated Hardee's strike against Logan's well-entrenched unit, which could be quickly reinforced. Hours passed and nothing happened. Howard finally told Logan to probe forward at three o'clock when, just before that hour, Hardee's attack materialized at last.

As the tired graybacks waited for the signal to attack they watched Federal artillery hurl shells their way. They also observed that Logan's men had "chosen a strong position and entrenched within rifle shot of our own breastworks." Johnny Green and his fellow Kentuckians were told not to fire until they closed on the Union line, then fire and use their bayonets.

Hardee's plan called for Cleburne to strike the Union right with Lee assaulting the enemy front. Lee was to charge when he heard Cleburne's artillery begin its bombardment. Unfortunately for the Rebels, Lee heard skirmish fire, took it to be the signal, and threw his men forward. Logan concentrated his fire on Lee, clawing huge holes in the attacking force.

One Illinois captain never forgot the sound of the Rebel yell and the sight of red battle flags streaming as Lee's men attacked. Orders were given to hold fire until the assault line closed on Union works, and the commander of the Fifty-seventh Ohio reported of the enemy, "Many fell, but with a stubborness and determination that showed no value was attached to human life, the gaps were soon closed, as if by magic." He also reported that a number of Confederates ran into his lines with hands raised in surrender rather than risk what appeared to be certain death. General Logan said the Federal defenders produced "[t]he most terrible and destructive fire I ever witnessed." In front of his works Rebel dead and wounded were heaped in piles. Observing another battlefield covered with the wreck of a Confederate army, Major Charles Wills of the One Hundred and Third Illinois wrote: "Besides losing a host of men in this campaign, the Rebel Army has lost a large measure of *vim*, which counts a good deal in soldiering."

Lee's attack at Jonesboro was mistimed and irresolute. The imposing Federal lines led Rebel soldiers to surrender in droves, to cower in gullies on the field, and to refuse to charge. One regimental leader found his troops "possessed of some great horror of charging breastworks, which no power, persuasion, or example could dispel." General H. D. Clayton reported, "Never was a charge begun with such enthusiasm terminated with accomplishing so little." General Patton Anderson was badly wounded riding forward to lead his men in the face of withering fire. Of Anderson Logan said, "he did all that a commander could to make the assault a success. . . . I could not help admire his gallantry, though an enemy."

When Lee struck, Cleburne, his blue battle flags on high, joined in the advance, first encountering Kilpatrick who had dismounted his five regiments. "Little Kil's" troopers and his artillery stopped two Rebel attacks before retreating across the Flint River Bridge in his rear. The men of Mark Lowery's division, pursuing the troopers, raced across the Flint "too full of impetuosity," and, as Howard wrote in his *Autobiography*, "Nothing, even if I had planned it, could have been better done to keep an entire Confederate division away from the main battlefield."

Lowery did recross the stream but the "impetuosity" was costly. When he finally joined Lee in assaulting Logan's works, Cleburne found them formidable and the Confederate attack became confused and listless. Yelling defiantly, the Federals unleashed a torrent of fire that covered the field with smoke and tore gaps in the grayclad line. The storm of shells and minié balls, swirling smoke, and the very uneven terrain confused the assault force.

Pinned down in a ditch, one Florida officer yelled to his men, "You boys can stay here, but I'm getting out!" Taking a drink of whiskey he raced to the rear, but was shot and fell. One Rebel remembered, "The air seemed literally swarming with screaming and bursting shells." One of those shells found the chaplain of the Tenth Tennessee as he kneeled to comfort the dying colonel of a South Carolina regiment. He was decapitated by a Federal projectile.

As the Confederates fell back late in the afternoon, soldiers of the Sixth Kentucky paused to bury their regimental standard rather than have it captured. That night they returned, dug it up, and went back to camp feeling that they had saved the honor of the regiment. With both Confederate corps stalled, Howard reinforcing the Fifteenth Corps and Lee arguing that his corps was too badly beaten to continue the attack, Hardee cancelled a further advance and set his men in a defensive line.

The bloody afternoon ended and the guns muttered toward silence, as the agonized cries of the wounded rose from the field. Several graybacks braved enemy fire to race onto the field to recover the wounded. When the Yankees realized what they were doing they held fire and cheered.

In the afternoon clash on the last day of August, casualties were very uneven. The Confederates lost 1,725 men; Logan and Kilpatrick counted less than 200 casualties. Of this battle one Wisconsin private said: "They had to come out of their works and fight us. We gave them a hard whipping then."

So much of what happened on August 31 seemed to repeat a familiar pattern of Confederate command bungling. Once again communications between Hardee and Hood broke down. Once again Hood remained far from the battlefield, out of contact with rapidly changing events, and, therefore, out of the control of his army. Once again Hardee's handling of an independent command was slow and confused. Once again Hardee disobeyed Hood's orders. Three times on the thirty-first Hood had ordered him to attack, yet after two feeble moves forward, Hardee, without informing Atlanta, assumed a defensive position. Once again, as at Ezra Church, Stephen D. Lee managed his men poorly, attacking at the wrong place on July 28 and at the wrong time on August 31.

Hood had one method of deciding why Hardee had failed. It reveals a great deal about the Confederate commander. On September 3 he wrote to General Braxton Bragg: "Our loss on the evening of the 31st was so small that it is evident that our effort was not a vigorous one." Two days later the Kentuckian wrote Bragg again, this time labeling the effort by Hardee and Lee "disgraceful." Twenty years later he had not changed his mind: "the general attack . . . must have been rather feeble, as the loss incurred was only about fourteen hundred in killed and wounded—a small number in comparison to the forces engaged."

Both during and after the war charges and recriminations ricocheted off of the Confederate principals involved in this first day of the Battle of Jonesboro. Hood charged that Hardee had been fooled by Sherman, was unaware of the location of the Union force, and led his men badly. The corps commander made the same charges against Hood. Both men tried to defend their actions, going so far as to distort the record.

While the two armies struggled at Jonesboro that afternoon, Schofield's Army of the Ohio was marching toward the Macon & Western. At three o'clock General Jacob D. Cox's division reached the railroad, shoved aside cavalry defenders, and almost captured a train. Commissary officer Joseph Semmes, taking supplies to Hardee, narrowly avoided capture. His train raced by just ahead of Cox's bluecoats, their guns, and their wrecking bars.

It was the last train from Atlanta. After the Yanks began dismantling the railroad another train approached. Realizing the danger, the engineer quickly reversed, racing back to Atlanta to carry news of Yankees on the line at Rough and Ready. When Sherman discovered that Schofield had reached the rail line he told his army commander, "Don't get off the track; hold it fast." He instructed Schofield, "We will get our whole army on the railroad as near Jonesborough as possible and push Hardee and Lee first, and then for Atlanta."

By the night of August 31 Hood, like Hardee, had abandoned plans for a further attack on the Army of the Tennessee. He ordered Lee to march his corps back to Atlanta to reinforce Stewart in expectation of Sherman's attack on the city using Thomas and Schofield. Hardee later denounced the Kentuckian for moving Lee away from the real danger point, but when Hood made his decision he did not yet know that Sherman was near Jonesboro in force—and neither did Hardee. In light of this lack of information, the Confederate commander's decision was not unreasonable. However, after dark Hood received disturbing reports that made him change his plans again. Word reached Atlanta that Union troops had cut the Macon railroad at Rough and Ready, and were across Hood's last rail line in strength at several other points. When Lee reached East Point at dawn he reported that Thomas and Schofield were both south of Atlanta attacking the railroad.

Hood knew that Atlanta was doomed, and he set his staff to prepare for evacuation as quickly as possible. A second and more disquieting possibility came with the latest word of Sherman's position. The Union army lay between Hardee and the remainder of the Confederate forces. A vigorous concentration might demolish Hardee, seriously wounding the Army of Tennessee. The Kentuckian had to rush Stewart and Lee southward to join Hardee before Sherman could crush Hardee's 12,500 men at Jonesboro.

September 1 was an important day in the long Atlanta campaign. It was a day on which the two commanders, Sherman and Hood, groped toward Jonesboro, the former determined to destroy the divided and reeling Rebel army, the latter determined to save his army to fight another day and not to add the loss of the army to the loss of Atlanta.

Sherman had begun the campaign with two objectives: "knocking Joe Johnston" and capturing Atlanta. His sweep toward the Macon & Western was aimed at forcing Hood to pull his army out of the Gate City, leaving it in Union hands. On September 1, with that objective almost in his grasp, the first returned to his thoughts. Howard was told to send the Sixteenth Corps across the Flint to join Logan with Blair's corps and Kilpatrick's horsemen to wreck the railroad, thereby blocking Hardee's escape route southward. Then he ordered Thomas and Schofield to join Howard at Jonesboro.

On September 1 it was Sherman's turn to wait anxiously as his men slowly responded to orders. The Federals rose on the battle field to feel a hint of the coming autumn in a cool morning breeze. Although it was warm by afternoon, the respite was a relief. It was three o'clock before the Fourteenth Corps, led by General Jefferson C. Davis, reached Jonesboro. Trailing Davis, Stanley's Fourth Corps was lost and stumbling down the wrong road while Schofield's Army of the Ohio, still tearing up track, was moving slowly toward Jonesboro. If there was going to be an attack on Hardee it would have to come from far fewer men than Sherman had intended to use, although he still outnumbered Hardee by more than two to one.

Hardee's men had moved into the works Lee had left when he marched toward Atlanta. The line was poorly constructed and so close to the enemy that as Rebel pickets deployed, thirty-three were easily captured. The morning continued the previous day's confusion. One Confederate brigade was ordered to entrain for Atlanta, only to be sent back to the lines when a Union advance seemed imminent. Kentuckian Johnny Green knew what was expected: "We must hold off the enemy until night, by which time our forces in Atlanta could be withdrawn and the army reunited about Lovejoy Station."

Fortunately for Sherman the Fourteenth Corps leader—Davis—was an aggressive general who, once on hand, wasted little time in striking. He set his three divisions facing Hardee's left where the Confederate corps abruptly turned in a ninety-degree angle and swung across the railroad. Davis's right connected with Howard's army. At four o'clock Davis's men charged with a yell. They found themselves slowed by blackberry vines and thick undergrowth, grown luxuriant by the late summer. The terrain and Cleburne's withering fire threw them back, but they rallied and charged straight into the works held by Brigadier General Dan Govan.

Confederate artillery tore holes in the assault line, but it reformed and kept on coming. As Johnny Green fired at the bluecoats he thought: "I never saw men more defiant." Union guns also raked the Rebel defense and Green realized: "Their fire is thinning our slender ranks." To urge the Tenth Michigan to charge, its drummers "beat out the charge, raising such a daddy-mammy as they felt their men must hear above the whistling bullets and the unearthly yells made by the Rebel soldiers." Henry Ingraham, charging in an Illinois regiment, did not have drums to inspire him when his unit wavered under the heavy fire: "I remembered that both of my grand fathers died defending that same emblem of liberty. The thoughts inspired my soul with courage, we rallied and the day was ours."

As the armies closed the men fought hand-to-hand in desperation. Union brigadier Absalom Baird reported, "On no occasion within my

knowledge has the use of the bayonet been so general." One Union soldier leaped on the works and demanded: "Surrender you damn rebels!"
"The hell you say," replied a Kentuckian, who shot the bold Yank. Through
the smoky haze, balls flew, bayonets struck sparks, and men bludgeoned
their foes with clubbed muskets. Govan's Arkansans were not a match
for the Yankees. "They ran over us like a drove of Texas beeves, by sheer
force of numbers," recalled an Arkansas private. Two batteries were captured and more than half of the Arkansas brigade, including General
Govan, were taken prisoner. Sherman, watching Davis's advance, cried
out in joy, "They're rolling them up like a sheet of paper."

Pat Cleburne fell back, repositioned his remaining units, and held on.
Granbury's Texas brigade stopped Davis's onslaught; but with some daylight left, Sherman still had an opportunity to wreck Hardee. Stanley
had not yet made his appearance, and the Union commander felt that
he needed the Fourth Corps to join Davis in collapsing the weakened
Rebel right. Thomas had been sending couriers all afternoon in search
of Stanley and finally, in response to Sherman's rising anger, rode off
himself in search of his laggard corps. "It was the only time during the
campaign I can recall seeing General Thomas urge his horse into a gallop," wrote Sherman after the war.

Stanley did not arrive until after sundown and Sherman let daylight
pass without sending the Fifteenth Corps forward, fearing the results of
a charge against Hardee's well-constructed works. Logan's corps occupied
Hardee's left to prevent the Rebel corps commander from sending reinforcements to the right. Rather than waiting for Stanley, Sherman might
have used the Fifteenth and Sixteenth corps to aid Davis. He did not do
so, and the Battle of Jonesboro was over. Sherman had lost 1,275 men
on the first while the enemy had suffered about 1,000 casualities. The
Union army had failed to crush Hardee's corps.

Rebel captain Tom Key observed, "The defense of the Confederates
was noble, but they were too weak to contend against such numbers." In
the victorious camp Illinois major James A. Connolly, still charged with
the exhiliration men often feel in battle, sat down to describe the feeling
in words reminiscent of *Henry V:* "I have no language to express the
rapture one feels in the moment of victory, but I do know at such a
moment one feels as if the joy were worth risking a hundred lives to
attain. Men at home will read of the battle, but they can never feel as
we felt, standing there quivering with excitement." In a less literary manner
Indianan Ben Mabrey gloated: "Old Clabron was the bragg fighter of the
rebel army. They sed that all they wanted was to get to fight the fourteenth corps in an open field fight. They sed they wanted to nock some

acorns, that is the badge of our Corps. But the acorns was to hy for the Johnies to nock."

There would be no second chance to hammer Hardee. That night the corps left its positions, ordered to march south to Lovejoy's Station to link up with the remainder of Hood's army on its way down the McDonough Road from Atlanta. It was a discouraged force that wearily marched away from Jonesboro, but a lucky one. Had Sherman hurled forward all of his troops in the area, Hardee surely would have been smashed.

The Confederate military's evacuation of Atlanta was badly bungled. Journalist Wallace Reed saw the city "almost in a state of anarchy." Hood ordered his ordnance train south but it was not moved before the road was cut. Eighty-one cars, including those holding the army's entire reserve supply of ammunition, five locomotives, thirteen pieces of heavy artillery, and a large amount of supplies and equipment were destroyed. Also wrecked were the Western & Atlantic's roundhouse, the cannon foundry and irreplaceable materials at the Confederate Arsenal, the Confederate Rolling Mill, and the Atlanta Machine Company.

After the distant firing on the thirty-first, Atlantans had heard rumors of a victory halting Sherman's latest thrust at their city. There were no announcements from Hood, however, and by the following afternoon word filtered through the city that the army was preparing to evacuate. Atlanta's citizens were confused and shocked. Their alarm increased when explosions began to rock the quiet they had enjoyed since August 25. This time the explosions were created by their own soldiers. Since they were a prelude to evacuation and Union occupation, they were even more threatening than the crashing Union shells endured the previous month. The exploding buildings, locomotives, and cars "sent a thrill of alarm through the city." Flames shot hundreds of feet into the air and fragments flew in all directions, endangering nearby buildings. Houses rocked, windows shattered, and "[t]housands of people flocked to high places and watched with breathless excitement the volcanic scene on the Georgia Railroad."

There were other causes for alarm. Deserters from the army at Jonesboro, bringing word of defeat, began moving quietly into the city. Strange Negroes appeared in the streets; although they caused no trouble, their presence was unsettling. Public drunkenness increased as some soldiers reeled through the city on their way south. "Something was up," wrote Wallace Reed, "but the citizens could not tell what was coming. They could not believe that the city was to be given up." "The sun went down looking like a great ball of fire as it shone through the thick haze of red dust," continued Reed. "It was a hot, stifling night, and the people found it impossible to sleep. Shortly after dark the streets resounded with the heavy tread of marching soldiers. . . . It soon became evident that they were moving out of the city." To Samuel Richards, September 1 "was a day of terror and a night of dread."

In the early hours of the second, General Sherman's thoughts of renewing the attack at Jonesboro were replaced by concerns raised by unidentified sounds in the still night air from the direction of Atlanta. Sherman and much of his army were awakened after midnight when, as he remembered, "there arose toward Atlanta sounds of shells exploding, and other sounds like that of musketry." The Union commander's first fear was that Hood had unleashed his two remaining corps against Slocum. Members of Sherman's staff disagreed with his assessment, hearing instead the explosions of planned destruction. The Union army was made up of veterans of many a campaign, and members of the Sixth-third Ohio had heard those sounds before: "Many of us think it resembles the noise we heard when Beauregard blew up his ammunition and evacuated Corinth in 1862," reported Colonel O. L. Jackson. To help resolve the dispute, and calm his apprehension, Sherman went to a nearby farmhouse and roused the occupants. A surprised farmer came outside in his nightshirt and listened with Sherman to the distant booms. When the general

Destruction of Hood's Ordnance Train.

asked if he had heard such sounds before, the farmer responded at once that those were the sounds of battle around Atlanta. Off and on all night long the distant thunder continued. At four in the morning the thudding shattered the night's peace, rolling on for some time before dying away before daybreak.

With first light the Federal leader sent his army after Hardee only to discover that the Rebel corps was gone. With a band blaring "Hail Columbia," Sherman entered the badly damaged little town of Jonesboro. He marched on through the town in pursuit along the Macon & Western when he received a message from Schofield expressing the belief that the night sounds had been made by Hood's destruction of property as he evacuated Atlanta. By midmorning, the Army of the Ohio's commander sent Sherman word that a Negro fleeing Atlanta had just arrived with the story of a Rebel flight in great confusion and disorder. In spite of these reports Sherman continued to chase Hardee. Federal units found the woods full of Rebel wounded and roads clogged with burned wagons and abandoned ambulances. Confederate wounded, "some of them fairly butchered," drew the sympathy of the Yanks. Hundreds of Rebel stragglers fell into Union hands.

Sherman's pursuit ended near Lovejoy's Station where he found Hardee in works "as well constructed and as strong as if these Confederates had a week to prepare them." Still worried about Slocum, Sherman advised both Howard and Thomas that he would not strike Hardee as long as he was unsure of the fate of the Twentieth Corps. Another day ended and there were no further sounds from the north. Late on the evening of September 2 Sherman told Schofield, "Nothing from Atlanta and that bothers me."

Another restless night ended for Sherman when, before first light on September 3 a dispatch rider from Slocum reached the Union commander's campfire. Slocum was inside Atlanta; Hood had marched away to the south. The previous night's thunder? It was the destruction of ammunition and stores. Slocum had heard the detonations far more clearly than had Sherman and he had gingerly moved toward Atlanta after dawn.

Inside the Gate City, Mayor James M. Calhoun watched Atlanta's defenders leave and called the city council and several other prominent citizens together. Hood had provided for no formal surrender of Atlanta, so Calhoun decided it was a responsibility of the city government. The council agreed and they all mounted for a ride out the Marietta Road toward what they believed was Union headquarters. They went under a white flag and unarmed. After a short ride the party reached deserted Union lines, quiet in the morning sunlight. "Not a human being, not a living thing, was in sight. Two, three, four miles, and not a sign of the enemy." Finally, around a turn in the road, they came face to face with a detachment from the Thirty-third Indiana, Colonel John Coburn commanding. Calhoun approached the colonel and said with a formal bow, "The fortunes of war have placed the city of Atlanta in your hands. As mayor of the city I ask protection for non-combatants and private property."

Shortly before noon a signed surrender was in the hands of Brigadier General W. T. Ward, commanding Slocum's Third Division. By one o'clock Slocum knew of it, and he sent the welcome news to Washington: "General Sherman has taken Atlanta." Union troops marched into the battered city, the Stars and Bars was hauled down from the Court House, and the Stars and Strips raised in its place. As the Federals marched in "the Old Flag caught the breeze . . . [and] such a cheer went up as only a conquering army, flushed with victory, can give."

When the Union commander received Slocum's dispatch he examined the writing carefully to ensure that it was genuine. Then he sent a staff officer to Thomas with the note. Thomas immediately joined Sherman, who watched as the Army of the Cumberland's commander uncharacteristically "snapped his fingers, whistled and almost danced." The good news spread through the army like wildfire, and Sherman smiled as he heard the "shouts that arose from our men, the wild hallooing and glorious laughter."

The "glorious laughter" sounded for the Union soldiers' pride and joy at their victory. When Sherman's mail service began rolling again on September 4 his men told their families that they were safe and victorious. Back home in Indiana, Jonathan Carter's wife read her husband's simple words of happiness: "We have whoop the rebs and got Atlanta." Both officers and men spoke with respect and affection for their commander. Benjamin Taylor of the Eighty-fourth Illinois told his sister: "Sherman took one of his crazy spells," ordered a flank march, and the Rebels "got whipped and sent on their way further into dixie." They hailed the redhead with the ragged beard as "the general of the day," said that he had "done wonders," was "the man for this army," and that he was "a masterly genius." One soldier thought "it was a very cute trick that Billy Sherman played on Hood, whose whole army is completely demoralized and routed. So much for being a damn traitor." Another proclaimed that "Sherman has Hood under his thumb nail as completely as ever one man had another." "Vive la Sherman," shouted Robert Finley of the Thirtieth Illinois.

The men in blue were satisfied with the campaign's results. Thomas Taylor, who fought with the Fifteenth Corps, believed "the primary object

City of Atlanta.

of the campaign had been attained." Ohio's Andrew Rose agreed that "Gen. Sherman has accomplished what he started for."

Nothing about "Uncle Billy" gained as much respect as the men's deep conviction that he valued their lives and would not waste them. His opponent had wasted Confederate lives and had been beaten. "Old Sherman" had conserved lives and was victorious. The general from Ohio "was a *great military genius* who depends upon his brains to win his victories instead of the lives of his men," Ohioan C. B. Welton wrote his parents. Samuel Bachtell, serving at Thomas's headquarters, told his wife of the general's "*Grand Tactics*" that had discovered "it is sometimes much easier to fight with the legs and feet than with muskets and cannon." Is there any wonder that John D. Ferguson of the Second Iowa wrote in his diary the day Atlanta fell: "Our confidence in Sherman has been fulfilled to the uttermost. Gen. Sherman is loved by all."

Along with Slocum's news that Atlanta had fallen came the first picture of Hood's withdrawal. The battered Kentuckian had begun the evacuation at five o'clock on the afternoon of the first, moving his first units down the McDonough Road. Stewart's veterans and "Joe Brown's Pets" of the Georgia Militia "filed through the streets with a steady tread it is true, but nevertheless with sorrow depicted on their weatherbeaten countenances." On the first and second Hood had marched Stewart and Lee across the Union front several miles away to the east, and by the third those two corps had joined Hardee at Lovejoy's Station.

After fighting for months to defend Atlanta, the Confederate evacuation was demoralizing. A Louisiana soldier may have expressed the feeling of the army when he asked, " 'ood's played 'el 'asn't he?" George B. Blakemore wrote a few days later: "Well old Sherman flanked us out of Atlanta most beautifully and scientifically. I don't know what is to blame but the counter movement on our side was very bunglingly executed." A. T. Holliday, his feet "worn out to a blister," carrying only "raw meat and crackers," to eat, moved along with the Georgia Militia and wished he was at home on his Wilkes County plantation. The grim, forced march through the night was exhausting and, according to one ragged Reb, "like to kild us every won." When the Army of Tennessee had retreated in May and June there was hope that General Johnston was withdrawing to fight in a place of his choosing. Victory was possible across the next river. This was the retreat of defeat.

On September 4 Hood was still convinced that his army's morale remained high. He telegraphed Bragg: "I think the officers and men of this army feel that every effort was made to hold Atlanta to the last. I do not think the army is discouraged."

In *Advance and Retreat* Hood said that he was more upset "by the *recurrence* of retreat" and its demoralizing effect on his army than by losing Atlanta. He also attempted to excuse his failure by explaining the evacuation, in part, as being brought about by the need to impose his force between Sherman and Andersonville Prison. He believed that Sherman was on his way to the stockade to release Union captives "to wreak [their] ill-will upon our people." He also said that but for his desire to check the vengeful Yankee prisoners he might have crossed the Chattahoochee and "destroyed the enemy's communications and supplies." By 1879 Hood's memories of the last days in Atlanta were fanciful indeed.

While the Twentieth Corps marched into Atlanta, explosions continued to roar through the city as the abandoned ammunition blew up. Few Atlantans were visible; the ones who peeked from behind shutters were amazed by the quiet and orderly occupation. Everyone was leery of cavalrymen, Blue or Gray, and little Carrie Berry wrote, "the cavalry came dashing in. We were all frightened. We were afraid they were going to treat us badly. But when the infantry marched in they were orderly and behaved very well, I think I shall like the Yankees very much."

Sherman would not pursue Hood's reunited army. Instead he would go to Atlanta, taken at last after four months of hard fighting across the hills and rivers and through the woods of north Georgia. "I shall not push much farther in this raid, but in a day or so will move to Atlanta and give my men some rest," he informed Halleck. He also told Halleck and a cheering Union, "Atlanta is ours, and fairly won."

# 14

# I Am Not Brutal or Inhuman

THE lean Ohioan with the grizzled, short-cropped beard must have felt vindicated. Those newspaper allegations early in the war that he was insane were eclipsed by success; so too the fact that he was surprised by the Rebels at Shiloh; and for that matter, any other unpleasantness from the first years of the conflict. William Tecumseh Sherman was now famous, and about to become more so. He had captured Atlanta. General Grant wrote Sherman that he had accomplished the most gigantic undertaking given to any general in the war. Halleck called the campaign the most brilliant of the war, and Charles Francis Adams was ranking Sherman with Napoleon and Frederick the Great. Praise from newspapers, telegrams, and letters was pouring in.

And soon Sherman planned another bold stroke, something that had been in his mind a long time. At the opening of the spring campaign Sherman reportedly had been questioned about what he would do after taking Atlanta and made the reply: "Salt water. Salt water." In early September, with a view toward marching into the interior of Georgia from Atlanta, Sherman began to correspond with Grant about his future operations.

Sherman realized that Grant, since becoming general-in-chief of the armies of the United States with responsibility for the strategic direction of the war, was the only person he really had to convince in order to get what he desired. At every chance Sherman pursued the subject. On September 20, he wrote Grant: "If you can whip Lee, and I can march to the Atlantic, I think Uncle Abe will give us twenty days leave of absence to see the young folks."

On October 1, Sherman asked Grant, "Why would it not do for me to leave Tennessee to the force which Thomas has and the reserves soon to come to Nashville and for me to destroy Atlanta and then march across Georgia to Savannah and Charleston, breaking roads and doing irreparable damage?" For several weeks Grant and Sherman exchanged telegrams about the proposal and considered various aspects of the strategic situation.

Sherman had also been busy exchanging communiqués with another general—although these were of an entirely different nature from his correspondence with Grant. Since mid-August Sherman and Hood had been waging a heated duel of words through letters, some of which were several pages in length and increasingly hostile. After thousands of shells delivered by Sherman's newly-arrived siege guns from Chattanooga struck Atlanta in a single day, leaving few blocks undamaged and numerous casualties, Hood began sending bitter letters about the increased bombardment. Contending that all Confederate armed forces were entrenched at least a mile from the center of the city and that no military gains could be expected from shelling civilians, most of them women and children, Hood charged Sherman with violating "all rules of civilized warfare."

Defending himself strongly, Sherman replied to each message that came from Hood. He said he had no intention of changing his military procedures. Women and children had no business staying in Atlanta, a city which was a principal Confederate depot for materials and instruments of war. The Federal commander declared that he intended to render Atlanta incapable of war activity.

When Sherman actually entered Atlanta in early September the correspondence with Hood became even more bitter. Sherman ordered the "entire, complete and prompt evacuation" of the city by the civilian population. The Union army would require all homes and buildings, he said. "If the people raise a howl against my barbarity and cruelty," he wrote, "I will answer that war is war and not popularity-seeking." Sherman at once sent a letter to Hood, who had retreated south of the city, stating that the citizens then residing in Atlanta should leave; those who preferred could go south and the rest north. He told Hood that he would provide food and transportation for the latter. For those who went south Sherman said he could "provide transportation by cars as far as Rough and Ready, and also wagons; but—it will be necessary for you to help the families from Rough and Ready to the cars at Lovejoy's. . . . Atlanta is no place for families or non-combatants—I will consent to a truce in the neighborhood of Rough and Ready."

On September 9 Hood answered, reluctantly agreeing to the evacuation ("I do not consider that I have any alternative in this matter"), discussing its specifics, and concluding with two indignant paragraphs. He said Sherman's action transcended, "in studied and ingenious cruelty, all acts ever before brought to my attention in the dark history of war" and he protested the evacuation measure "in the name of God and humanity."

Sherman's response on the following day ran to more than six hundred words, calling upon Hood "in the name of common sense . . . not to appeal to a just God in such a sacrilegious manner." The Federal commander proceeded, personalizing the South and focusing upon Hood, to castigate the Confederacy for causing the war: "You who, in the midst of peace and prosperity, have plunged a nation into war—dark and cruel war—who dared and badgered us to battle, insulted our flag, seized our arsenals and forts that were left in the honorable custody of peaceful ordnance sergeants, seized and made 'prisoners of war' the very garrisons sent to protect your people against negroes and Indians, long before any overt act was committed by the (to you) hated Lincoln Government; tried to force Kentucky and Missouri into rebellion, in spite of themselves; falsified the vote of Louisiana; turned loose your privateers to plunder unarmed ships; expelled Union families by the thousands, burned their houses, and declared, by an act of your Congress, the confiscation of all debts due Northern men for goods had and received!"

Hood did not reply until September 12—probably because his epistle contained nearly seventeen thousand words and must have taken a long time to prepare. Sherman's evacuation order, stated the Confederate general, was "pre-eminent in the dark history of war for studied and ingenious cruelty." (The latter was a phrase that Hood seemed to relish.) Nothing Sherman had written had changed Hood's mind; on the contrary, it only strengthened him in his low opinion of Sherman's actions. Furthermore, the Confederate commander said he did not feel "called upon to discuss with you the causes of the present war." Having so said, Hood then proceeded, one by one, to discuss and deny all of Sherman's accusations. Finally he wrote: "I close this correspondence with you . . . and again humbly and reverently invoke his Almighty aid in defence of justice and right."

To this long letter Sherman replied briefly. Sherman reminded Hood that the Southern commander began the controversy, restated his own position, and concluded: "I was not bound by the laws of war to give notice of the shelling of Atlanta, a fortified town, with magazines, arsenals, foundries, and public stores; you were bound to take notice. See the books. This is the conclusion of our correspondence, which I did not begin, and terminate with satisfaction."

About the time Sherman was writing this last letter to Hood, Right

Reverend Henry C. Lay, bishop of Arkansas, visited the Union commander's headquarters. Lay reported that Sherman complained that Hood had treated him harshly, and said: "To be sure I have made war vindictively; war is war, and you can make nothing else of it; but Hood knows as well as anyone I am not brutal or inhuman."

For what it was worth to his peace of mind, Sherman had the sanction of the administration in Washington and of the War Department. General Halleck wrote him: "The course which you have pursued in removing rebel families from Atlanta . . . is fully approved by the War Department." Not only did the laws of war justify removing the people, but Halleck said he considered it Sherman's "duty to your own army to do so. . . . We certainly are not required to treat the so-called noncombatant rebels better than they themselves treat each other. . . . We have fed this class of people long enough." Saying that he had tried to impress these views upon Federal commanders for the last two years, Halleck complimented Sherman, stating, "You are almost the only one who has properly applied them."

No doubt the long and heated exchange with Hood was frustrating to Sherman, but certainly it was not the Union commander's main concern. He "would infinitely prefer to . . . move through Georgia, smashing things to the sea," wrote Sherman to Grant on October 11. Grant worried about preparing a coastal base to supply the army, but Sherman replied that his troops would need no supplies, and no base. They would take what they required from the countryside. "I can make the march and make Georgia howl!" said Sherman.

Grant was also concerned that Sherman might be "bushwhacked by all the old men, little boys, and such railroad guards as are still left at home." Sherman, however, intended to be very strong, planning, as he worded it, to take only "the best fighting material" on his trek. The matter was considered by Lincoln, Secretary of War Stanton, and Halleck, as well as Grant. The president was quite concerned, but willing to accept Grant's decision.

After weeks of Sherman's pleadings, Grant's earlier fears for Sherman's safety and success subsided. Sherman got what he wanted. Grant advised Lincoln that he considered the proposed march to be sound and telegraphed Sherman that his plan was approved and that he had the "confidence and support of the government" and might "go on as you propose." General George H. Thomas, at Nashville in command of the Department of the Cumberland, was to oppose Hood's advance northward should the Rebel general march into Tennessee instead of following Sherman.

After the fall of Atlanta, General Thomas had favored a campaign south from the city, with his own Army of the Cumberland, which had composed about two-thirds of Sherman's total force in the advance from Chattanooga. But he was opposed to Sherman's plan of marching to the Atlantic coast while Hood was still moving westward, along the Tennessee River. Now that Sherman had Grant's approval for the march, he wrote to Thomas, arguing that simply to pursue Hood would wear out his army. "I know I am right," Sherman stated. "I think Hood will follow me, at least with his cavalry. . . . If, however, he turns on you, you must act defensively on the line of the Tennessee."

Thomas certainly possessed ample strength at his command to handle the situation, if he could bring all the troops together rapidly. In Nashville he already had some 8,000 to 10,000 soldiers under arms, plus about that many more employees in the quartermaster's department who were available to man the fortifications about the city in case of attack. Also, there were various detachments that could be marshalled at Nashville. There would be James B. Steedman's 5,000 men at Chattanooga; Lovell H. Rousseau's 5,000 at Murfreesboro; Gordon Granger's 4,000 at Decatur; and a number of other smaller garrisons—Spring Hill for instance, with 1,200 to 1,500 men. The two divisions under General Andrew Jackson Smith, numbering about 14,000, were ordered to return from Missouri; and Sherman sent the Fourth Corps, under Stanley, numbering 12,000, and the Twenty-third Corps, under Schofield, numbering 10,000, back to Tennessee to further strengthen Thomas's forces. Including a cavalry command of some 10,000 being assembled in the Tennessee capital, Thomas would have more than 70,000 men available.

Nevertheless, when Hood began to cross the Tennessee River, a movement Sherman had thought improbable, Sherman was irritated; and Grant and Thomas were alarmed. Thomas did feel confident, however, that with Stanley's and Schofield's troops added to those already at hand, and if Smith was hurried forward from Missouri, he would be able to drive Hood back. Sherman did not think that Hood was in any condition to march on Nashville, but if he did, Sherman also thought that Thomas would have sufficient time to concentrate his forces and repel him. The Union commander was heard to exclaim of Hood, "Damn him, if he will go to the Ohio River, I'll give him rations. . . . let him go North, my business is down South." Thus Sherman marched out of Atlanta, torching the city, and proceeded "to ruin Georgia," as he phrased it, "and bring up at the sea-coast." Hood and the Army of Tennessee were left for Thomas to stop, if an invasion of middle Tennessee should really occur.

By this time November was at the midpoint and Abraham Lincoln had been reelected president of the United States, itself a major Union victory—and one to which Sherman had contributed immeasurably, perhaps decisively, with the conquest of Atlanta. Before the fall of Atlanta, the Civil War appeared likely, in the eyes of a war-weary North, to drag on for several years. The critics of the Union war effort and the Lincoln administration were most vocal, and seemed most powerful, in the disheartening spring and summer months of 1864, when Grant's casualties mounted astronomically, yet without victory over Lee in Virginia, while Sherman seemed also unable to defeat his opponent, even if taking less casualties and compelling Confederate retreats.

Because Lincoln had control of the federal patronage and of the party machinery, he was renominated in June. The mere fact of renomination was misleading. It did not mean that the Republican party, or those who had supported the war effort, whatever their political stripe, were solidly united behind Lincoln. Not only was the unsuccessful attempt to run Salmon P. Chase as a rival of Lincoln evidence of this fact; there was also the third-party movement in support of the 1856 Republican nominee, John C. Fremont. Even as late as early September, some of the opposition were trying to reconvene the Republican convention in the hope of ousting Lincoln as the party's nominee. It was not merely that some party leaders disliked the president: they did not think he could be reelected. Lincoln himself, astute politician that he was, sincerely doubted his reelection. So dark was the outlook that the president, a few weeks before the election, conceded that the Democratic nominee, General George B. McClellan, was likely to win.

The fall of Atlanta changed the bleak atmosphere. Sherman's telegraph to Washington, "Atlanta is ours and fairly won," had a pulsating effect on the North. News of the victory made the Democratic platform's assertion that the war was a failure seem ridiculous. Sherman had directed a hundred thousand men into the heart of the Confederacy, capturing a major city, railroad hub, and supply base. But even greater, in some respects, than the military achievement was the psychological and political impact of Atlanta's fall—both because Atlanta had stood as a symbol to the North of Confederate strength, and because Atlanta's capture strongly affected the presidential election.

There are historians who have flatly stated that the fall of Atlanta was decisive in the 1864 election. For example, the four authors of the recent *Why the South Lost the Civil War* state: "The fall of Atlanta changed the whole complexion of events, for Sherman had provided a needed victory—expected more from Grant than from him—that indicated the beginning of substantial progress. As a result, in 1864 the Union voters reelected the administration." Possibly this is claiming too much for the impact of Atlanta's capture, great as it was, because Lincoln did win handily, gaining a substantial 55 percent of the popular vote, and dominating in the electoral college by a margin of 212 to 21, with McClellan carrying only New Jersey, Kentucky, and Delaware. Obviously there is no way to know either how many people changed their vote to Lincoln or decided to vote rather than stay at home because of the Atlanta triumph.

Whether decisive or not, Sherman's Atlanta victory clearly gave a welcome and substantial boost to Lincoln's campaign for reelection. It also happened early enough that Sherman could furlough many soldiers to return home and vote in key states, such as Illinois and Indiana, which did not allow absentee voting by soldiers. Interestingly, of eighteen Northern states that allowed soldiers to vote in the field, twelve tabulated the soldier vote separately; and in these twelve, a massive 78 percent voted for Lincoln.

One of those furloughed home to Illinois was General John A. Logan, the prewar Democrat. Illinois Republican congressman Elihu Washburne had written Logan immediately after the fall of Atlanta, "We want your clarion voice to echo over our state and arouse the Union and patriotic people to the salvation of the country." The general did stump the state, and Washburne—who had written to Lincoln early in the election of the "imminent danger of losing" Illinois—wrote just before election day of his rising confidence since "Logan is carrying all before him."

The Atlanta campaign was also highly significant from another perspective: its impact on both the South's ability and will to make war. The Confederate Army of Tennessee had not been destroyed or captured, but it had suffered severely. Its base had been devastated. The army's losses could not be easily replaced, even with inexperienced soldiers. The Army of Northern Virginia was also severed from supplies provided by Georgia, Florida, and Alabama. Worse, the fall of Atlanta, especially when coupled with the reelection of Lincoln, convinced many a Confederate that the war could not be won.

Confederates had looked hopefully to the United States presidential election of 1864, believing that the defeat of Lincoln would signify the failure of support for the Union war effort, and ultimately lead to negotiations with a new administration that could end the struggle with the recognition of Southern independence. The fall of Atlanta, combined with Lincoln's triumph at the polls, constituted a devastating blow to Confederate morale. Desertion rates, already serious, increased significantly. Many Southerners were convinced the cause was lost.

It is an irony that Sherman, the general perceived to be more hostile to politics and politicians than any Union military leader, had won the victory whose political consequences were as great as those of any single campaign in the war.

And then Sherman began to deliver still another blow to the Southern will to win: his sixty-mile swath of devastation as he marched to the sea at Savannah. More than anyone else, Sherman seemed to understand that total war was required to defeat the Southern people. The will of the people who sustained the Confederate armies in the field must be destroyed. "We cannot change the hearts of those people of the South," Sherman had written earlier, "but we can make war so terrible," he thought, that generations would pass away before they would again think of appealing to war. Now his march would be, he said, "a demonstration to the world . . . that we have a power which [Jefferson] Davis cannot resist."

With the smoking ruins of Atlanta at his back, Sherman set out through central Georgia, destroying railroads, factories, farms, all manner of supplies, and many private houses. There was little resistance, and before Christmas he had captured Savannah—dramatically offering it as a holiday present to Lincoln—before turning his army northward and pushing toward the Carolinas, demonstrating to his enemy what it meant to fight "to the last ditch." The news of Sherman's capture of Savannah was published in Northern newspapers on Christmas Eve and triggered another round of celebration, which was coupled with joy at recent news of Federal triumphs in middle Tennessee.

There Hood had proceeded in mid-November, hoping to draw Sherman after him. The Confederate general had decided to try to capture Nashville and gain supplies and reinforcements. Plans after that were vague. Perhaps he would continue on into Kentucky advancing to the Ohio River, or turn to meet Sherman if he should come back from Georgia, or maybe even move eastward and join forces with Lee in Virginia by attacking Grant from the rear. Lee could then choose whether to, in Hood's words, "annihilate Sherman" or march on Washington. The strategy stemmed from desperation—a desperation born of Hood's costly failures to stop Sherman in front of Atlanta.

Advancing with about 40,000 soldiers—approximately 7,000 of whom were cavalry, and poorly equipped for marching, especially in a winter campaign—Hood's army came to disaster twenty miles south of Nashville at the little town of Franklin on the bank of the Harpeth. Ignoring his corps and cavalry commanders, who urged him to flank the Federal troops under Schofield, Hood stubbornly launched a frontal assault on November 30. Two-thirds of Stephen Lee's corps and most of the army's artillery were far to the rear, and the Confederates did not have any more troops at hand than did the Federals. Still worse, Hood did not organize his infantry to have the weight of his strength at the point where he hoped to break the Union line. The Rebels suffered 7,000 casualties, more than three times as many as the Yankees. Ten times as many Confederates were killed as Federals. The loss of officers in the Army of Tennessee was devastating. Among the six Confederate generals killed or mortally wounded was Patrick Cleburne. In Mobile, his fiancée Susan Tarleton fainted when she heard a newsboy cry on a nearby street the tidings of the battle at Franklin and of Cleburne's death.

Then in defeat, as well as desperation, the one-legged Hood, having misled the Confederate government into believing that he had won a victory at Franklin while neglecting to inform them accurately of the extent of his losses, was once more strapped to his saddle and riding toward Nashville, where Schofield had fallen back to join up with the forces of Thomas. Hood was too weak to assault the Nashville defenses. Entrenching his troops on the hills south of the city, he waited for the Yankees to attack.

On December 15 Thomas's massive force moved out of the Nashville earthworks. With excellent execution, the Federals hurled more troops against the Confederate left flank than Hood had in his whole army, which by then probably had less than 20,000 effectives to contest the Union juggernaut. The Rebels fought with determination, but were compelled to retreat. On the bleak afternoon of December 16, Hood's second line gave way and the army collapsed in panic, soldiers streaming to the south on the Granny White and Franklin Pikes. Only Stephen Lee's corps retained any organization. Shocked to see the army evaporating before his eyes, Lee ably pulled back his troops to the Overton Hills. While a young drummer beat the long roll, Lee held firm until his entire corps could be placed in retreat. Still, the end had come so quickly that sixteen of Lee's guns were captured before the artillery horses could be brought up from the rear. For the most part, the broken remnants of a once-great army scrambled and struggled southward, the vanguard crossing the Harpeth River on December 17.

There would be no stand at Columbia as Hood had hoped might be possible. The road from Nashville was strewn with abandoned wagons, artillery, baggage, and small arms. Thousands of men were barefoot and dressed in thin clothing. The weather, after a brief moderation from the miserable cold just before the battle at Nashville, changed again on December 21, and a driving snow pelted the ragged Confederate column while icy roads slashed the bare feet of hundreds. With a rear guard commanded by Forrest, the suffering army marched on toward the Tennessee River, bound for supply bases at Tupelo and Corinth. It was Christmas day—while Sherman still celebrated his Savannah triumph—when the Confederates began crossing the Tennessee River near Florence, Alabama.

Hood was soon removed from command. He did request to be relieved, although only after Lieutenant General Richard Taylor visited the army on January 9 and enabled the Confederate government to learn the truth about the campaign and the condition of the army. The survivors of the Army of Tennessee rejoined General Johnston who was then in the Carolinas, hoping to blunt Sherman's continuing onslaught with his second march of destruction.

From the point of view of many a Yankee, South Carolina, the home of secession, deserved more vengeful treatment than Georgia. Wrote Sherman to Halleck: "The truth is the whole army is burning with an insatiable desire to wreak vengeance upon South Carolina." A number of South Carolina towns were burned in whole or in part, with the worst destruction coming in the capital city of Columbia. Whether or not the fire was accidental (Sherman said in his memoirs that it was) it is a fact that Sherman did little to restrain his 60,000-man army as it gradually trudged northward leaving vast destruction in its wake.

Moving into North Carolina, Sherman encountered Joseph Johnston once more. Johnston had been restored to command by Robert E. Lee, now general-in-chief of the Confederate armies. But Johnston, who had little more than 20,000 men, could hardly hope to thwart Sherman, whose 60,000 were soon to be joined by 30,000 more soldiers moving inland from the North Carolina coast. Johnston did attack a portion of Sherman's army at Bentonville on March 19. These Federals, however, had as much strength at hand as the Rebels and they entrenched and held their ground. On the following day the rest of Sherman's troops began arriving and the Confederates retreated northward.

Grant, meanwhile, clamped down ever tighter on Lee's forces at Petersburg. At last Lee tried to break away in the hope of joining with Johnston, only to be cut off by Grant; and on April 9 at Appomattox he surrendered. Johnston too, unable to do more against Sherman than aggravate him, could see no point in continuing the struggle and asked Sherman for an armistice on April 14.

The Northern jubilation that followed the wonderful news of Lee's capitulation was suddenly stifled by the shocking, senseless assassination of Lincoln. Just before Sherman boarded a train in Raleigh for the short journey to Durham's Station, from which he would continue on horseback to the meeting arranged with Johnston, the Union commander received a cipher dispatch from Washington that began: "President Lincoln was murdered about 10 o'clock last night in his private box in Ford's Theater in this city." Sherman firmly instructed the telegrapher to tell no one the awful news, and proceeded to the meeting with Johnston.

The two generals conferred in the little farmhouse of Mrs. Daniel

Bennett, where Sherman showed Johnston the dispatch about Lincoln's assassination. Johnston was visibly moved. Neither general knew what this deeply disconcerting event would ultimately mean, and both feared for the possible repercussions. A more somber atmosphere would scarcely have been conceivable as the generals discussed the surrender of Johnston's army. The proceedings went on until sunset, when they agreed to meet again the next day. With Sherman's consent, Confederate general John C. Breckinridge, once vice-president of the United States and then serving as Confederate secretary of war, would join them when negotiations were resumed.

Hurrying back to Raleigh, and ordering all soldiers to their camps, Sherman then issued a carefully worded announcement of the president's assassination. He clearly stated that the Confederate army had nothing to do with the crime. The Federal soldiers were shocked. Some wanted vengence and hoped that the surrender negotiations would collapse. But they remained relatively quiet and did not attempt any reprisal measures on their own. Sherman had succeeded in maintaining order.

The next day, doubtless thinking he was acting in the spirit of Lincoln's lenient policy for reconstruction, and attempting to satisfy Johnston as well, Sherman went far beyond Grant's surrender terms for Lee's army. He negotiated what amounted to a reconstruction policy, something he had no authority to do. The general, although he had conducted a hard war, believed in a soft peace, and certainly hoped to prevent any postwar reprisals. Also, he may not have understood all the implications of what he agreed to, which could be interpreted as recognizing Southern state governments, guaranteeing political rights of former Confederates—and property in slaves. When one recognizes that Sherman disliked politicians generally, opposed the radical program of reconstruction, had little faith in black equality, and had opposed the arming of blacks, then it is not too difficult to understand why he blundered as he did in the matter of the armistice.

When Sherman's terms reached Washington, the government was enraged. The most vocal critic was the secretary of war. Edwin M. Stanton denounced Sherman, all but accused him of treason, and repudiated what he had done. Grant was sent to confer with Sherman and see that Johnston's terms of surrender were essentially the same as those for Lee. Thus Sherman and Johnston were forced to negotiate a new surrender agreement, which was accomplished on April 26. Sherman never forgave Stanton for the things Stanton said about him. Indeed, Stanton's distorted version of the affair, whether sincerely motivated or not, was unjust to the general who, beginning in the spring of 1864 and continuing until the end of the war, had contributed more than any other Union military man to bring the Confederacy to her knees.

WHILE there are many reasons for the perennial interest in the Civil War, as well as war in general, one major factor is found in the intriguing realm of analysis. Why were particular decisions made or not made? If some event, or series of events, had developed differently, would that have changed the final outcome of the struggle? Did the decision of battle or campaign hinge upon internal dissension? Was it determined by a strong personality—or perhaps a weak personality? Considering such factors as terrain, weather, time, numbers, and so on, what tactical possibilities might have yielded greater success than those employed? Might campaign strategy have been better conceived or implemented? Did the simple factor of luck, good or bad, constitute a significant part in the end result? These are the kind of questions that bring freshness, vitality, and fascination to the study of war.

Clearly the preceding chapters have been interlaced with analysis, and the authors do not propose to reiterate the book in the last chapter. There are points, however, both implied and stated, that deserve emphasis and clarity of focus. Sherman's campaign, in essential respects, was the more important movement in Grant's two-pronged grand design for crushing the Confederacy by placing continual and simultaneous pressure on the South's two major armies. Sherman's campaign was the more difficult endeavor. Sherman had to rely on a long railroad line from Louisville to Nashville to Chattanooga and southward, while Grant had relatively short, water communications. Sherman also had no one coming up behind Johnston, as Grant did Lee, to threaten the enemy's rear. (Originally there was supposed to have been an expedition from Mobile up the Alabama River, but it was turned aside to the Red River.) Sherman was much farther into enemy territory than Grant and in the event of defeat would have a correspondingly more difficult time extricating his army, a fact that had to be upon Sherman's mind as the campaign progressed. Sherman's army, deep in the Confederate heartland and dependent on some 350 miles of railroad for supplies, had to stand or fall alone— and if Sherman failed, Grant's grand strategy failed. Thus the significance of Sherman's campaign, especially when set against the background of long overemphasis on the eastern theater of war, deserves to be underscored in the interest of historical objectivity.

Sherman's campaign—like Grant's in Virginia—was different from anything yet experienced in the course of the war. Previously armies had met in battle for a day or two or a week at the most, with long periods of time between these clashes. In the western theater, such was the case with Fort Donelson, Elk Horn Tavern, Shiloh, Perryville, Stones River, Chickasaw Bluffs, Champions Hill, Chickamauga, and others. Some of these engagements saw few casualties, while others were very bloody indeed; but all were relatively brief. In the Atlanta campaign the armies were continually facing one another, day after day and week after week. Certainly this is not to say that the soldiers of the Atlanta campaign experienced every day the intensity of a Shiloh or a Chickamauga, or had as high a percentage of their total force involved in fighting as in those battles. Definitely not. But from early May until Hood retreated from Atlanta in September the Union and Confederate armies were virtually never out of violent contact with one another. The action varied from skirmishing to heavy fighting. Sometimes the skirmishing was light and at other times it was intense. Sometimes the heavy fighting involved a few divisions and at other times a large portion of the armies was engaged. The point is that the frequency of battle was much greater than it had ever been in the first three years of conflict. Some degree of fighting occurred nearly every day, and neither army had experienced anything like such a campaign previously.

The Atlanta campaign also discredits further the traditional concept that the South had better generals than the North. This legend stems, unquestionably, from the long overemphasis on the Virginia theater and, particularly, the impressive exploits of Lee. It is well illustrated by the following statement, typical of both popular writers and academics, which comes from David Donald's *Liberty and Union*: "It would be hard to argue that Northern generalship was superior to that of the South. While Grant has his admirers, to most students Robert E. Lee is unquestionably the greatest Civil War commander."

Without contesting Lee as the greatest commander, the history of the war in the western theater—where of course Lee never fought—clearly demonstrates that the alleged superiority of Southern generals is largely a myth. Actually, it would be hard to argue that Southern generalship was superior to that of the North in most major western actions, such as Fort Donelson, Shiloh, Stones River, and Vicksburg. The Chattanooga campaign was a prime example of the failures of Confederate generalship, and the Atlanta campaign only contributes still more evidence that top-ranking Southern generals were certainly no better than—if indeed they were as good as—their Northern counterparts.

General Johnston fully expected Sherman to move around his right flank at Dalton when the campaign began in early May. With Snake

Creek Gap not guarded, only good fortune rescued Johnston from the trap that Sherman envisioned. Throughout the campaign Johnston seemed to lack a competitive, aggressive temperament, retreating from positions where he might have fought well, defending and even counterattacking. Far from being offensively minded, he apparently followed a general retreat policy, hoping the Union commander would make a fundamental mistake. Johnston seemed oblivious too about the political implications of his continued retreat. At the Chattahoochee River Johnston was alarmingly complacent. There, as at Dalton, he was totally deceived by Sherman's movement, seemingly focusing once more on a preconceived idea of the enemy's intent. With the unfolding of the campaign, it becomes difficult to believe that Johnston had any overall plan—unless merely reacting to an enemy's actions can be considered a plan. He allowed the Federal commander to seize the initiative and control the momentum of the struggle. A more imaginative, competitive Confederate general would have recognized the psychological pressure that could have been exerted upon Sherman, deep in enemy territory, by refusing to simply react to the Yankee general's moves. If ever a true "offensive-defensive" strategy was needed by the Confederates, this was that time.

Johnston's lack of a competitive, aggressive temperament becomes clearer after the historian has the Atlanta campaign to complete the picture of the general's military career. After all, when he took command at Dalton, Johnston's supporters could argue he would have defeated McClellan on the Peninsula except for the Seven Pines wound. It was possible to argue that his western theater command had failed only because the Davis government had not given him real power. Indeed, so strong was the Johnston mystique that it would long be argued that he would have defeated Sherman before Atlanta but for his removal by Davis.

The support of Johnston as a capable general became deeply involved with the anti-Davis bloc, a fact that, it seems reasonable to assume, was beneficial to Johnston's image as a successful military leader—if only, so ran the argument, he had not been thwarted time and again by Davis. Some people really were not so concerned with whether or not Johnston was a good general as with trying to destroy Davis. Johnston himself once commented that perhaps the anti-Davis bloc of congressmen were less his friends and more Davis's enemies.

During the war and especially after the war, Johnston was probably not scrutinized as carefully as he might have been had he not become, in a sense, an automatic hero of the Confederacy due to his clashes with Jefferson Davis. In defeat Davis was blamed much more than he deserved. Since Johnston was an enemy of Davis, and Davis was pilloried as a "loser," it was an easy and natural oversimplification to contend that General Johnston must have been a "winner." Johnston's image benefited further from the debacle of Hood.

General Hood was indeed less impressive than Johnston. Before replacing Johnston, his reckless, repeated attacks at Kolb's Farm—where the Yankees were behind defensive works—did not portend well for the future. After he was elevated to the position of army commander, Hood's attacks of July 20, 22, and 28 at Atlanta were either delayed or uncoordinated—or both. Hood did not bear all the responsibility for these failures. He lashed out at Hardee for taking a lethargic role in the Peachtree Creek and Decatur battles, and clearly Stephen Lee blundered badly at Ezra Church.

Yet it is a fact that Hood established his headquarters in Atlanta, where he was not easily accessible to his generals, did not understand the battlefield situation, and was in no position to direct the development of the engagements. Only after his army had suffered terribly in casualties and morale, and was forced out of Atlanta, did Hood move northwestward, menacing Sherman's railroad. This movement, had it been tried earlier and from strength when Johnston commanded, might possibly have forced Sherman to retreat. Under Hood it was a desperation measure. It came after Sherman already had captured Atlanta and was in a position to abandon rail communications, something he would not have dared while still in north Georgia in the earlier stages of the campaign—especially if Johnston, when he was 70,000 strong, had moved into north Alabama, where he could have had a supply line and threatened to actually destroy Sherman's rail communications.

Finally, the railroads deserve more attention. The railroads were indispensable for Sherman's Atlanta campaign. Sherman himself stated in his memoirs: "I repeat again and again that the Atlanta campaign would not have been possible without these railroads, and also, because we had men and means to maintain and defend them." The Atlanta campaign demonstrates that Sherman appreciated the value of the railroads more than the Confederates did. Whether as Sherman also claimed—"we had men and means to maintain and defend them"—is a question that was never really tested.

The two historians who have published most extensively on the Confederate aspect of the Atlanta campaign differ markedly concerning what the Rebels might have done to Sherman's railroad. Richard McMurry, in a 1976 *Civil War History* article, implied that Mississippi's abandonment would have been necessary in order to concentrate cavalry against Sherman's railroad; that such could have been disastrous to the Confederates because of the impact on the doctrine of States' Rights; and that

Tunnel, 2,228 Feet Long, through the Cumberland Mountain, South of Cowan, Tennessee. *(Photo John Hursh.)*

the railroad probably could not have been disrupted long enough to affect Sherman's operations in Georgia anyway. Thomas Connelly, in a lengthy discussion of the railroad question in *Autumn of Glory* (1971) concluded that Stephen Lee, in his Alabama-Mississippi command, had more than 15,000 effective troops (mostly cavalry) in the spring of 1864, while Simon Buckner, in east Tennessee, who might also have contributed, had 4,000 effective cavalry. Building a case for the weakness of Federal garrisons in Tennessee, together with many vulnerable points on the railroads, Connelly persuasively implies that Confederate cavalry provided the potential manpower for significant action against Sherman's communications.

Clearly the railroads were vulnerable in scores of places. While restoring over 100 miles of track on the Nashville-Decatur line, for example, General Grenville M. Dodge repaired or rebuilt 182 bridges. Obviously many were minor spans, but a lot were major structures. There were twelve important bridges on the 40-mile stretch between Nashville and

Columbia alone. Also, midway between Pulaski and Athens, the railroad first went through a curving tunnel, soon crossed a 700 foot bridge over the Elk River, and then traveled a long and narrow trestle just south of Elkmount. The long rail link of the Memphis & Charleston from Decatur through Huntsville, Scottsboro, and Stevenson presented many opportunities (dozens of creek crossings, for example) for attack and destruction. On the more direct route to Chattanooga—the 151-mile Nashville & Chattanooga line—the destruction of the long tunnel at Cowan, Tennessee, would surely have been a significant setback for Sherman's food and supplies. Just as with the Nashville & Decatur, and the Memphis & Charleston, so too the Nashville & Chattanooga road had numerous important bridges that were vulnerable to attack.

In truth, the Yankees do not appear to have had sufficient forces to defend both routes against determined Rebel assaults without detaching significantly from Sherman's command while he contended with Johnston in Georgia. Not to be forgotten, too, is that only a single track existed between Stevenson and Chattanooga. This line was exceedingly vulnerable. One particular wooden trestle, 780 feet long and 116 feet high in the center of its span, located at the pass in the Raccoon Range near Whiteside, Tennessee, would have been a good target. A long, flimsy trestle across Running Water Ravine would have been another highly vulnerable point of attack.

But the Confederates never mounted a campaign in earnest to destroy Sherman's railroads. They did not really grasp the fundamental truth that upon rail communications depended the success of the Atlanta campaign. Also, Confederate cavalry, accustomed to riding and raiding and riding again, were generally not capable—with the possible exception of Forrest's command—of destroying rail lines so that they could not be quickly repaired. Lastly, the Confederates failed to damage Sherman's railroads significantly because of the strategically incapacitating, territorially binding, States' Rights philosophy.

Even Bedford Forrest—so often cited as an advocate of falling upon Sherman's communications in middle Tennessee—actually wished to strike off into west Tennessee, and was willing to undertake the mission against Sherman's rail lines only if northern Mississippi were secure from Federal invasion.

Thus Sherman, by sending out expeditions from Memphis into north Mississippi, neutralized the Mississippi cavalry of Forrest, and Stephen Lee as well. While four Union thrusts from Memphis were tactical failures, they were strategic successes. As Sherman told General Cadwallader C. Washburn, the unfortunate Yankee commander at Memphis who fled from his bedroom in nightclothes to escape Forrest's raiders: "If you get a chance [Could this be a touch of sarcasm?] tell Forrest that I admire his dash but not his judgment. The oftener he runs his head against Memphis the better."

From the strategical point of view, even Forrest's greatest victory of the war—at Brice's Cross Roads—was well worth the cost to the Federals, for Sherman was achieving his primary objective of keeping Forrest off his communications. While Forrest's mind was on northern Mississippi and west Tennessee, Sherman visualized the whole war and acted accordingly. Sherman's success, coupled with the success of Grant and Meade in Virginia, meant the ruin of the Confederacy, and Sherman did not lose sight of that fact. In the final analysis, although Sherman more than once demonstrated tactical shortcomings in his military career, from the standpoint of strategy, logistics, and communications, the general had no superior on either side of the war; possibly no equal.

GENERAL WILLIAM TECUMSEH SHERMAN and General Joseph Eggleston Johnston both lived for a quarter of a century after the Civil War. Both wrote memoirs of their military experiences. They sometimes corresponded and occasionally visited with each other. Mutual respect led to the development of genuine friendship. At the funeral of General Grant in New York, Sherman and Johnston stood side by side, "a picture of American fraternity," wrote a reporter for *Harper's Weekly*, "astonishing almost to ourselves who remember terrible conflict within the present generation."

Sherman lived to see his seventy-first birthday, February 8, 1891—although it was hardly an occasion of celebration, as he was attended by two physicians on that day. His ailments were more than one, but it was apparently his longtime nemesis, asthma, that finally overcame him and he died on February 14. The general had asked that none except the family view his face when he was dead, but it was felt that the veterans should not be denied the paying of their last respects in this manner. On February 18 thousands viewed his remains.

All of New York seemed to be in mourning, flags at half-mast on buildings and ships. Members of the Grand Army of the Republic, many of them Sherman's veterans, were in line, uniformed and armed. Behind them were regiments of the National Guard and the West Point cadet corps—30,000 soldiers or former soldiers.

President Harrison and former presidents Hayes and Cleveland were present. Members of the cabinet, congressmen, senators, governors, mayors, and friends were in attendance. The sidewalks were filled with crowds of people. Among those who made the journey to New York for the funeral was Joseph Johnston, who had observed his eighty-fourth birthday on February 3.

General Johnston took his place as an honorary pallbearer. The day was very cold following a winter rain, but Johnston stood bareheaded with the other pallbearers while the flag-draped coffin was carried from Sherman's residence to the waiting caisson. A bystander, concerned about Johnston, urged the general to "please put on your hat; you might get sick."

Johnston replied: "If I were in his place and he were standing here in mine, he would not put on his hat." Johnston left New York with a severe cold that aggravated a bad heart condition. About a month later, on March 21, 1891, Johnston too was dead.

# Epilogue

# Frankly, Margaret Mitchell Did Give a Damn!

WHAT most people know about Sherman's Atlanta campaign was acquired at some point between "Tara's Theme" and "Frankly, my dear, I don't give a damn!" David O. Selznick's film of Margaret Mitchell's novel *Gone with the Wind* has had an audience larger than the total population of the United States. By 1983 the novel itself had sold twenty-five million copies and had been translated into twenty-seven languages. Richard Current, in his article, "Fiction as History," wrote: "novelists may have a much greater influence than historians do on popular conceptions of the past." He might have added, "especially if their novels become cinematic giants." No historian can write about Sherman's months in Georgia without discussing *Gone with the Wind*, for few readers will not have read the book or seen the film, or done both. We recognize that as readers follow Sherman to Atlanta it is inevitable that they will recall images from Margaret Mitchell's story: Aunt Pittypat shrieking as Sherman's shells plunged into the red clay; the terrible scene of Confederate wounded at the Atlanta depot; Prissy's admission that "Lawsy Miss Scarlett, I don't know nothin' 'bout birthin' babies!"; Rhett's rescue of Scarlett, Melanie and her baby, and Prissy, and their dramatic flight down the McDonough road as Hood's ammunition explodes.

Fifty years ago *Gone with the Wind* was published by an Atlanta woman who, from childhood, had been fascinated by stories of the Civil War and her city's darkest days. In "Why, Miss Scarlett, How Well You've Aged," Tom Wicker wrote: "The Civil War remains a prime source of American myth and drama not least because Margaret Mitchell, growing to maturity in a land not yet healed, among a people many of whom could remember the war's devastation recreated it in one of the most memorable of American fictions."

Margaret Mitchell was always the first to insist that she was a novelist, not a historian. After her historical novel had become a success, Georgia governor Eugene Talmadge asked her to write a history of Georgia to be used in the state's public schools. Mitchell declined: "I am a novelist and a newspaper reporter not a scholar or historian, and I do not consider myself qualified to write a history." Her letters indicate great respect for historians, and a hope that they would find her work historically reliable and would respect her novel of war and reconstruction. She once even thought historians might find her book useful, writing: "At first I thought the book might sell a few thousands to people who were interested in the history of that period. A few hundreds to college libraries for use in collateral readings in American History." Her letters reveal a determination to make the novel's historical background as accurate as possible. It is doubtful if any author of a work of historical fiction spent as much time researching the times in which she placed her fictional characters as did Mitchell.

Research for *Gone with the Wind* "started in my cradle," wrote Margaret Mitchell. She admitted that she was "raised on" Civil War diaries and "when most children were reading 'Peter Rabbit' and the 'Rover Boys' " she was devouring Eliza Andrews's *The War Time Journal of a Georgia Girl*. As a child Margaret often was taken by her parents to see the Cyclorama, the huge painting of the July 22, 1864, Battle of Atlanta in Grant Park. The painting produced wonder in the little girl who was to learn so much about the events it depicted.

Mitchell's lifelong research continued when as a child she "sat on the bony knees of veterans" and listened to their experiences of the Civil War and Reconstruction. She and her brother heard endless arguments among their elders over "why Jeff Davis didn't put Hood in command at Dalton instead of waiting till the last ditches of Atlanta." She considered her father "an authority on Atlanta and Georgia history of that period," adding, "and Mother knew about as much as he did." Those family stories provided Mitchell with a great deal of information as well as with some of her basic attitudes toward the war. Such stories, while valuable, are often distorted by personal prejudice and fading memory. But old Sunday afternoon yarns were not her only sources.

In 1936 Margaret Mitchell told a South Carolina fan of her blockbuster novel: "I have always liked Southern literature and Southern history, and since I could first read I have read everything I could find on the subject of the Civil War. In later years, I have hunted down private letters and diaries of that period." To a New Yorker she boasted, "my bibliography runs into the thousands of volumes"; and to a woman from Minnesota she wrote, "The historical background of War and Reconstruction are as accurate as I could possibly make them after ten years of reading thousands of books, documents, letters, diaries, old newspapers and interviewing people who had lived through those terrible times."

In the months after *Gone with the Wind's* publication on June 30, 1936, Margaret Mitchell wrote dozens of letters to admirers, reviewers, and historians. Since she often mentioned the material she had consulted, these responses that poured out as *GWTW* fever swept the land provided a source list almost as if she had included a bibliography after page 1037 of her gigantic work.

She recalled being "laden down with 'Records of the War of the Rebellion' (each book weighed three pounds)," a real burden for the tiny author. Mitchell read and reread Hood's *Advance and Retreat,* Johnston's *Narrative,* and Sherman's *Memoirs.* She told Stephen Vincent Benét, who wrote to praise her novel, "I used everybody from Myrta Lockett Avary to Eliza Andrews and Mary Gay and Mrs. Clement Clay and Miss Fearn and Eliza Ripley [all published diaries of the war years] and the Lord knows how many unpublished letters and diaries." She also "studied [Union general Jacob D.] Cox's Atlanta campaign harder than I ever did Caesar's Gallic Wars." "And, if there was even a sergeant who wrote a book about that retreat, I read it," she reported. One of her favorites was "my old friend Sam Watkins, author of 'Co. Aitch.' " who "left a record to show what the dryly humorous foot soldier thought about it all." *Gone with the Wind's* author also used Civil War reports of the Georgia adjutant general, *Battles and Leaders of the Civil War,* and Robert S. Henry's *The Story of the Confederacy;* the latter she pronounced "grand and readable." To better understand the war in Virginia, Mitchell closely perused two classic studies of the eastern theater: Douglas Southall Freeman's four-volume *Robert E. Lee* and G. F. R. Henderson's *Stonewall Jackson and the American Civil War.*

Through the twenties the future novelist haunted Atlanta's Carnegie Library. She hauled armloads of books to her apartment and remembered the library's staff as "indefatigable, accurate, obliging and courteous." Day after day she lugged books to her trolley stop in front of Loew's Grand Theater, never imagining the honors that would be showered upon her in that theater a little more than a decade later. One day in 1926, when she came home with her latest stack of books, it appeared to her husband John Marsh that she was about to exhaust the library's holdings. He greeted her with: "It looks to me, Peggy, as though you'll have to write a book yourself if you're to have anything to read."

In the library's manuscript collection she found a number of letters and memoirs adding to her knowledge of the city's past. One, a letter written by Clark Howell, editor of the *Atlanta Constitution,* was especially informative. Howell, as a small boy, went with his father and a group of Confederate veterans to call on General Sherman when he visited the city after the war. One veteran asked the general, "Why were you so hell bent on capturing Atlanta? You had established your base at Chattanooga. Wasn't that enough?" Sherman rose and "holding up his left arm with the fingers of his hand spread out," he said:

> The answer is simple. Atlanta, say, is on my wrist. At the end of each of my fingers are Norfolk, Savannah, Jacksonville, Pensacola and New Orleans. Atlanta was the only place in the South from which every city on the South Atlantic and the Gulf Coast between Norfolk and New Orleans could be reached over night. . . . I knew when I had Atlanta the war would be at an end.

In addition to her voluminous reading, Margaret Mitchell had firsthand familiarity with the land through which Sherman's campaign was fought. She had often gone over the battlefields from Chattanooga to Atlanta. Just before MacMillan published *Gone with the Wind,* she reported "trailing the way the campaign from Tennessee to Atlanta was fought and wondering mournfully how I was ever to compress such an epic and heartbreaking affair into a few lines instead of giving it a whole book as it deserved." Before choosing a site for Tara (the O'Hara plantation in Clayton County, just south of Atlanta) Mitchell, with one of Sherman's 1864 maps in hand, "travelled the roads of the County in the backwoods time and again," eventually locating the antebellum South's best-known plantation, "in my imagination."

Margaret Mitchell's determination to make her book historically accurate was created both by her devotion to accuracy and by her fear of being discovered in mistakes by historians and the Confederate veterans still alive. On the eve of publication she confided to a friend: "However lousy the book may be as far as style, subject, plot, characters, it's as accurate historically as I can get it. I didn't want to get caught out in anything that any Confederate Vet could nail me on, or any historian either." She laboriously checked on the rainy weather before Kennesaw, fearing that if she "didn't get it right, seven hundred old vets would rise up out of Soldiers' Homes and denounce me." She once stated that she could "cite at least four sources for each nonfictional statement in my book." Five months after *GWTW* was published Mitchell admitted, "I have been waking up screaming in the night after dreaming that someone *has* caught me out, in spite of my efforts to be accurate."

One of her favorite reviews was that by historian Henry Steele Commager in the *New York Herald Tribune Books* on July 5, 1936. Commager praised the book, calling it "the prose to 'John Brown's Body.' " It was the highest kind of praise, because Mitchell loved Benét's poem. "Soon Sherman is battering his way into Georgia and Atlanta is besieged," wrote Commager, adding, "Never has a chapter of the war been more realistically recreated, more vividly described." Mitchell sent her thanks:

> You speak of my book not 'ruffling your historical feather.' Thanks for that. I positively cringed when I heard that you, a historian, were going to review me. I cringed even though I knew the history in my tale was as water proof and air tight as ten years of study and a lifetime of listening to participants would make it. Historians, like those who deal in the exact sciences, are prone to be tough!

Commager was not alone in praising the results of her research for *GWTW*. John Peale Bishop, who called the novel, "neither very good nor very sound," added in his *New Republic* review, "The historical background is handled well and with an extraordinary sense of detail."

But some contemporary historians were "tough." Bernard De Voto, whose *Across the Wide Missouri* would win the Pulitzer Prize for history in 1948, saw little to praise in the novel, writing, "It has too little thought and no philosophical overtones. . . . The size of its public is significant; the book is not." W. E. B. Du Bois, one of the nation's best-known black historians, said the novel was guilty of "conventional provincialism about which Negroes need not get excited."

Between the novel's publication in 1936 and Margaret Mitchell's tragic death in 1949, she maintained contact with a number of well-known Civil War historians. Robert Selph Henry became a friend, as did Clifford Dowdey, John W. Thomason, and Douglas Southall Freeman. When Freeman praised her work, Mitchell replied, "To have you say such things about my book is the highest accolade the book or I can receive." The novelist also continued to read the latest historical works as they appeared. In 1943 she recommended Ella Lonn's *Foreigners in the Confederacy* and had high praise for Bell Wiley's pioneering *The Life of Johnny Reb*. She wrote Dowdey after reading Wiley's profile of the common soldier of the Confederacy: "It was letters such as these which made me decide to write a more realistic war story than I had ever read."

Margaret Mitchell never wavered in her confidence that her history was accurate. She admitted to a California journalist a fear that her book "might not set well upon Southerners," but hastened to add: "I had written nothing that was not true, nothing that I could not prove."

What was Mitchell's "true' picture of the Civil War that served as a frame for Scarlett, Rhett, Melanie, and Ashley? Her portrayal of Tara's

Clayton County and of Atlanta emphasized their newness, vigor, and lack of sophistication. Early in chapter 1 the reader is told the region is "crude" and that the citizens of coastal Georgia and South Carolina "looked down their noses at the up-country Georgians." In chapter 3 she returned to that theme, using such words as "rugged," "hardy," "sturdy," and "virile" to describe north Georgia and its people.

In chapter 8 Mitchell introduces Atlanta and compares the city to Scarlett O'Hara: "crude with the crudities of youth and as headstrong and impetuous as herself." This linking of city and heroine is made throughout the novel so that the personality of the city through the antebellum years, the Civil War, and Reconstruction, is also that of this most famous of fictitious Southern women.

Atlanta was inseparable from its railroads, a fact Mitchell is quick to point out. She traces the development from Terminus to Marthasville to Atlanta, and writes: "Born of a railroad, Atlanta grew as its railroads grew." On pages 142 and 143, Atlanta's "restless, energetic people" live in a town whose streets were "winding rivers of mud," even though "fine homes on Whitehall and Washington streets" had been built by the out-break of war.

Margaret Mitchell was determined to write of north Georgia without adding the often-used, and she feared expected, adornments of life in the antebellum South. "I tried not to hammer on the theme of Atlanta and its growth and its railroads and its differences from other Southern cities of the time but I wanted it there in the background of Scarlett," she wrote *New York Times* critic Donald Adams. To historian Gilbert E. Govan, later a biographer of Joseph E. Johnston, she was even more detailed:

> Most Southerners (and most North Georgians too) find it difficult to understand how the Atlanta neighborhood differed from the rest of the South. People persist in believing that magnolias, moonlight, Spanish moss and enormous white columns were to be found everywhere in the old South. Some people became incensed at being told that the old South was not a hundred per cent white columns. This section of North Georgia was undeniably crude in spots. Another generation of cotton money would perhaps have given us a lot of white columns, but during the period of which I wrote the cotton money was going back into the land and into Negroes, and not into architectural gems.

*Gone with the Wind*'s author wanted to make sure that "Tara wasn't a movie set but a working plantation," as she wrote Stephen Vincent Benét in 1936. "It's hard to make people understand that North Georgia wasn't all white columns and singing darkies and magnolias, that it was so new,

so raw," she continued in her letter to the author of *John Brown's Body*.
Mitchell was especially concerned about Tara's architecture in her book,
a concern that would eventually turn to mirth when she saw the film.
She did not make Tara a Greek revival house, because few existed in
Clayton County in the 1850s.

One of the greatest controversies to swirl about *GWTW* was its picture
of slavery. In his biting 1936 review, Malcolm Cowley wrote: " 'Gone
with the Wind,' is an encyclopedia of the plantation legend." Cowley's
words have been repeated in virtually every study of the novel. Mitchell
was faulted by others who believed that her work failed to probe the
sociology of the antebellum plantation. She was quick to reply that she
had not intended to write a sociological study of plantation life.

"Mitchell is a child of her time, not ours and is unfairly judged by the
70's or 80's view of racism," wrote Tom Wicker in 1986. Historian Albert
Castel, in an article on *Gone with the Wind* as history, echoes Wicker:
"Most of the inaccuracies in *Gone with the Wind* are either excusable on
grounds of literary need or explainable as the consequences of the author's
sources and of the time and place she lived." Mitchell wrote her book in
the 1920s, when the best-known study of slavery was U. B. Phillips's
*American Negro Slavery*. There is no evidence in her letters that Mitchell
had read Phillips's work and much evidence that her view of slavery had
come through oral tradition, passed on by family and friends, that pictured slavery as a benign institution. When criticized for her portrait of
the old South, Mitchell wrote her friend, novelist and historian Clifford
Dowdey: "I've always been slightly amused by the New York critics who
referred to GWTW as a 'moonlight and magnolias romance.' My God,
they never read the gentle Confederate novel of the Nineties, or they'd
know better."

There is no denying that her slaves—Mammy, Pork, Dilcey, Prissy,
and Big Sam—were stereotypes. They were happy, humorous, loyal, often
silly, and doggedly loyal to "Mr. Rhett and Miss Scarlett." The brutaliz-
ing nature of the institution is never evident. Yet Mitchell's attempt to
remind her readers that Tara was a "working plantation" took her beyond
many earlier novels in which slaves appeared only to laugh and play in
the quarter.

As war clouds gathered in Charleston harbor, Mitchell's Georgians
were disdainful. Scarlett told the Tarleton twins "the Yankees are too
scared of us to fight" and that there would be no war. Later Scarlett's
father reported that in Atlanta people are "talking nothing but war. . . .
the news from Charleston is that they will be putting up with no more
Yankee insults." When Rhett Butler, the mysterious stranger from
Charleston, arrives in Clayton County he brings reality to this boastful

atmosphere. Butler has spent some time in the North and has "seen many things you all have not seen. The thousands of immigrants who'd be glad to fight for the Yankees for food and a few dollars, the factories, the foundries, the shipyards, the iron and coal mines—all the things we haven't got. Why, all we have is cotton and slaves and arrogance. They'd lick us in a month." The overconfident inhabitants of Tara and Twelve Oaks were mirrored across the South and most did not have the words of a Rhett Butler to intrude on their dreams of easy victory.

Once the war is under way, Mitchell's Atlanta is a city filled with excitement. When Scarlett goes there in May 1862, Mitchell describes Atlanta's role in the Confederacy with historical accuracy and keen insight. "From the minute the fighting first began, Atlanta had been transformed," she wrote. From page 145 through page 148 the bustling "turntable of the Confederacy" comes alive:

> The same railroads which had made the town the crossroads of commerce in time of peace were now of vital strategic importance in time of war. Far from the battle lines, the town and its railroads provided the connecting link between the two armies of the Confederacy. . . . And Atlanta likewise linked both of the armies with the deeper South from which they drew their supplies. Now, in response to the needs of war, Atlanta had become a manufacturing center, a hospital base and one of the south's chief depots for the collecting of food and supplies for the armies in the field.

The youthful Scarlett had often gone to a young Atlanta, but in May 1862, Scarlett, widow and mother, a woman not a girl, "looked about her for the little town she remembered so well. It was gone. The town she was now seeing was like a baby grown overnight into a busy, sprawling giant." Atlanta had grown up and so had Scarlett. And Scarlett loved it: "I'm going to like it here! It's so alive and exciting!"

The theme of Atlanta's growing importance is continued. On pages 280 and 281 Mitchell's analysis of this growth and of a shift of power from the tidewater to the interior brought on by war and blockade stands with the best historical writing on Atlanta, Georgia, and the Civil War's impact:

> Atlanta's ten thousand population had grown to double that number during the war. Even the blockade had added to Atlanta's prestige. From time immemorial, the coast cities had dominated the South, commercially and otherwise. But now with the ports closed and many of the port cities captured or beseiged, the South's salvation depended upon itself. The interior section was what counted, if the south was going to win the war, and Atlanta was

now the center of things. . . . Atlanta, the city, had gained rather than lost as a result of the war.

From Scarlett's arrival in Atlanta in May 1862, to May 1864, when Sherman moved south, Mitchell brings news of the as yet distant conflict to the city in bits. She treats the war's campaigns as remote but increasingly menacing as they near Georgia. They are also menacing in that Ashley Wilkes, loved by both Scarlett and Melanie, is in Cobb's Legion in Virginia. As she expands the war beyond Georgia's borders, on page 146, Mitchell overestimates the number of immigrants serving in the Union army. On the same page she writes that, "the Confederate ports were stoppered with Yankee gunboats, only a trickle of blockade-run goods was slipping in from Europe," in 1862. She makes the blockade effective far earlier than it was, and accords it too much impact on the Confederate war effort. Twenty-five pages later she unleashes Rebel raider Raphael Semmes on the Yankees well before his ship, the *Alabama*, had begun to take its toll of Union shipping.

As she traces the conflict, Mitchell omits Antietam, one of the war's most important struggles, but mentions Lee's victories at Fredericksburg and Chancellorsville. After Fredericksburg, the South knew that in the spring "the Yankees would be crushed for good and all," and following Chancellorsville, "the South roared with elation." She also mentioned Nathan Bedford Forrest's crushing defeat of a Union cavalry force near Rome in north Georgia.

But Gettysburg is the battle that gets the most attention. Dismissing Grant's triumph at Vicksburg in passing, she follows Lee into Pennsylvania, bringing on what Atlantans believed would be "the last fight of the war!" Mitchell effectively conveys the slow receipt of news from Pennsylvania, followed by the dramatic arrival of word of Lee's withdrawal. One of the book's best-known scenes (no doubt enhanced by the film) is that of Scarlett and Melanie outside the *Daily Examiner* as part of a large crowd awaiting casualty lists from Gettysburg. On pages 278 and 279 the author recounts the Confederate victory at Chickamauga in September 1863, adding that "the South had needed the cheering news from Chickamauga to strengthen its morale through the winter." Nowhere does she follow Chickamauga with Bragg's humiliating November defeat at Missionary Ridge, which left the Southern populace with defeat, not victory, as it faced the winter. This omission is one of the most serious historical errors in the Civil War portion of *Gone with the Wind*.

Mitchell traced the war somewhat unevenly, making occasional mistakes; but she was not writing a military history of the Civil War, and her material was successful in permitting her readers to view the war through the eyes of Civil War Georgians.

Chapter 17 of *Gone with the Wind* begins, "May of 1864 came . . . and the Yankees under General Sherman were in Georgia again." For the next 130 pages Margaret Mitchell is a historian describing Sherman's inexorable drive to Atlanta. In "The Unwritten War," Daniel Aaron called the novel "that blend of solid journalism, dogged research and personal fanticizing." Tom Wicker replied: "Anyone who thinks as Aaron does, that Mitchell's account of the Civil War reflects mere 'dogged research' should return to chapters 18 through 24—her splendidly imagined account of the siege, capture and burning of Atlanta and Scarlett's escape to Tara."

In following Yankee advance and Rebel retreat across Georgia's hills and rivers, Mitchell had her best opportunity to use notes from the *Official Records*, Sherman, Johnston, Hood, and Sam Watkins, as well as her trips through the region. Through the eyes of her heroines in Atlanta she watched with hope, disappointment, hope again, and finally terror as "a small, dark cloud . . . appeared in the northwest, the first cloud of a summer storm," which soon blew "up swiftly into a large, sullen storm cloud and it was as though a faint, chilling wind blew from it." Her tracing of the campaign and the attitudes toward the two Confederate commanders, Johnston and Hood, is done with color and is generally accurate.

As the campaign opens in May, Dr. Meade expresses his faith in the Gray army's ability to defend the state: "Johnston and his army stands there . . . like an iron rampart. . . . Sherman will never pass. He'll never dislodge Old Joe." But Johnston retreats to Resaca as Sherman flanks him. Mitchell emphasizes Sherman's numerical superiority, which permits him to force the Confederates to retreat by outflanking them. Yet, in estimating the size of the Rebel army she says Johnston had 40,000 men when he actually had almost 70,000. (In fairness to the novelist, historians writing in the 1920s wrote that the Confederates were outnumbered about two to one.) Mitchell is also in error when she states that Johnston's defense at Dalton forced Sherman to flank toward Resaca. Sherman planned from the campaign's inception to send McPherson marching for Resaca.

Through Resaca, Calhoun, Adairsville, and Cassville to New Hope Church Mitchell moved the armies. At Calhoun she has the Yankees "beaten back," when all that occurred was a skirmish between withdrawing Confederates and a small advance unit of Yankees. She also writes that Johnston's army "could and did lick the Yankees every time the Yankees would stand and fight." Actually, the May losses in the two armies were about equal and attacking grayclads at Resaca and Dallas were soundly beaten. Mitchell also inflates the fighting at Big Shanty into a more significant encounter than occurred there.

Through May her Atlantans retain their faith in the army, but faith in Johnston dies and demands for his removal begin. Soon the armies reach Kennesaw Mountain and there once again, "The Yankees couldn't dislodge Old Joe's men. . . . Atlanta breathed more easily, but—but Kennesaw Mountain was only twenty-two miles away."

When the armies reach Kennesaw Scarlett and Melanie can hear the guns for the first time, according to Mitchell. The earlier firing around New Hope Church had also been audible in Atlanta. In the city, "Panic lay just beneath the surface. . . . No one spoke of fears. That subject was taboo, but strained nerves found expression in loud criticism of the General." Now the rains came, rains Margaret Mitchell had researched so carefully. Sherman halted and, according to the novel, "Everyone grew more cheerful and spoke more kindly of General Johnston." Parties and dances, Scarlett's reason for coming to Atlanta, began again and she was happy.

Mitchell does not specifically mention the June 27 Battle of Kennesaw Mountain, reporting only that after twenty-five days there had been "enormous" Union losses. On the Confederate side Mitchell reported that Johnston "had lost a third of his men." This overestimate would have placed Rebel losses at about 20,000, whereas they were only about one-third of that figure. Sherman then flanked again. With the retreat from Kennesaw, "a fresh wave of terror swept the town." GWTW's Atlantans thought, "But surely the General would hold the Yankees on the opposite bank of the river. Though God knows the river was close enough, only seven miles away!" Sherman crossed the river quickly and in early July, "Atlanta was in agony and panic."

"Richmond knew that if Atlanta was lost the war was lost," writes Mitchell, perhaps attributing to her city more significance in Jefferson Davis's strategic thoughts than was realistic. Johnston is removed "and the town breathed a little easier. Hood wouldn't retreat. Not that tall Kentuckian, with his flowing beard and flashing eye!" Mitchell, echoing the scholarly works of her time, presents the view that the Army of Tennessee was overwhelmingly opposed to the command change and roared " 'Give us back Old Joe!' " In reality, although many Rebel soldiers favored Johnston, a large number believed in Hood. In discussing the evacuation of Atlanta, Mitchell twice repeats words, attributed to Johnston, which ring hollow as the city is abandoned: " 'I can hold Atlanta forever!' " There is no evidence that Johnston said anything of the kind. Had he done so perhaps Davis would not have removed him.

Hood does fight, and the city listens to the struggle along Peachtree Creek. The outcome is uncertain while the city is filled with "wounded and dying men, dripping blood into the red dust."

"Not for Hood the cautious tactics of General Johnston," Margaret Mitchell writes as she moves on to the battles of Atlanta and Ezra Church. She judges that these two struggles "made Peachtree Creek seem like a skirmish," a slight misreading of the relative military significance of Hood's three sorties. In her discussion of the battles around Atlanta, GWTW's author tends to overestimate Sherman's casualties when compared to those of his enemy. But she does add: "General Hood had lost almost as many men as Johnston had lost in seventy-four days . . . and Atlanta was hemmed in on three sides." Only one railroad remained uncut and it "ran through the County, through Jonesboro. And Tara was only five miles from Jonesboro!"

And then came the terror of the siege. It was a terror of instant death from the skies mixed with rising optimism, since Hood appeared to be holding Sherman at bay. Scarlett was terrified of the Yankees at her gates, because rumors that the Northerners "raped women and ran bayonets through children's stomachs" circulated through the city. Rhett Butler scoffed: "My dear girl, the Yankees aren't fiends. They haven't horns and hoofs, as you seem to think. They are pretty much like Southerners—except with worse manners, of course, and terrible accents."

In late August the Union bombardment "abruptly ceased" and "the stillness, after the screaming days . . . if possible, made the strain even worse." The last days of August for Mitchell's characters were days of rumor and uncertainty. The rumors of Sherman's retreat mingled with rumors of a new Union threat. "At last, news came from the south to the strained town and it was alarming news, especially to Scarlett," writes the author. Sherman was moving in force toward the railroad at Jonesboro. The Yankee hordes were heading for Tara.

"On the morning of the first of September, Scarlett awoke with a suffocating sense of dread upon her." The city was quiet. Later that day the sound of distant cannon rumbled up from the south, "and they might be tolling the knell of Atlanta's fall. But to Scarlett . . . fighting to the South only meant fighting near Tara." That afternoon the silence was broken by a horseman racing down Peachtree Street. Scarlett stopped him, and he told her of corps commander William Hardee's dispatch to Hood: "I have lost the battle and am in full retreat."

With Atlanta's defenses collapsing and Melanie in labor, Scarlett faces some of the best-known moments of the novel. She searched for Dr. Meade at the depot where, "Lying in the pitiless sun . . . were hundreds of wounded men. . . . The smell of sweat, of blood, of unwashed bodies, of excrement rose up in waves of blistering heat until the fetid stench almost nauseated her." To Mitchell the scene was "an inferno of pain and smell and noise." The dozens of romantic novels about the lost cause to which *Gone with the Wind* is compared never approached the reality of Scarlett O'Hara's trip across Atlanta.

As night fell on the first and Hood began burning his supplies, Scarlett prepared to flee to Tara. Aided by Rhett Butler, who warns her of the fighting in Clayton County, and accompanied by her son Wade, Melanie and her newborn son, and Scarlett's slave Prissy, she leaves the city. Riding by the rail yard and its cars loaded with ammunition, Rhett angrily shouts in language Mitchell must have heard as a child from Hood's critics: "That must be the last of the ammunition trains. . . . Why didn't they get them out this morning, the fools!" As they pass the evacuating Confederate rear guard Rhett tells her: "Take a good look at them . . . so you can tell your grandchildren you saw the rear guard of the Glorious Cause in retreat." Through the dark and the flames, down the McDonough road, clogged with the retreating army, drive the refugees. Rhett leaves them to go join the Confederate army at last, and Scarlett drives on toward home. In her mind she asked: "Was Tara still standing? Or was Tara also gone with the wind which had swept through Georgia?" She arrived to find her mother dead, her home wrecked, and her life changed forever. As Margaret Mitchell writes at the end of chapter 24: "somewhere along the long road to Tara, she had left her girlhood behind her. . . . She was a woman now and youth was gone."

Using her research and stories of Atlanta's fall she had heard sitting on the "bony knees" of old men who had fled the burning city, in combination with the vivid characters of her imagination, Margaret Mitchell gave Americans their most memorable picture of the Civil War. Richard Current is correct in his appraisal of the comparative popular influence of novelists and historians. Margaret Mitchell's one book has had greater influence than any history of the period. For the Civil War portion at least, if not for her portrayal of the antebellum South and certainly not for her historical approach to Reconstruction, the public has been well served by Mitchell's determination to make her work historically accurate.

And then came David O. Selznick.

Within one month of *Gone with the Wind*'s publication Selznick bought the story from Macmillian for $50,000. As Richard Harwell has written in his introduction to *GWTW: The Screenplay*: "*Gone with the Wind* was David Selznick's film. No matter how entertaining and exciting Miss Mitchell's novel, no matter how felicitous Sidney Howard's screenplay, no matter what directors and actors contributed—the film was Selznick's through and through." From July 1936 to December 1939, when the film premiered in Atlanta, the production of *GWTW* (initials that became instantly recognizable around the world) was news, often commanding more column inches than such stories as Edward VIII's marriage to Mrs. Simpson and appeasement at Munich. The search for an actress to play Scarlett, ending in the selection of Vivien Leigh, gripped the United States. From the first, Mitchell made it clear that she wanted nothing to do with filming her novel. She refused to influence the movie's casting, played no role in writing the script, and never set foot on the Selznick lot in California. Mitchell was afraid of what Hollywood would do to her novel, "but in the end she was genuinely pleased with the movie."

The Atlanta novelist's two concessions to requests for aid from the Selznick Company were to guide film makers around Georgia sites (though none of the film was shot on location) and to recommend technical advisors to work with the film's writers, directors, and producer. George Cukor, Selznick's first director, went to Atlanta in April 1937, and Mitchell guided him "all over the red rutted roads of Clayton County." She reported that Cukor and his staff were disappointed in the houses they saw. Mitchell did carry on a correspondence with Sidney Howard, the playwright chosen to write the script, and answered his technical and historical questions—even trotting back to the Carnegie Library to check 1864 newspapers for him.

Margaret Mitchell's greatest contributions to the motion picture were her recommendations of Wilbur Kurtz as historical advisor and Susan Myrick as technical advisor. Kurtz, an artist and architect, described by Mitchell as "perhaps the world's leading authority on the Atlanta campaign," was a native of Indiana who had walked all the Georgia battlefields and published a number of articles about the Civil War in the state. "His job," in Hollywood, reported Mitchell, "was picking flaws in the old Atlanta sets, fighting to keep too many tall, white columns off of houses." Sue Myrick was a feature writer for the *Macon Telegraph* whose specialty was Southern accents and general regional usages. Replying to Sue Myrick in February 1939, as the film neared completion, Mitchell laughed "when you described Twelve Oaks. I had feared . . . that it would end up looking like the Grand Central Station, and your description confirms my worst apprehensions. I did not know whether to laugh or throw up at the *two* staircases." She added: "All that stands between them [the moviemakers] and a violent Southern revolt is you and the Kurtzes in Hollywood." The pair of Georgians also served, according to Richard Harwell, as "conduits through which Miss Mitchell kept in far closer touch with the filming of *GWTW* than she was willing to admit."

Kurtz and Myrick fought for accuracy, and won some of their battles.

Selznick demanded that Tara have columns, but Kurtz and Myrick argued that at least they be squared not rounded so as to conform with the north Georgia style. Selznick surrendered on Tara but threw all of his fantasies of the Old South into Twelve Oaks. The producer wanted Tara's slaves picking cotton in the movie's early scenes, but the two advisors were quick to point out that Sumter and Lincoln's call for troops occurred in April—planting time, not harvest time. The producer had even hired a Negro chorus to sing as the slaves picked, but grudgingly he abandoned the idea. Instead the slaves ploughed. No one was more familiar with 1864 Atlanta than Kurtz, so the street scenes have buildings placed exactly where they were during the war. Few period movies have made greater efforts at historical accuracy in creating their sets. To recreate Georgia's red clay on a California set, tons of red earth were brought in from Arizona along with red bricks pounded into dust.

Sue Myrick's major task was to advise on Southern accents. Mitchell did not want the exaggerated "you all" drawls used in many Hollywood productions, and she urged her friend to curb these extremes. After scenes were shot Selznick's second director, Victor Fleming, would turn to Myrick and ask: "Okay for Dixie?" Vivien Leigh and Olivia De Havilland mastered the accent, while Clark Gable and Leslie Howard were much less successful.

Selznick went to great lengths for some scenes—notably the overhead shot of Rebel wounded, writhing and moaning at the depot. He hired a huge crane and demanded 2,500 extras to play the soldiers. When not enough extras could be mustered on short notice, he was content with 949 live extras and more than 1,000 dummies, rocked gently by the live extras for animation.

The film that opened in Atlanta in December 1939 differed from Margaret Mitchell's novel. From the first titles with the huge block GONE WITH THE WIND, and the romantic surge of Max Steiner's music, soon to be known as "Tara's Theme," the movie is far more romantic and one-dimensional than Mitchell's novel. An even clearer indication of this difference follows the credits. Selznick's imprint is evident in the prologue attributed to both Selznick and his second writer, Ben Hecht. The titles, which roll across the screen accompanied by "Dixie" in the background, are not Mitchell's words. They envelope *Gone with the Wind's* Old South segment in the kind of moonlight and magnolias the novelist had sought to avoid.

> There was a land of Cavaliers and
> Cotton fields called the Old South . . .
> Here in this pretty world

Gallantry took its last bow . . .
Here was the last ever to be seen
of Knights and their Ladies Fair,
of Master and Slave . . .
Look for it only in books, for it
is no more than a dream remembered,
a Civilization gone with the wind.

Behind the credits and early in the movie are views of Tara's cotton fields, peach blossoms, and lazy streams. As the field hands end their day's work and move toward home, Steiner's idyllic music conjures up Selznick's dream of the Old South.

In his article, "From *The Clansmen* and *Birth of a Nation* to *Gone with the Wind*: the Loss of American Innocence," Gerald Wood finds the film far more romantic than the "pessimistic and fatalistic" novel. Wood writes, "David Selznick purged *Gone with the Wind* of Mitchell's ambiguity," and concludes: "Rather than dramatize, as Mitchell does, an inconclusive conflict between aristocratic idealism and lumpish realism, the filmmaker makes a clear preference for days-gone-by when, in the prologue, he described the prewar South as a chivalric and orderly world that has tragically been lost, 'a dream remembered.' The present and future, the film implies, are no match for the past portrayed in the story about to be told."

Mitchell, who had insisted so often that she had struggled "to describe North Georgia as it was," was frustrated "by finding [herself] included among writers who pictured the South as a land of white-columned mansions whose wealthy owners had thousands of slaves and drank thousands of juleps." In frustration she told Virginius Dabney, liberal editor of the *Richmond Times-Dispatch* and author of "The South that Never Was," "People believe what they like to believe and the mythical Old South has too strong a hold on their imaginations to be altered by the mere reading of a 1,037 page book." Since David O. Selznick was one of those people she might have added, "Especially after Mr. Selznick had finished his film."

There are a number of changes made in the novel's characters by Selznick and his writers. Many who appear in Mitchell's 1,037 pages are, understandably, omitted; others are changed. To alter and simplify Scarlett's character for the first half of the movie, she is left childless with the death of her first husband—Charles Hamilton. Those who have seen the film but have not read the book are invariably shocked to learn that Scarlett bore a son after Charles's death. Few can imagine Vivien Leigh's Scarlett, in her flirtatious wartime scenes, as a mother.

There might have been more differences between novel and film had it not been for the work of F. Scott Fitzgerald. The famous novelist made few contributions to the dialogue, but when asked to read Howard's script he often advised a return to Mitchell's words. One of his marginal notes read, "Book restored. It is infinitely more moving."

While there is a difference of attitude between the book and the film in both the antebellum and Reconstruction footage, there are fewer conflicts in the material on the Civil War. Perhaps Wilbur Kurtz's insistence on accuracy kept the studio from straying too far. It may also be that there is less opportunity for differences in interpretation in the war years than in material on either slavery or Reconstruction.

Both book and film might have indulged in a favorite Southern occupation, turning Sherman into a satanic figure. The novel presents the Union commander as a figure hated and feared by Atlantans, but the film, while making him the leader of a powerful and menacing army, does nothing with the general personally. Mitchell calls the soldier shot by Scarlett in the act of plundering Tara one of "Sherman's Raiders," but, when a Union veterans organization protested, Selznick called him simply a "deserter."

The major military issue facing the Confederates in the Atlanta campaign—the Johnston-Hood controversy—is discussed often in the novel by Mitchell's characters, but completely ignored in the film. Selznick and Howard never mention Johnston, and Hood is mentioned only once, by Dr. Meade, who assures Scarlett the Yanks will "never get through old Peg Leg Hood."

One of the film's greatest failures in dealing with Sherman's campaign is the failure to convey the growing sense of menace, the "small cloud on the northwest" image done so well in Mitchell's novel. Ashley comes home for Christmas, 1863, and, with little transition and no comment on the May–June fighting between Chattanooga and Atlanta, the Union army is suddenly lobbing shells into the city and Aunt Pittypat is shrieking. Mitchell believed Sherman's growing cloud on the horizon had great dramatic possibilities, and she used them well. She wrote, "I was trying to give a picture of how it felt to be in a city a hundred miles away from the war, with the war coming closer every day." Selznick ignored the dramatic possibilities in juggling hope and fear among Atlanta's citizens, thus making his film less comprehensible historically as well.

There are ten major scenes in the film's footage of the war years: war talk at Twelve Oaks; the Atlanta Bazaar; Rhett's gift of a hat to Scarlett after returning from Paris; Atlanta waiting for Gettysburg's casualty lists; Ashley's Christmas leave; Sherman's arrival outside of Atlanta; the siege; Scarlett's visit to the car shed and the birth of Melanie's baby; the flight from Atlanta; and the arrival at Tara. All ten are taken from the novel, although there are alterations of language, characterization, and emphasis in each.

In the initial scene—talk of the imminence of war—the film's version is stronger and more effective. Amid the Rebel bluster Rhett Butler's chilling words of reality are more challenging and confrontational than in the novel. They also remain one of the clearest summations of Confederate disadvantages ever written:

> GERALD O'HARA: Now, now, Mr. Butler's been up north I hear. Don't you agree with us Mr. Butler?
>
> RHETT: I think it's hard winning a war with words gentlemen.
>
> CHARLES HAMILTON: What do you mean sir?
>
> RHETT: I mean, Mr. Hamilton, there's not a cannon factory in the whole South.
>
> MAN: What difference does that mean sir to a gentleman?
>
> RHETT: I'm afraid it's going to make a great deal of difference to a great many gentlemen, sir.
>
> CHARLES: Are you hintin', Mr. Butler, that the Yankees can lick us?
>
> RHETT: No, I'm not hinting, I'm saying very plainly that the Yankees are better equipped than we. They've got factories, shipyards, coal mines and a fleet to bottle up our harbors and starve us to death. All we've got is cotton and slaves and arrogance.
>
> CHARLES: Just listen to that renegade talk.
>
> RHETT: I'm sorry if the truth offends you.

The Atlanta Bazaar and Rhett's visit to Scarlett differ little with the book. Selznick uses Dr. Meade in the former and Rhett in the latter to give the viewer the latest war news. When Rhett tells Scarlett "there's a little battle goin' on right now that ought to pretty well fix things," she expresses fear for Ashley's safety and asks "where?" Rhett snarls, "Some little town in Pennsylvania called Gettysburg." The wait for casualties is similar to the book with the exception of Rhett's words about the Confederacy's "dying right in front of us." Ashley's Christmas furlough also closely follows Mitchell's actions and words. When Major Wilkes leaves Scarlett, his "We shall need all our prayers now that the end is coming" speech is different but just as defeatist as the one in the novel.

When Sherman's army reaches Atlanta's northern perimeter, Selznick's titles roll across the screen: "Panic hit the city with the first of Sherman's shells. Helpless and unarmed the populace fled from the oncoming Juggernaut." Without the preparation provided in Mitchell's book the filmgoer is left to wonder, What happened to the Confederate army? Although it faced superior numbers, Confederate Atlanta was certainly not "helpless and unarmed."

Once Selznick abruptly moves Sherman to Atlanta, his segments on the siege and the flight to Tara follow the novel more closely and are also more faithful to the historical events. On a number of occasions in the film its producers used titles rolling across the screen to explain the war's progress and to smooth transitions. They were Ben Hecht's idea and he wrote them from historical data prepared by Wilbur Kurtz. These titles were used instead of action scenes from the Battle of Gettysburg, Lee's surrender at Appomattox, and Lincoln's assassination that Selznick planned to include until he realized they were making his motion picture far too long.

As the bombardment of Atlanta intensifies, viewers read: "SIEGE! The skies rained death . . . for thirty-five days. A battered Atlanta hung on grimly hoping for a miracle. Then there fell a silence . . . more terrifying than the pounding of the cannon." Following the titles the camera cuts to the conversation between Scarlett and the young officer who informs her of the army's evacuation. This scene and the scene at the car shed mirror Mitchell's descriptions and use many of her words. That is also true of the birth of Melanie's baby and the entire escape from burning Atlanta. Mitchell's Prissy says, "Fo' gawd, Miss Scarlett! We's got ter have a doctah. Ah-Ah-Miss Scarlett. Ah doan know nuthin' 'bout bringin' babies." Selznick obviously wanted to sustain the excitement of the passage through Atlanta and the flight to Tara, so he added to the menace by including looters who tried to seize Rhett's stolen horse, and by having Scarlett and the refugees hide under a bridge being crossed by Yankee horsemen during a driving rain.

GONE WITH THE WIND's impact on popular conceptions of the antebellum South, the Civil War, and Reconstruction has been enormous. David O. Selznick was warned when he bought the property that Civil War films do not sell. He proved those prophets of doom wrong in this case, but there have been few other well-made Civil War films and none with a fraction of GWTW's impact. In the 1980s viewers of such television Civil War miniseries as *Blue and Gray* and *North and South* look back to *Gone with the Wind* with the same kind of nostalgia with which Scarlett looked back to antebellum Tara in the years after the war.

Fortunately for scholars of Civil War military history in the 1980s the image of the conflict in Georgia presented in novel and film is better history than either its treatment of the antebellum South or of Reconstruction. Students of slavery and the pre–Civil War South find the novel simplistic and incomplete and the movie awash in moonlight and magnolias. Students of the post–Civil War South, who have long ago abandoned the *Tragic Era* ideas of Claude Bowers (a contemporary of Margaret Mitchell's), find the novel and film monuments to old prejudices and bad history.

*Gone with the Wind* has been such a great success in large part because it is a novel about the American Civil War, an event viewed by millions of Americans and by Margaret Mitchell as the central event in the American experience. The Civil War brought change and loss to a nation, a region, a city, and to Scarlett O'Hara. The world viewed the way the nation, region and city dealt with change and loss with interest; it viewed Scarlett's way with fascination. *GWTW* was published in a time of change and loss, the chaotic 1930s. Readers wanted to escape, and they found parallels between Scarlett's world and their own. They also had known a loss of wealth and jobs, and lived in a world filled with growing hate and uncertainty.

The worldwide appeal of *Gone with the Wind* came from the same sources. In blitzed and battered London *GWTW* ran at the Ritz Theater almost the entire length of the war. In postwar Europe, the film played to packed houses, whose response to Scarlett's vow as she knelt in Tara's ravaged fields, "As God is my witness, I'll never be hungry again," must have been instant identification. Tom Wicker, himself author of a Civil War novel, believes, "the idea of loss is at the heart of the novel. A world irrevocably vanished, whether real or not, and Scarlett's personal losses—the ideal of Ashley, the reality of Rhett—evoke the losses in our own lives, those we comprehend as well as those we only sense."

Margaret Mitchell focused her novel of change and loss on what she believed was an event that brought great change to the Civil War and great loss to the Confederacy—Sherman's Georgia campaign ending in the capture of Atlanta. She clearly believed that with Atlanta's fall the Confederacy's doom was sealed. In April 1936, two months before her novel appeared, she mused to a friend, "I wonder why the military historians concentrate so much on the Virginia and Mississippi River campaigns and slight Johnston's retreat which has, to me, at least, far more drama than anything else in the whole war." After June 30, 1936, with the publication of *Gone with the Wind*, few would disagree.

# Critical Bibliography

## Primary Sources

### MANUSCRIPTS

Much of this study is based on unpublished manuscripts. The William Tecumseh Sherman Papers in the Library of Congress are indispensable for studying the Federal commander. Other important Sherman papers are in the Henry E. Huntington Library, San Marino, California, and the holdings of the Ohio Historical Society, as well as the Sherman Family Papers in the University of Notre Dame Archives. The most significant papers of the Confederate commander, Joseph Eggleston Johnston, are in the Huntington Library; the Miami University Library, Oxford, Ohio; the Duke University Library; and the Library of the College of William and Mary. Although the papers of Sherman and Johnston are widely scattered across the nation, they are extensive, especially those of Sherman. General Johnston's successor, John Bell Hood, is somewhat frustrating to study because his papers are meager. Apparently, as his biographer Richard McMurry points out, there is no collection of Hood's personal papers. Letters to, from, and about General Hood are found in many collections, from coast to coast, but none of these contain many materials written by Hood himself. Even the personal letters he wrote to Sally "Buck" Preston, which might have been both interesting and enlightening, were destroyed, according to Mary Chesnut.

The Braxton Bragg Papers, Western Reserve Historical Society, provide background information on the western theater command problems of 1864, which so hampered the Confederate war effort. One should also consult the Jefferson Davis Papers, Duke University; the William J. Hardee Papers, Alabama State Department of Archives and History; and the P. G. T. Beauregard Papers in the National Archives and the Library of Congress.

In addition to the Sherman collections, the papers of several of his lieutenants add to an understanding of the Union command. The immense John A. Logan collection in the Library of Congress affords an excellent view of one of Sherman's critics. Also in the Library of Congress are the John M. Schofield Papers and the James B. McPherson Papers. Both collections are small but useful. The Orlando Poe Papers in the Library of Congress, often overlooked by Civil War scholars, contain informative letters from Sherman's young chief engineer.

The manuscript collections of four other Federal generals were used in this study. They are the Oliver O. Howard Papers, Bowdoin University Library, Brunswick, Maine; Jefferson C. Davis Papers, Indiana Historical Society Library, Indianapolis; John Geary Papers, Atlanta Historical Society; and Jacob D. Cox Papers, Kennesaw Mountain National Military Park Library. The Howard Papers, containing letters between the general and his wife, are especially frank and revealing.

Letters and diaries provide much human-interest material and are invaluable in conveying the thoughts and feelings of lower-ranking officers and men in the ranks. Ten libraries across the nation supplied the diaries and collections of letters for this study.

The Library of Congress collections include the Alpheus Bloomfield Papers, James A. Congleton Papers, John Cope Papers, Josiah Cotton Papers, John D. Ferguson Papers, James L. Gillette Papers, Gist Family Papers, James Goodnow Papers, John Law Papers, Joseph Lester Papers, John Wesley Marshall Papers, Marshall M. Miller Papers, and Henry Clay Weaver Papers. Also available in the Library of Congress are the papers of Mother Bickerdyke of the U.S. Sanitary Commission.

The Illinois State Historical Library, Springfield, houses an enormous collection of soldiers' letters and diaries, mostly of men from the Prairie State. Used in this book were the Francis R. Baker Papers, John Batchelor Papers, Andrew Bush Papers, George N. Compton Papers, Thomas J. Frazee Papers, Theodore H. Jansen Papers, Robert B. Parks Papers, Will Pepper Papers, Joshua D. Rilea Papers, William Robinson Papers, James P. Suiter Papers, Benjamine F. Taylor Papers, Lysander Wheeler Papers, John A. Widney Papers, and William Wilson Papers.

The holdings of the Indiana State Historical Society Library, Indianapolis, also include a large number of primary sources from men in Sherman's army. Most of the collections are from Hoosiers serving in the Georgia campaign. Adding to the picture of life among the Federal invaders were the Jonathan J. Carter Papers, Orville T. Chamberlain Papers, John Finton Papers, Alva C. Grist Papers, Saunders R. Hornbrook Papers, Henry R. Ingraham Papers, Andrew Jackson Johnson Papers, James H. Kelly Papers, William F. King Papers, Charles P. Lesh Papers, John D. Lowman Papers, Benjamin B. Mabrey Papers, Eli Sherlock Papers, Thomas M. Small Papers, Joseph Taylor Smith Papers, Edward P. Stanfield Papers, Augustus VanDyke Papers, William D. Ward Papers, John A. Wilkens Papers, and Walter P. Wilson Papers.

The Flowers Collection of the Duke University Library, Durham, North Carolina, made available nine collections, which included manuscripts of both Union and Confederate soldiers. They are the Ellison Capers Papers, Elijah T. D. Hawkins Papers, George Metz Papers, Seaborn Montgomery Papers, James Nourse Papers, Charles R. Pomeroy Papers, Andrew K. Rose Papers, Frank E. Spencer Papers, and W. H. Tucker Papers.

The Southern Historical Collection of the University of North Carolina, Chapel Hill, also contained manuscript collections of participants on both sides. Used were the Edward W. Allen Papers, J. C. C. Black Papers, Irving Buck Papers, George H. Cadman Papers, Robert S. Finley Papers, George Gegner Papers, Charles M. Hopper Papers, George Mercer Papers, Joseph Semmes Papers, and C. B. Welton Papers.

Much of the manuscript research for this study of the Atlanta campaign was carried out in and around the city of Atlanta. Three manuscript collections in the library of the Atlanta Historical Society are vital contemporary records of the city under siege. They are the Carrie Berry Papers, Thomas Maguire Papers, and Samuel Richards Papers. The A. T. Holliday Papers are the literate, humorous letters of a Confederate volunteer and member of "Joe Brown's Pets." Also found in the Atlanta Historical Society are the Samuel Bachtell Papers, Colin Dunlap Papers, and James P. Snell Papers.

Four collections of soldiers' manuscripts from the Georgia Department of Archives and History, Atlanta, were consulted. They are the Alfred A. Atkins Papers, A. J. Jackson Papers, Lawrence Vetsch Papers, and William K. Watson Papers.

From Emory University's excellent collection of Civil War manuscripts the authors used the Alexander M. Ayers Papers, William G. Baugh Papers, Sidney Champion Papers, W. B. Corbitt Papers, Mumford Dixon Papers, R. M. Gill Papers, O. P. Hargis Papers, John Humphrey Papers, Moses Kirkland Papers, Leonidas W. Mackey Papers, Chauncey Mead Papers, Andrew Jackson Neal Papers, G. W. Peddy Papers, Albert Quincy Porter Papers, Elias J. Prichard Papers, Lavender Ray Papers, Bear Slagle Papers, Thomas T. Taylor Papers, and James W. Watkins Papers.

The Kennesaw Mountain National Military Park Library has collected soldiers' letters and diaries of men active throughout Sherman's Georgia campaign. The authors used the James A. Baird Papers, Allen L. Fahnestock Papers, Alonzo Miller Papers, Charles M. Smith Papers, Columbus Sykes Papers, W. T. Trask Papers, and Lyman Widney Papers.

## DOCUMENTS

Any serious study of a Civil War military campaign is greatly indebted to the United States Department of War for *The War of the Rebellion: A Compilation of the Official Records of the Union and Confederate Armies* (Washington, 1880–1901). In 128 massive volumes, the government printed thousands of documents from both armies, including dispatches, reports, orders, letters, telegrams, circulars, organizational tables, manpower tabulations, and casualty statements. The papers relating to the Atlanta campaign are found in Series 1, Volume 38, Parts 1–5, and in Volume 52, Part 2. Both authors have used these six volumes extensively in preparing this study. Obviously some After Action Reports are better than others, dependent upon the ability and objectivity of the officer reporting, as well as the role of his command in a particular fight. For instance, a researcher soon learns to seek eagerly for a report from Confederate general Patrick R. Cleburne, if his division was engaged, because Cleburne's report will invariably be rewarding. For complete, accurate reporting, Cleburne was seldom surpassed by any officer on either side. If one turns to a report from Union general John W. Geary, it probably will be longer than any report on either side and contain a great amount of detail—but also be generally accurate, if one allows for Geary's bias in favor of his own command. One soon learns the officers who, for whatever reasons, will normally submit reports that are of little or no value to the researcher.

It should also be noted that a good documentary study of the war in the western theater is provided by Stanley F. Horn, editor, *Tennessee's War, 1861–1865, Described by Participants* (Nashville, 1965). And the *Atlas to Accompany the Official Records of the Union and Confederate Armies of the War of the Rebellion* (Washington, 1891–1895) contains several good maps for the campaign and the different battles, with troop positions noted. An examination of Sherman's objective, the city of Atlanta, was aided by the use of the *United States Census* for 1850 and 1860 for Fulton and DeKalb counties.

## NEWSPAPERS

NEWSPAPERS have a somewhat limited value as a research tool for Civil War military history. They are often filled with inaccuracies, rumors, and false reports. In this study, however, the often-interrupted runs of Georgia journals provided a picture of civilian fears and concerns as well as daily life in central Georgia as the Yankee storm clouds gathered. Newspapers were also used in the study of prewar Atlanta. Consulted were the Atlanta *Weekly Intelligencer*, Atlanta *Daily Intelligencer*, Atlanta *Daily Examiner*, Atlanta *Southern Confederacy*, Macon *Daily Telegraph*, Augusta *Daily Constitutionalist*, and Memphis (Tennessee) *Daily Appeal*. The Tennessee journal, known as the "Moving Appeal" as it fled ahead of Federal armies, published its last issues in Georgia.

## MEMOIRS

SHERMAN, Johnston, and Hood all wrote memoirs in which they dealt with the Atlanta campaign. In evaluating memoirs or autobiographies penned years after the war, readers should remember that generals usually strive to justify their war record. Also, their memory may not be accurate and, like many veterans, generals are not immune to romanticizing their war experiences. Sherman wrote his *Memoirs* about ten years after the war, approximately the same time that Johnston penned his. Sherman's work was published in a two-volume edition and is very readable. Candid and vigorous, Sherman does not engage in much of the contentiousness that characterizes the books of Johnston and Hood. Of course, Sherman commanded the winning army, doubtless a fact of no little import in explaining the Federal general's style.

General Johnston, in his *Narrative of Military Operations*, devotes almost as much space to attacking Hood and Jefferson Davis as he does to narrating and analyzing the military operations of the Atlanta campaign. In *Advance and Retreat*, published fifteen years after the war, General Hood reciprocated, writing a lengthy and impassioned rebuttal to Johnston. Hood maintained that Johnston's unaggressive campaign and continual retreats led to Confederate defeat despite all of Hood's efforts to reverse the campaign.

Two figures who greatly influenced the campaign wrote memoirs that add to an understanding of the 1864 action in Georgia. Jefferson Davis's *The Rise and Fall of the Confederate Government* (New York, 1881) presents the view from Richmond while Ulysses S. Grant, *Personal Memoirs of U. S. Grant* (New York, 1895) gives the reader an evaluation of Sherman's campaign from the Union army in Virginia. Also consulted was J. B. Jones, *A Rebel War Clerk's Diary* (Philadelphia, 1866).

Other generals besides the army commanders also wrote reminiscences. Jacob D. Cox's *Military Reminiscences of the Civil War* (1900) includes materials on the Atlanta campaign. Cox also wrote the first volume devoted exclusively to that subject. Cox's *Atlanta* (New York, 1882) is useful, but its focus is on the Federal army, and particularly Cox's own command in the Army of the Ohio, resulting in a relatively narrow perspective of the campaign. Other Federal generals whose autobiographies include material on Atlanta are Grenville M. Dodge, *Personal Recollections of General William T. Sherman* (Des Moines, 1902), William B. Hazen, *A Narrative of Military Service* (Boston, 1895), Oliver O. Howard, *Autobiography* (New York, 1907), Richard W. Johnson, *A Soldier's Reminiscence in Peace and War* (Philadelphia, 1886), John M. Palmer, *Personal Recollections* (Cincinnati, 1901), John M. Schofield, *Forty-Six Years in the Army* (New York, 1897), and David S. Stanley, *Personal Memoirs* (Cambridge, Mass., 1917). The books by Howard and Schofield are probably the most valuable for the Atlanta campaign. Also available is a journalist's reminiscences: Donn Piatt, *Memories of the Men Who Saved the Union* (New York, 1887). To add to an understanding of civilian apprehensions around Atlanta and across Georgia see Robert Manson Myers's brilliantly edited *The Children of Pride: A True Story of Georgia and the Civil War* (New Haven, Conn., 1972).

Only two Confederate generals involved in the Atlanta campaign, besides Johnston and Hood, penned memoirs: Samuel G. French and Arthur Middleton Manigault. French's *Two Wars: An Autobiography* (Nashville, 1901) is especially useful for 1864, because the account of that year is based on a diary which

French kept. Manigault's memoir, A Carolinian Goes to War: The Civil War Narrative of Arthur Middleton Manigault, Brigadier General, C.S.A., edited by R. Lockwood Tower (Columbia, S.C., 1983), is very valuable. Written soon after the war ended, when events were still fresh in his mind, and never intended for publication, Manigault's memoir offers some useful insights to the Confederate campaign. Manigault was a capable officer and a keen observer who, as a brigadier general, knew things that men of lesser rank could not.

Besides memoirs and autobiographies, there are two significant collections of writings by participants in the Atlanta campaign. Robert U. Johnson and Clarence C. Buell edited Battles and Leaders of the Civil War. 4 vols. (New York, 1887). Volume four contains eight articles on the Atlanta campaign. A number of reminiscences of the campaign by Union officers were collected by Syndey C. Kerksis and published under the title of The Atlanta Papers (Dayton, Ohio, 1890). Most of these papers were read in the late nineteenth century at gatherings of Federal veterans.

## UNIT HISTORIES AND MEMOIRS BY SECONDARY FIGURES

FEDERAL regimental histories and memoirs by lower-ranking officers and enlisted men are numerous. Many of these were consulted in this study. Listed alphabetically by author or editor, they are George W. Bailey, A Private Chapter of the War (St. Louis, 1880); James A. Barnes et al., The Eighty-sixth Regiment Indiana Volunteer Infantry (Crawfordsville, Ind., 1895); William W. Belknap, History of the Fifteenth Regiment Iowa Veteran Volunteer Infantry (Keokuk, Iowa, 1887); Andrew I. Boies, Record of the Thirty-third Massachusetts Volunteer Infantry (Fitchburg, Mass., 1880); Thaddeus Brown et al., Behind the Guns: The History of Battery I, Second Regiment Illinois Light Artillery (Carbondale, Ill., 1965); Edwin E. Bryant, History of the Third Regiment Wisconsin Veteran Volunteer Infantry (Madison, Wis., 1891); Charles T. Clark, Opdycke's Tigers, the 125th Ohio Volunteer Infantry: A History of the Regiment and of the Campaigns and Battles of the Army of the Cumberland (Columbus, Ohio, 1895); Captain George K. Collins, Memoirs of the 149th Regiment New York Volunteer Infantry (Syracuse, N.Y., 1891); Alexis Cope, The Fifteenth Ohio Volunteers and Its Campaigns (Columbus, 1916); Samuel H. Hurst, Journal History of the 73rd Ohio Volunteer Infantry (Chillicothe, Ohio, 1866); John A. Joyce, A Checkered Life (Chicago, 1883); B. F. Magee, History of the 72nd Indiana (Lafayette, Ind., 1882); Francis M. McAdams, Every-day Soldier Life or, A History of the One Hundred and Thirteenth Ohio Volunteer Infantry (Columbus, 1884); Samuel Merrill, The Seventh Indiana Volunteer Infantry in the War of the Rebellion (Indianapolis, 1900); Sergeant Henry C. Morhous, Reminiscences of the 123rd Regiment, New York State Volunteers (Greenwich, N.Y., 1879); W. S. Morris, History of the 31st Regiment Illinois Volunteers, Organized by John A. Logan (Evansville, Ind., 1902); H. H. Orendorff et al., Reminiscences of the Civil War From Diaries of Members of the One Hundred and Third Illinois Volunteer Infantry (Chicago, 1904); Captain Hartwell Osborn et al., *Trials and Triumphs: the Record of the 55th Ohio Volunteer Infantry* (Chicago, 1904); Nelson A. Pinney, *History of the 104th Regiment Ohio Volunteer Infantry, 1862 to 1865* (Akron, Ohio, 1886); Nixon B. Stewart, *Dan McCook's Regiment, 52nd Ohio Volunteer Infantry* (Alliance, Ohio, 1900); Samuel Toombs, *Reminiscences of the War: Comprising a Detailed Account of the Experiences of the Thirteenth New Jersey Volunteers* (Orange, N.J., 1878); Charles W. Wills, *Army Life of an Illinois Soldier* (Washington, 1906); Henry H. Wright, *A History of the Sixth Iowa Infantry* (Iowa City, 1923).

Although Confederate regimental histories and memoirs by lower-ranking officers and enlisted men are much less numerous than Union accounts, there are some worth consulting. The reader should look at the following: Ephraim McD. Anderson, *Memoirs Historical and Personal Including the Campaign of the First Missouri Confederate Brigade* (St. Louis, 1868); Walter A. Clark, *Under the Stars and Bars: or Memories of Four Years Service with the Oglethorpes, of Augusta, Georgia* (Augusta, Ga., 1900); R. M. Collins, *Chapters From the Unwritten History of the War Between the States* (St. Louis, 1893); Lilla Mills Hawes, ed., "The Memoirs of Charles H. Olmstead," *Georgia Historical Quarterly* (1960, 1961); Albert D. Kirwan, ed., *Johnny Green of the Orphan Brigade: The Journal of a Confederate Soldier* (Lexington, Ky., 1956). One may wish to read this in conjunction with William C. Davis's *The Orphan Brigade: The Kentucky Confederates Who Couldn't Go Home* (New York, 1980) and Ed Porter Thompson, *History of the Orphan Brigade* (Louisville, Ky., 1898). Also see W. J. McMurry, *History of the Twentieth Tennessee Regiment Volunteer Infantry, C.S.A.* (Nashville, 1904); James C. Nisbet, *Four Years on the Firing Line*, edited by Bell I. Wiley (Jackson, Tenn., 1963); Bromfield Ridley, *Battles and Sketches of the Army of Tennessee* (Mexico, Mo., 1906); and W. J. Worsham, *The Old Nineteenth Tennessee Regiment, C.S.A.: June 1861–April, 1865* (Knoxville, Tenn., 1902). Finally and best known of all, but requiring much caution in its use because the author was frequently inclined to exaggeration, is Samuel R. Watkins, *"Co. Aytch," Maury Grays, First Tennessee Regiment* (Jackson, Tenn., 1952).

## PUBLISHED LETTERS AND DIARIES

AMONG Federal letters and diaries that have been published, some of the most useful are: Byron R. Abernethy, ed., *Private Elisha Stockwell, Jr., Sees the Civil War* (Norman, Okla., 1958); Paul M. Angle, ed., *Three Years in the Army of the Cumberland: The Letters and Diary of Major James A. Connolly* (Bloomington, Ind., 1959); Robert G. Athearn, ed., *Soldier in the West: The Civil War Letters of Alfred Lacey Hough* (Philadelphia, 1957); John D. Barnhart, ed., "A Hoosier Invades the Confederacy: Letters and Diaries of Leroy S. Mayfield," *Indiana Magazine of History* (1943); K. Jack Bauer, ed., *Soldiering: The Civil War Diary of Rice C. Bull, 123rd New York Volunteer Infantry* (San Rafael, Calif., 1978); Wilfred W. Black, ed., "Marching with Sherman Through Georgia and the Carolinas, Civil War Diary of Jesse L. Dozer," *Georgia Historical Quarterly* (1968);

Frank L. Byrne, ed., *The View from Headquarters: Civil War Letters of Harvey Reid* (Madison, Wis., 1965); Thaddeus H. Capron, "War Diary," *Journal of the Illinois State Historical Society* (1919); Wirt Armistead Cate, *Two Soldiers: The Campaign Diaries of Thomas J. Key, C.S.A., December 7, 1863–May 17, 1865, and Robert J. Campbell, U.S.A., January 1, 1864–July 21, 1864* (Chapel Hill, N.C., 1938); David P. Conynghan, *Sherman's March Through the South* (New York, 1865); Corydon E. Foote, *With Sherman to the Sea: A Drummer's Story of the Civil War* (New York, 1960); Richard B. Harwell, ed., "The Campaign from Chattanooga to Atlanta as Seen by a Federal Soldier," *Georgia Historical Quarterly* (1941); M. A. DeWolfe Howe, ed., *Home Letters of General Sherman* (New York, 1909); David P. Jackson, ed., *The Colonel's Diary* (Sharon, Penn., 1922); Charles F. Morse, *Letters Written during the Civil War* (n.p., 1898); James A. Padgett, ed., "With Sherman Through Georgia and the Carolinas: Letters of a Federal Soldier," *Georgia Historical Quarterly* (1948); Milo M. Quaife, ed., *From the Cannon's Mouth: The Civil War Letters of General Alpheus S. Williams* (Detroit, 1959); Margaret B. Roth, ed., *Well Mary: Civil War Letters of a Wisconsin Volunteer* (Madison, Wis., 1960); Robert J. Snetsinger, ed., *Kiss Clara for Me* (State College, Penn., 1969); Rachel Sherman Thorndyke, ed., *The Sherman Letters: Correspondence Between General and Senator Sherman from 1837–1891* (New York, 1894); and Theodore F. Upson, *With Sherman to the Sea* (Bloomington, Ind., 1943).

For the better published letters and diaries on the Confederate side, one should consult Norman D. Brown, ed., *One of Cleburne's Command: The Civil War Reminiscences and Diary of Captain Samuel T. Foster, Granbury's Texas Brigade, C.S.A.* (Austin, Tex., 1980); W. M. Cash and L. S. Howarth, eds., *My Dear Nellie: The Civil War Letters of William L. Nugent to Eleanor Smith Nugent* (Jackson, Miss., 1977); Weymouth T. Jordan, ed., "Matthew Andrew Dunn Letters," *Journal of Mississippi History* (1939); Donald W. Lewis, ed., "A Confederate Officer's Letters on Sherman's March to Atlanta," *Georgia Historical Quarterly* (1967); Elizabeth H. Marshall, ed., "Watch on the Chattahoochee: A Civil War Letter," *Georgia Historical Quarterly* (1959); Andrew F. Muir, ed., "The Battle of Atlanta as Described by a Confederate Soldier," *Georgia Historical Quarterly* (1958); George C. Osborn, ed., "Civil War Letters of Robert W. Banks: Atlanta Campaign," *Georgia Historical Quarterly* (1943); H. E. Sterkx, "Civil War Letters of Joel Murphree of Troy, Alabama," *Alabama Historical Quarterly* (1957); and Bell I. Wiley, ed., "The Confederate Letters of John W. Hagan," *Georgia Historical Quarterly* (1954).

## CONFEDERATE VETERAN

EVERY ONE of the forty volumes of the *Confederate Veteran*, published annually beginning in 1893, contains something about the Atlanta campaign. Typically, there are five to ten, sometimes fifteen or twenty articles per volume. The quality varies markedly, from brief, human-interest reminiscences of veterans to detailed accounts by officers, such as Confederate brigadier general Francis A. Shoup's account of his discussions with General Joseph E. Johnston about the Rebel defensive works at the Chattahoochee River, together with a detailed description of those works. Valuable articles such as Shoup's, as one might expect, are not the norm.

## Secondary Sources

### BOOKS

THERE are few books devoted solely to the Atlanta campaign. Samuel Carter III's *The Siege of Atlanta, 1864* (New York, 1973) is valuable for its accounts from eyewitnesses, and those who were close to the events, especially during the siege of the city. When dealing with the military campaign, however, Carter's work is brief, lacking in analysis, and sometimes inaccurate. William Key's *The Battle of Atlanta and the Georgia Campaign* (New York, 1958) offers a touch of drama, but is very short and superficial. A. A. Hoehling's *Last Train From Atlanta* (New York, 1958) is an excellent book about the life of Atlanta's civilians during the campaign and siege. Hoehling does not treat the campaign itself. Earl S. Miers's *The General Who Marched to Hell* (New York, 1951) is not a biography of Sherman, as some might conclude from the title, but a broad consideration of the Atlanta campaign, quoting extensively from contemporary letters and diaries. Detailed, analytical, military coverage of the campaign was not the author's purpose.

Two unpublished doctoral dissertations, directed by Professor Bell I. Wiley, may be consulted for extensive and critical evaluation of the campaign: Richard M. McMurry, "The Atlanta Campaign, December 23, 1863, to July 18, 1864" (Emory University, 1967), and Errol M. Clauss, "The Atlanta Campaign, July 18–September 2, 1864" (Emory University, 1965).

Certainly one should study the standard works on the Army of Tennessee. Stanley F. Horn's *The Army of Tennessee* (Indianapolis, 1941) contains fifty pages on the Atlanta campaign and provides a good introduction to the many Rebel controversies about the proper strategy. Thomas L. Connelly's *Autumn of Glory: The Army of Tennessee, 1862–1865* (Baton Rouge, 1971) devoted almost two hundred pages to the Atlanta campaign, providing the most in depth and perceptive assessment of the Confederate side of the struggle. His evaluations are well supported by extensive research and they are usually balanced and fair. Any history of the Atlanta campaign must take account of Connelly's work.

Unfortunately, there is no study of the Federal side of the campaign that even begins to approach the quality of Connelly's assessment of the Confederates. The largest of Sherman's three armies is the subject of Thomas B. Van Horn's two volumes, *The History of the Army of the Cumberland* (Cincinnati, 1875). There is no history of either the Army of the Ohio or the Army of the Tennessee.

Numerous biographies of the generals who participated in the Atlanta campaign may be consulted, some of which provide valuable material. Among the Sherman biographies, Lloyd Lewis, *Sherman: Fighting Prophet* (New York, 1932) is still the best. Basil H. Liddell Hart's *Sherman: Soldier, Realist, American* (New York, 1958) deserves attention, because the astute British military historian was always thought provoking, even if noticeably pro-Sherman. James M. Merrill's *William Tecumseh Sherman* (Chicago, 1971) concentrates on the general's personal life and is weak in analysis of military operations. John B. Walters's *Merchant of Terror: General Sherman and Total War* (Indianapolis, 1973) is basically the author's 1947 doctoral dissertation. It emphasizes the general's destruction of Southern resources. John F. Marszalek's *Sherman's Other War: The General and the Civil War Press* (Memphis, 1981) deals with an important subject and offers some interesting insights to what Sherman was like. No biography has yet adequately covered the life of this man who was perhaps both the most significant and the most colorful of Union commanders. Because of the close relationship between Sherman and Grant, the excellent biography of the latter by William S. McFeely, *Grant: A Biography* (New York, 1981), should be consulted.

But Sherman has fared much better than the first of the two Confederate commanders who opposed him in the Atlanta campaign. On General Joseph E. Johnston there is only one biography worthy of the term. Gilbert E. Govan and James W. Livingood, *A Different Valor: The Story of General Joseph E. Johnston, C.S.A.* (Indianapolis, 1956) recounts the general's life well enough, only to be marred by the authors' almost unqualified acceptance of Johnston's position in his quarrels with Davis and Hood. A modern, critical biography of Johnston is needed.

There are three biographies of General Hood. The best and most recent is Richard M. McMurry, *John Bell Hood and the War for Southern Independence* (Lexington, Ky., 1982), which devotes three of its twelve chapters to the Atlanta campaign. Two older biographies provide background material. John P. Dyer's *The Gallant Hood* (Indianapolis, 1950) is more useful than Richard O'Connor's *Hood: Cavalier General* (New York, 1949), but both are superficial in treating the Atlanta campaign.

Among the biographies of subordinate commanders, first on the Federal side, Francis F. McKinney's *Education in Violence: The Life of George H. Thomas and the History of the Army of the Cumberland* (Detroit, 1961), is one of the best. Other Thomas biographies are by Freeman Cleaves, *Rock of Chickamauga: The Life of General George H. Thomas* (Norman, Okla., 1948), Wilbur Thomas, *General George H. Thomas, The Indomitable Warrior* (New York, 1964), and Thomas B. Van Horn, *The Life of Major General George H. Thomas* (New York, 1882). In consulting biographies of Thomas, one soon becomes aware of an often-bitter debate among high-ranking Federals, involving the extent to which Sherman's successes were allegedly attributable to the work of Thomas.

For other Federal leaders who played key roles in the Atlanta campaign, see James P. Jones, *"Black Jack": John A. Logan and Southern Illinois in the Civil War*

(Tallahassee, Fla., 1967), James L. McDonough, *Schofield: Union General in the Civil War and Reconstruction* (Tallahassee, Fla., 1972), John A. Carpenter, *Sword and Olive Branch: Oliver Otis Howard* (Pittsburgh, 1964), Stanley P. Hirshson, *Grenville M. Dodge: Soldier, Politician, Railroad Pioneer* (Bloomington, Ind., 1967); Walter H. Hebert, *Fighting Joe Hooker* (Indianapolis, 1944); George T. Palmer, *A Conscientious Turncoat: The Story of John M. Palmer* (New Haven, Conn., 1941). One of the most significant of the Federal subordinates, General James B. McPherson, who led the second largest of Sherman's three armies in the campaign, is in need of an adequate biography. Elizabeth J. Whaley's *Forgotten Hero: General James B. McPherson* (New York, 1955) is weak.

On important Confederate subordinates, the reader should consult Nathaniel Cheairs Hughes, Jr., *General William J. Hardee: Old Reliable* (Baton Rough, La., 1965), Joseph H. Parks, *General Leonidas Polk, C.S.A.: The Fighting Bishop* (Baton Rouge, La., 1962), Herman Hattaway, *General Stephen D. Lee* (Jackson, Miss., 1976), and John P. Dyer, *From Shiloh to San Juan: The Life of "Fightin' Joe" Wheeler* (Baton Rouge, La., 1941). Two books must be consulted about General Cleburne. First in importance is the work of Irving A. Buck, who was a member of Cleburne's staff, entitled *Cleburne and His Command* (Jackson, Tenn., 1958). Much more detailed but less useful, is Howell and Elizabeth Purdue's *Pat Cleburne Confederate General: A Definitive Biography* (Hillsboro, Tex., 1973). Marshall Wingfield's *General A. P. Stewart: His Life and Letters* (Memphis, 1954), will not be of much help.

For an understanding of Confederate and Georgia politics as Sherman invaded the state see T. Conn Bryan *Confederate Georgia* (Athens, Ga., 1953) and Rudolph Von Abele, *Alexander H. Stephens, A Biography* (New York, 1946).

For the Union cavalry in the Atlanta campaign, see Stephen Z. Starr, *The Union Cavalry in the Civil War*, Volume 3: *The War in the West, 1861–1865* (Baton Rouge, La., 1985). There is no comparable work on the Confederate cavalry. Also check John W. Rowell, *Yankee Cavalrymen: Through the Civil War with the Ninth Pennsylvania Cavalry* (Knoxville, Tenn., 1971). On Federal artillery, see Rowell's *Yankee Artillerymen: Through the Civil War with Eli Lilly's Indiana Battery* (Knoxville, Tenn., 1975) and Richard Harwell and Philip N. Racine, eds., *The Fiery Trail: A Union Officer's Account of Sherman's Last Campaigns* (Knoxville, Tenn., 1986). Larry Daniel, *Cannoneers in Gray* (Tuscaloosa, Ala., 1984) deals in part with Confederate artillery in the Atlanta campaign.

Consulted for general information on some participants in the campaign were Ezra J. Warner, *Generals in Gray* (Baton Rouge, La., 1959) and Ezra J. Warner, *Generals in Blue* (Baton Rouge, La., 1964).

For an increased understanding of life among the common soldiers in both armies in the Atlanta campaign and throughout the war the authors consulted Bell I. Wiley's two pioneering studies, *The Life of Johnny Reb* (Indianapolis, 1943) and *The Life of Billy Yank* (New York, 1971).

The history of Atlanta has been chronicled by a number of professional and amateur historians. The most complete study is Franklin Garrett, *Atlanta and Environs: A Chronicle of Its People and Events*, 2 vols., (Athens, Ga., 1982).

Volume 1 deals with Atlanta from its founding through Sherman's visit. Also used in this study were: Ivan Allen, *Atlanta from the Ashes* (Atlanta, 1928); I. W. Avery, *The History of Georgia from 1850 to 1881* (New York, 1881); Fannie A. Beers, *Memories* (Philadelphia, 1889); Walter G. Cooper, *Official History of Fulton County* (Atlanta, 1934); Mary Cumming, *Georgia Railroad and Banking Company, 1833–1945* (Augusta, Ga., 1945); Sarah Huff, *My 80 Years in Atlanta* (Atlanta, 1937); James H. Johnston, *Western and Atlantic Railroad of the State of Georgia* (Atlanta, 1931); Thomas H. Martin, *Atlanta and Its Builders*, 2 vols., (n.p., 1902); and Wallace P. Reed, *History of Atlanta, Georgia* (Syracuse, N.Y., 1889).

The most important sources for the Epilogue were the first edition of the novel, Margaret Mitchell, *Gone with the Wind* (New York, 1936), and a videotape of the film produced by David O. Selznick in 1939. To clearly understand Mitchell's research for GWTW and her response to the instant fame the book brought her, see Richard B. Harwell, ed., *Margaret Mitchell's Gone with the Wind Letters, 1936–1949* (New York, 1976). Also see Sidney Howard, *GWTW, the Screenplay*, edited by Richard B. Harwell (New York, 1980). Three studies of the novel, the motion picture, and the author that are helpful are: Darden A. Pyron, ed., *Recasting: "Gone with the Wind" in American Culture* (Miami, 1983); Roland Flamini, *Scarlett, Rhett and a Cast of Thousands: The Filming of Gone with the Wind* (New York, 1975); and Finis Farr, *Margaret Mitchell of Atlanta, the Author of Gone with the Wind* (New York, 1965).

Richard N. Current's article, "Fiction as History: A Review Essay," *Journal of Southern History* (1986), is a fine analysis of the impact of fiction on the interpretation of history. In "Why, Miss Scarlett, How Well You've Aged," *New York Times Book Review* (May 25, 1986), Tom Wicker reviews the staying power of this best-known novel of the Civil War.

Two recent studies that attempt to explain the outcome of the Civil War are: Herman Hattaway and Archer Jones, *How the North Won: A Military History of the Civil War* (Urbana, Ill., 1983) and Richard E. Beringer, Herman Hattaway, Archer Jones, and William N. Still, Jr., *Why the South Lost the Civil War* (Athens, Ga., 1986). We consulted these two controversial works both for their material on the Atlanta campaign and for their overall treatment of the war.

And finally, it might seem amiss to some readers if nothing were said about the work of the two preeminent popularizers of the Civil War during and since the centennial of the 1960s: Bruce Catton and Shelby Foote. The latter's massive, three-volume, three-thousand-page effort, *The Civil War: A Narrative* (New York, 1958–1974), devotes about one hundred pages of the final volume to the Atlanta campaign. Foote's treatment of the subject does not equal the quality of some of his best work, like the discussion of Gettysburg, for instance, in his second volume, but is superior to any of Bruce Catton's efforts on Atlanta. Catton did his best work on the eastern theater, emphasizing the Federal side, as in *A Stillness At Appomattox* (New York, 1953), for instance, whereas Foote gave a generally more balanced account, Union and Confederate, East and West. But neither did justice to Atlanta.

## ARTICLES

THERE is a large number of secondary articles concerning various aspects of the Atlanta campaign. For campaign overviews the reader should consult Thomas R. Hay, "The Atlanta Campaign," *Georgia Historical Quarterly* (1923); Allen P. Julian et al., "The Campaign for Atlanta," a special issue of *Civil War Times Illustrated* (July 1964); Alan Keller, "On the Road to Atlanta: Johnston vs. Sherman," *Civil War Times Illustrated* (December 1962); Richard McMurry, "The Atlanta Campaign of 1864: A New Look," *Civil War History* (March 1976); and George C. Osborn, "The Atlanta Campaign, 1864," *Georgia Historical Quarterly* (1950).

Many articles concern personalities, both army commanders and subordinate officers. General Sherman, of course, has been a fascinating subject. See Stephen E. Ambrose, "William T. Sherman," *American History Illustrated* (January 1967); Albert Castel, "The Life of a Rising Sun," *Civil War Times Illustrated* (July, August, October, 1979); E. Merton Coulter, "Sherman and the South," *Georgia Historical Quarterly* (1931); and Otto Eisenschiml's "Sherman: Hero or War Criminal?" *Civil War Times Illustrated* (January 1964). The last article is a scathing anti-Sherman essay.

Articles about General Johnston or General Hood often address the other also. Sometimes President Davis and General Bragg will be included as well. A good starting point is Thomas R. Hay, "Davis, Bragg, and Johnston in the Atlanta Campaign," *Georgia Historical Quarterly* (1924). One should also consult Alfred P. James, "General Joseph E. Johnston, Storm Center of the Confederate Army," *Mississippi Valley Historical Review* (1927–1928) and Richard M. McMurry's "The Enemy at Richmond: Joseph E. Johnston and the Confederate Government," *Civil War History* (1981). Two articles by Phillip L. Secrist are of interest: "Prelude to the Atlanta Campaign: The Davis-Bragg-Johnston Controversy," *Atlanta Historical Bulletin* (Spring–Summer, 1972) and "Jefferson Davis and the Atlanta Campaign: A Study in Confederate Command," *Atlanta Historical Bulletin* (Fall–Winter, 1972). See also David G. Chollett, "Advance and Retreat: Rage or Reason?" *Atlanta Historical Bulletin* (Spring, 1976).

Other articles about significant officers are Charles M. Cummings, "Otho French Strahl: 'Choicest Spirit to Embrace the South,'" *Tennessee Historical Quarterly* (1965); Stephen Davis, "A Georgia Firebrand: Major General W. H. T. Walker, C. S. A.," *Georgia Historical Quarterly* (1970); James P. Jones, "General Jeff C. Davis, U.S.A., and Sherman's Georgia Campaign," *Georgia Historical Quarterly* (1963); James P. Jones, "The Battle of Atlanta and McPherson's Successor," *Civil War History* (1961); Holman D. Jordan, "The Military Career of Henry D. Clayton," *Alabama Review* (1960); Wilbur G. Kurtz, "The Death of Major General W. H. T. Walker, July 22, 1864," *Civil War History* (1960); and Robert D. Little, "General Hardee and the Atlanta Campaign," *Georgia Historical Quarterly* (1945). The last is a defense of Hardee against Hood's allegations of mistakes by the corps commander in the fighting before Atlanta.

For articles on particular battles, the reader should begin with the publications of Richard M. McMurry: "The Affair at Kolb's Farm," *Civil War Times Illustrated* (December 1968); "Kennesaw Mountain," *Civil War Times Illustrated* (January 1970); "Resaca: 'A Heap of Hard Fiten,' " *Civil War Times Illustrated* (November 1970); "Cassville," *Civil War Times Illustrated* (December 1971); "The Hell Hole," *Civil War Times Illustrated* (February 1973); "Sherman's Meridian Campaign," *Civil War Times Illustrated* (May 1975); and "The Opening Phase of the 1864 Campaign in the West," *Atlanta Historical Journal* (Summer, 1983). Other useful articles on battles are Albert Castel's "Union Fizzle at Atlanta: The Battle of Utoy Creek," *Civil War Times Illustrated* (February 1978); Bruce Catton, "Battle of Atlanta," *Georgia Review* (1956); Errol M. Clauss, "The Battle of Jonesborough," *Civil War Times Illustrated* (November 1968); Sydney C. Kerksis, "Action at Gilgal Church, Georgia, June 15–16, 1864," *Atlanta Historical Bulletin* (Fall, 1970); and Philip L. Secrist's two articles, "Scenes of Awful Carnage," *Civil War Times Illustrated* (June 1971); and "Resaca: For Sherman a Moment of Truth," *Atlanta Historical Journal* (Spring, 1978). Also valuable is Wilbur G. Kurtz's unpublished article "Why was Snake Creek Gap Left Unguarded?" in the Chickamauga-Chattanooga National Military Park Library. Also see H. David Williams, "On the Fringes of Hell: Billy Yank and Johnny Reb at the Siege of Kennesaw Mountain," *Georgia Historical Quarterly* (1986).

The significance of railroads in the Atlanta campaign is discussed by Robert C. Black III, "The Railroads of Georgia in the Confederate War Effort," *Journal of Southern History* (1947); James G. Bogle, "The Western & Atlantic Railroad—1864," *Atlanta Historical Journal* (Summer, 1981); Errol M. Clauss, "Sherman's Rail Support in the Atlanta Campaign," *Georgia Historical Quarterly* (1966); and Armin E. Mruck, "The Role of Railroads in the Atlanta Campaign," *Civil War History* (1961).

For cavalry operations see John P. Dyer's "Some Aspects of Cavalry Operations in the Army of Tennessee," *Journal of Southern History* (1942); John W. Rowell's "McCook's Raid," *Civil War Times Illustrated* (July 1974); and especially Philip L. Secrist's "The Role of Cavalry in the Atlanta Campaign, *Georgia Historical Quarterly* (1972).

Several other articles involving such matters as background, incidentals, human interest stories, and controversy may be worth consulting. Listed alphabetically, these are: Steven J. Adolphson, "An Incident of Valor in the Battle of Peach Tree Creek, 1864," *Georgia Historical Quarterly* (1973); William G. Bentley, "The Great Snowball Battle," *Civil War Times Illustrated* (January 1967); Hartwell T. Bynum, "Sherman's Expulsion of the Roswell Women in 1864," *Georgia Historical Quarterly* (1970); Errol M. Clauss, "Sherman's Failure at Atlanta," *Georgia Historical Quarterly* (1969); Steve Davis, "The Great Snow Battle of 1864," *Civil War Times Illustrated* (June 1976); Bruce S. Eastwood, "Confederate Medical Problems in the Atlanta Campaign," *Georgia Historical Quarterly* (1963); Robert Gibbon, "Life at the Crossroads of the Confederacy: Atlanta, 1861–1865," *Atlanta Historical Journal* (Summer, 1979); Richard B. Harwell, "Civilian Life in Atlanta in 1862," *Atlanta Historical Bulletin* (1944); Wilbur

Kurtz, "Embattled Atlanta," *Atlanta Constitution* (1930); Earl J. Hess, "Civilians at War: The Georgia Militia in the Atlanta Campaign," *Georgia Historical Quarterly* (1982); Richard M. McMurry, "Confederate Morale in the Atlanta Campaign," *Georgia Historical Quarterly* (1970), and "More on Raw Courage," *Civil War Times Illustrated* (October 1975); William J. McNeill, "A Survey of Confederate Soldier Morale During Sherman's Campaign Through Georgia and the Carolinas," *Georgia Historical Quarterly* (1971); John M. Morgan, "Steedman's Action at Dalton, 1864," *Northwest Ohio Quarterly* (1981); Peggy Robbins, "Hood vs. Sherman: A Duel of Words," *Civil War Times Illustrated* (July 1978); Philip L. Secrist, "Life in Atlanta," *Civil War Times Illustrated* (July 1970); and John R. Smith, "The Day Atlanta Was Occupied," *Atlanta Historical Bulletin* (Fall, 1977).

# Index